THE COMPLETE IDIOT'S GUIDE TO

ECDL

THE COMPLETE IDIOT'S GUIDE TO

ECDL

by James Moran
Victoria Hull
and Donna Wheeler

Prentice
Hall

An imprint of Pearson Education

London • Boston • Indianapolis • New York • Mexico City • Toronto • Sydney • Tokyo •
Singapore • Hong Kong • Cape Town • Madrid • Paris • Amsterdam • Munich • Milan

PEARSON EDUCATION LIMITED

Edinburgh Gate
Harlow, Essex CM20 2JE
Tel: +44 (0)1279 623623
Fax: +44 (0)1279 431059
Website: www.pearsoned.co.uk

First published in Great Britain in 2003

Reprinted 2004

© Happy Computers 2003

The rights of James Moran, Victoria Hull and Donna Wheeler to be
identified as the Authors of this work has been asserted by them in
accordance with the Copyright, Designs and Patents Act 1988.

ISBN: 0-130-39916-7

British Library Cataloguing in Publication Data
A CIP catalogue record for this book can be obtained from the British Library

'European Computer Driving Licence' and ECDL and Stars device are registered
trademarks of the European Computer Driving Licence Foundation Limited.
All products and company names are ™ or ® trademarks of their respective owners.
All Websites reproduced herein are copyright of their owners.

10 9 8 7 6 5 4

Typeset by Land & Unwin (Data Sciences) Ltd.
Printed and bound in Great Britain by Biddles Ltd, King's Lynn, Norfolk

The Publishers' policy is to use paper manufactured from sustainable forests.

Contents

Module 4: Spreadsheets 271

Module 6: Presentations 523

xiii

Acknowledgements

Compiled/edited/mismanaged by James Moran, based on manuals written by Victoria Hull, Donna Wheeler and James Moran.

This book could not have existed without the hard work, team spirit and good teeth of the Happy Computers and LearnFish teams, specifically:

Alison Bellamy – for beating the website into shape using programming

Cathy Callus – for manuals, caring, and being lovely

Kate Cary – for checking spelling, and for to monitoring my word usement grammarness

Victoria Hull – for keeping all us Fishies safe and warm, being fab, and remembering things

Jodie Kearns – for all your help and support (and it's probably in the cupboard, by the way)

Debbie Lampon – for more website battering using programmy code stuff

Christina Onyett – for hitting the PC when it crashed and making it work

Jane Rostron – for e-Tutoring people and keeping them away from us

Donna Wheeler – for manuals and bot missiles

... and Henry Stewart who, thankfully, didn't listen to all the people who said that you could never run a business being nice to the staff, or with a silly name like Happy

Computers. Thanks for starting such a great place to work, and giving all us troublemakers jobs.

Happy Computers (www.happy.co.uk) is a computer training company who believes that learning should be fun. It was established to combine technical expertise and excellent training skills with an enjoyable learning environment. In 2001 they were named as IT Training Company of the Year by the Institute of IT Training. All Happy Computers' training is based around the following age-old principle:

➤ Tell me and I will forget

➤ Show me and I will remember

➤ Involve me and I will understand.

LearnFish is the online division of Happy Computers. In partnership with eCampus, we have created a complete range of online learning materials for ECDL, under the LearnECDL brand. Contact us via the Website:

www.learnecdl.com

For more details of classroom training contact Happy Computers:

Website: www.happy.co.uk

E-mail: happy@happy.co.uk

Phone: 020 7375 7300

And seeing as I spent ages fiddling about with putting the pages together, coping with a constantly crashing PC and a deadline of about 12 seconds, I think I deserve a paragraph all to myself.

And that was it. Oh well.

Introduction

What Is This Book For?

This book is designed to teach you everything you need to know to be able to pass the ECDL (European Computer Driving License) exam. It is aimed at users of Microsoft Office 2000, and all screenshots will reflect this. If you are using any other packages, for example Star Office or Lotus, then the screenshots will look completely wrong. It is recommended that you use Office 2000 while using this book. The File Management section of the book is based on Windows 98 and above.

How Do I Use This Book?

Open the first page of the book, and read the words from left to right, starting at the top of the page, and working your way down to the bottom. Proceed to the next page, ensuring that the page numbers are ascending as you go along. When you have finished the book, close it.

That's Very Funny. Now How Do I Really Use It?

As this book is aimed at helping you to pass the exam, you really need to read every scrap of information in it. There is nothing less, nothing more than you need. If you are very confident that you know, for example, how to mail merge, then it should be okay to skip that part. But it is worth checking through just in case – you may know how to mail merge using an Excel data document, but the ECDL syllabus assumes that you know how to do it using a Word data document. So even if you think you know everything, it won't hurt to read everything just in case.

If you know lots of things, but just need to know one particular thing, you can just flick around and pick up the piece of information. Feel free to dip in and out, but some things will require you to know something else first – taking the mail merge example, the section on merging will assume you know how to create a data document and a main document. The book also assumes that you can switch a PC on and off, and can use a mouse.

Instead of just reading the book, try and go through it when you have access to a PC and Microsoft Office. Have a go at anything you learn, or anything you're not sure of – it's the best way to understand it.

Module 1
Basic Concepts Of Information Technology

Chapter 1

Getting Started

Computer Terms

What Is A Computer?

A computer is a machine that can run programs to carry out a wide range of tasks. Unlike, say, a calculator, it can be programmed to do more or less anything. However, it can only do what you tell it to do. It cannot take over the planet; unless you tell it to.

The First Computer

The first computer was called the Atanasoff-Berry Computer (ABC), after its inventors John Vincent Atanasoff and Clifford Berry. It was made between 1937–1942, and originally designed to solve equations. Later on, computers got much bigger, heavier and more complex. Information was fed into them with punched cards, and bits of the machines tended to pop and explode. As computers became more advanced, they became smaller, faster, more reliable, and less likely to explode. Nowadays they are much smaller, and never explode at all.

Hardware And Software

A computer, and all the physical, solid objects that come with it, is a piece of hardware. If you can touch it, or feel it, it is hardware. Software is the name for the programs that run on the computer, or that come supplied with it.

Other Names For Computers

➤ **PC/Microcomputer**: a computer is usually called a PC – this stands for Personal Computer. Back in the olden days (the 1970s and 1980s) it was called a microcomputer. Just like computers themselves, they've managed to make the words smaller as well.

➤ **Desktop/Laptop**: the two main types of PC are desktop and laptop. Desktop PCs are used on or near a desk, and consist of a large box base, a screen, a keyboard and a mouse. Laptop PCs are very small, and contain everything in one small package – they are a lot more expensive than desktops.

➤ **Mainframe**: this is a large, expensive computer used by, for example, NASA for critical, complex operations like launching the space shuttle. Mainframes can run several different programs simultaneously, and allow hundreds or even thousands of people to connect to them at the same time.

➤ **Minicomputer**: halfway between a mainframe and a normal computer, this is typically used by large companies, such as banks, to keep the business running smoothly.

➤ **Network Server**: like a minicomputer, this controls a company network, letting users access company files and communicate with each other.

➤ **Dumb/Intelligent terminals**: a dumb terminal is connected to a network server but you can only access it and read/write to it, it cannot do anything on its own. An intelligent terminal can do this and also perform other functions – a normal PC connected to a company network would also be called an intelligent terminal.

Computer Hardware

Computer Types

➤ **Tower**: a tower-style PC is slightly larger than a normal one, and usually stands on one side. Network servers are usually tower PCs.

➤ **Desktop**: a desktop-style PC is one that sits flat on a desk.

Parts Of A Computer

The external parts of a computer comprise the following:

➤ **Base unit**: this is the square box that all the other parts plug into. It contains all the components that make the PC work.

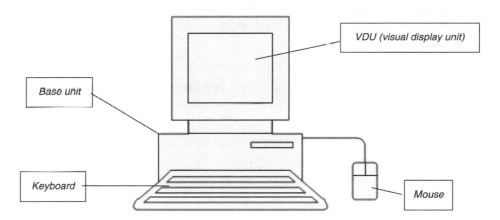

➤ **VDU**: the screen/monitor/visual display unit (VDU) is the part of the computer that shows you what is going on, and what you are doing. For example, in a word processing program, you would see the letters you type appearing on the screen.

➤ **Keyboard**: this is what you use to type information into the computer.

➤ **Mouse**: the mouse is used to point and click on things on the screen – when you move the mouse, a pointer on the screen moves as well. If you press the mouse button while the pointer is on certain icons or buttons, you can run programs or open menus.

The internal parts of a computer comprise the following:

➤ **CPU**: the CPU, or Central Processing Unit, is the brains of the computer. All the 'thinking', calculating and processing is done here. Its speed is measured in megahertz (MHz), which measures the amount of complete circuits a signal can travel around the processor in one second, or the millions of simple calculations it can make in a second. If it has a speed of 600 MHz, this means it can do 600 million things in one second.

➤ **Hard disk**: the hard disk drive is used to store programs and information. When you save a file, it is saved onto your hard disk.

➤ **Floppy disk**: a floppy disk drive is like a hard disk, but with removable disks called floppies or floppy disks. Floppies can be used to transfer small files from one PC to another. Older floppies really were floppy, as they came in soft plastic or card cases. Today's floppies are a bit more sturdy, although the disk itself is very floppy and wobbly, which is why it comes in a strong plastic case.

➤ **Memory**: when a program is run, it is loaded into the computer's memory. The more memory a PC has, the more things it can do at one time.

Computer Accessories

Disks

➤ **Floppy disks**: these are used when you need to transfer a small file from one PC to another. If the file is a bit too big, you need something that will hold more information.

➤ **Zip drives**: these are another type of floppy drive, that use zip disks instead of floppy disks. Zip disks can hold about 100 times as much information as a floppy disk.

➤ **CDs**: if you have a CD writer/burner, you can put files on to a CD (Compact Disc), which can hold over 400 floppies' worth of files. A DVD (Digital Versatile Disc) is a higher quality form of a CD, and can hold 6 to 7 times as much as a normal CD.

Backup Tapes

Another way of backing up large amounts of information is a backup tape. This is a magnetic tape, like a video or audio cassette, which has the files streamed onto it. It usually takes a long time, and is only used for large backups. They are sometimes called data cartridges.

Printers

Printers are used to transfer information from the computer onto paper, for example, if you typed a letter in a word processor you would probably want to print it out. Printers come in many different shapes and sizes:

➤ **Laser**: these are generally large, expensive printers that work like a photocopier. They usually have very high quality printouts.

➤ **Inkjet**: these are smaller, cheaper printers that use a little cartridge to spray a jet of ink onto the paper. They are fairly quiet and of good quality, but are not as fast or good as lasers.

➤ **Dot matrix/impact**: the old type of printer uses a ribbon and a print head, like a typewriter. They are very loud and extremely slow. However, they are very cheap to buy.

Modems

A modem is a device that allows a computer to connect to a telephone line and access the Internet, send and receive e-mails, or dial into a computer network. Most PCs have a modem built inside them, but external ones are also available.

Network Cards

A network card is used to link up one PC to another PC, or several PCs in a network.

Talking To The PC

Apart from the mouse and keyboard, there are other ways of communicating with your PC:

➤ **Trackball**: like an upside-down mouse – it sits on the desk, and you move the ball with your fingers to control the movement of the pointer on the screen.

➤ **Light pen**: a special pen that lets you draw directly onto the screen, or click on buttons and menus.

➤ **Touch screen**: like a normal screen, but with a thin, transparent, touch-sensitive layer of plastic covering it. When you touch a part of the screen, it has the same effect as if you had clicked on that area with a mouse.

➤ **Joystick**: a knob that can be moved around in any direction. Used mainly for playing games.

Multimedia

Multimedia is a fancy word for something that uses sound, music, pictures, video and animation. Multi means many. A medium is a thing, like sound or video, that is used to communicate. Multimedia literally means 'many types of communication'. Most modern PCs are multimedia machines, and need certain things to work:

➤ **Sound card**: a special controller inside the PC that translates sound into a form the computer can understand.

➤ **Microphone**: a device that lets you record your voice, or other sounds.

➤ **Speakers**: the objects that let you hear the sounds and music playing.

➤ **Scanner (optional)**: a bit like a photocopier, this scans your own pictures or drawings into the computer so that you can edit them.

➤ **Digital camera (optional)**: this works like a normal camera, but doesn't use film – instead it lets you transfer the pictures directly into your PC.

Input And Output Devices

All of the above extra bits and pieces are input and output devices. This means that they are used to get information into the PC, or take information out of it.

➤ An **input** device lets you put information **in** to a PC – keyboard, mouse, microphone, scanner, etc.

➤ An **output** device takes information **out** of the PC – printer, screen/VDU, speakers, etc.

Some items, like floppy disk drives and modems, are both input **and** output devices – they are used to get information in as well as out of a PC.

What Is A Peripheral Device?

A peripheral device is anything which you can attach to the main part of your computer. Some of the accessories we have looked at so far are peripheral devices, such as:

➤ printers

➤ scanners

➤ modems

➤ speakers.

Memory And Storage

RAM

When a computer runs a program, it loads it into its RAM (Random Access Memory). The amount of RAM a computer has affects its performance – the more RAM, the more things it can do, faster. You can read and overwrite the RAM, but everything in it disappears when the computer is switched off.

It works a bit like your own memory – when you eat a packet of crisps, your brain loads up the programs about how to open the packet, how to pick up crisps, how to chew, how to swallow, etc. You don't need those 'programs' in your mind all the time, only when they're needed. When you have finished the crisps, your brain 'closes' the eating program, and loads up something else.

ROM

ROM (Read Only Memory) contains all of the information that the computer needs to switch itself on, and check that all its systems are working. It cannot be changed or overwritten by you, and keeps its contents even when the PC is switched off.

Hard Disks

A hard disk drive contains a hard, round disk covered in a magnetic layer. Special arms, like record player needles, read and write the magnetic information whenever you run a program or save a file. They don't actually touch the surface of the hard disk – if they did, they would damage it. A hard disk is very delicate and complicated. It is sealed in a hard, airtight case, so that no dust can get in and damage it.

Bits And Bytes

Computer memory and hard disk space is measured in bits and bytes. One bit is the smallest unit, and represents either 1 or 0, depending on its magnetic charge. Eight bits make one byte, which is roughly the space you would need to store one letter of the alphabet. Basically:

8 bits = 1 byte

1,000 bytes = 1 kilobyte (KB)

1,000 kilobytes (KB) = 1 megabyte (MB)

1,000 megabytes (MB) = 1 gigabyte (GB)

So 1 GB = 1,000 MB = 1,000,000 KB = 1,000,000,000 bytes = 8,000,000,000 bits

If a PC has 64MB of RAM, it is capable of keeping 64 million letters in its memory at once. If its hard disk had 4GB of space, it could store 4 billion letters.

Check This Out...

1,024 Not 1,000 Bytes In A Kilobyte

Actually there are 1,024 bytes in a kilobyte, 1,024 kilobytes in a megabyte, etc. This is because memory is based on a binary system not one based on the number 10, (2, 4, 8, 16, 32 ... 1,024). However, most people use 1,000 because it is easier to multiply and makes life easier.

Let's try to understand this in terms of what you will be using a computer for. Imagine that you produce a file in Word.

➤ Each character that you type will be roughly one byte.

➤ If you type 3,000 characters to a page then each page will be roughly 3,000 bytes, or 3KB.

➤ Let's say that you type 3 pages – your file will be 9,000 bytes, or 9KB.

➤ Imagine that you type 500 pages – your file will be roughly 1,500,000 bytes or 1.5MB.

➤ Now, if you save two 500 page files into the same folder, that folder will be 3,000,000 bytes or 3MB.

My File Is Bigger Than That!

Word saves lots of other information along with your file – formatting, tables, etc. These will make the file bigger. Pictures will also dramatically increase the size. Try saving it as a plain text file, to see how big it really is.

Comparing The Capacity Of Different Memory Devices

Memory device	Average capacity
Hard disk	5GB
Zip disk	100MB
CD-ROM	650MB–1GB
Floppy disk	1.38MB
DVD-ROM	4.7 GB (single sided) or 9.4 GB (double sided)

Comparing The Cost Of Different Memory Devices

Memory device	Average cost
Hard disk	£50–£150
Zip disk	£20
CD-ROM	£0.50
Floppy disk	£0.10
DVD-ROM	£5–10

What Should I Consider When Buying A PC?

The performance of the PC depends on various factors. When you are buying a PC, consider the following:

➤ **CPU speed**: this is measured in megahertz (MHz) and is usually included in the name of the chip. The higher the number of megahertz, the faster your PC will run. 33MHz used to be considered quite fast, these days 1GHz (gigahertz) is the norm.

➤ **RAM**: this is temporary memory. The more RAM your computer has, the faster it will run. You should look for at least 128MB, more if possible – memory is usually very cheap, and can dramatically improve PC performance.

➤ **Hard disk space**: hard disk space used to be measured in megabytes (MB), and a 200MB hard disk drive used to be a lot. These days the operating system normally takes up at least 200MB, and hard drives come in gigabytes (GB). The more bytes your hard disk has, the better your computer will perform. The average is about 8GB, but the more you have, the better.

➤ **Sound card and graphics card**: if you just want to write letters and do your accounts, then these are not important. But if you want to play the latest games or create music, then you will need a decent sound card and a good graphics card. These can be expensive, but you should be able to pick them up for around £50 each.

Volatile And Non-volatile Memory

Volatile memory is memory that loses its contents when the computer is switched off – like RAM.

Non-volatile memory is memory that keeps its contents, even when the computer is switched off – like ROM.

Smart Cards

A smart card is a small card that contains memory and a tiny circuit board, which lets you store personal information and other details. These are usually very small, about the size of a normal credit card.

Computer Software

What Is Software?

Software refers to the programs that are loaded onto a computer. Microsoft Word and Excel are software programs, as is Internet Explorer and Windows.

➤ **Systems software** is the software that runs the computer – this is usually called the operating system. Windows is the operating system a lot of people use.

➤ **Application software** is the programs that run on the PC. Word and Excel are applications, for example.

Examples Of Application Software

Type of software	What does it do?	Examples
Word processors	Has the same function as a typewriter – for producing letters, reports or other written documents.	Word, WordPerfect
Spreadsheets	Lets you perform calculations on a table containing text and figures. Spreadsheets are usually used for budgets, statistics, etc.	Excel, Lotus 1-2-3
Databases	Stores information, e.g. the names and addresses of all your clients.	Access, FileMaker Pro
Presentation tools	Creates presentations by allowing you to produce slides or handouts.	PowerPoint
Desktop publishing (DTP)	Lets you produce magazines, newsletters, etc.	Quark, PageMaker, Publisher
Multimedia applications	Lets you produce multimedia presentations, e.g. Websites, animations, videos.	Dreamweaver, FrontPage, Flash

The GUI

Older operating systems, like DOS (Disk Operating System) were purely text-based – if you wanted to do something, you had to type in a string of commands. Recently, the Windows-style operating system was introduced, which is called a GUI (Graphical User Interface).

The GUI is a system that lets you use the PC without knowing too much about it. Programs and commands are represented as little pictures, called icons. To run a program, you move the pointer over it using the mouse, and click on it with the mouse button.

Microsoft Windows is a GUI, as is MacOS (the operating system on Macintosh computers), SunOS (used on Sun workstation computers) and Workbench (used on Amiga computers).

Data

Data is not the same as software – for example, if you wrote a letter using a word processor like Word, Word would be the software, but the letter you wrote would be called data. Anything you create or save onto your hard disk or a floppy disk is data.

Software Development

Software programs don't just appear on trees, or out of thin air. First of all a group of people called **systems analysts** analyse the market, figure out what software is needed, and decide what sort of things should be done.

After that, the **programmers** sit in dark rooms for months and actually write the program. Once they have written the program, it has to be tested and have any mistakes fixed. Only then is it released to the public, to worldwide celebration and rejoicing.

Bugs

Nobody's perfect. Software programs are so big and complex, most of the time the people testing them can't find all the errors and problems, and they have to be released at some time. After a program has been out for a while, people notice that there are little things wrong with it – these things are called *bugs* for some reason (there are 'amusing' alternative words for most computer terms, you'll discover).

When the number of bugs gets too embarrassing for the software company, they release a *patch*, *service pack* or *bugfix*. This is a little add-on program that fixes most of the bugs that people have found.

If a program is big and complex enough, it will need several service packs as time goes by. Nearly every single software product released has bugs of some kind in it. This is why even though you have bought the latest brand-new PC, and have only had it switched on for half an hour, it can still crash, or freeze for no reason.

Chapter 2

Using
Information
Technology

Using Networks

What Is A Network?

A computer network is two or more computers connected together. They could be in the same room, in the same building, or on opposite sides of the world. There are several reasons for using a network:

➤ If you have two PCs but only one printer, the PCs can both connect to the printer and share it. You could have a whole company full of computers with only one printer, and everyone would be able to use it.

➤ As well as sharing things like printers, PCs on a network can also share files and data. Instead of making lots of copies of a file, like a company letter, one copy could be stored on a particular PC, and everyone could read it.

➤ To help people work together, users can send messages to each other through their connected computers – this is called electronic mail, or e-mail.

LANs And WANs

There are two main types of network:

➤ **LAN (Local Area Network):** this is a small network, connecting computers spread out over a fairly small, local area – either in the same building or in a few buildings.

➤ **WAN (Wide Area Network)**: this is a larger network, connecting computers spread out over a wide area – usually around the whole country, or around the world.

Connecting Computers Together

LANs are connected by a system of cables that let the computers talk to each other. The computers must also have network cards installed in order to get them to connect to the network.

WANs use the telephone cables (the PSDN – Public Switched Data Network), as well as satellites and other clever bits and pieces. This saves companies having to lay loads of extra cable, but it means they have to use special equipment to send their information down the phone lines.

Analogue And Digital

Computer information is digital, other information (like sound, voices, etc.) is analogue. For example, a digital watch measures the time digitally, while a wind-up watch uses analogue parts like springs, cogs, etc.

When a computer sends information down the telephone line, it has to convert it to analogue first. Once it reaches the other end, the receiving computer has to convert it back into digital information so that the information can be understood.

Modems

A modem is a device that lets a computer convert information into analogue sounds, and back again. This is referred to as **mo**dulation and **dem**odulation.

Suppose you wanted to send a file down the phone line. Your modem modulates it, or converts it into analogue noise, and relays it down the phone line. At the other end, another modem demodulates it, or converts it back into a digital file, so that the other PC can read it properly.

Modem speed, or baud rate, is measured in bits per second – how many bits of data it can transfer in one second. Most modems have a speed of 56kbps, which is 56,000 bits per second.

ISDN

ISDN (Integrated Services Digital Network) is a similar way of transferring data between PCs, but is all digital. It doesn't need to convert the information to analogue and back again, so it is a lot faster, running at 128kbps, or 128,000 bits per second. The digital line doesn't have the problems with interference and quality that a normal telephone line does.

Fax

A fax works in a similar way to a modem – in fact, it's like a scanner or photocopier combined with a modem. You put a piece of paper in it, the fax scans the words or pictures on the paper, and sends it down the telephone line. A fax machine at the other end receives the information, and prints out an exact copy of the original.

Telex

The telex was an ancient piece of technology dating from the 1970s. You would type in what you wanted to say on your telex machine (like an electronic typewriter), it would send that down the telephone line, and the telex machine at the other end would type out what you originally typed. Telexes are no longer in popular use. If you have one in your attic, take it to an antique dealer and get it valued.

The Internet And E-mail

The Internet

The Internet consists of lots and lots of computers and networks all connected together by telephone lines and cables. People use it to share information with other users around the world. There is information available on nearly every subject imaginable – it's like a massive electronic library.

The Internet is also sometimes called the **World Wide Web**, or the **Information Superhighway**, or any one of a number of trendy words and phrases, depending on what's cool this week. However, the Internet is **not** the same as the World Wide Web – the Internet is the huge network system that connects everything together, while the World Wide Web is the method of accessing information over the Internet (using browsers like Internet Explorer or Netscape). E-mail, FTP, newsgroups and the Web all use the Internet to communicate.

Websites

The information on the Internet is stored in Web pages and Websites. A Web page is like a normal page of text and pictures, but in a special file format that any computer can read. A program called a browser is used to read these pages. The two main types of browser are Internet Explorer and Netscape Navigator.

A Website is a collection of Web pages on the same topic, or by the same person. Like references or footnotes in books, Web pages can link to other sites – but if you click on the link with your mouse, it will take you directly to that page. These links are called hyperlinks.

What You Need

Accessing the Internet is just like accessing a normal network (LAN or WAN). You need a modem, or ISDN connection, and a cable to connect to it. You also need to subscribe to an ISP (Internet Service Provider). This is a company you have to go through to get on the Internet, using a user name and password (a bit like the way you get a telephone service – you can't have a telephone line until you sign up with a telephone company). Once you have connected, you can use your browser to look at the Websites.

Searching

There are more than one billion Web pages on the Internet. If you were browsing for something in particular, it could take you several hundred years to find it just by guessing. A search engine is a special Web page that lets you find what you're looking for quickly.

You type in a word or phrase, and the search engine quickly looks though all the Web pages for ones that match what you're after. It then shows you a list of likely Websites, which you can look through to see if they are of any use.

E-commerce

E-commerce (electronic commerce), basically, is doing business on the Internet. Most companies have their own Websites, and a lot of them allow people to do business with them this way. For example, most airline companies have a Website that lets you check flight schedules, and book tickets using your credit card details. It's all done online (on the Internet) and you don't even have to get out of your chair.

Imagine you had booked a flight to another country. You could book your hotel by contacting the hotel's Web page, you could arrange for a hired car to be waiting for you at the airport, book a meal in a local restaurant, check maps of the area for the best places to go – the opportunities are endless.

E-mail

E-mail can be sent over the Internet, just like in a company network. Unlike a company network though, you can send it to anyone in the world, as long they have access to the Internet and e-mail software.

When you want to send an e-mail to a friend, you simply type your letter into your e-mail software, enter your friend's e-mail address, and send it. The software sends it off down the phone line to your ISP, they forward it to your friend's ISP, which then sends it on to your friend. The next time your friend 'logs on' to the Internet and checks their e-mail, your message will be sitting waiting for them.

Chapter 3

Computers In Everyday Life

Home, Work And Education

Computers In The Home

Many people have a PC at home, either for work or entertainment. Some of the common uses for a home PC are:

- ➤ playing games
- ➤ doing school work
- ➤ working from home
- ➤ managing your finances, Internet banking, etc.
- ➤ writing letters
- ➤ e-mailing friends and relatives
- ➤ using the Internet.

Computers In Business

Nearly every single business or office has some sort of a computer in it. Most businesses depend on them. Here are some of the ways they use them:

- ➤ **Offices:** companies can use computers to store their records, keep track of their customers, or even help to run the business. A room full of old reports and files could be easily stored on a PC – and this would make it quicker to find something too. Computers are used to pay employees, send out letters to customers and communicate with branches in other areas.

➤ **Factories**: factories can use computers for the same tasks that an office would, and also control large machinery safely, collect customer orders, order supplies, etc.

➤ **Shops**: in addition to using computers in the same way that offices and factories do, shops and supermarkets use them on their checkout counters to scan in the price barcode on the things you buy. This information is shared with the warehouse, so that the stock is always kept up to date. They also use magnetic strip readers if you pay by credit card. These check that you have enough money to pay, and then take the money from your account.

Schools

It is very important to have some computer skills in today's working world. As well as storing student details, names, addresses, academic records and so on, most schools now have some form of computer education. Pupils can learn about the computer world, and also make use of the ability to connect up to other learning institutions around the world. Pupils can also write reports using the computers, or start school newspapers.

Hospitals

Hospitals use computers to help them in their day-to-day running. Patient records are stored on PCs for ease of access, appointments are booked for them, and their vital signs can be constantly monitored.

Government

Like any other large business, the government relies on computers to help it run things. Apart from the normal uses, it needs heavy computing power to keep track of the population, tax records and the voting register, for example.

Everyday Life

Computers, Computers Everywhere

We all recognize computers when they are a big box on a desk with a screen and keyboard. But these aren't the only computers in the world – some of them are much smaller, some of them you will never see, some of them you will use without even knowing that they are there.

When you set your video to tape The Simpsons (and miss the last 10 minutes because the snooker dragged on a bit), a tiny computer chip controls the timer and the programming. When you do your laundry, a computer works out how long to spin the drum for (and how to lose one of your socks). When you take money out of a cashpoint machine, a computer checks your PIN (Personal Identification Number), works out if you have enough money and hands out the cash.

When you try and telephone most companies now, a computer controlled message gives you different options which you can access by dialling certain numbers on your telephone. Somebody has to sit and say all the words into a recorder, so that the computer can play them back in that strange, jerking way that they have. Another way of doing this is a speech synthesizer, which mimics the human voice.

The Information Society

Due to the many areas in which computers are being used, the world we live in now is sometimes referred to as the Information Society. Information and data are very important, and so are the machines we use to work with them – computers. Information Technology refers to computers, accessories, gadgets – anything used to work with information.

Computers are used at work, in the home, in shops, at school. They are everywhere. But you still have a choice, whether or not to use them, or how you use them. You can have a full, happy life without ever using a computer. You may want to use one every single day.

It is important to remember though, that of all the information out there, on the Internet, in e-mails, stored on computers – most, if not all, of it is created by people. Just because it is on a PC or a Website doesn't mean it is true, or important. Treat this information just as you would treat articles in a newspaper, things you see on television or stories you hear from real people.

Remember: a lot of people have access to the Internet, and the ability to create Websites. Some of them are good people, some are bad, and this is reflected in the content of these Websites. Before you blame computers and the Internet for promoting hatred, prejudice or dangerous subjects, remember that PCs only do what people tell them to do. Banning the Internet won't stop bigots from trying to spread their message around.

The Year 2000 Problem

Although this is not an issue any more, you may not know what all the fuss was about. Basically, when computers were invented, programmers used 2 letters to store the year (79 instead of 1979, etc.) to save space and memory. Unfortunately, when the year 2000 arrived, some PCs thought it was the year 1900, as all they had to represent the year were the digits '00'. There was also a leap year issue – i.e. was it or wasn't it a leap year (people still argue about this, as well as those who say 'it's not the real millennium you know', as if they expected everyone not to have a big party when the year 2000 hit – it didn't matter if it was the 'correct' millennium or not, we all just wanted to watch the numbers change).

This caused some problems (although not as many as the panicmongers were telling people) with some software and hardware. Many people were convinced this meant that 'all the bombs would go off'. This would have been true if, for some reason, 'all the bombs' had been programmed to explode if it ever became 1900 again. As with many computer panics, it was a bit of a river of fire (the supposed 'river of fire' on the Thames when the year 2000 arrived, which turned out to be more like a sparkler in a bucket of water). At the time of writing this (July 2002), the world hasn't ended yet, and none of 'the bombs' have gone off.

I suppose the lesson here is 'plan ahead', and don't panic when someone tells you that the world is going to end, because it usually won't.

Computers Or Humans?

Which is better for a job, a computer or a human being? That all depends on the job. If the job is storing millions of pieces of information, finding and sorting them quickly and doing mindless tasks 24 hours a day, then obviously a computer is better. If the job requires any creative or artistic input, then of course a real person is needed.

Computers are wonderful machines, but they can't do everything. They're not going to take your job away from you. They can't sing, dance, understand, think, or reason. You'll never find a computer police officer (apart from RoboCop, who is, of course, real) or a computer author. There's no substitute for the human touch.

Working Safely With Computers

Common Sense

Computers are never going to rebel against humanity and attack you while you sleep. However, as with any objects that use electricity, or objects that you use a lot, you must use your common sense. Computers are usually safe to use, but there are some things you must look out for.

RSI

RSI stands for Repetitive Strain Injury. If you are typing and/or using the mouse a lot, you can strain the muscles in your hand, arm or back. Take a short break every fifteen minutes, so that your muscles can relax. Do not go longer than an hour without a break. Try to arrange your day so that you break up your computer time by doing tasks away from the screen.

Eyes

Like your hands and arms, your eyes can get strained if you have been working on a PC for a long time without taking break. Look away from the screen whenever you can, focus on things further away, and remember to blink – it sounds silly, but when you get heavily involved with any screen (television included) you blink a lot less. You should have adjustable controls on your screen so you can change the brightness and contrast.

Lighting

It is very important that the lighting is correct when you look at your computer screen as this can help reduce eyestrain. It's a bit like when you're watching television inside on a bright sunny day and you have to draw the curtains. Light should be soft – so fit blinds on windows and diffusers over lights.

Sit Properly

Your mother always used to tell you to sit up straight – it turns out that she was right all along and ahead of her time.

➤ Your PC screen should be at a level where you can see it without leaning forward or backward. You should be able to adjust your screen – tilt it or swivel it in any direction.

➤ You should have an adjustable chair that supports your back properly.

➤ Think about getting a footrest.

➤ Your keyboard should be at a level where your arms are parallel to the floor.

➤ Make sure you have enough space on your desk to have your mouse and keyboard in a comfortable position.

Cables

There are roughly twenty-seven million cables coming out the back of your PC. Modern technology, while making everything else smaller, has somehow increased the size and amount of the wires. It is very easy to trip over them, so make sure they are all out of the way tidily. Besides, it looks nicer.

Another thing worth mentioning, is try not to plug everything into one adapter. That goes for any electrical equipment, as you can overload your fuses or even start a fire. Plugging several adapters into each other is also a bad thing. Just because you can, doesn't mean that you should. Watch those 1970s public information adverts at 3am, they'll tell you the same thing: fire bad, tree pretty.

Protecting Your Work

Your Data

Your data is very valuable. It may not have a cash value, but if you had spent 3 hours typing in a letter or big report, you wouldn't want to lose it. It is up to you to look after it.

Passwords

You probably don't want people reading your documents, especially confidential information. You may want to put a password on them for security. Most software lets you password protect a document so that only you, or someone who knows the password, can read them.

➤ Choose a password that is easy to remember – if you forget the password, then the document is lost to you forever. Sure, it will be secure, but that's no consolation.

➤ Do not write the password down anywhere – passwords are supposed to be secret. If you start writing them down so you don't forget, then why bother having one at all?

➤ **Never** make the password your birthday, girlfriend/boyfriend/wife/brother's name, pet's name, or a football team, etc., etc. Most people's passwords can be guessed after about 5 goes. Choose an obscure word or number that means something to you but that nobody else will know. Better still, use a combination of letters and numbers – something that nobody will guess.

Backups

If you came to work one day to find that the building had burned down, you would lose all of your data (and have a day off). However, if you had copied your important files onto floppy disks or some other form of storage the night before, you wouldn't lose anything. Make regular backups and keep them **away** from the office – it won't help you much if the building burns down with your backups inside. You can't insure your data – you can never get it back once it has gone.

Viruses

You've probably heard a lot of wild stories about viruses in the press. While they are not as ominous and disastrous as they sound, they are a very real threat to you. They are programs written by 'Bad People' that copy themselves around sneakily and damage computers.

Some viruses merely display a message telling of the programmer's prowess, which are full of spelling mistakes, LOTS OF CAPITAL LETTERS and terrible grammar that it am not good. Some display a message and delete data from your hard disk. The damage levels vary from virus to virus.

Your PC can catch a virus by opening an infected e-mail attachment (a program sent within an e-mail message), using an infected floppy disk or getting an infected file from the Internet (not as common as the other two methods).

Your PC **cannot** get a virus by looking at Web pages, or by using e-mail normally.

To keep your PC safe from viruses:

➤ Make sure your PC has the latest virus software installed, and regularly update its data files so that it can recognize new viruses (roughly 300 new viruses appear every month).

➤ Always scan floppy disks for viruses before using any information on them.

➤ Never run an e-mail attachment unless you are sure who it is from and have scanned the attachment itself for viruses.

➤ Keep an emergency disk nearby just in case – your anti-virus software will create one for you. If your PC becomes infected, reboot with the emergency disk in the drive, and it will try to clean the infection for you.

Virus Hoaxes

This is a fairly recent problem, and a very annoying one: you get an e-mail from a friend telling you about a scary new virus that has just come out. Apparently it has been reported by Microsoft, or IBM, or AOL or someone like that, it is even worse that the last virus that came out and has no cure. The message then tells you to forward the message on to all of your friends. You later find out the whole thing was made up.

This is a type of virus in itself. It is designed to create a panic, and get everyone sending the same message to all of their friends, who then send it to all of their friends and so on and so on. It ties up your company mail PC with hundreds of e-mails going around and wastes everyone's time. Sometimes the e-mail traffic is so heavy, it can crash a company network.

The e-mail text usually goes along these lines:

WARNING: If you receive an e-mail with the subject line *InsertSubjectHere*, do not open the file. The file contains the *InsertVirusNameHere* virus. This information was announced yesterday morning at IBM/Microsoft/*InsertCompanyNameHere*. This is a very dangerous virus, much worse than 'Melissa', and there is NO remedy for it at this time. If you open/read/look at the e-mail, it will completely delete your hard drive/do some other ridiculously frightening thing. This is a new, very malicious virus and not many people know about it. Pass this warning along to EVERYONE in your address book ASAP so that this threat may be stopped.

If you receive an e-mail like this, do not send it to all of your friends – if you do, the hoaxer has won. Check and find out if it is a hoax, with an online virus library:

The Network Associates Virus Library:

http://vil.nai.com/vil

F Secure Hoax Warnings:

http://www.f-secure.com/virus-info/hoax

Urban Legends – Virus Hoaxes Page:

http://urbanlegends.about.com/science/urbanlegends/msubvir.htm

The last site also contains information about other e-mail hoaxes you will receive, for example, the one about the businessman falling asleep in a hotel and waking up with his kidneys stolen, etc. These are never true, and your friends have probably received them 50 times already. If you insist on sending them on, you will lose all your friends and become a hermit.

Do Not Delete A File If A Virus Warning Tells You To!

Some virus hoaxes pretend that if you have a certain file on your PC, then you are infected – this is not true! The file is usually an important one, and removing it will damage your system. Never delete files or forward virus alerts without checking the above Web pages, or talking to an IT support person.

Save, Save, Save

This is the most important thing you will ever learn in computing. **Ever**.

➤ If you are working on a document, and your PC crashes or has a power cut, **if you haven't saved your document, you will lose it.**

That's it, simple really, but for some reason, this little fact escapes everyone. One of the most common PC support issues goes along these lines:

Person: 'I was typing this letter, and the PC crashed/the plug came out, and I lost it. Can you get it back?'

PC Support Person: 'Did you save the letter?'

Person: 'No. Can you get it back for me?'

PC Support Person: 'No.'

Person: 'But …'

PC Support Person: 'This conversation is over.'

If you haven't saved it, you haven't saved it and that's it. Repeat this to yourself 1,000 times. YOU MUST SAVE YOUR WORK EVERY 10 MINUTES. Then if it all explodes, you've only lost 10 minutes' work. If you are typing a letter for 2 hours and, just before you save it, the machine dies, you have just lost all 2 hours' worth. Bye bye.

Good practice: as soon as you create the document, before you've even typed one word, save it. Find out the keyboard shortcut or find the **Save** icon and, every 5 or 10 minutes, click **Save**, hit **Ctrl+S**, or whatever it is in that particular program.

Another good tip: never type a document and think 'I'll just print it first, then I'll save it'. This is a very bad thing to do. Save it first, then print it. Don't tempt fate. PC's often crash when you try to print something without saving it first – there might be a good reason for this but, then again, they might just do it to annoy you.

Always save every 10 minutes. I realize I've already said that, but it's worth repeating, several times. Save – your – work, all the time. There is **nothing** more important than this.

The problem: you won't listen. I didn't. I never bothered, until one day, 7 years ago, I lost 4 hours' work due to a power cut. Since then, I do Ctrl+S every 5 minutes, no matter what I'm doing. But you won't start doing this until you lose a large amount of work. That's just the way it is, really. Unless you start saving now, get the practice in before it's too late. Not for me – for your data.

Save Your Work Every 10 Minutes!

Have I mentioned that already? I wasn't sure. Save! Save! Save! Tear this page out and tape it to your PC so that you never forget. Save!

Protec-

Wait, I'm not finished talking about saving. Save! SAVE! Save your work! Every ten minutes! Okay, you can start the next section now.

Protecting Your PC

➤ Try not to eat or drink while using your PC – spilt drinks and dropped biscuit crumbs make your keyboard sticky and unusable, but if you spill them on your PC they can destroy it completely.

➤ Don't leave the PC in a place where it will get very hot or very cold. Many computer parts are only designed to operate within a certain range of temperatures. For example, if a CPU overheats it will usually shut down, but some types will be irreparably damaged.

➤ When you have finished using your PC, shut it down properly and wait until it shuts down completely. It will normally display a message when it is safe to switch it off, although some PCs switch themselves off when you shut them down. Don't pull the plug out or switch it off while it's still doing something. The RAM empties when the PC is switched off, and you will lose your work. Switching it off without shutting it down can damage the hard disk.

➤ Water and electricity don't mix. If it's plugged in, it will explode or catch fire. If it isn't plugged in, the circuits will still get damaged.

➤ Try to keep dust away from your PC – it clogs up the insides.

➤ See those air vents and holes in the case? They're there for a reason. Don't block them. Keep at least a foot between them and any walls, shelves, etc.

➤ Don't move the PC base unit while it is switched on. The hard disk is very delicate, and moving it can cause the read/write arms to come into contact with the disk surface. This will badly damage it.

➤ Keep floppy disks away from the screen, speakers, and magnets – any data on them can be erased. Similarly, keep magnets away from the base unit.

➤ Although this should go without saying, never ever hang clothes on a PC or monitor to dry. That's not a joke, some people actually do it.

Chapter 4

Legal Issues

Copyright And Software

Copyright

The same copyright laws that apply to newspapers, books, television and film apply to data on computers or the Internet. If someone has created something and put it on their Website, you cannot take it and pass it off as your own, or even distribute it without permission from the person who made it. It remains their property. If it's a computer program you are not allowed to change the code – even if it is an improvement.

Licensing

Software is licensed instead of sold – this means that you are paying to use it and must agree to certain conditions (the license agreement most programs ask you to agree to). If a company had 200 PCs, and needed Microsoft Office on them all, it would be silly to buy 200 copies of it – they would take up a whole room. But it would be illegal to buy one copy and install it on all 200 PCs. This is where licensing comes in. There are various types of multi-user licence depending on whether you want it to cover one building, or several branches, or a certain number of users at one time. A company can have only one copy of the software, but will have paid to use it on 200 machines.

Piracy

In days of old, pirates attacked ships and stole their treasure. For some bizarre reason, the word 'pirate' is now used to refer to someone who illegally makes a copy of a piece of software. The only similarity is that theft is involved, but the word is in common use now, so it's too late to question it. Software theft/copying is piracy. Don't do it. Someone has worked long and hard to create it and if you just steal it then they lose out. Some people distribute illegally copied software over the Internet or other sources, but it's up to you to refuse it. Be responsible.

Freeware And Shareware

Some software is written by people who then give it away, totally free – this is called freeware. It is usually only for your personal use; if a company uses it for profit, then they will normally have to pay for it.

Shareware is similar – the program is given out free for you to try out for a month or so. If you want to keep it after that, you have to pay for it. If not, you must delete it. This relies on people's honesty, unfortunately it doesn't always work. Some software is designed to stop working after the trial period or is missing certain features; once you have paid you are given the code to unlock it, or given a complete version.

Other forms of freeware/shareware are cardware/postcardware/e-mailware – instead of paying, you send the programmer a card or an e-mail saying thanks. A lesser-known version is hugware – if you like the program and want to keep it, you have to give someone a hug.

The Data Protection Act

Big Brother

As so many businesses use computers to keep records, there are probably a lot of computers that have stored your name, address, and other details. When you apply for a mortgage or for credit, companies check with your bank or a credit agency, who look up your credit records. If they show you're a high risk, you get refused the loan. If not, then you are approved. Sometimes these companies have the wrong information – this can cause you to be wrongly refused credit.

Some companies sell their lists of names and addresses to marketing companies, which explains why you get loads of junk mail – such as offers of credit cards, 'You Could Have Won Ten Million Pounds', etc., etc. The same goes for e-mail addresses, leading to junk e-mail – this is called spam (a reference to the Monty Python sketch where absolutely everything on the menu is served with a certain brand of luncheon meat).

Data Protection

The Data Protection Act 1998 is intended to safeguard the information about you.

Anyone who holds personal details about an individual on computer must register with the Data Protection Registrar, giving details of the information they hold, what it is used for, etc.

Companies who have your personal details are not allowed to use them for illegal purposes or even for a different purpose from that stated. They must be kept secure and out of the wrong hands. They must also be kept up-to-date and disposed of when no longer needed.

If a company has your details stored on computer, you are allowed to write to them requesting a copy of all the information about you. They must respond within 40 days, so even if they cannot give you the details immediately they have to write back and tell you this. You also have the right to correct the information if the details are incorrrect or get rid of it completely.

Module 2
File Management

Chapter 1

The Desktop

Introduction To The Desktop

The desktop is the screen you first see when your computer has started. It can be customized to look how you want and make it easier for you to do your work.

The Desktop Screen

A picture of the desktop screen is shown on the next page, although each desktop will look a little different.

What Is Each Part For?

The table below explains what the parts of the screen are for.

Part of the screen	What is it?
Icons	Pictures that represent a part of your computer, or applications or tools available on your computer. Double-click on them to run programs.
Background	This is the main desk part, and can be customized in many different ways – you could display a picture of your pet, for example (see page 46).

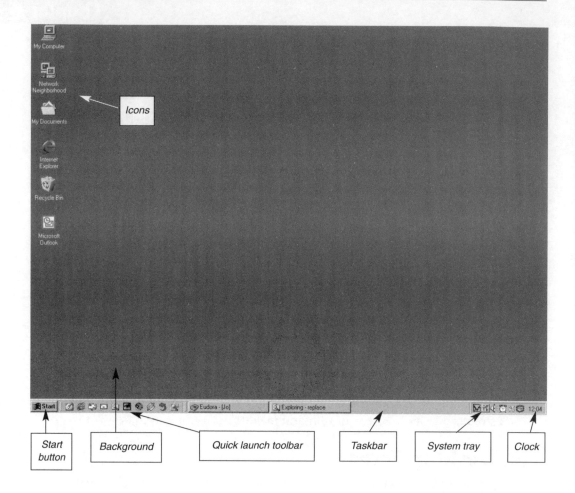

Start button	The place that contains icons to run all your programs and tools.
Taskbar	The bar that shows you what applications you have open. It also provides a way of switching between all open applications.
Quick launch toolbar	This is a toolbar that can be positioned anywhere but often sits somewhere on your taskbar. It provides quick access to applications on your computer.

Start button/Start menu   The place that contains icons to run all your programs and tools.

Taskbar   The bar that shows you what applications you have open. It also provides a way of switching between all open applications.

Quick launch toolbar   This is a toolbar that can be positioned anywhere but often sits somewhere on your taskbar. It provides quick access to applications on your computer.

System tray	A tool that can be used to change some of your computer's settings, and also provides information (such as whether you have certain software in use, or, if you are using a laptop computer, if you are low on battery).
Clock	A normal clock that tells the time (or at least the time that your computer thinks it is).

Desktop Icons

The little pictures you have on your desktop are all for different things:

My Computer

This lets you get at the computer's filing system. It gives you access to the different parts of your computer where information is stored (the drives). You can also change your computer settings from here (using the Control Panel).

Network Neighborhood

If your PC is on a network, this contains a list of all the resources available to you, i.e. printers, folders.

Recycle Bin

When you delete a document, it goes in here. You can then take it out if you didn't really mean to delete it!

My Documents

When you save a document, unless you instruct the machine otherwise, it will be saved in this folder.

The Taskbar

At the bottom of the screen there is a grey bar that runs from left to right. When you open a window a button for that window will appear on the bar. The **Start** button is on the far left in the following figure.

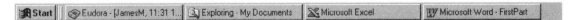

Having More Than One Window Open

You can work with a number of different windows at the same time. For example, you might have both Word and Internet Explorer open at the same time. To switch between the windows you have opened, just click on the button that refers to it on the Taskbar.

If You Can't See The Whole Description On The Taskbar

As you open more windows or programs in Windows, the buttons that represent them on the Taskbar become smaller. Just hold the mouse over the Taskbar for a second or two, and a note will pop up with a full description.

Moving The Taskbar

The Taskbar can be at the top, bottom, left or right of your screen. To move your Taskbar:

1   Position the mouse pointer on an empty part of the Taskbar (where there are no buttons).

2   Click and hold your left mouse button and drag to the edge of the screen (left, right, top or bottom) that you'd like it to be.

3   Release the mouse button – your Taskbar will be in its new position!

The Start Button

Clicking on the **Start** button shows the **Start** menu. From here you can open applications, view files, get help, find files, access your favourite Websites, run programs, change your settings and shut down or restart your computer. Just about everything you might want to do!

Using The Start Menu

1   Click on the **Start** button.

2   Click on the option you require (see below) – a sub-menu may appear.

3   If necessary, click on the option you require in the sub-menu.

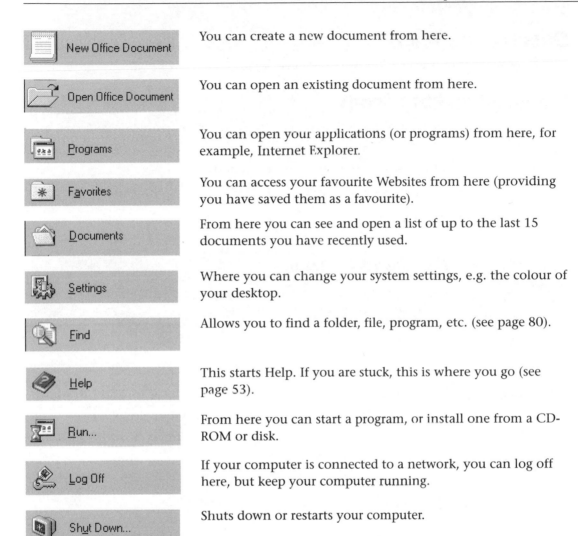

You can create a new document from here.

You can open an existing document from here.

You can open your applications (or programs) from here, for example, Internet Explorer.

You can access your favourite Websites from here (providing you have saved them as a favourite).

From here you can see and open a list of up to the last 15 documents you have recently used.

Where you can change your system settings, e.g. the colour of your desktop.

Allows you to find a folder, file, program, etc. (see page 80).

This starts Help. If you are stuck, this is where you go (see page 53).

From here you can start a program, or install one from a CD-ROM or disk.

If your computer is connected to a network, you can log off here, but keep your computer running.

Shuts down or restarts your computer.

Desktop Icons

Selecting Icons

Click on the icon to select it – it will turn blue.

Deselecting Icons

Click away from the icon – it will no longer be blue.

Moving Desktop Icons

You can rearrange your computer's desktop, just as you might rearrange your desk at work.

1 Position your mouse over the icon you wish to move.

2 Click and drag to a new position.

3 Release the mouse.

My Icons Won't Move!

Right click anywhere over the desktop and choose Arrange Icons. Make sure there is no tick next to Auto Arrange.

Arranging The Icons

You can let Windows tidy up your desktop by getting it to automatically arrange your icons.

1 Right-click anywhere over the desktop.

2 Click on Arrange Icons.

3 Click on Auto Arrange.

How Do I Know When It's On?

When Auto Arrange is on it will have a tick before it in the menu. Click it again to switch it off!

Opening A Window Using A Desktop Icon

The desktop icons can be used to open a window. Just double-click on the icon, and a window will open.

What Are Desktop Shortcuts?

➤ You can create shortcuts that allow you to open programs, folders or documents that you use frequently. You can put a shortcut onto your desktop.

➤ Shortcuts always have a little curly arrow in the bottom left corner of the icon.

➤ Shortcuts are only a link to the folder, document or program and not the actual file.

➤ If you delete a shortcut, it does not delete the original object.

My Received
Files

Creating A Shortcut On The Desktop

1 Open My Computer and find the icon for the program, folder or document that you want to create a shortcut for.

2 Restore or resize the My Computer window so you can see the desktop as well.

3 Hold the mouse over the icon you wish to create a shortcut to.

4 Click and drag the icon onto the desktop using the **right** mouse button.

5 Release the mouse – a shortcut menu will appear.

6 Click **Create Shortcut Here**.

or

1 Find the item that you want to create a shortcut for, using My Computer.

2 Right-click on the item – a menu will pop up.

3 Click **Send To**.

4 Click **Desktop (create shortcut)**.

Renaming Shortcuts

As a shortcut just points to a document, folder or program (and is not the actual thing) you can rename the shortcut without renaming the file. So you can call it whatever you like.

1 Position your mouse over the shortcut you wish to rename.

2 Right-click on the shortcut – a menu will pop up.

3   Click **Rename** – the name of the shortcut is highlighted.

4   Type in the new name for the shortcut.

5   Click away from the shortcut or press **Return**.

Deleting Shortcuts

You might wish to remove shortcuts that you no longer require. Deleting shortcuts does not delete the item to which the shortcut is pointing.

1   Right-click on the shortcut.

2   Click **Delete**.

3   Click Yes to confirm it.

The Desktop Settings

Customizing Your Desktop

Aside from creating new icons that are shortcuts to things that you frequently use, you can also change:

➤ The colour scheme your computer uses.

➤ The pattern or pictures (wallpaper) on you desktop background.

➤ The images that pop up when you don't use your computer for a while (the screen saver).

Changing The Wallpaper

The wallpaper is a picture you can have on your desktop background. To change the wallpaper:

1   Right-click on a blank part of the desktop.

2   Click **Properties**.

3   Click on the **Background** tab.

4   Click your choice in the list of Wallpaper – a preview will appear in the box above the name.

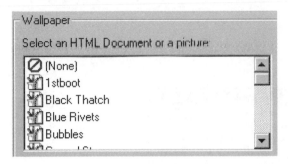

5   Click **OK**.

Tile, Centre Or Stretch?

You can have your picture repeated (tiled) over your desktop, stretched to fit or positioned as a picture in the centre of your desktop. After you choose your wallpaper from the list, click on the drop-down arrow at the end of the display box and click on the option you require.

Changing The Pattern

If you prefer patterns to wallpaper:

1   Right click anywhere on the desktop.

2   Click **Properties**.

3   Click on the **Background** tab.

4   Make sure the wallpaper chosen is *None*.

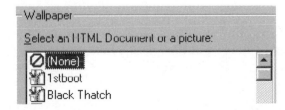

5   Click on **Pattern**.

6   Click your choice in the list of patterns. A preview will appear to the right of the list.

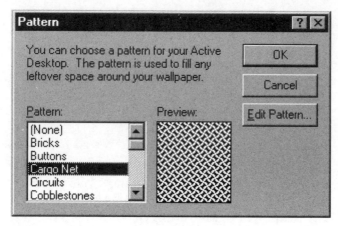

7   Click **OK**.

8   Click **OK** again.

Applying ...

If you want to apply any of your changes without losing the *Display Properties* dialog box, click on the **Apply** button!

Changing The Colour Scheme

If you would like a different colour scheme for your windows, icons, background, etc.:

1   Right click anywhere on the desktop.

2   Click **Properties**.

3   Click on the **Appearance** tab.

4   Click on the drop-down arrow at the end of the *Schemes* box.

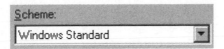

5 Click your choice.

6 Click **OK**.

Changing The Screen Saver

These pop up as full screen images or animations if your computer is left alone for a while. They save wear and tear on your screen and protect your work when you're away from the computer. To change the screen saver:

1 Right-click anywhere on the desktop.

2 Click **Properties**.

3 Click on the **Screen Saver** tab.

4 Click on the drop-down arrow at the end of the *Screen Saver* box.

5 Click your choice.

6 Click **Preview** button and don't move the mouse! Wait a few seconds and you will see a full-screen preview of the screen saver.

7 Sit for a minute, and decide if you like it.

8 Move the mouse to make it go away.

9 Change timing if required by clicking the up and down arrows next to the number.

10 Click **OK.**

Getting The Computer Screen Back

To get back to your normal computer screen when a screen saver is on, just press any key on the keyboard or move the mouse around. If the screen saver is protected you may need the password to stop it – see below.

Protecting Your Computer With A Screen Saver

If you do not want people to use your computer while you are away from your desk then you can specify a password that must be entered to clear the screen saver.

1 Right-click anywhere on the desktop.

2 Click **Properties.**

3 Click on the **Screen Saver** tab.

4 Select a screen saver.

5 Click the box next to *Password protected* so that it is ticked.

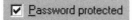

6 Click **Change.**

7 Type your password in the box next to *New.*

8 Type your password again in the box next to *Confirm password.*

9 Click **OK.**

10 Click **OK.**

Don't Forget It!

Don't password protect your screen saver unless you can be absolutely sure you won't forget it! Once protected, a screen saver can't be broken into without the password – ever! (If you do this and can't remember the password, your techies will have to reinstall Windows for you! So make sure you remember it.)

Be Responsible!

If someone is coming to fix your PC, don't just go off for a coffee break – the PC support person is not a mind-reader, and will get very cross if they can't access your computer. If you don't need a password, don't set one up.

Chapter 2

Finding Out More

Using Help

Accessing Help In Windows

1   Click the **Start** button.

2   Click on **Help**.

Note: this feature will only work if it has been installed when Windows was installed. If it doesn't work, ask your techies to help you, or telephone the support number you were given when you bought your computer.

Help Using The Contents Tab

The Help Contents tab is organized like a table of contents and allows you to find topics grouped by subjects. If you know the subject area you want to look up:

1   Bring up the Help feature (see above).

2   Click on the **Contents** tab.

3   Click on the subject area you require.

4   Click a topic in the list to see the help – it will appear on the right.

Topics And Subject Headings

Help topics have a question mark before them:

 Print a document

Subject headings (under which topics are grouped) have a book before them:

Open books are the subjects you are currently looking into:

Help Using The Index Tab

The **Index** tab allows you to find Help topics. It is organized like a book index.

1   Click on the **Index** tab.

2   Type the first few letters of the subject you need help in.

3   Click the index entry you want help on.

4   Click the **Display** button. Help is displayed on the right.

Help Using The Search Tab

Use this if you couldn't find what you wanted in the **Index** tab. It allows to you search for Help using a 'keyword' rather than a topic.

1   Click the **Search** tab.

2   Type in a 'keyword' or phrase for the help you are looking for, e.g. Taskbar.

3   Click **List Topics** – the topics are displayed below.

4   Double-click a topic – help is displayed on the right.

What's This?

Whenever you see a little ? icon in the top right of a dialog box, you can click it, then click on part of the dialog to find out what it does (try it out and see).

System Information And Settings

Viewing Your System Information

If you want to find out what operating system, RAM and processor your computer has:

1   Click on the **Start** button.

2   Click on **Settings**.

3   Click on **Control Panel**.

4   Double-click on the **System** icon, the *System Properties* dialog box will appear.

5   Click on the **General** tab (if you are not already there).

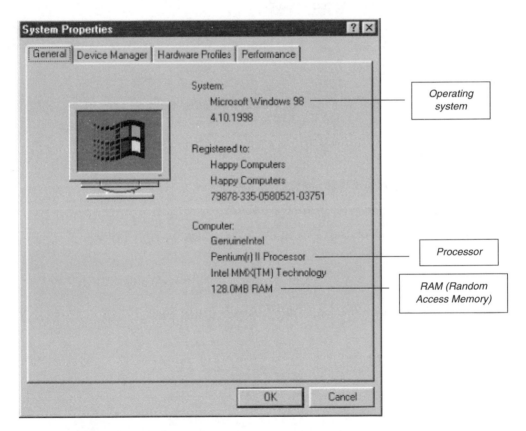

When you have finished looking:

1   Click **OK**.

2   Click on the X to close the **Control Panel** window.

How Does My Computer Know The Date And Time?

The date and time is just one of your computer's settings, and you can change it if it's wrong. You may find that your network resets the date and time (if you are connected to one).

Viewing The Date And Time

The time is shown on your Taskbar.

To view the date:

Hover your mouse over the clock – a yellow label will pop up with the date

Setting The Date And Time

If the month, date, year or time is wrong:

1   Double-click on the clock in the System Tray on your Taskbar.

12:21

This will open the *Data/Time Properties* dialog box.

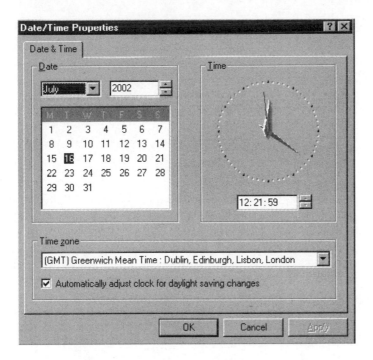

2   Click on the drop-down arrow at the end of the month box.

3   Select the correct month.

4   Click on the up or down arrows to change the year

or

click on the correct date from the calendar

or

double-click on the hour, the minutes or the seconds in the *Time* box to select which you need to change; then click the up or down arrow to change it.

5   Click **OK.**

Changing The Volume

If you have speakers for your computer you may find that the volume disturbs you or those around you.

1   Click on the **Volume** icon in your System Tray on your Taskbar.

2　When the volume control appears, click and drag the slider to adjust the volume.

3　Click in the box next to *Mute* to turn mute on or off – it will appear ticked if on.

4　Click away from the volume control – it will disappear.

Or

1　Double-click on the **Volume** icon in the System Tray .

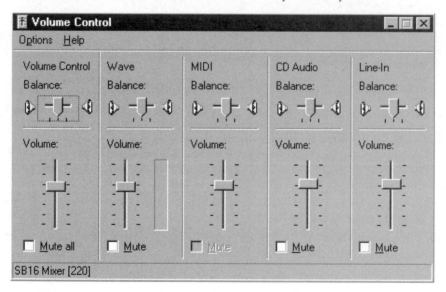

2　Click and drag the sliders to adjust the volume settings

　　or

　　click in the boxes before *Mute* to turn volume settings on or off.

3　Click X at top right of the *Volume Control* dialog box.

58

Changing The Regional Settings

Your regional settings affect the way that dates, numbers and times are displayed and which currency symbol is displayed in the programs you use. They are chosen by which country you are in:

1   Click on the **Start** button.

2   Click on **Settings**.

3   Click on **Control Panel**.

4   Double-click on the **Regional Settings** icon.

Regional
Settings

5   Click on the drop-down arrow at the end of the country.

English (United Kingdom)

6   Click on the country you are in.

7   Click **OK**.

Check This Out...

Changing The Default Conventions

If you want to override any of the settings for your country, click on the other tabs and change any settings you wish.

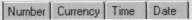

| Number | Currency | Time | Date |

Chapter 3

Working With Files And Folders

Drives, Files And Folders

The Computer's Filing System

➤ The computer's filing system is very much like an ordinary filing cabinet.

➤ The whole of the filing cabinet is your computer.

➤ The drawers in the filing cabinet are known as **drives**.

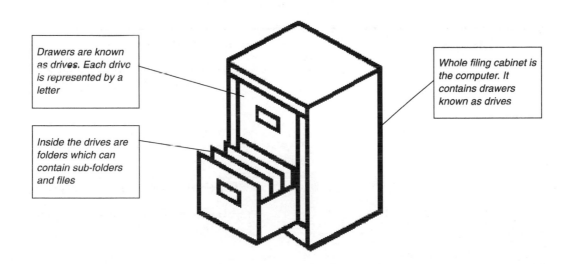

Drawers are known as drives. Each drive is represented by a letter

Inside the drives are folders which can contain sub-folders and files

Whole filing cabinet is the computer. It contains drawers known as drives

➤ **Drives** are represented by letters of the alphabet (see below).

➤ Inside the drawers are **folders** that hold your documents.

➤ Inside some of the folders may be **subfolders** to make things more organized.

➤ Inside the folders are the pieces of paper that you have written on, known as **files**. Word files are known as **documents**.

Imagine you are filing your work documents inside these drives. You may have a main folder which contains all of your work. Inside that, you may have subfolders to contain your memos, reports and letters. Inside those sub-folders are the actual files that you have written on.

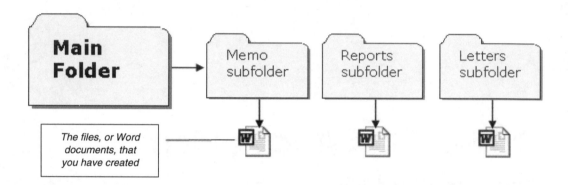

Main Folder

Memo subfolder

Reports subfolder

Letters subfolder

The files, or Word documents, that you have created

What Drives Do I Have?

The drives you have and the letters assigned to them can be different. The table below describes what you will find on most computers.

Letter	Drive	What do you use it for?
A:	Usually the floppy disk drive	➤ Saving onto the floppy disk means that you can take the document to another machine.
		➤ It is also useful to make copies of documents onto the floppy disk as a backup.
C:	Usually the hard disk drive	➤ The hard disk is your main disk drive.
		➤ It is situated inside the box that makes up your PC.

> ➤ If you save onto the hard disk, you can only access that file from that machine, but there is much more space on the hard disk than on a floppy disk.

D:	Usually the CD-ROM drive	➤ You cannot save onto the CD-ROM.
		➤ It is used for installing software from CDs.
F:–Z:	Usually network drives	➤ If you can see these drives you are probably connected to a network.
		➤ A network is a group of computers connected to each other through a server. If you save onto a network drive, the information will go to the server and everyone else who is connected to the network will be able to access your document.

What Are Files?

All the information on your computer will be stored as some type of file. There will be lots of different files on your computer. Some that you have created yourself and some that were already there before! For instance, if you write a letter in Microsoft Word, when you save it, it will be stored as a file, as a Word document file type.

File Icons

The following are some of the file icons that you might see on your computer:

 Microsoft Word (Word Processing)

 Microsoft Excel (Spreadsheet)

 Microsoft PowerPoint (Presentation)

 Microsoft Access (Database)

 Text

  Pictures

 Movies

  Sound/Music

What Are File Name Extensions?

Each different type of file, (e.g. Word document, Excel spreadsheet) has three letters stuck on the end of its name. This is called the file name extension. The extension for a type of file lets Windows know what type of file it is, so it knows which icon to display and which program to open the file in.

Underneath the icon for the file you will see the name of the file, sometimes followed by a full stop and then the filename extension. For example, this Word icon has a filename of **report**, and an extension of **.doc**.

Some of the filename extensions you might see are:

.doc	Microsoft Word document	.xls	Microsoft Excel spreadsheet
.ppt	Microsoft PowerPoint presentation	.txt	Plain text (e.g. Notepad file)
.mdb	Microsoft Access database	.htm	Internet Explorer Web page

Which Filing System?

There are two places where you can manage your files:

➤ Windows Explorer (see below).

➤ My Computer (see page 66).

Windows Explorer is more or less the same thing as My Computer. They both contain the same things, they are just arranged slightly differently. You'll see the differences over the next few pages. It's up to you which one you use – they're both effectively the same program, so use the one you feel more comfortable with.

Windows Explorer

Starting Windows Explorer

1 Click on the **Start** button.

2 Click on **Programs**.

3 Click on **Windows Explorer**.

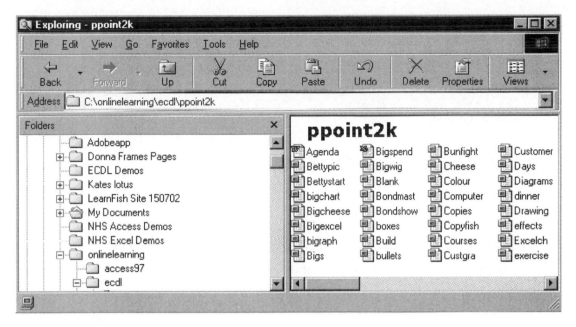

What You See In Windows Explorer

➤ The screen is divided into two 'panes'.

➤ The left-hand side shows the hierarchical structure of your folders on your computer.

➤ The right-hand side represents the contents of the selected item in the left pane.

➤ If you click on a folder in the left pane, the contents of it will appear in the right pane.

Expanding And Collapsing

You can expand and collapse the hierarchical view of the left pane to see more or less detail:

➤ **Expanding:** if you see a plus (+) by an item in the left pane then it has an additional folder within it. To display it, just click on the plus.

➤ **Collapsing:** if you see a minus (–) by an object then you can hide its contents by clicking on the minus.

Click the plus next to the folder to see what's inside.

Click the minus sign to 'close' open it and the folder again.

Looking In A Drive Or Folder

Click on the drive or folder in the left-hand pane. The contents will be displayed in the right-hand pane.

Opening A Folder In The Right-Hand Pane

Double-click the folder you wish to open (in the right-hand pane).

courses

My Computer

Windows organizes all of your hard drives, floppy drives, network drives and settings into an area called My Computer. Remember the idea of your computer as a big filing cabinet? Well, this is it. Let's have a look inside to see what it does.

Opening My Computer

Double-click the **My Computer** icon on the desktop.

My Computer

What You See In My Computer

The picture below shows the main drives and folders you might see in My Computer.

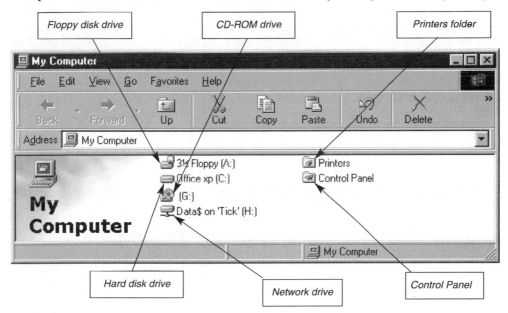

Floppy disk drive

CD-ROM drive

Printers folder

Hard disk drive

Network drive

Control Panel

Opening A Drive

If you want to see what's inside a drive; double-click on the drive icon.

(C:)

Is There A Disk In the Floppy Disk Drive?

You'll need to have a disk in your computer's floppy disk drive to be able to see what's in it! Otherwise you might hear a funny whirring noise and get the following message ...

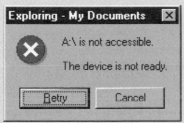

Opening A Folder

Double-click on the folder icon to look inside.

courses

Closing A Folder

Each time you double-click on a folder, the contents are opened in a new window. To close it, click on the X at the top right of the folder window.

Changing The View

Showing The Standard Buttons Toolbar

This toolbar allows you to navigate around My Computer and Windows Explorer. To switch the toolbar on and off:

1   Open My Computer or Windows Explorer.

2   Click on the **View** menu.

3   Click on **Toolbar**.

4   Click on **Standard Buttons** – a tick appears next to it in the menu when it is displayed.

Changing The View Of Your Files And Folders

To change the way you see your drive, folder and files displayed:

1   Click on the **View** menu

or

click on the **View** button – if the toolbar is displayed, see above.

2   Click on the option you require.

Large Icons

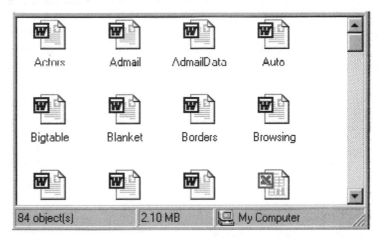

Small Icons

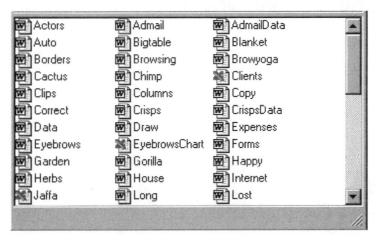

List

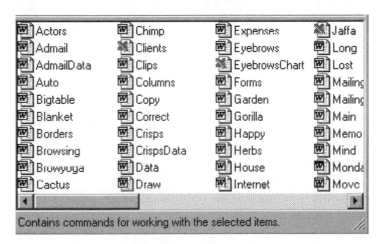

Details

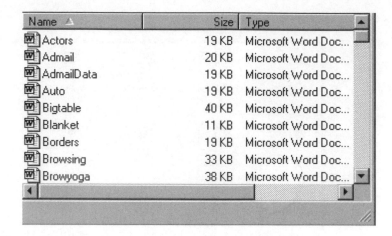

Arranging Your Drives

If you are looking in My Computer you can have your drives arranged by drive letter, type, size or free space:

1 Click on the **View** menu.

2 Click on **Arrange Icons**.

3 Click on the option you require.

Auto Arrange

To make sure that all icons are evenly spaced you can choose *Auto Arrange* from the list.

Sorting Your Files And Folders

You can have your files and folders arranged by name, type, size or date:

1 Click on the **View** menu.

2 Click on **Arrange Icons**.

3 Click on the option you require.

Auto Arrange

To make sure that all icons are evenly spaced you can choose *Auto Arrange* from the list.

Viewing The Properties Of A File

To find out when a file was created or last modified, its size, etc.:

1   Click on the file to select it.

2   Click on the **File** menu.

3   Click on **Properties** – a box will appear displaying the file's properties.

4   Click on the **General** tab.

Click **OK** to close the box when you have finished looking.

Viewing The Properties Of A Folder

If you want to find out the size of a folder, when it was created and how many files and other folders it contains:

1   Click on the folder to select it.

2   Click on the **File** menu.

3   Click on **Properties** – a box will appear displaying the folder's properties.

Click **OK** to close the box when you have finished looking.

Opening A File

Double-click the file to open it.

Navigating Your Folders

Going Back

If you want to move back through the drives and folders you have already looked at:

Click on the **Back** button.

Where Was I?

If you want to know what the next folder 'back' is, position the mouse pointer over the tiny black downward arrow for a second and a little yellow flag will pop up and tell you!

Going Forward

If you want to return to the drives and folders you have already looked at after going back:

Click on the **Forward** button.

What's Next?

If you want to know what the next folder 'forward' is, position the mouse pointer over the tiny black downward arrow for a second and a little yellow flag will pop up and tell you!

Going Up A Level

If you want to go up a level (e.g. if you look in a folder in the C: drive and then want to go back again to see the other folders in the C: drive):

Click on the **Up** button.

Or

Click on the **Back** button.

Back And Up

Up performs the same function as the **Back** icon!

Chapter 4

Managing Your Files

File Management

Creating A Folder

Once you start getting a lot of files you might want to create different folders to store them in to help you locate them quickly.

1   Open My Computer or Windows Explorer.

2   Open the folder or drive where you would like this folder to be stored.

3   Click on the **File** menu.

4   Click **New**.

5   Click **Folder** – a new folder will appear.

6   Type the name for the new folder.

7   Press **Enter** to create the folder.

Check This Out...

Subfolders

You can have folders inside other folders. You create them in exactly the same way!

Selecting A File Or Folder

You may need to select files or folders if you want to delete, move or copy them:

Click on a file or folder to select it – it will appear blue.

Selecting Adjacent Files And Folders

If you want to select several files or folders that are next to each other:

1 Select the first file or folder.

2 Press and hold the **Shift** key on the keyboard.

3 Click on the last file or folder of the group you want to select.

4 Release the **Shift** key.

Selecting Non-Adjacent Files And Folders

If you want to select several files or folders that are not next to each other:

1 Select the first file or folder.

2 Press and hold the **Ctrl** key on the keyboard.

3 Click on the next file or folder you want to select.

4 Continue clicking on files until all the files or folders you want are selected.

5 Release the **Ctrl** key.

Selecting All Files And Folders

1 Click on the **Edit** menu.

2 Click on **Select All**.

Or

Press **Ctrl+A** on the keyboard.

Deselecting Files And Folders

Click into an empty space anywhere in the window.

Renaming A File Or Folder

1 Right-click the file – a menu will pop up.

2 Click on **Rename**.

3   Type a new name for the file.

4   Press **Enter.**

Not Including The Filename Extension ...

If the filename extensions are visible in your window (see page 64) and you don't include it at the end when you rename a file, you may see this error message ...

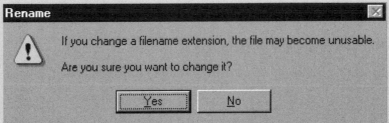

Click **No** and rename it again to include the existing filename extension. If you can't remember the original extension, press **Escape (Esc)** to go back to the original file name and start again.

Moving A File Or Folder Using Cut And Paste

1   Select the file(s) or folder(s) you want to move.

2   Click **Cut** – the file(s) or folder(s) will be moved to the Windows clipboard.

3   Open the folder where you want to place the file(s) or folder(s).

4   Click **Paste** – the file(s) or folder(s) will be pasted from the Windows clipboard.

Copying A File Or Folder Using Copy And Paste

1   Select the file(s) or folder(s) you want to copy.

2   Click **Copy** – the file(s) or folder(s) will be copied to the Windows clipboard.

3   Open the folder where you want to place the file(s) or folder(s).

4   Click **Paste** – the file(s) or folder(s) will be pasted from the Windows clipboard.

The Windows Clipboard

This is a temporary storage area in your computer where items are placed when they are cut or copied. It can only hold one selection at a time, so when you cut or copy something else this will replace the previous selection on the clipboard.

Deleting And Using The Recycle Bin

Deleting A File

1   Select the file you wish to delete.

2   Press **Delete** on the keyboard

or

click on the **Delete** icon.

3   Click on **Yes** to confirm the deletion.

Deleting A Folder

When you delete a folder you will also delete all of its contents (any files or folders inside that folder):

1   Select the folder you wish to delete.

2   Press **Delete** on the keyboard.

or

click on the **Delete** icon – a dialog box will appear to confirm the deletion.

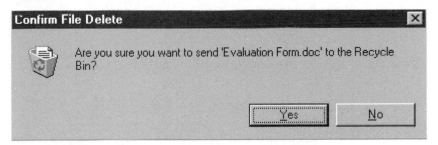

3   Click on **Yes**.

Recycle Bin

When you delete anything from your hard disk drive (C: drive or desktop) it gets sent to the Recycle Bin. This bin doesn't empty itself, so if you delete something by accident you can retrieve it from here.

Paper In The Bin ...

You can tell when there are files or folders in the Recycle Bin because the icon looks as though it has paper in it.

Opening The Recycle Bin

Double-click the **Recycle Bin** icon on the desktop.

Retrieving A File Or Folder

1   Double-click the **Recycle Bin** to open it.

2   Click on the file or folder you want to retrieve.

3   Click on the **File** menu.

4   Click on **Restore** – the file or folder will be returned to where it was deleted from.

Emptying The Recycle Bin

You may want to empty the Recycle Bin occasionally to free up some more space on your computer.

1   Right click on the **Recycle Bin**.

2   Click on **Empty Recycle Bin**.

3   Click on **Yes**, to confirm the deletion of all items in the bin.

No Paper In The Bin ...

When the bin is empty the icon looks empty too!

Recycle Bin

Are You Sure You Want To Empty The Bin?

If you empty the **Recycle Bin**, you cannot get back what you deleted – ever! Make absolutely sure you want to permanently delete it. Once it's gone, it's really gone.

Finding Files

Why Might I Need To Find A File?

The Find File tool is very useful if you cannot remember the exact name of a file, or where you stored it. You can tell Windows everything you can remember about the file from its file name, date created, modified or accessed to the type of file and a keyword that the file contains. The more you can tell it, the quicker the search!

Starting A Find

1   Click on the **Start** button.

2   Click on **Find**.

3   Click on the **File** menus or **Folders**.

Finding Files Or Folders By Name

1   Click on the **Name & Location** tab (if not already there).

2   In *Named*, type the name of the file or folder.

Check This Out...

Using A Wild Card

If you can only remember the first few letters of the name of a file, type those in followed by an asterisk, e.g. 'letter*'. (The asterisk can represent any number of letters). Find File will then pick out every file whose name begins with 'letter'. It won't however find files that are just called 'letter'!

Finding Files By Type

If you know the type of file it is (e.g. Excel workbook) you can use the filename extension to speed up your search. This tells Windows to ignore files of any other type.

1   Click on the **Name & Location** tab (if not already there).

2   In *Named* type the file name (see above), followed by a full stop and the filename extension (see the examples below).

Type of file	What to type after the filename
Word document	.doc
Excel workbook	.xls
PowerPoint presentation	.ppt
Access database	.mdb

Combine File Types And Wild cards

If you know you're looking for a Word document which starts with the letters 'cat', you can type "cat*.doc" into the Named box. This will find any Word files that begin with the letters 'cat'.

Finding Files Using A Keyword

You can search for files containing a particular word. For example, if you're looking for a letter about cheese, you can search for any files containing the word 'cheese'.

1   Click on the **Name & Location** tab (if not already there).

2   In **Containing Text**, type a keyword.

Uncommon Words ...

The search will be quicker if the word you are searching for is less common and doesn't appear in lots of your files. 'The' would not be an example of a good keyword!

Choosing Where To Look

1   Click on the **Name & Location** tab (if not already there).

2   Click the down arrow at the end of the *Look in* box.

3   Click on the drive you wish to look in.

4   Click in the box before *Include subfolders* if it is not ticked already.

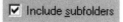

Include Subfolders

If the *Include subfolders* box is not ticked, the Find tool will only search for files saved directly onto that drive (not in a folder).

What If I Want To Search Through A Folder?

You do not have to search through the whole drive. Just follow the steps below to search through a folder or subfolder.

From the *Find* dialog box:

1 Click **Browse**.

Browse...

2 Click on the folder you require from list (see below).

Click Plus(+) and Minus(–) signs to collapse or expand folders.

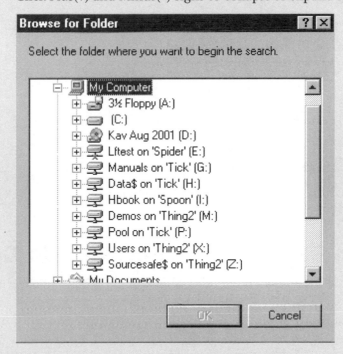

3. Click **OK**.

Finding Files Between Two Dates

You can limit your search to files created, accessed or changed between certain dates. For example, if you know what date you created the file on, you can narrow the search down a bit.

1   Click on the **Date** tab (if not already there).

2   Click in the circle before *Find all files*.

3   Click the down arrow at the end of the box.

4   Click on created, accessed or modified as required.

5   Click in the circle before the word *between*.

6   Click the first drop-down arrow – a calendar will appear.

7   Click on the required date.

8   Click on the second drop-down arrow.

9   Click on the required date.

Finding Files For Previous Months Or Days

You can limit your search to files created, accessed or changed during a specified number of the preceding months or days.

1   Click on the **Date** tab (if you are not already there).

2   Click in the circle before *Find all files*.

84

3   Click the down arrow at the end of the box.

4   Click on created, accessed or modified as required.

5   Click in the circles for months or days as required before the words *during the previous.*

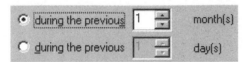

6   Click on the up or down arrows to change the number of days or months.

Finding The Files

Once you have set the criteria for the search, click on the **Find Now** button. Any files that are found will appear in the box below, and the status bar will display the number of files found.

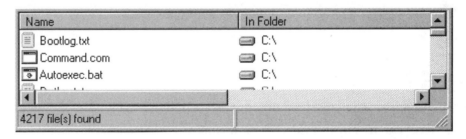

Name	In Folder
Bootlog.txt	C:\
Command.com	C:\
Autoexec.bat	C:\

4217 file(s) found

Watch The Magnifying Glass

While the magnifying glass is moving, 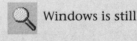 Windows is still searching.

You can see where it is currently searching by looking at the status bar of the window.

Searching C:\WINDOWS\Temporary Internet Files\Content.IE5\SBD23Y7H

If your file has already been found you can stop the search by clicking on **Stop!**

Opening A Found File

If the file you were looking for is displayed:

Double-click the file to open it.

Find Box Stays Open ...

The *Find* dialog box will stay open until you close it. Click the X on the title bar to close the window.

Modifying Your Search

If the file you were looking for isn't found, you can modify the information you have put in and try again.

Starting A New Search

If you still have the *Find* dialog box open and want to look for something different:

Click on **New Search** – the information in the box will be cleared.

New Search

Using Floppy Disks

What Is A Floppy Disk?

You can save your files onto floppy disks and use them in your floppy disk drive (see page 62). Although they store a lot less information than your computer, floppy disks are small and therefore portable and can be used in any PC. You can use them to:

➤ Make copies of your files (in case something happens to your computer).

➤ Share files with friends and colleagues.

➤ Copy a file from one computer to another.

Looking At What Is On A Floppy Disk

1   Insert the floppy disk into your floppy disk drive.

2   Open My Computer or Windows Explorer.

3   Double-click on the A: drive – the files on the disk will be displayed.

3½ Floppy (A:)

Formatting A Floppy Disk

Before you can use a floppy disk it must be formatted for use on your computer. Although you can buy floppy disks already formatted, it is cheaper to buy them unformatted. To format a floppy disk:

1   Insert the floppy disk into your floppy disk drive.

2   Open My Computer or Windows Explorer.

3   Right-click on the A: drive.

4   Click on the **Format** menu.

5   Click in the circle before *Full*.

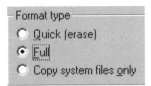

6   Click on **Start**.

Formatting may take a few minutes, check the progress under the word *Formatting*.

When the format is complete, a box displaying the results will appear.

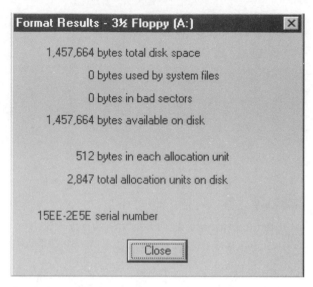

Format Results - 3½ Floppy (A:)

1,457,664 bytes total disk space

0 bytes used by system files

0 bytes in bad sectors

1,457,664 bytes available on disk

512 bytes in each allocation unit

2,847 total allocation units on disk

15EE-2E5E serial number

Close

7   Click on **Close**.

8   Click on **Close**.

Make Sure There Are No Files On The Disk

Formatting a disk will overwrite any files already stored on it. If it is not a brand new floppy disk, make sure there are no files on it that you need before formatting!

Make Sure There Are No Files Open

If there are files already on the disk and you have one of them open, you will get an error message

Click **OK**, close the file and carry on formatting if you don't require the file any more, or insert another floppy disk to format.

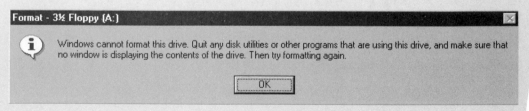

Format - 3½ Floppy (A:)

Windows cannot format this drive. Quit any disk utilities or other programs that are using this drive, and make sure that no window is displaying the contents of the drive. Then try formatting again.

OK

Copying A File To A Floppy Disk

If you want to make a copy of a file, for backup, to give to someone else or to transfer to another computer:

1   Insert a disk into your floppy drive.

2   Open My Computer or Windows Explorer.

3   Find the file you wish to copy.

4   Right-click on the file – a menu will pop up.

5   Click on **Send To**.

6   Click on *3¹/₂ Floppy (A)* – the file will be copied to your floppy disk.

Copying More Than One File

You can copy several files to your floppy disk at once in this way by selecting the files first (see page 76).

Using Save As

If the file you want to copy is already open, you can make a copy of it using **Save as** and choose to save it to the A: drive (see page 110).

Chapter 5

Programs and Printing

Starting Applications

Using The Start Menu Programs

1   Click on the **Start** button.

2   Click on **Programs**.

3   Click on the program you want – the ▶ symbol indicates that there is more to see.
Follow the direction of the arrow to get to the next menu.

Using The Start Menu For A New Office Document

1   Click on the **Start** button.

2   Click on **New Office Document**.

3   Click on *Blank Document* (to open Microsoft Word)

    or

    click on *Blank Workbook* (to open Microsoft Excel)

    or

    click on *Blank Presentation* (to open Microsoft PowerPoint).

4   Click **OK**.

Using A Desktop Shortcut

If you have a shortcut to a file or a program you can open it using the shortcut. Just double-click on the shortcut to open it.

Opening A File From The Documents List

If you have used a file recently it may be displayed in the Documents list (see page 42):

1   Click on the **Start** button.

2   Click on **Documents** – the last 15 documents you used will be displayed.

3   Click on the document you require and the file will open.

What Programs Do I Have?

All the programs you have on your computer will be listed in Programs on the **Start** menu. The following table explains what some of these applications are used for:

Program (application)	Type of application	Used for ...
Microsoft Word	Word Processing	Creating letters, memos, faxes, reports, etc.
Microsoft Excel	Spreadsheet	Creating graphs, managing accounts, stock control, or other mathematical or financial calculations.

| Microsoft PowerPoint | Presentation | Creating presentations, slide shows, organization charts, etc. |
| Microsoft Access | Database | Creating databases which hold information that can be queried or used to create reports. |

Switching Between Open Windows

You can have several programs open at once. For every program you have open there will be a button for it on the Taskbar. Whichever program is 'active', the button will look as if it is pushed in on the toolbar. If you want to switch to looking at another window:

Click on the button for the window on the Taskbar.

Closing An Application

Click on the top X on the title bar.

Using Word

What You Need To Know

If you are only learning Module 2 (File Management), you will still need to know a few things about Word. These can be found in the Word section, which is on page 99. The topics you need to know are:

➤ Starting Word
➤ Opening a document
➤ Typing text
➤ Insert or overtype
➤ Typing a space
➤ Creating a new line
➤ Saving a document
➤ Saving changes
➤ Saving to a floppy disk

➤ Using Save As

➤ Closing a document

➤ Closing Word.

Don't worry, most of them are quite small and simple.

Printing

Printing From A Program

Most programs let you print in the same way:

Click on the **Print** icon.

or

1 Click on the **File** menu.

2 Click on **Print**.

3 Click **OK**.

The Default Printer

If you are connected to a network you may find that there are several printers that you could print to. This could be useful if one is broken or is often busy!

When you print from Word (or any other program) the document will be sent to the default printer. This is the printer you will see in the *Print Options* dialog box when you click on **Print** in the **File** menu.

Changing The Default Printer

1 Click on the **Start** button.

2 Click on **Settings**.

3 Click on **Printers** – a window will appear showing all the printers that are available for you to print to.

4 Right-click on the printer you wish to set as default.

5 Click on **Set as Default**.

Which Is My Default Printer?

The default printer has a tick at the top of the icon.

Acrobat PDFWriter

Checking The Progress Of Printing

Lots of people may print to the same printer as you, and you'll find all of these files form a queue. You can have a look at the print queue to see where your file is, and how far the printer has got with printing your document:

1   Click on the **Start** button.

2   Click on **Settings**.

3   Click on **Printers**.

4   Double-click on the printer you require – usually the default printer (see above).

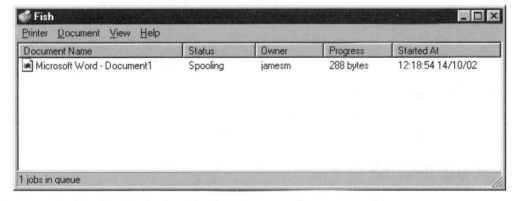

Look In The System Tray

When you are waiting for something to print there will be a little printer icon in your System Tray. You can double-click on this as a shortcut to seeing the print queue!

Cancelling Printing

1 Make sure you can see the print queue your file has been sent to (see above).

2 Click on your file to select it.

3 Click on the **Document** menu.

4 Click on **Cancel Printing**.

Mouse Techniques

The mouse is designed to perform certain functions. This section explains some of the basic terms and the purpose of using the mouse.

Click

A click with the mouse will always refer to the LEFT mouse button. A single click is generally used to open something on the **Desktop** or in **My Computer** (i.e. a program or a document).

Or

A single click is used to select something once you are inside a program, such as Word or Excel.

Right-Click

A right-click is a click with the RIGHT mouse button. Right clicks are only used to bring up a pop-up menu.

Double-Click

A double-click is used to open documents inside a program like Word or Excel.

Click And Drag

This means click on something, hold the mouse button down, drag to another area of the screen and then release the mouse button.

Module 3
Word Processing

Chapter 1

Getting Started

Word

Word is a word processor. You can use it to type letters, write stories – in fact, pretty much anything you could do on a normal typewriter. The great thing about a word processor is that, unlike a typewriter, you can edit your words as you go along, copy sections, rearrange bits, and do all sorts of fancy things with the text. It is also much, much quieter than a typewriter.

Starting Word

1   Click on the **Start** button.

2   Click on **Programs**.

3   Click on **Microsoft Word.**

If you see an icon for Word in the middle of your screen, you can use that instead. Just double-click on it to run Word.

Or you might have the Office shortcut bar on the edge of your screen. Just click on the Word icon to start Word.

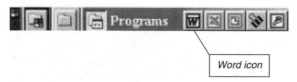

Word icon

100

How Do I Know If Word Has Opened?

You should be able to see the Word window on the screen (see the section on The Word 2000 Screen, on page 00).

You should also be able to see Word as one of the tasks on the Taskbar at the bottom of the screen.

Exiting Word 2000

1   Click on the **File** menu.

2   Click on **Exit**.

Or

Click on the X at the top right-hand corner of the screen.

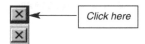 Click here

How Do I Know That Word Is Closed?

The Word window should disappear from the screen and you should no longer be able to see it on the Taskbar.

Word 2000 Options

Word 2000 has several options that can change the way you carry out simple tasks.

Standard And Formatting Toolbars Sharing The Same Row

You may find that you cannot separate the *Standard* and *Formatting* toolbars – which means that you will not be able to see all the icons you need.

To turn this option on and off:

1   Click on the **Tools** menu.

2   Click **Customize**.

3   Click on the **Options** tab.

4   Add or remove the tick next to *Standard and Formatting toolbars share one row*.

Toolbars will become separated when the option is turned off.

Menus Showing Most Recently Used Commands First

You may find that you cannot see all the commands available on your menus, unless you pause for a short while after clicking the menu. If you can see a double-headed arrow at the bottom of your menu, it means that this option is turned on.

This is designed to help you see which options you use most often, and to hide the ones you don't use that much, or don't need. In theory, this is a great idea. In practice, it is just annoying and weird, and seems to bear no relation to the options you actually use or, in fact, to anything at all. If you want to turn this option on and off:

1   Click on the **Tools** menu.

2   Click **Customize**.

3   Click on the **Options** tab.

4   Add or remove the tick next to *Menus show most recently used commands first.*

5   Click **OK**.

The Word 2000 Screen

The following is a picture of the Word screen in Normal view. Use it as a reference throughout the course and mark your own comments onto it. The Appendix contains a description of the different icons at the top of the screen.

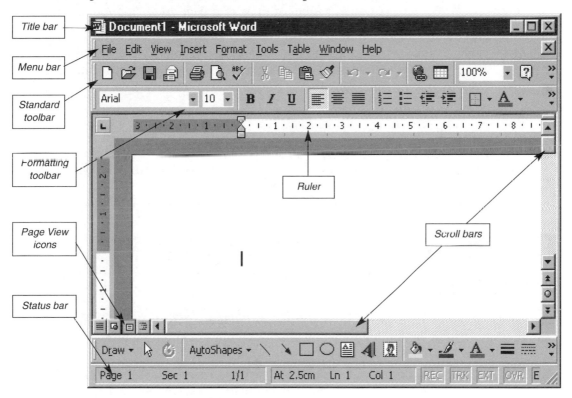

Part of the screen	What does it do?
Title bar	Tells you the name of the document you are working on. Before you have saved your document this will be something like 'Document 1'.
Menu bar	Gives you access to the commands available in Word. All commands are grouped under one of the menus.
Standard toolbar	Provides a quick way of carrying out standard commands using the icons.
Formatting toolbar	Provides a quick way of changing the format, or the appearance, of your document.
Ruler	Shows you the width of your page and helps you set things like margins and tabs.
Scroll bars	Helps you to move around a document – the vertical scroll bar allows you to move through a long document, whilst the horizontal scroll bar allows you to move across a wide document.
Page View icons	Changes the way you are looking at the document depending on the task that you wish to carry out.
Status bar	Tells you whereabouts your cursor is in the document and what mode Word is working in.

Entering And Deleting Text
Typing Text

➤ When you start Word a blank document appears ready for you to start typing.

➤ A blinking vertical bar called the Insertion Point (or cursor) indicates where text will come out when you type.

➤ Unlike using a typewriter, you do not have to press the carriage return when you get to the end of the line. Word will automatically wrap the text onto the next line. But if you want to finish a line and go to the next one, just press **Enter** or **Return**.

➤ You can delete text to the left or the right of the cursor.

➤ To type text, position your cursor where you would like to start typing and just start typing!

Insert Or Overtype?

➤ Normally when you type you will be in Insert mode. This means that if your cursor is in the middle of an existing sentence and you start typing, nothing will be deleted. The text that is already there will shuffle along to make way for the new text.

➤ If you are in Overtype mode, then any text you type will go over the top of existing text.

To change modes:

Press the **Insert key** on the keyboard

or

double-click the OVR mark on the status bar at the bottom of the screen.

Creating A Space

Press the **Space Bar** at the bottom of the keyboard – it is the long, blank key between the **Alt** keys.

Creating A New Paragraph

1   Make sure your cursor is flashing where you would like a new line.

2   Press the **Enter** or **Hard Return** key (found on the right of the keyboard).

Creating Capital Letters

Hold down the **Shift** key while you type the letters.

There are two **Shift** keys on the keyboard, one at the bottom left and one at the bottom right.

Capitalizing All the Text You Are Typing

1   Press the **Caps Lock** key on the left of the keyboard – a light will appear above Caps Lock on the top right-hand side of the keyboard.

2   To turn it off, press **Caps Lock** again.

Moving The Cursor Around With The Keyboard

Use the Cursor keys at the bottom right of the keyboard.

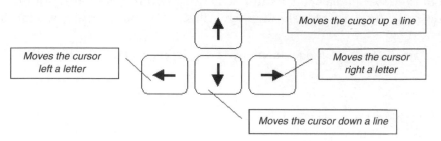

Adding Extra Text To What You Have Typed

1   Position your cursor where you would like to start typing.

2   Start typing!

As long as you are in Insert mode (see page 105), the rest of the text will shuffle along to make way for your new text.

Delete And Backspace

To get rid of text, use the Delete and Backspace keys.

1   Position your cursor next to the text you would like to get rid of.

2   Press **Delete** if the text is to the **right** of the cursor

or

press **Backspace** if the text is to the **left** of the cursor.

Selecting Text To Delete

1   Select the text to delete (see page 117).

2   Press **Delete**.

Deleting Spaces And Hard Returns

Just because you can't see them doesn't mean that hard returns and spaces are not there. They are just as easily deleted as normal letters.

1   Click on the **Show/Hide** icon to see spaces and hard returns

The·quick·brown·fox·jumped·over·the·lazy·dog¶
¶
The·quick·brown·fox·jumped·over·the·lazy·dog¶

Spaces will appear as dots, and hard returns will appear as back-to-front Ps.

2   Position your cursor next to the space or hard return you wish to delete.

3   Press **Delete** if it is to the **right** of the cursor

or

press **Backspace** if it is to the **left** of the cursor.

4   Click on the **Show/Hide** icon to hide spaces and hard returns again.

Saving, Closing, Opening And New

Saving a document creates a copy inside the computer that you can use again at a later date.

Saving A Document

1   Click on the **File** menu.

2   Click **Save**.

Or just click on the Save icon.

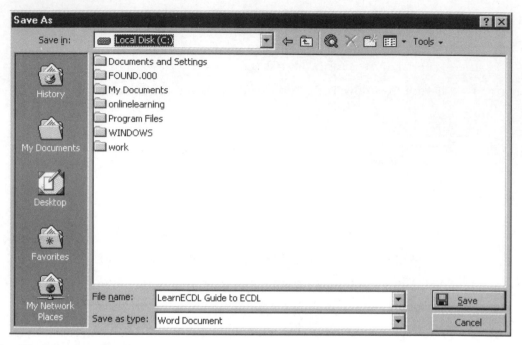

3   Type in your filename

➤ You do not need to click into the *File name* box if the name is highlighted in blue.

➤ You can have up to 255 letters in a file name.

➤ Ensure that your file name is relevant to the document.

4   Click the drop-down arrow in the *Save in* box.

5   Click the drive/folder you wish to save into.

6   Click on **Save**

or

press **Enter**.

How Do I Know The Document Has Been Saved?

You should be able to see the file name you have given the document on the blue title bar at the top of the screen.

Word Adds The Extension .doc To The End Of Your File Name ...

This is to distinguish the file as a Word document.

How Do I Change The File Name?

Click into the File name box and the existing file name should go blue. If you press Delete whilst it is blue, the file name will disappear, and you can type a new one.

If you cannot get the file name to go blue, just use Delete and Backspace to get rid of the existing file name.

Saving A Document Again After Changes

After you have saved the document for the first time, you must continue to save any changes you make to it. Word does not save your changes automatically.

1   Click on the **File** menu.

2   Click **Save**.

Or

Click on the **Save** icon – the changes will be saved.

You Will Not Be Asked To Enter A Filename Or Specify The Folder You Wish To Save In

You specified these things when you first saved the document, so Word will just save the document in the same place and with the same file name. If you want to change these things, you must use the **Save As** command from the **File** menu.

Save Regularly!

As you are working on a document, get into the habit of clicking the **Save** icon every few minutes. This will update the document and protects it if your PC crashes.

Creating A Copy Of A Document Using Save As

If you want to create a copy of your document with a different name or in a different folder, you can use **Save As**. Your original document will remain intact.

Save As is often used to create a copy onto a floppy disk. Floppy disks are very beneficial as a backup because they can be stored separately from your main computer. They also allow you to take your work to a different computer, if you need to.

1   Click on the **File** menu.

2   Click **Save As**.

3   If required, type in a name for the document next to *File name*.

4   Click the down arrow next to *Save in* box.

5   Choose location to save into.

6   Click on **Save**

    or

    press **Enter**.

Word Uses The Last Folder You Saved Into

When you first use **Save As**, the *Save in* box will show you the last folder you saved into.

If I Make Changes – Where Will They Be Saved?

When you use **Save As** and type a different file name, you are creating a copy. If you make any changes, and then click on **Save**, only the version you are working on will change.

Closing Documents

Closing a document takes it off the screen and files it away inside the computer if it is to be saved, or gets rid of it if it is not to be saved.

1   Click on the **File** menu.

2   Click **Close**.

Or

Click on the lower X at the top right-hand side of the screen.

The Screen Has Gone Grey And I Can't Use The Menus Or Toolbars

This means that you have closed all documents, which is a bit like having an empty desk. You can't use menus and toolbars because there is no piece of paper for the commands to be carried out on. Start a new document, or open one that you have already created.

Did You Remember To Save?

If you have made changes to a document and forgotten to save them, Word will prompt you and ask if you would like to save when you close. If you do not want to save, just click **No**.

Opening Documents

You can only open documents which you have saved previously.

1   Click on the **File** menu.

2   Click **Open**.

Or

Click on the **Open** icon

3   If required, click the down arrow next to the *Look in* box to change the folder Word is looking in.

4   Double-click on the name of the file to be opened

or

click on the name of the file to be opened, then

click **Open**.

When I Double-click The File Name, A Box Appears Around It And A Cursor Starts Flashing

It's very easy to just miss doing a double-click and end up performing two single clicks. This signifies to Word that you want to rename the document rather than open it! Just press the **Escape (Esc)** key on the keyboard, or click into a white space to go back to normal.

You Can Open More Than One File At A Time

You can select and open as many files as you want in one go. To select more than one file, click the first file, then hold down **Ctrl** whilst you click on the others. Then just press **Enter** or **Return**!

Creating New Documents

1   Click on the **File** menu.

2   Click **New**.

3   Click on the **General** tab.

4   Click *Blank Document.*

5   Click **OK.**

Or

Click on the **New Document** icon.

How Do I Know I've Created A New Document?

Look at the blue title bar at the top of the screen. Your file name should be something like Document 1, Document 2, etc., and you should be able to see a blank white space to start typing in the middle of the screen.

Creating New Documents Based On A Template

Templates give you a head-start in creating documents. When you create a new document based on a template, some of the text will already be there and you just have to fill in the rest.

1   Click on the **File** menu.

2   Click **New**.

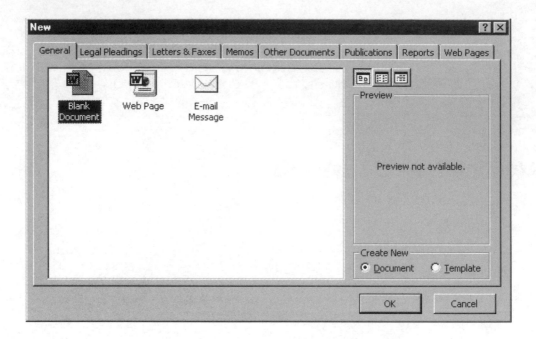

3 Click on the tab you require, e.g. **Letters & Faxes**.

4 Click on the template you wish to use, e.g. *Elegant Letter*.

5 Click **OK.**

Moving Around Documents

Where Am I?

Check the status bar at the bottom left of the screen. It tells you what page you are on, what section you are in and how many pages there are in your document.

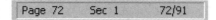

| Page 72 | Sec 1 | | 72/91 |

Using Scroll Bars

➤ Scroll bars **do not always move the cursor**. Sometimes they only change what you are **looking** at.

➤ There are two scroll bars. The vertical scroll bar will move you up and down, and the horizontal scroll bar will move you left and right.

114

The Vertical Scroll Bar – Moving Up And Down

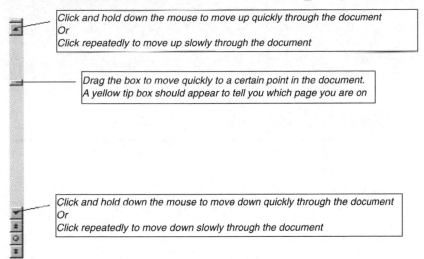

Click and hold down the mouse to move up quickly through the document
Or
Click repeatedly to move up slowly through the document

Drag the box to move quickly to a certain point in the document.
A yellow tip box should appear to tell you which page you are on

Click and hold down the mouse to move down quickly through the document
Or
Click repeatedly to move down slowly through the document

Using The Scroll Bar To Move To A Particular Page

Click on the **Next Page/Previous Page** icon at the bottom of the vertical scroll bar.

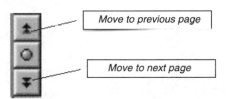

Move to previous page

Move to next page

Using The Horizontal Scroll Bar

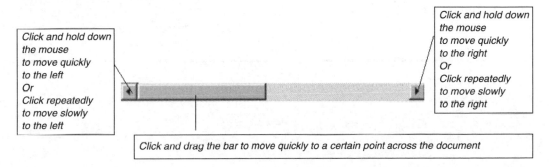

Click and hold down
the mouse
to move quickly
to the left
Or
Click repeatedly
to move slowly
to the left

Click and hold down
the mouse
to move quickly
to the right
Or
Click repeatedly
to move slowly
to the right

Click and drag the bar to move quickly to a certain point across the document

115

Everything Has Disappeared!

If you scroll too far to the right, you may find that all your text disappears. When in Normal view, Word just keeps on going to the right, long past the right-hand edge of the page. This means that your text will go off the screen. Try scrolling back to the left.

Moving The Cursor Using Shortcut Keys

Where do you want to go?	Press these keys at the same time
To the top of the document	Ctrl Home
To the end of the document	Ctrl End
To the beginning of a line	Home
To the end of a line	End
Up a page	Ctrl Page Up
Down a page	Ctrl Page Down
To the previous word	Ctrl ←
To the next word	Ctrl →

Selecting Text

Selection is the way of letting Word know which text you want to work with. If you want to make some text bold, for example, Word doesn't know which text you mean unless you select it. You can use selection to format, move, copy or delete text.

To Select Text

1   Place your mouse at the start of the text you wish to select. The mouse should look like the **I** bar.

 I

2   Click and drag over text. The text will become white surrounded by black, `like this`.

Smart Selection

When you click and drag over text, Word uses smart selection. This means that if you start dragging from the middle of a word and carry on to other words, the beginning of the first word gets selected automatically.

My Text Has Moved Around!

If you select text and then release the mouse, it is possible to click back on the selected text and drag it to a different place. You will see a fuzzy grey line appear if this is happening. Click **Undo** to put it back.

To Deselect Text

Click once into any white space on the right-hand side of your document.

To Select A Word

Double-click on the word.

To Select A Sentence

1   Hold down **Ctrl**.

2   Click anywhere in the sentence.

To Select A Line

Click to the left of the line – the cursor will change to a right-pointing white arrow when you are in the right place.

To Select A Paragraph

Double-click to the left of the paragraph – the cursor will change to a right-pointing white arrow when you are in the right place

or

triple click the paragraph (click three times quickly in the paragraph).

Selecting Multiple Words, Lines Or Paragraphs

1   Select in one of the ways described above.

2   Do not let go of the mouse.

3   Drag over the rest of the text you wish to select.

Check This Out...

You Cannot Select Pieces Of Text That Are Not Next To Each Other

It is not possible to select two separate pieces of text. You just can't do it. Sorry. Unless you buy Word XP, but it would be a bit extravagant just to buy it for that one thing …

To Select The Entire Document

Press **Ctrl+A**.

Selecting Text With The Keyboard

1   Place the cursor at the start of what you wish to select.

2   Hold down the **Shift** key.

3   Use the cursor keys to move along the text you wish to select.

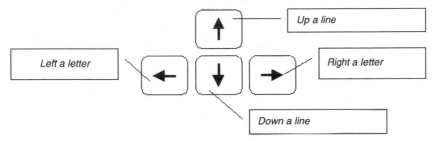

Deselecting With The Keyboard

Press a cursor key again without holding down **Shift**.

Using Help In Word

Getting Help

Word comes with an Office Assistant to help you if you get stuck. There is also a normal Help tool you can use, with a contents and searchable index. Excel, PowerPoint, Access and Outlook all have the same features, so this section applies to them too.

To display the Office Assistant, click on the Office Assistant icon.

The Office Assistant will appear, all bright-eyed and eager to help.

Asking A Question

If the Office Assistant has just appeared by itself ('It looks like you're writing a letter!' etc.), just click on the blue circle next to the topic you are interested in and the answer will appear. If you want to ask a question:

1   Type your question into the space provided.

2   Press **Enter**.

3   Click the blue circle next to the topic you are interested in.

Printing The Answer

From the Help window ... click on the **Print** icon.

Moving The Office Assistant

Click and drag it to a new position.

Hiding The Office Assistant

1   Click on the **Help** menu.

2   Click on **Hide Office Assistant**.

Check This Out...

Hide The Office Assistant One Too Many Times ...

And it will ask you whether you want to hide it permanently.

Don't worry, if you do turn it off you haven't lost it for ever, just click on the **Help** menu and **Show Office Assistant**. Even if you really hate it and never want to see it again, you can be sure that it will still pop up now and again. It wants to be your friend.

Turning off the Office Assistant.

You've hidden me several times now. Would you like to permanently turn me off or just hide me again?

⦿ No, just hide me

⦿ Yes, turn me off

⦿ Change other options

Changing The Office Assistant's Character

If you get bored with the behaviour of the paper clip, you can completely change its personality and appearance. Wouldn't it be nice if we could do that with real people? OK, maybe not.

1   Display the Office Assistant.

2   Right-click on the Office Assistant.

3   Click **Options**.

4   Click the **Gallery** tab at top of the dialog box.

5   Click **Next** to move through the assistants.

6   Click **OK** when you've found the assistant you require.

Using The Help Tool

If you want some help that is a bit more in depth, try the Help tool. Click on the **Help** menu and choose **Microsoft Word Help**, or just press **F1**. Once you have opened Help, use it in the same way as the normal Windows Help. See page 53 for more on how to use it. If you are using Excel, PowerPoint, Access, Outlook or Internet Explorer, you can access the Help in the same way – click on the **Help** menu and choose the first option ('Microsoft Excel/Access/etc. Help'), or press **F1**.

Correcting Mistakes

Undo And Redo

Word provides 500 levels of undo and redo. This means that not only can you undo the last thing you did, but also the one before that, and the one before that, and so on up to 500 actions. If you undo something that you didn't mean to, you can redo up to 500 times as well!

Undoing The Last Thing You Did

Click the **Undo** icon

or

press **Ctrl+Z.**

Redoing The Last Thing You Undid

Click the **Redo** icon

or

press **Ctrl+Y.**

Undoing Up To 500 Actions

1   Click on the down arrow next to the **Undo** button.

2   Use the scroll bar to scroll to the last action you wish to undo.

3   Click on the action – all the actions up to and including that one will be undone.

It Will Undo All Of The Actions!

You cannot pick out an isolated action from the list and just undo that. If you undo the action you did 10 steps ago, your last 9 steps will be undone as well.

Redoing Up To 500 Things You Undid

1   Click on the down arrow next to the **Redo** icon.

2   Scroll to the last action you wish to redo.

3   Click on the action.

Repeating An Action

Imagine that you have to type the same piece of text several times. Rather than typing it out again and again, you can just use the repeat command!

1   Carry out the action you wish to repeat, e.g. typing.

2   Click on the **Edit** menu.

3   Click on **Repeat Typing**.

Or

1   Carry out the action you wish to repeat.

2   Press **Ctrl+Y**.

What Is The Difference Between Redo And Repeat?

Redo is used to cancel the effects of an undo. So if you make a mistake and undo your action, you can redo it again!

Repeat is for repeating your last action – it has nothing to do with the Undo command.

Views

Word provides four different ways of looking at your document depending on the task you are carrying out. Each view allows you to concentrate on a different aspect of your work.

Which View Am I In?

Check which icon is pushed in of the view icons at the bottom left of the screen.

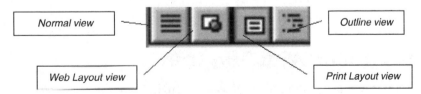

Changing The View With The Icons

Click on the icon required from the bottom left of the screen.

Why Do I Use Normal View?

➤ It shows you the text **only**, you cannot see the margins or the way it will look on the page.

➤ At the end of the page you will see a dotted line.

➤ Normal view shows you hidden characters, such as page breaks (see page 168).

➤ You will not be able to see your headers and footers in Normal view (see page 172).

Use Normal view when you want to concentrate on typing and editing text.

Why Do I Use Print Layout View?

➤ It shows you the margins and the way it will look on the page.

➤ At the end of a page, you will see a grey gap.

➤ You can only see headers and footers in Print Layout view (see page 172).

➤ You cannot see hidden characters such as page breaks (see page 168).

This view allows you to see how your document will print while you are working on it.

The Zoom Control

The zoom control allows you to stand up close to your document, or stand back so that you can see more of it. It does not change the size that it will print out at.

To check your current zoom:

Look at the **Zoom Control** icon on the *Standard* toolbar.

Changing The Zoom With The Icon

1   Click the drop-down arrow next to the **Zoom Control** icon

2   Click on the zoom level you require.

Each View Has Its Own Zoom

Normal view, Print Layout view and Print Preview all have a separate zoom control.

Toolbars

You can choose which toolbars you want displayed, depending on what you are doing.

Displaying Toolbars

1　Click on the **View** menu.

2　Click on **Toolbars**.

3　Click on the name of the toolbar you want to display.

Hiding Toolbars

1　Click on the **View** menu.

2　Click on **Toolbars**.

3　Click on the name of the toolbar you want to hide.

Hidden Or Displayed?

When you go to the **Toolbars** sub-menu on the **View** menu, you will see a list of all the toolbars which are available in Word. Those which are currently displayed will have a tick next to them.

Print Preview

Print Preview lets you see what your document will look like when it prints out. You can check for any mistakes before you print it, saving paper, time, money and probably the world. To see a Print Preview of your document, just click on the Print **Preview** icon. Or you can click on the **File** menu, and click **Print Preview**. The choice, as they say, is yours. Print Preview works the same way in all other Microsoft applications, so whenever you see the icon, you'll know what to do.

The Print Preview Toolbar

When you are in Print Preview you will be able to see the *Print Preview* toolbar at the top of the screen.

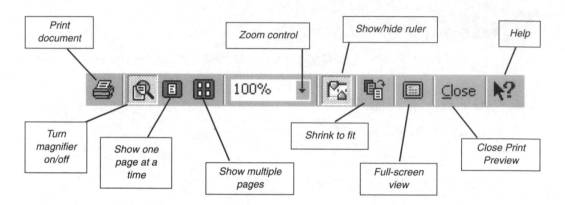

Be Careful With Shrink To Fit

Shrink to Fit will shrink your document by one page, which is useful if you have a document that goes just over one page. However, it may make changes that you don't want or expect if you use it on longer documents.

Zooming In On Your Document

1   Position your mouse at the point on the page where you want to zoom in – the mouse will change to a magnifying glass with a plus(+) sign.

2   Click the left mouse button once.

Zooming Out Of Your Document

1   Position your mouse over the document where you wish to zoom out – your mouse will change to a magnifying glass with a minus(–) sign.

2   Click the left mouse button once.

Closing Print Preview

Click on **Close** on the *Print Preview* toolbar.

Printing

To print a document once, just click on the **Print** icon. Yes, it's that simple.

Be Careful Not To Click The Print Icon More Than Once!

Sometimes it can take a while for your document to reach the printer and be printed out. If you click on the Print icon again you will get two copies. Some people get impatient and think it hasn't worked, so they click a million times – then they end up with a million copies, and the forests cry.

Printing More Than One Copy

1   Click on the **File** menu.

2   Click on **Print**.

3   Change the number of copies to the number you require – click on the up or down arrows in the box next to *Number of copies*, or just click inside the box and type a new number.

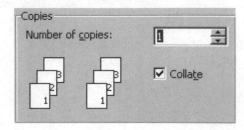

4   Click **OK**.

What Does Collate Mean?

This box is ticked by default, but what is it? Well, if you wanted 2 copies of a 3 page file, leave this box ticked. The printer will print pages 1 to 3, then pages 1 to 3 a second time. These copies are 'collated'. If you untick the box, it will print out both page 1s, then both page 2s, then both page 3s. So, if in doubt, just leave the box ticked.

Printing The Current Page

1   Click on the **File** menu.

2   Click on **Print**.

3   Click in the circle next to *Current page*.

4   Click **OK**.

Current Page Means The Page Your Cursor Is On!

You must check that your cursor is on the page you wish to print out. If you have used the scroll bar to move somewhere else, what you see on the screen may not be the page the cursor is on!

Printing Selected Text

1   Select the text you wish to print.

2   Click on the **File** menu.

3   Click on **Print**.

4   Click in the circle next to *Selection*.

5   Click **OK**.

Printing Certain Pages

1   Click on the **File** menu.

2   Click on **Print**.

3   Type in the pages you require into the *Pages* box (see below).

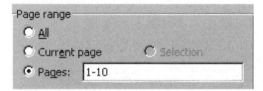

4   Click **OK**.

Individual pages can be separated by a comma, e.g. **1,2**. If you are printing a range of pages, you can use a hyphen – for example, typing in **5–10** will print pages 5, 6, 7, 8, 9 and 10.

Chapter 2

Formatting Text

Changing The Look Of Text

Changing the look of text is known as **formatting**. Formatting makes your documents look more professional and allows you to give emphasis to the important parts.

Applying Bold, Italic And Underline

1   Select the text to change.

2   Click on the icon you require (shown below).

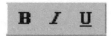

If you want to remove bold, italics or underline, just select the text and click the relevant icon, i.e. if you want to remove the bold, just click on the **Bold** icon, and so on.

What Is A Font?

A font is the style of the letters in your document.

This font is Arial and has a size of 10 points.

This font is Arial, 16 points.

This font is Times New Roman, 10 points.

This font is Times New Roman, 16 points.

This font is Courier, 12 points.

This font is Courier, 18 points.

Which Font Am I Using?

1   Position the cursor inside the text you wish to check.

2   Check the *Font* boxes on the *Formatting* toolbar.

In the figure below, the font face is Arial and the size is 10 point.

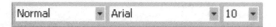

Changing The Font Size

1   Select the text you wish to change.

2   Click on the down arrow next to the *Font Size* box.

3   Click on the size you require – the bigger the number, the bigger the text.

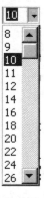

Changing The Font

1   Select the text you wish to change.

2   Click on the down arrow next to the *Font* box.

3 Click on the font you require.

You Can Display Font Names In The Actual Font...

... so that you can see what the font looks like before you apply it.

1 Click on the **Tools** menu.

2 Click **Customize**.

3 Click the **Options** tab.

4 Add a tick next to *List font names in their font*.

5 Click **Close**.

Aligning Text

What Is Alignment?

➤ Alignment decides how your text will line up on the page.

This is left-aligned for normal text.

      This is centre-aligned for headings.

            This is right-aligned for dates.

And this is a piece of fully justified text that has straight edges at both sides. It looks very neat and tidy, doesn't it?

➤ Alignment will change the whole paragraph that your cursor is in. Word thinks that paragraphs are where you have pressed **Return**, even if it is only a blank line.

Using The Icons

1 Click into the paragraph you wish to change.

or

select several paragraphs.

2 Click on the icon you require (shown below).

Left align — Centre align — Right align — Fully justified

You Can Change The Alignment At Any Time!

For example, if you have made a piece of text justified, you can left-align it by following the instructions above again!

Special Text Effects
Changing The Underline Options

1 Select the text you wish to change.

2 Click on the **Format** menu.

3 Click on **Font**.

4 Click on the drop-down arrow next to the *Underline* box.

Underline:

(none)

5 Click on the *Underline* option you require.

6 Click **OK**.

Check This Out...

Watch The Preview Box

The Preview box at the bottom will show you how your text will look, e.g.

> Preview
>
> *Preview*

Changing The Text Effects

1 Select the text you wish to change.

2 Click on the **Format** menu.

3 Click on **Font**.

4 Click in the box next to the effect you require.

> Effects
>
> ☐ Strikethrough   ☐ Shadow   ☐ Small caps
> ☐ Double strikethrough   ☐ Outline   ☐ All caps
> ☐ Superscript   ☐ Emboss   ☐ Hidden
> ☐ Subscript   ☐ Engrave

5 Click **OK**.

Check This Out...

When Would I Use Special Text Effects?

➤ Use strikethrough to cross out mistakes, or show that something has been done. ~~This is strikethrough~~

➤ Use superscript to produce smaller characters above the normal letters, e.g. 3^3, 2^2, Idiot's Guide^{TM}.

➤ Use subscript to produce smaller characters below the normal letters, e.g. H_2O.

135

Fields, Special Characters And Symbols

What Are Fields?

Fields are special codes in Word that you use when information changes automatically – some examples would be a Page Number field, which changes according to what page you are on, or a Date field, which changes constantly so that it always shows the correct date.

Inserting Fields

1   Click on the **Insert** menu.

2   Click on **Field**.

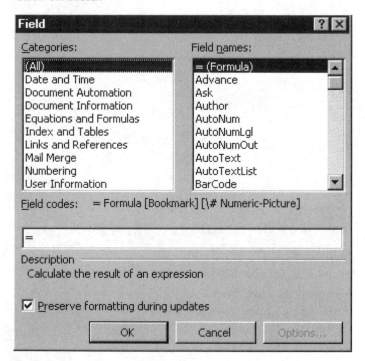

3   Click on the *Category* you require on the left.

4   Choose the *Field name* you require on the right.

5   Click **OK**.

Updating Fields

To update a single field:

1   Select the field you wish to update.

2   Press **F9**.

To update all fields:

1   Click on the **Edit** menu.

2   Click on **Select All**.

3   Press **F9**.

Deleting Fields

1   Select the field you wish to delete.

2   Press the **Delete** key.

The Two States Of A Field

A field can either show the results of the field or the special codes that describe what the field does. The usual setting is to show the results.

Toggle Field Codes/Results

1   Select the **field**.

2   Press **Shift + F9**.

Or

To toggle field codes for all fields, press **Alt + F9**.

Adding Switches To Fields

Switches are optional instructions that modify the format of, or prevent changes to, the information that results from a field. To add a switch to a field, you must first delete the field and reinsert it.

1   Delete the field you wish to add the switch to.

2   Click on the **Insert** menu.

3   Click on **Field**.

4   Choose the field category and name you wish to insert.

5   Click on **Options**.

6   Choose your field switch – a description of the switch will appear under *Description*.

7   Click on **Add to Field**.

8   Click **OK**.

9   Click **OK**.

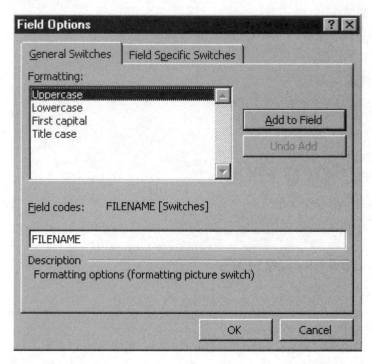

Inserting Symbols

Symbols can be particularly useful for foreign words and names containing accented letters that don't exist in English.

1   Position the cursor where you require the symbol.

2   Click on the **Insert** menu.

3   Click on **Symbol**.

4   Click on the **Symbols** tab.

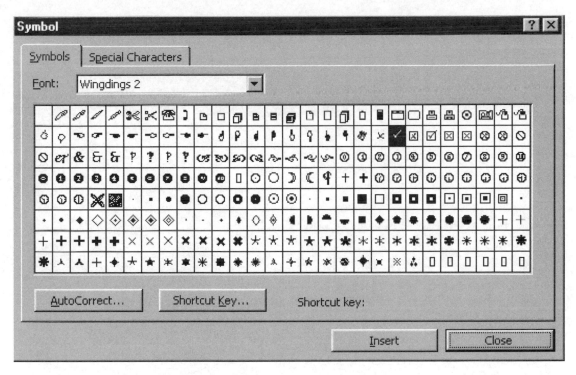

5   Under *Font*, click on the font to use.

6   Click on the symbol to insert.

7   Click on the **Insert** button.

8   Click on **Close**.

Creating Shortcut Keys For Symbols

1   Click on the **Insert** menu.

2   Click on **Symbol**.

3   Click on the **Symbols** tab.

4   Choose the font and symbol you require a shortcut key for.

5   Click on **Shortcut Key**.

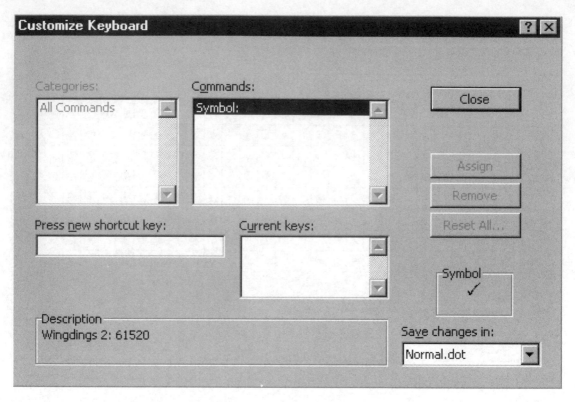

6   Type in the shortcut key you wish to use.

7   Click on **Assign**.

8   Click on **Close**.

Inserting Special Characters

As well as providing special characters such as © or ™, this is also useful for different types of spaces between words.

1   Click on the **Insert** menu.

2   Click on **Symbol**.

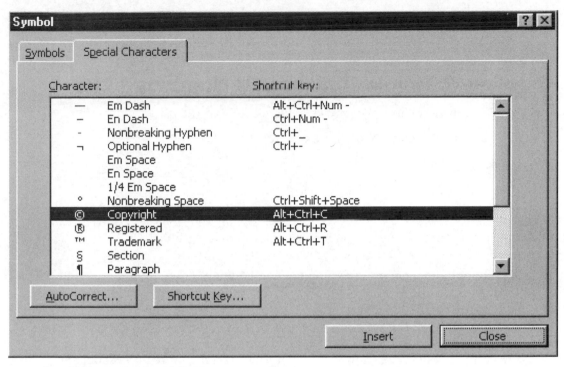

3   Click on the **Special Characters** tab.

4   Choose the special character you require.

5   Click on the **Insert** menu.

6   Click on **Close**.

Bullets And Numbering

Bulleted And Numbered Lists

Bulleted and numbered lists are basically just lists. Bulleted lists have little symbols, or 'bullets' at the start of the lines, and numbered ones have – can you guess? – numbers.

➤ This is

➤ a bulleted

➤ list.

1   And this is

2   a numbered

3   list.

Word will create these lists automatically for you, if you ask it nicely.

Creating A Simple Bulleted Or Numbered List

1   Position your cursor where you would like to start the list.

2   Click the **Bullets** or **Numbers** icon.

3   Type your first point.

4   Press **Return** whenever you require a new number or bullet.

Turning Bullets Or Numbers Off

Press **Return** twice.

Or

1   Position your cursor in the paragraph where you do not require a bullet or number.

2   Click the **Bullets** or **Numbers** icon again.

Applying Bullets Or Numbers To Existing Text

Word will put a number or a bullet wherever there is a paragraph.

1   Select the text to change.

2   Click the **Bullets** or **Numbers** icon.

Adding Extra Points In The Middle Of A Numbered List

1   Place your cursor at the end of the point where you require the new point.

2   Press **Return** – Word will automatically renumber!

Creating Blank Lines In The Middle Of A List

Word is programmed to give you a number or a bullet wherever you press the Return key. To get a blank line, don't press Return – enter a soft return instead!

1   Position your cursor at the end of the point before you require a blank line.

2   Hold down the **Shift** key and press **Return** at the same time to create a soft return.

3   Press **Return** on its own to get the next number.

If Your Text Is Fully Justified ...

Then this method will cause the alignment to go a little strange. Change the alignment back to left, or

1   Create list as normal, so that the lines which are meant to be blank have numbers or bullets.

2   Click your cursor into any paragraph which has an unwanted number or bullet.

3   Click on the **Bullets** or **Numbers** icon to turn them off.

4   Make sure your cursor is still in the paragraph you wish to be blank.

5   Drag the square at the bottom of the indent marker on the ruler inwards to make the text line up with the numbered or bulleted text (see below).

Removing Bullets Or Numbers

1   Select text you wish to remove bullets or numbers from.

2   Click **Bullets** or **Numbers** icon.

Customizing Bullets
Changing The Style Of Bullets

1   Select the text you want to change.

2   Click on the **Format** menu.

3   Click **Bullets and Numbering**.

4   Click on the **Bulleted** tab if you are not there already.

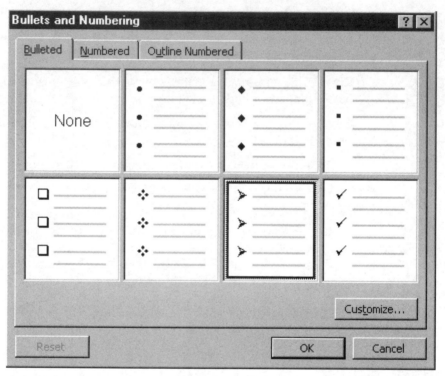

5   Click on the bullet style you require.

6   Click **OK**.

Getting Even More Bullet Styles!

If the bullet style you require isn't listed:

1   Select the text you want to change.

2   Click on the **Format** menu.

3   Click **Bullets and Numbering**.

4   Click on the **Bulleted** tab if you are not there already.

5   Click on an existing style of bullet, if you have not done so already.

6   Click **Customize**.

7   Click **Bullet**.

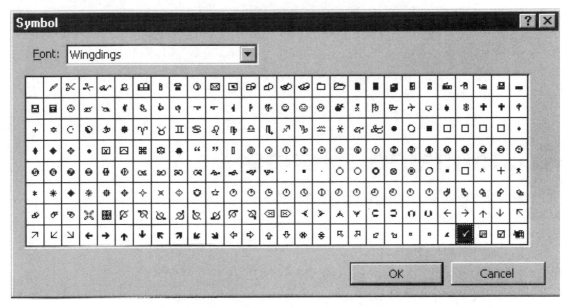

8   Click on the drop-down arrow next to *Font* and change the font if required.

9   Click on the bullet you require from the grid.

10   Click **OK**.

11   Click **OK**.

Changing The Indentation Of Bullets

1   Select the text you want to change.

2   Click on the **Format** menu.

3   Click **Bullets and Numbering**.

4   Click on the **Bulleted** tab if you are not there already.

5   Click an existing type of bullet if you have not done so already.

6   Click **Customize**.

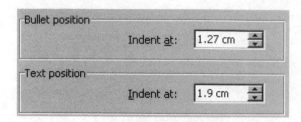

7   To increase or decrease the distance from the margin, change the number in the *Indent at* box under *Bullet position*.

8   To increase or decrease the distance between the text and the bullet, change the number in the *Indent at* box under *Text position*.

9   Click **OK**.

Customizing Numbers

Changing The Number Style

1   Select the text you want to change.

2   Click on the **Format** menu.

3   Click **Bullets and Numbering**.

4   Click on the **Numbered** tab if you are not there already.

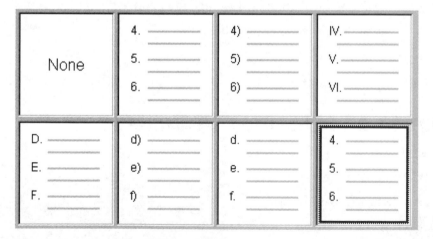

5   Click on the number style you require.

6   Click **OK**.

Changing The Indentation Of Numbers

1 Select the text you want to change.

2 Click on the **Format** menu.

3 Click **Bullets and Numbering**.

4 Click on the **Numbered** tab, if you are not there already.

5 Click a style of numbers, if you have not done so already.

6 Click **Customize**.

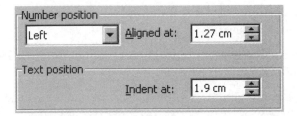

7 Change the number in the *Aligned at* box under *Number* position to increase the distance between the number and the margin.

8 Change the number in the *Indent at* box under *Text position* to increase the distance between the text and the number.

9 Click **OK**.

Continue And Restart Numbering

If your numbering does not work correctly and you find that you are getting the wrong number, you can choose to restart it again at 1, or continue a list that you were doing previously.

1 Click the cursor into the paragraph where you would like to restart or continue the numbers.

2 Click on the **Format** menu.

3 Click **Bullets and Numbering**.

4 Click on the **Numbered** tab.

5 Click in the circle next to *Restart numbering*

or

click in the circle next to *Continue previous list.*

Indenting Text

What Are Indents?

This is a normal paragraph with no sort of indentation whatsoever. It is just straightforward and normal and not a single thing is special about it. Sad, really, isn't it?

> This is an indented paragraph. When I type, the text is **indented from the left-hand margin**, and when I get to the next line it remains indented.

> This paragraph is different again because it is **indented from the left and also from the right**.

> This paragraph has a **first line indent**. The first line is indented from the left and the rest of the paragraph has no indent.

And finally here is a **hanging indent**, which we often use for numbers because the first line is normal, but the rest of the paragraph is indented slightly from the left hand side. This means that if you had a numbered list, it would line up nicely. The moral of this story? It's good to be different.

You would use indents to give emphasis to a paragraph, for quotes or for creating numbered or bulleted lists manually (although Word will do these for you automatically, see page 141).

Indents Affect Paragraphs

Word does not see paragraphs in quite the same way as you would expect. To Word, a paragraph is wherever you have pressed the **Return** key, so even blank lines are paragraphs.

Indenting A Paragraph From The Left

1   Position your cursor in the paragraph you want to change

or

select the paragraphs you wish to change.

2   Click on the **Increase Indent** icon.

You Can Indent More Than Once

Every time you click the **Increase Indent** icon, the text is indented by half an inch more.

Removing The Left Indent From A Paragraph

1   Position your cursor in the paragraph you want to change

or

select the paragraphs you wish to change.

2   Click on the **Decrease Indent** icon

Understanding The Indent Markers

On the ruler you will see several grey triangles – an upper and lower one on the left, and a lower one on the right. These represent different indents. The top triangle lines up to the first line of the paragraph you are in. The bottom triangle lines up to the rest of the paragraph which you are in, i.e. anything but the first line. If the paragraph you are in is indented from the right hand side, as well as the left, the bottom triangle will be dragged in from the right-hand margin.

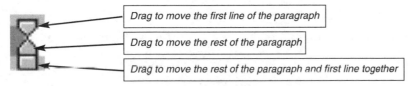

Drag to move the first line of the paragraph

Drag to move the rest of the paragraph

Drag to move the rest of the paragraph and first line together

Indent Markers Will Change Depending On Which Paragraph Your Cursor Is In

If your document has paragraphs with different indents, you must click into the paragraph you require to see the indents it contains.

149

Indent Markers In Action!

So I says to Mabel, I says, Mabel – what do you think you're doing, putting the chips on the bean shelf? So she says to me, she says, Bernie, she says, there's no room on the chip shelf, I've got to put the chips on the bean shelf.

> Of course, once she'd pointed out the space difficulties on the chip shelf, I was forced to agree with her. Mabel, I says to her, your powers of observation and bean/chip shelf management are beyond reproach.

But it was too late. The damage was done. Mabel never spoke to me of beans, or chips, ever again. The days stretched out into winter, and our conversations, while enjoyable, were never quite as sparkling as they were during the chip and bean days.

Look at the example above. The cursor is positioned in the middle paragraph, so it is the indents for that paragraph that show on the ruler.

Changing Indents With The Ruler

1   Position your cursor in the paragraph to change

    or

    select the paragraphs to change.

2   Click and drag the indent marker you require:

➤ Drag the top-left triangle to move the first line of the paragraph.

➤ Drag the bottom-left triangle to move the rest of the paragraph.

➤ Drag the square to move the rest of the paragraph and the first line together.

➤ Drag the bottom-right indent marker to indent the right-hand side of the paragraph.

Set The Indents <u>After</u> The Paragraphs Are Typed!

Otherwise the indents you set will affect everything you type afterwards and you will have to change them back again.

Creating A First Line Indent With The Keyboard

1   Position your cursor at the start of the paragraph.

2   Press the **Tab** key.

Creating A Hanging Indent With The Keyboard

1   Position your cursor in the paragraph to change

or

select the paragraphs to change.

2   Press **Ctrl+T.**

Removing Hanging Indents With The Keyboard

1   Position your cursor in the paragraph to change

or

select the paragraphs to change.

2   Press **Ctrl+Shift+T.**

Borders And Shading

Sometimes you might want to add a bit of colour to a paragraph or maybe a nice border, and there's absolutely nothing wrong with that. Let's have a look at how to do it.

Adding Shading To Paragraphs

1   Select the text you want to change.

2   Click on the **Format** menu.

3   Click **Borders and Shading**.

4   Click on the **Shading** tab.

5   Click on the colour you require.

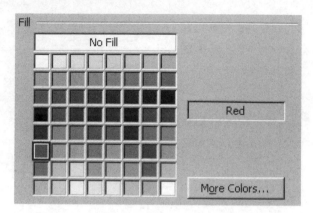

6   Choose *Pattern*, if required (see next section, Applying Patterned Shading).

7   Click **OK**.

If The Colour You Require Is Not Available ...

1   Click on the **More Colors** button.

2   Click on the **Standard** tab.

3   Click on the colour you require.

4   Click **OK**.

5   Click **OK**.

What Is The Shading Being Applied To?

Check the *Apply to* box.

This whole paragraph is shaded.

Only this text is shaded, but not the paragraph.

Applying Patterned Shading

1   Select the text you want to change.

2   Click on the **Format** menu.

3   Click **Borders and Shading.**

4   Click on the **Shading** tab.

5   Click on a colour underneath *Fill* to become the background of your pattern.

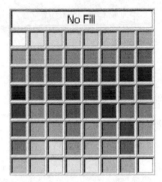

6   Click on the down arrow underneath *Style.*

7   Click on the style you require.

8   If required, click the down arrow underneath *Color* and click on a foreground colour for your pattern.

9   Click **OK.**

Removing Shading

1   Select the text you wish to remove shading from.

2   Click on the **Format** menu.

3   Click **Borders and Shading.**

4   Click *No fill.*

5   Click **OK.**

Applying Borders To Paragraphs

1   Select text to apply borders to.

2   Click on the **Format** menu.

3   Click **Borders and Shading.**

4   Click on the **Borders** tab.

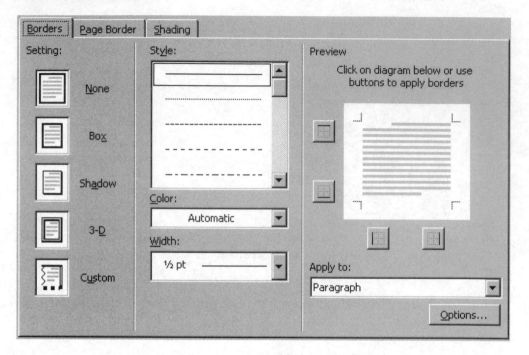

➤ The Box, Shadow and 3-D settings give you a border all the way around your selection.

➤ With the Custom setting, you do not have to have a border all the way around – for example, you can choose just to have a top and bottom border.

➤ The *Preview* box shows you what your borders will look like.

➤ Click on the **Border** buttons (in and around the *Preview* box) to specify which borders you require.

5   Choose the setting you require from the left-hand side (under *Setting*).

6   If required, choose a different style of line from the list underneath *Style*.

7   If required, click on the down arrow underneath *Color* and choose a different colour for your border.

8   If required, click on the down arrow underneath *Width* and change the width of your border.

9   If you have chosen **Custom** settings, click the **Border** buttons (in and around the *Preview* box) to add selected borders.

10   Click **OK**.

Adding A Picture For A Border

1   Position the cursor where you would like a picture border.

2   Click on the **Format** menu.

3   Click **Borders and Shading**.

4   Click on the **Borders** tab.

5   Click on the **Horizontal Line** button to open the Clip Art Gallery.

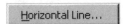

6   Click on the line you require.

7   Click on the **Insert Clip** icon.

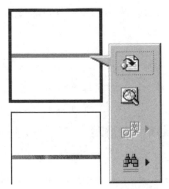

Removing Borders

1   Select the text you wish to remove the borders from.

2   Click on the **Format** menu.

3   Click **Borders and Shading**.

4   Click on the **Borders** tab.

155

5   In *Setting*, click on the *None* box.

6   Click **OK**.

This Will Not Remove A Picture Border

Instead, you must click on the picture, and then press the **Delete** key.

Format Painter

Format Painter provides a quick way of copying formatting, such as borders and shading, to other text in your document. For example, if you had a heading with lots of fancy formatting on it, you could copy those formats in one go and apply them to a different piece of text.

Using Format Painter Once

1   Select some text that is already formatted.

2   Click on the **Format Painter** icon – a paintbrush appears next to your mouse.

3   Drag your mouse over the text you wish to copy the formatting to.

Using Format Painter More Than Once

1   Select some text that is already formatted.

2   Double-click on the **Format Painter** icon – a paintbrush appears next to your mouse.

3   Drag your mouse over the text you wish to copy the formatting to.

4   Click on the **Format Painter** icon again when you have finished.

Styles

A style is a collection of formats which you can apply to your text. For example all your main headings could be in **Arial, Bold, 16 point** and **centred** Taken together these formats would be your **Heading 1 Style**.

Styles are closely connected to the template you are using. Different templates will have different styles. (For more information on templates, see page 237)

Why Use Styles?

Styles make working with Word a lot easier. Once you have mastered them you can:

➤ Format your documents quickly and consistently.

➤ Change the formatting in your documents quickly and consistently.

➤ Use the styles you create in other documents and templates.

➤ Create a table of contents.

➤ Use Outline View to work with long documents.

Which Style Is My Text In?

1   Position your cursor in the text you wish to check.

2   Look at the *Style* box on the formatting toolbar – in the example shown below, the selected text is in the Normal style.

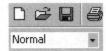

Applying An Existing Style

1   Position your cursor in the paragraph you wish to change

or

select the text you wish to change.

2   Click on the drop-down arrow next to the **Style** box.

3   Click on the style you require.

Changing A Style

1   Select some text that is in the style you wish to change.

2   Make any formatting changes you require.

3   Click on top of the style name in the *Style* box to make it go blue.

4   Press **Enter.**

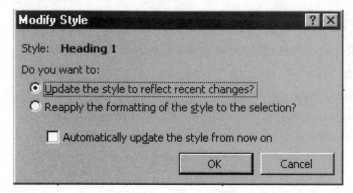

5   Make sure *Update the style to reflect recent changes?* is selected.

6   Click **OK** to make all the text in this style change.

Changing Styles Will Only Affect The Document You Are In

If you wish to change the styles for the template (so that all new documents based on this template use the styles you create) then read the section on page 239.

Creating A New Style

1   Type some text and format it as required.

2   Select the text.

3   Click on top of the style name in the *Style* box to make it go blue.

4   Type in a name for your style.

5   Press **Enter.**

158

Copying Styles To The Normal Template With The Organizer

1   Open the document you wish to copy the style from.

2   Click on the **Format** menu.

3   Click on **Style**.

4   Click on **Organizer**.

5   Ensure that the document you wish to copy from is displayed on the left (see Check This Out below).

6   Ensure that the Normal template is displayed on the right (see Check This Out on next page).

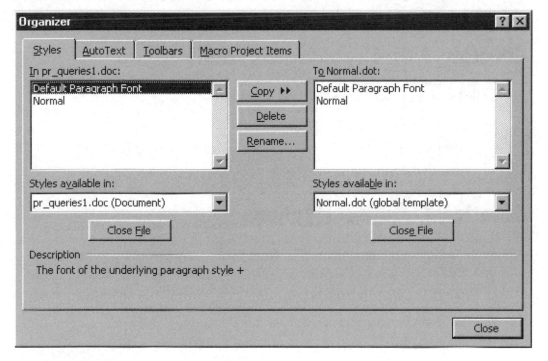

7   Click on the style you wish to copy.

8   Click on **Copy**.

9   Click **Close**.

Check This Out...

How Do I Make Sure The Correct Documents Are Displayed?

If the correct documents are not displayed, click on the **Close File** button, then the **Open File** button and choose the correct document.

Hyphenation

A hyphen is something that you use to join certain words together, like co-operate. If the word is near the end of a line, Word might use it to split the word up, like this: co-operate.

Creating Non-Breaking Hyphens

A non-breaking hyphen does not split at the end of the line. The hyphenated words will always stay together on the same line.

1   Delete the original hyphen if necessary.

2   Position your cursor where you require the non-breaking hyphen.

3   Press **Ctrl+Shift+Hyphen**.

Creating Optional Hyphens

Use optional hyphens when you have two words that may be split up over two lines. If you insert an optional hyphen between them, a hyphen will appear if they do get split up.

1   Delete the original hyphen if necessary.

2   Position your cursor where you require the optional hyphen.

3   Press **Ctrl+Hyphen**.

Hyphenation And Justified Text

When you justify text sometimes it gets spread out in an attempt to keep the left and right margins in a straight line. This is particularly true if the text is in columns and contains long words. Hyphenation can be used to get rid of some of the white spaces. (See the example opposite.)

When using fully justified text particularly with long words, the text can spread out leaving unattractive white space. Using hyphenation and splitting words up over two lines can alleviate the situation.

When using fully justified text particularly with long words, the text can spread out leaving unattractive white space. Using hyphenation and splitting words up over two lines can alleviate the situation.

The options for avoiding this situation are:

➤ Typing in hyphens yourself.

➤ Using automatic hyphenation.

➤ Using manual hyphenation.

Automatic Hyphenation

This feature inserts the hyphens automatically as you type.

1   Click on the **Tools** menu.

2   Click **Language**.

3   Click **Hyphenation**.

4   Put a tick in the box next to *Automatically hyphenate document*.

5   If necessary, click on the **Manual** button to view and decide on each hyphen suggestion.

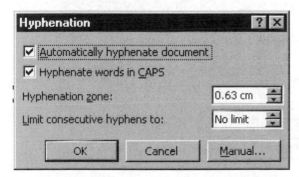

161

Manual Hyphenation

1   Position your cursor where you require a hyphen.

2   Click on the **Tools** menu.

3   Click **Language**.

4   Click **Hyphenation**.

5   Click **Manual** – Word will suggest hyphens and you can agree or reject each suggestion.

Typing In Hyphens

Note that if you use this method any subsequent changes to the text may alter the position of the hyphens.

1   Position your cursor where you require a hyphen.

2   Press the hyphen-key (-) on the keyboard.

Page Numbering

Page numbers are a good thing. They tell you what page you are on, and might prevent athlete's foot (though it's not likely). What page are you on now? See? If this book didn't have page numbers, you'd have been completely stumped.

Page Numbering With The Menu

1   Click on the **Insert** menu.

2   Click **Page Numbers**.

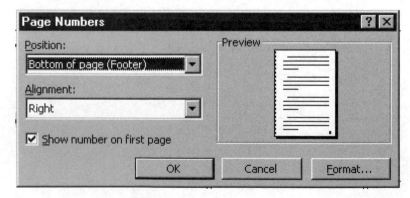

3 Click the down arrow under *Position* and choose where you would like to put your page numbers.

4 Click the down arrow underneath *Alignment* and choose the alignment for your page numbers.

5 Click **OK**.

You Can Only See Your Page Numbers In Print Layout View!

So don't panic if you can't see them, just check what view you're in. See page 123 for more details.

No Numbers On The First Page

If you have a title page on a report, you may wish to remove the numbers from the first page:

1 Click on the **Insert** menu.

2 Click **Page Numbers**.

3 Click in the box next to *Show number on first page* so that it is **not** ticked (see below).

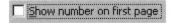

4 Click **OK**.

Changing The Format Of Page Numbers

1 Click on the **Insert** menu.

2 Click **Page Numbers**.

3 Click **Format**.

4 Click the down arrow next to the *Number format* box.

5 Click number style you require.

6   Click **OK**.

7   Click **OK**.

Deleting Page Numbering

1   Double-click on any page number – you will be taken into Header and Footer view.

2   Click on top of the number – diagonal lines should appear.

3   Click on top of the diagonal lines – black boxes should appear.

4   Press the **Delete** key on the keyboard.

Once You Have Deleted One Page Number, All The Others Will Be Deleted As Well!

Chapter 3

Working With Long Documents

Moving And Copying Text

Sometimes you might want to move a piece of text somewhere else or copy another piece of text to save yourself from having to type it out again. Word uses the Windows Clipboard to help you do this, which is a special area where copied and cut text goes to. Let's have a look at what this means.

Moving Text

1 Select the text you would like to move.

2 Click on the **Cut** icon – the text is moved to the Windows Clipboard.

3 Position the cursor in the place you would like to move the text to.

4 Click on the **Paste** icon.

Copying Text

1 Select the text you would like to copy.

2 Click on **Copy** icon – the text is copied to the Windows Clipboard.

3 Position the cursor in the place you would like to copy the text to.

4   Click on the **Paste** icon.

The Cut Or Copied Text Remains On The Clipboard

If you click **Paste** more than once, whatever was last cut or copied will appear again.

Switching Between Documents

1   Click on the Window menu to display a list of open documents.

2   Click on the document you require.

Or

Press **Ctrl+F6** to cycle through the open documents.

Or

Click on the button for that document on the Taskbar.

Copying Text Between Documents

1   Open the document you are copying from.

2   Open the document you are copying to – they will appear as icons on the Taskbar.

3   Select the text you would like to copy.

4   Click on **Copy**.

5   Click on the document you would like to copy to on the Taskbar.

6   Position the cursor where you would like to copy to.

7   Click on **Paste**.

Copying Or Moving More Than One Thing

Word 2000 gives you the option of putting lots of things on the clipboard, so that you can copy many separate pieces of text at once.

1   Select the first piece of text you wish to cut or copy.

2   Click **Cut** or **Copy** – the text is sent to the Windows clipboard.

3   Select the second piece of text you wish to cut or copy.

4   Click **Cut** or **Copy** – the text is sent to the Office clipboard, and a new toolbar will appear.

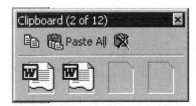

5   Continue cutting and/or copying up to 12 times.

6   Position the cursor where you would like to paste the text.

7   Click the icon for the text you would like to paste

or

click on **Paste All** to paste everything – hover your mouse pointer over the icon to see which piece of text it is.

 **Eventually The Clipboard Will Get Full Up**

Once you have cut or copied 12 pieces of text, the clipboard will get full. Click on the Clear Clipboard icon to empty it.

Page Breaks

A page break forces Word to end the current page and start a new one. This is useful if you need to start a new page without filling up the page you are on. Sometimes people press Return lots of times to create blank lines to get onto the next page, but this is A Very Bad Thing. If you add text to the page later on, it will push all those blank lines further down, and the next page will have a big gap at the top. This makes the document look bad.

Creating A Page Break

1   Position the cursor where you would like a page break.

2   Press **Ctrl+Enter**.

Or

1   Click on the **Insert** menu.

2   Click **Break**.

3   Click the circle next to *Page break*.

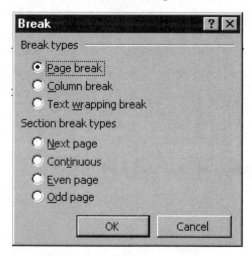

4   Click **OK**.

Deleting A Page Break

1   Make sure you are in Normal view.

2   Position your cursor on the page break.

3   Press the **Delete** key.

Margins

Margins are the gaps between your text and the edge of the page. There are four margins on your page: top, bottom, left and right. Word usually determines their size automatically, but you may want to change them. Here are some of the reasons why:

➤ If you increase the size of the margins you create more white space on the page. This makes your document more legible and also provides room for people to make notes.

➤ You may have a document which only has one or two lines on the last page. If you decrease the size of the margins, you create more space for text in the document, and the lines may fit back onto the previous page.

Changing The Margins With The Menu

1   Click on the **File** menu.

2   Click **Page Setup**.

3   Change the margins as required.

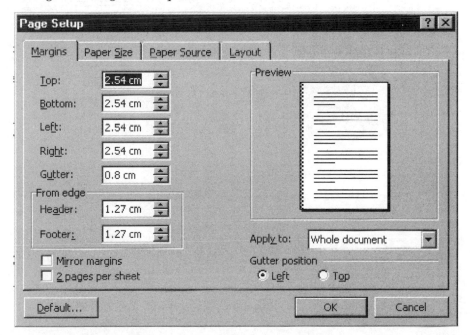

➤ In the box next to *Top*, *Bottom*, *Left* or *Right*, use the up or down arrows or type in the size of your new margin.

➤ If necessary, change the *Gutter* margin to make room for binding – if you are not sure about this, just ignore it.

➤ Tick *Mirror margins* if you are printing on both sides of the paper – again, if you are not sure if you need this, just leave it unticked.

➤ A preview of your margins is shown on the right-hand side of the box.

➤ Under the preview, look at the box marked *Apply to* – you can change the margins for the whole document, just the section you are currently in or from that point forward.

4   Click **OK**.

Changing The Paper Size

1   Click on the **File** menu.

2   Click **Page Setup**.

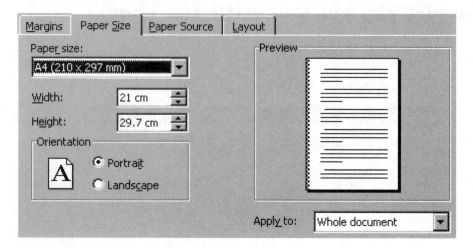

3   Click on the down arrow underneath *Paper size*.

4   Click on the paper size you require, e.g. *A4*.

5   Click **OK**.

170

Line Spacing

Line spacing, funnily enough, refers to the spacing between lines. Normally, single line spacing is fine, but sometimes you might want to space text out a bit to make it easier to read.

This is single (1) line spacing.	This is 1.5 line spacing.	This is double line spacing.

Changing The Line Spacing

1   Position your cursor in the paragraph you wish to change

or

select several paragraphs

or

press **Ctrl+A** to select the whole document.

2   Click on the **Format** menu.

3   Click **Paragraph**.

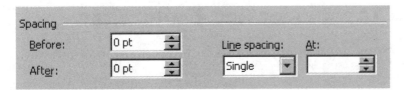

4   Click on the *Line spacing* drop-down arrow to choose the spacing you require.

5   Click **OK**.

Changing The Spacing Around Paragraphs

1   Position your cursor in the paragraph you wish to change

or

select several paragraphs

or

press **Ctrl+A** to select the whole document.

2   Click **Format**.

171

3   Click **Paragraph**.

4   Change the options as required in the *Spacing* section.

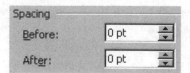

➤ In the *Before* box, use the up and down arrows or click inside the box and type the amount of space you require before the paragraph.

➤ In the *After* box, use the up and down arrows or click inside the box and type the amount of space you require after the paragraph.

5   Click **OK**.

Headers And Footers

Headers and footers appear at the top and bottom of every page. They are usually used to display information such as page numbers, the title of the document, the date, the file name and path, the author's name, etc. If you have something that you want to appear on every page, then the header or footer is the place to put it.

Going Into The Header And Footer Area

1   Click on the **View** menu.

2   Click on **Header and Footer**.

3   Position your cursor in the dotted area.

4   Start typing! What you type will appear on every page of the document.

Or, if you are getting back to Headers and Footers that you have already created …

Double-click on the header or footer area on any page.

Using Headers And Footers

If you want to move to the middle of the header/footer, press the **Tab** key. Press it again to move to the right-hand side. If you are on the header and want to go to the footer (or vice versa), click on the imaginatively named **Switch Between Header and Footer** icon.

Inserting Items

Position your cursor where you want to insert something. If you want to insert the date or time, click on the **Insert Date** icon or the **Insert Time** icon. If you want to insert the page number, click on the **Insert Page Number** icon. To insert the number of pages, click on the **Insert Number of Pages** icon. To add the author, page number and date all in one go, place your cursor at the left of the header or footer, click on the **Insert AutoText** icon on the *Header and Footer* toolbar, then click on **Author, Page #, Date**.

Date   *Time*   *Page Number*   *Number of Pages*

Closing The Header And Footer View

Click **Close** on the *Header and Footer* toolbar.

 **You Can Only See Headers And Footers In Print Layout View!**

Setting Alternate Headers And Footers

If your document is going to be printed on both sides of the page, you might want different headers and footers on the odd and even pages to make it look better.

To set alternate headers and footers:

1   Click on the **File** menu.

2   Click on **Page Setup**.

3   Click on the **Layout** tab.

4   Click in the *Different odd and even* box so that it is ticked.

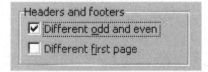

5   Click **OK**.

Adding Text Into Alternate Headers And Footers

1 Go to an odd page in your document.

2 Click on the **View** menu.

3 Click on **Header and Footer** – you will be taken to the *Odd Page Header*.

Odd Page Header

4 Enter any text you require into the *Odd Page Header*.

5 Click on the **Switch Between Header and Footer** icon.

6 Enter any text you require in the *Odd Page Footer*.

7 Click on the **Show Next** icon – you will be taken to the *Even Page Footer*.

8 Enter any text you require in the *Even Page Footer*.

9 Click on the **Switch Between Header and Footer** icon.

10 Enter any text you require in the *Even Page Header*.

Even Page Header

11 Click on **Close**.

Check This Out...

You Have Now Set Alternate Headers And Footers

All odd pages will have the odd page header and footer, and all even pages will have the even page header and footer. Aren't you clever?

First Page Header And Footer

If you are creating a document which has a title page, you may not want to have headers and footers on the first page.

To change the first page:

1   Click on the **File** menu.

2   Click on **Page Setup**.

3   Click on the **Layout** tab.

4   Tick the *Different first page* box.

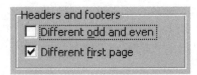

5   Click **OK**.

Once you have done that, it's time to change the first page:

1   Position your cursor on the first page.

2   Click on the **View** menu.

3   Click on **Header and Footer** – you will be taken to the *First Page Header*.

> First Page Header

4   Enter or delete any text in the *First Page Header*.

5   Click on the **Switch Between Header and Footer** icon.

6   Enter or delete any text in the *First Page Footer*.

7   Click on **Close**.

There you go – you now have a different header and footer on your first page. Show all your friends and bask in the glory of their admiration.

Section Breaks

Section breaks allow you to make the layout of a section of the document different from the rest. So a section can have different margins, orientation, page numbering and headers and footers.

You can have as many sections as you like inside a document and they can all have different layouts.

Page Orientation

The orientation of a page is, basically, which way up it is. Usually the pages in a Word document are in portrait orientation (standing up). However, if you are creating a poster or you wish to display a wide table, you might want to change the orientation to landscape (on its side).

A portrait page   **A landscape page**

Changing The Orientation From This Point Forward

1   Position your cursor where you wish the new orientation to start, e.g. at the top of the last page.

2   Click on the **File** menu.

3   Click on **Page Setup**.

4   Click on the **Paper Size** tab.

5   Click in the circle next to *Landscape*.

6   Click on the down arrow next to *Apply to*.

7   Click on *This point forward*.

8   Click **OK**.

What Does 'This Point Forward' Mean?

This means that everything after your cursor will be changed.

Very clever – but how does it work? Well, Word has inserted a section break before the landscape part of your document. You now have two sections to your document – one is portrait, the other is landscape.

To see the section break, switch to Normal view and scroll to the point where your pages have become landscape. You will be able to see the portrait text before the section break and the landscape text after the section break.

Portrait Portrait Portrait Portrait Portrait Portrait Portrait Portrait Portrait Portrait
Portrait Portrait Portrait Portrait Portrait Portrait Portrait Portrait Portrait Portrait
Portrait Portrait Portrait Portrait Portrait Portrait Portrait Portrait Portrait Portrait

··· Section Break (Next Page) ···

Landscape Landscape Landscape Landscape Landscape Landscape Landscape Landscape Landscape La.
Landscape Landscape Landscape Landscape Landscape Landscape Landscape Landscape Landscape La.
Landscape Landscape Landscape Landscape Landscape Landscape Landscape Landscape Landscape La.
Landscape Landscape Landscape Landscape Landscape Landscape Landscape Landscape Landscape La.

Which Section Am I In?

1   Position your cursor in the part of the document you wish to check.

2   Check the status bar at the bottom left of the screen.

If you go to the end of the portrait section that you created above, you are in section 1. If you click into the landscape page, you will see that you have gone into section 2.

| Page 3 | Sec 1 | 3/4 |

| Page 4 | Sec 2 | 4/4 |

An Example Of Section Breaks – A Document With Portrait And Landscape Pages

Sometimes you cannot use *This point forward*, as the page you wish to make landscape is in the middle of two portrait pages. For example, if you had a document with four pages and you wanted to make page three landscape, you would need to use section breaks, similar to the ones shown in the diagram below. The dotted lines represent the section breaks

1   Position the cursor where you would like your first section break – in the example above, it would be at the end of page 2 or the top of page 3.

2   Click on the **Insert** menu.

3   Click on **Break**.

4   Choose the type of break you require – in the example above it would be *Continuous*.

5   Click **OK**.

6   Position the cursor where you would like your second section break – in the example above it would be at the bottom of page 3 or the top of page 4.

7   Click on the **Insert** menu.

8   Click on **Break**.

9   Choose the type of break you require – in the example above it would be *Continuous*.

10   Click **OK** – the document now has three sections.

11   Position your cursor anywhere inside the section you wish to make landscape (the middle of page 3 is safest) – you can check which section you are in from the status bar.

| Page 19 | Sec 2 | 19/192 |

12   Click on the **File** menu.

13   Click on **Page Setup**.

14 Click on the **Paper Size** tab.

15 Click in the circle next to *Landscape*.

16 Check that the *Apply to* box says *This section*.

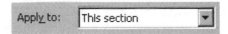

17 Click **OK** – section 2 will become landscape.

The Principle Of Section Breaks Is Always The Same

1 Insert section breaks around the part of the document you wish to be different.

2 Position the cursor inside the section you wish to be different.

3 Make the changes you require to that section.

Section Breaks Can Only Be Seen In Normal View!

You must switch to Normal View if you wish to see the section breaks you have created.

Types Of Section Break

Type of break	What it does
Next Page	Creates a section break and a page break, so any text after the section break will go onto a new page.
Continuous	Creates a section break with no page break.
Even Page	Inserts a section break and starts the next section on the next even numbered page.
Odd Page	Inserts a section break and starts the next section on the next odd numbered page.

Deleting Section Breaks

1   Make sure you are in Normal view.

2   Position your cursor on the section break.

3   Press the **Delete** key.

Tabs

Have you ever tried to line text up using the space bar? It may look nice and neat on the screen, but when you print, you'll find that it doesn't line up at all. Instead, you should use tabs. There are invisible markers across the page called tab stops. When you press the tab key, your cursor jumps to the next available tab stop. You can then line up text to these tab stops.

You would use tabs:

➤ For lining up text on the page.

➤ For creating neat columns of text or numbers.

➤ For creating forms with tab leaders (see page 183).

If you want to see tabs, have a look on the ruler – tabs are indicated by small black symbols:

Left	Centre	Right	Decimal
Text	Text	Text	Text
Words	Words	Words	Words
100.5	100.5	100.5	100.5
12.50	12.50	12.50	12.50
£1,343.54	£1,343.54	£1,343.54	£1,343.54

Types Of Tabs

Left tab (the start of the text will line up to the tab stop).

Centre tab (text will line up around the centre of the tab stop).

Right tab (the end of the text will line up to the tab stop).

   Decimal tab (the decimal point in figures will line up to the tab stop).

Lining Text Up With Tabs

Press the **Tab** key, and the cursor will jump to the next tab stop.

Moving Tabs With The Ruler

1   Select all the paragraphs that are affected by this tab.

2   Position your mouse on the tab mark at the bottom of the ruler.

3   Click and drag it to the new position.

Removing Tabs With The Ruler

1   Select all the paragraphs you wish to remove this tab from.

2   Click on the tab mark at the bottom of the ruler.

3   Drag down off the ruler.

Setting Your Own Tabs

1   Click into the paragraph where you require the tab.

2   Click on the **Format** menu.

3   Click **Tabs**.

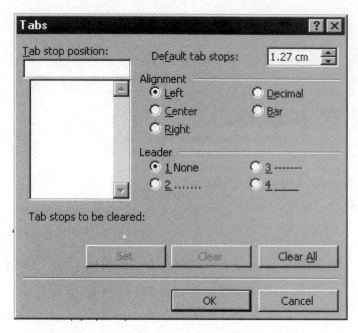

4   Type in the position of the tab underneath *Tab stop position*.

5   Click the circle next to the alignment you require.

6   Click **Set**.

7   Click **OK**.

Or

1   Click into the paragraph where you require the tab.

2   Click on the tab type selector on the top left of the ruler until it displays the type of tab you require (see page 180)

3   Position the mouse between the grey and white on the ruler where you wish the tab stop to be.

4   Click once.

Tab Leaders

Tab leaders let you create complex, perfectly lined up dotted lines like this:

Name . . . .

Address . . . . Birth date . . . .

Age . . . .

Marital status . . . .

Occupation . . . .

There are three types of tab leaders:

Dotted . . . .

Dashed -

Lined _____

Setting Tab Leaders

1   Position your cursor in the paragraph where you would like a tab leader

    or

    select several paragraphs.

2   Click on the **Format** menu.

3   Click **Tabs**.

4   Type the position for the tab underneath *Tab stop position*

    or

    click on an existing tab from the list on the left-hand side.

5   Click in the circle next to the tab leader style you require.

6   Click **Set**.

7   Click **OK**.

To use your tab leaders, type the text you require on the left-hand side, and then just press the **Tab** key – the dots will fill in the gap up to the next tab stop.

What Difference Does The Tab Type Make To A Tab Leader?

. . . . .This is a left tab at 7cm with a leader

. . . . .This is a right tab at 7cm with a leader

. . . . .This is a centre tab at 7cm with a leader

. . . .£1.00, this is a decimal tab at 7cm with a
leader

Spelling And Grammar

Nobody's perfect, even the best of us make the odd spelling mistake now and again. Luckily, we can get Word to check the spelling of our documents for us.

1   Click on the **Spell Check** icon.

➤ A word highlighted in red inside the white box at the top indicates a misspelling – just above this, Word says what it thinks is wrong (e.g. *Not in Dictionary*).

➤ A word or sentence highlighted in green at the top indicates a grammatical error.

➤ In the *Suggestions* box, Word offers you some words to choose from that might be correct.

➤ On the right-hand side, there are buttons that let you change the spelling, ignore the word, and so on – see later on in this chapter for more on these.

2   Click on the appropriate icon on the right-hand side.

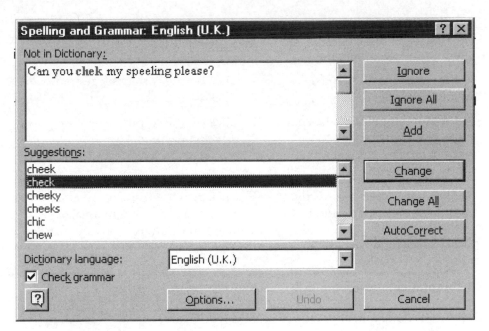

3   Click **Cancel** to finish the spell check early

or

click **OK** once the spell check is complete.

Word Is Not Perfect!

Don't just casually let Word change whatever it likes – keep an eye on it. Otherwise it will try to change someone's name, use American spellings, or mess up all your grammar.

How To Correct Your Mistakes With The Spell Check Buttons

Spelling error	Action
If the word is spelt correctly	Click on **Ignore.**
If the word is spelt correctly and occurs several times in the document	Click on **Ignore All.**

185

If the word is spelt correctly and is a word that you use very commonly, e.g. your name	Click on **Add**. This will add the word to the dictionary so that it is never seen as a misspelling again.
If the correct spelling is listed in the *Suggestions* box	1 Click on the correct suggestion. 2 Click on **Change**.
If the correct spelling is listed in the *Suggestions* box and the mis-spelling occurs commonly in the document	1 Click on the correct suggestion. 2 Click on **Change All**.
If the word is spelt incorrectly and the correct suggestion is not listed	1 Click into the white box containing the text. 2 Make the correction manually. 3 Click on **Change**.

Grammatical error	Action
If there is no grammatical error	Click on **Ignore**.
If there is no grammatical error and similar sentences appear in the rest of your document	Click on **Ignore Rule**.
If the correct grammar appears in the *Suggestions* box	1 Highlight the correct suggestion. 2 Click on **Change**.
If the grammar is incorrect, but the correct suggestion does not appear	1 Click into the white box containing the text. 2 Make the correction manually. 3 Click on **Change**.

Quick Spelling And Grammar Check

When you are typing the document, sometimes you will see that Word has put red or green squiggly lines under some of the words. Right click any of these words and a shortcut menu of suggested corrections will appear.

If You Have The American Dictionary ...

Try clicking on **Tools, Language, Set Language**, *English (UK)*, **OK**.

The Thesaurus

If you keep using the same word over and over, the thesaurus will help you to find other words that mean the same thing. This makes your documents look really attractive, appealing, remarkable, out of the ordinary, and fascinating. Do you see what I did there? I used the thesaurus for comic effect.

To change a word using the thesaurus:

1   Select the word you wish to change.

2   Click on the **Tools** menu.

3   Click **Language**.

4   Click **Thesaurus**.

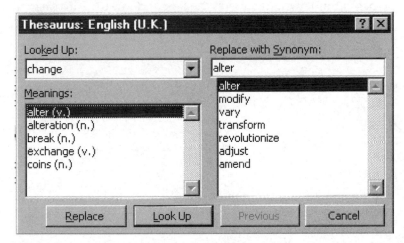

5   Click on the word you prefer on the right-hand side.

6   Click on **Replace**.

Go To, Find & Replace

It's fairly easy to work out what these three tools do, but I'm going to explain them anyway. Go To lets you go to a page or section. Find lets you find text. Replace lets you replace text. It's as simple as that, really.

Going To A Page

1   Press **Ctrl+G** to make the *Go To* box appear.

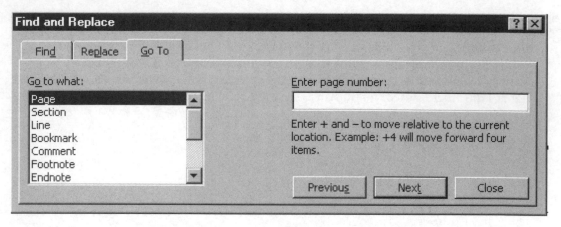

2   Type in the page number you require in the box underneath *Enter page number.*

3   Click the **Next** button – Word will move to the top of the page you typed in.

4   Click **Close**.

Closing The Go To Box

The *Go To* box does not disappear once it has gone to the correct page. You must close it by clicking on the **Close** button.

Finding Text

1   Click on the **Edit** menu.

2   Click on **Find**.

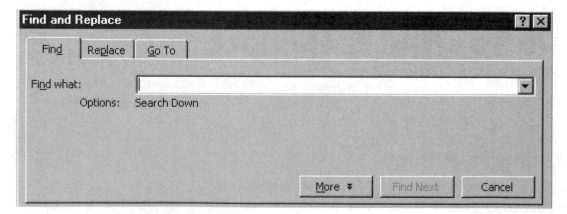

3   Type in the word you require in the box next to *Find what*.

4   Click on the **Find Next** button – Word will highlight the first occurrence of the word in the background.

5   Click on **Find Next** again – Word will highlight the second occurrence in the background, etc. When Word has found all occurrences it will display the message 'Word has finished searching the document'.

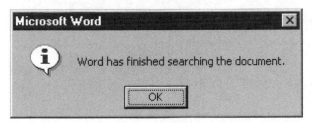

6   Click **OK**.

7   Click on **Cancel** to close the dialog box.

Replacing Text

1   Click on the **Edit** menu.

2   Click on **Replace**.

3   Type the word you wish to replace in the box next to *Find what*.

4   Type the word you wish to replace it with in the box next to *Replace with*.

5   Click on **Replace All** to replace all occurrences at once

or

click on **Replace** to replace the first occurrence. Click on **Replace** again to replace the second occurrence, etc.

When Word has finished it will display a message saying that it has completed its search, and tells you how many replacements it has made.

6   Click **OK**.

7   Click **Cancel** to close the dialog box.

Chapter 4

Tables

Creating And Editing Tables

Tables are little boxes divided up into smaller boxes, that help you to arrange text in a certain way. They look something like this:

Tables	Let	You
Line	Up	Things

Creating A Table With The Icon

1. Position the cursor where you would like the table to be.

2. Click on the **Table** icon, and **hold down the mouse button** – a set of boxes will appear just under the icon.

3. Still holding the mouse button down, click and drag over the number of columns and rows you require.

4. Once you have the size you require, release the mouse button.

Creating A Table With The Menu

This is useful if you require a large table:

1 Position the cursor where you require a table.

2 Click on the **Table** menu.

3 Click on the **Insert** sub-menu.

4 Click **Table**.

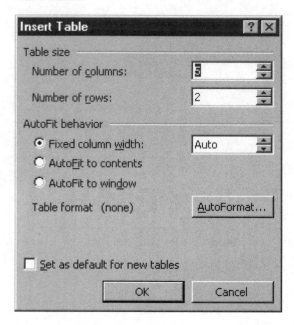

5 Type in the number of columns you require (or use the up and down arrows).

6 Type in the number of rows you require (or use the up and down arrows).

7 Change the *AutoFit* options as required.

8 If required, click **AutoFormat** to choose a preset format for your table.

9 Click **OK**.

The Parts Of A Table

A table has three parts: cells, columns and rows.

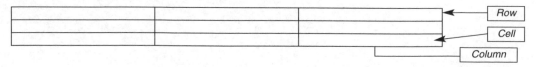

192

The Tables And Borders Toolbar

The *Table and Borders* toolbar allows you to do common table tasks quickly. To display

the toolbar, click on the **Tables and Borders** icon.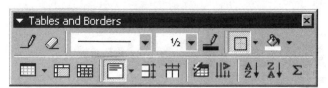

The *Table and Borders* toolbar will appear on the screen with the **Draw Table** icon

switched on, but you can click on it to switch it off if you don't need it.

Click on the **Tables and Borders** icon again to hide the toolbar.

Display The Table And Borders Toolbar!

It is easiest to insert rows and columns using the *Table and Borders* toolbar

Adding Text To A Table

To add text, position the cursor inside the cell you wish to add text to, and type the text.

Pressing Return Will Increase The Height Of A Row

You cannot use **Return** to get onto the next row of a table, it will just increase the height of the row you are in.

You can move around with the keyboard using these keys:

TAB	Moves to the next cell.
SHIFT/TAB	Takes you to the previous cell.
↑	Up a row.

↓	Down a row.
←	Left a cell.
→	Right a cell.

If you want to move around with the mouse, just click into the cell you require. The mouse must look like the I-bar just before you click.

I

Selecting Parts Of A Table

In order to work with tables, you must know how to select the different parts. Selection will allow you to:

➤ Format parts of the table.

➤ Delete parts of the table.

➤ Add extra rows and columns.

Selecting Cells

1 Click at the bottom left corner of the cell – the mouse changes to a black arrow

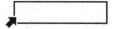

2 Click and drag to select more cells.

Or

1 Position the cursor at the start of the text inside the first cell.

2 Hold down the **Shift** key.

3 Press **End**.

4 Press **End** again to select the cell to the right

or

press arrow keys to select adjoining cells.

Selecting Rows

1   Position the mouse outside the table to the left of the row – it will change to a white arrow.

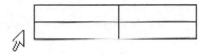

2   Click the left mouse button

or

click and drag to select several rows

Or

1   Click anywhere in the row you want to select.

2   Click on the **Table** menu.

3   Click on **Select**.

4   Click **Row**.

Selecting Columns

1   Position the mouse above the table. It will change to a black down arrow.

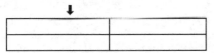

2   Click the left mouse button

or

click and drag to select several columns.

Or

1   Click anywhere in the column to select.

2   Click on the **Table** menu.

3   Click on **Select**.

4   Click **Column**.

Selecting The Whole Table

1   Click inside the table.

2   Click on the **Table** menu.

3   Click **Select**.

4   Click **Table**.

Or

1   Hold down the **Alt** key.

2   Double-click inside the table when the mouse looks like an I-bar I

Inserting And Deleting Rows And Columns

Display The Table And Borders Toolbar Before You Do This . . .

It is easier to insert rows with the **Insert** icon on the *Tables and Borders* toolbar. This icon changes shape depending on your last action. It is situated to the right of the **Shading** icon, and will look like this to start with:

Inserting Rows

To insert a row at the bottom of the table:

1   Position your cursor in the last cell.

2   Press the **Tab** key.

To insert a row somewhere else in the table:

1   Position the cursor in the row adjacent to where you require a new one.

2   Click the down arrow next to the **Insert** icon.

3   Click **Insert Rows Above**

or

click **Insert Rows Below.**

☐▤ Insert Rows <u>A</u>bove
☐▤ Insert Rows <u>B</u>elow

Inserting Several New Rows

For example, inserting six new rows:

1 Select six rows above or below where you require six new ones.

2 Click the down arrow next to the **Insert** icon.

3 Click **Insert Rows Above**

    or

    click **Insert Rows Below** – six new rows will be inserted.

Adjust the number from six to the number of rows that you require.

Inserting A New Column

1 Click inside the column next to where you require a new one.

2 Click the down arrow next to **Insert** icon.

3 Click **Insert Columns to the Left**

    or

    click **Insert Columns to the Right.**

▥ Insert Columns to the <u>L</u>eft
▥ Insert Columns to the <u>R</u>ight

Inserting Several New Columns

For example, inserting six new columns:

1 Select six columns next to where you require six new ones.

2 Click the down arrow next to the **Insert** icon.

3   Click **Insert Columns to the Left**

or

click **Insert Columns to the Right**.

Adjust the number from six to the number of columns that you require.

Deleting Rows And Columns

1   Click inside the row/column to delete

or

select several rows/columns to delete.

2   Click on the **Table** menu.

3   Click **Delete**.

4   Click **Rows**

or

click **Columns**.

Resizing Rows

Changing Row Height With The Mouse

If your rows are too big or too small, just resize them. Here's how:

1   Make sure you are in *Print Layout* view.

2   Position the mouse at the bottom border of the row you wish to resize, until the mouse pointer changes to a double-headed arrow.

3   Click and drag to the right or left to make the row bigger or smaller.

Or

1   Make sure you are in *Print Layout* view.

2   Click inside the table.

3   Position your mouse over a row marker on the vertical ruler to the left.

4   Click and drag it up and down to make the row bigger or smaller.

Using Table Properties For Rows

1   Click inside the row you want to resize

or

select several rows.

2   Click on the **Table** menu.

3   Click **Table Properties.**

4   Click on the **Row** tab.

5   Click inside the box next to *Specify height*.

6   Change the measurement to the size you require.

7   Click **OK**.

Putting Space Around Text

You can put extra space around the text in a table to make it easier to read:

1   Select the rows you wish to change.

2   Click on the **Format** menu.

3   Click **Paragraph**.

4   Specify a space *Before* and a space *After* in the appropriate boxes.

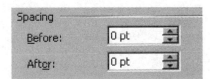

5   Click **OK**.

Distributing Rows Evenly

After fiddling about with your rows, you might want to make them all the same height. To do this, simply select the rows you want to make even, then click on the **Distribute Rows Evenly** icon on the *Tables and Borders* toolbar.

Resizing Columns

Changing Column Widths With The Mouse

1   Position the mouse between the border of two columns until the mouse pointer changes to a double-headed arrow.

2   Click and drag to the right or left to make the column bigger or smaller.

Or

1   Click inside the table.

2   Position your mouse over a column marker on the horizontal ruler at the top.

3   Click and drag to make the column bigger or smaller.

Be Careful Not To Select Any Cells!

Check This Out...

If you have any cells selected whilst you click and drag you will only resize that cell rather than the whole column.

If you are resizing the far right-hand column, you may accidentally select the end of the row marker (see below), which can lead to the same problem!

Using The Keyboard And The Mouse

➤ Holding down the **Shift** key while you drag means that only the column to the left will change its width.

➤ Holding down **Ctrl** and **Shift** while you drag means that the overall width of the table stays the same.

➤ Holding down **Alt** while you drag will show you the measurements as they change in the ruler area.

Using Table Properties For Columns

1 Click inside the column you wish to change

or

select several columns that you want to change.

2 Click on the **Table** menu.

3 Click **Table Properties**.

4 Click on the **Column** tab.

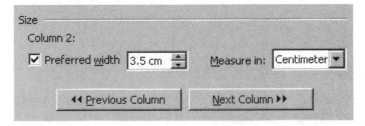

5 Tick the box next to *Preferred width*.

6 Type in the width you require.

7 Click **OK**.

Fitting Columns On The Page

1 Click inside the table.

2 Click on the **Table** menu.

3 Click **AutoFit**.

4 Choose the **AutoFit** option you require:

➤ **AutoFit to Contents:** makes the columns as wide as the text they contain.

➤ **AutoFit to Window:** makes the whole table as wide as the page.

Distributing Columns Evenly

If your columns are all different sizes, you might want to make them all the same. Simply select the columns you wish to make even, then click on the **Distribute Columns Evenly** icon.

Moving And Resizing Tables

Moving The Table

1   Position the mouse pointer in the middle of the table until a cross appears at the top left (a white box will also appear at the bottom right).

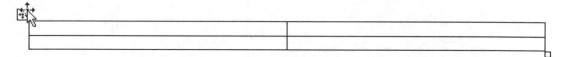

2   Move the mouse pointer towards the cross at the top left – you must not take the mouse outside the table or you will lose the cross!

3   Position the mouse pointer over the cross – it will change to a four-headed arrow.

4   Click and drag the table to a new position.

Resizing The Whole Table

1   Position the mouse pointer in the middle of the table until a cross appears at the top left (a white box will also appear at the bottom right).

2   Move the mouse pointer towards the box at the bottom right – you must not take the mouse outside the table, or you will lose the box!

3   Position your mouse pointer over the box – it will change to a double-headed arrow.

4   Click and drag to resize the table.

Changing Text Wrapping Around A Table

Once you have moved or resized the whole table you can make text flow around the edge of it.

1   Click inside the table.

2   Click on the **Table** menu.

3   Click **Table Properties.**

4   Click **Table** tab.

5   Click *Around* under *Text wrapping*.

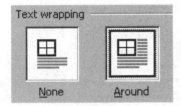

6   Click **OK.**

Putting Tables Next To Each Other

Once you have moved or resized tables, you can place them next to each other on the page.

1   Create your first table.

2   Resize it using the white box at the bottom right.

3   Click your cursor underneath the table.

4   Press **Return.**

5   Create your second table.

6   Resize it using the white box.

7   Move one of the tables next to the other using the cross at the top right.

Make Sure Your Tables Are Small Enough To Fit Next To Each Other On The Page!

If your tables are too big to go next to each other, Word will either refuse to place the tables where you require them, or it will put one of the tables inside the other!

Creating Nested Tables

You can create complicated table layouts by creating tables within tables:

1   Create your first table.

2   Position your cursor inside the first table where you would like to create a nested table.

3   Create a second table to insert the new table.

Gridlines And Borders

Gridlines And Borders – An Explanation

When you first create a table in Word it will have borders around it. **Borders print.** If you do not wish to print borders you can remove them, after which you will see gridlines to show you the structure of the table. **Gridlines do not print.**

Turning Printed Borders Off

1   Select the whole table.

2   Click the down arrow next to the **Borders** icon.

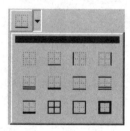

3   Click the **No Borders** icon.

Turning Gridlines On And Off

If you have removed the borders, you will see gridlines in their place. These appear as light grey lines around your table. **They do not print**. To see how your table will print, you can turn the gridlines off:

1 Click on the **Table** menu.

2 Click **Hide Gridlines.**

To bring gridlines back:

1 Click on the **Table** menu.

2 Click **Show Gridlines.**

Borders

Creating Borders Using The Menu

1 Select the part of the table you wish to add borders to.

2 Click on the **Format** menu.

3 Click **Borders and Shading.**

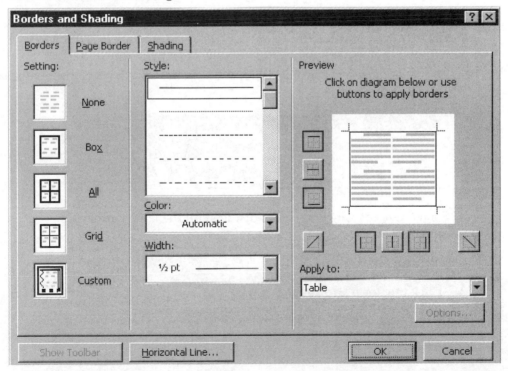

➤ The *Box* setting gives you a border all the way around your selection.

➤ The *All* setting applies inside and outside borders to selection.

➤ The *Grid* setting gives a thick outside border, and thin inside borders.

➤ With the *Custom* setting, you do not have to have a border all the way around – for example, you can choose just to have a top and bottom border.

➤ The *Preview* box shows you what your borders will look like.

➤ Click on the border buttons (in and around the Preview box) to specify which borders you require.

4   Choose the setting you require from left-hand side (see above).

5   If required, click on a different style from the list.

6   If required, click on the down arrow underneath *Color* and click a different colour for your border.

7   If required, click the down arrow underneath *Width* and click on a different width for your border.

8   If you have chosen the *Custom* setting, click the borders buttons to add selected borders (see above).

9   Click **OK**.

Using The Table Toolbar

1   Select the part of the table you want to change.

2   If it is not displayed already, click on the **Tables and Borders** icon to display the toolbar.

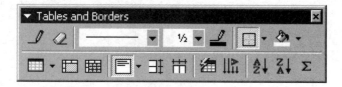

3   Make sure the **Pencil** icon (the first icon on the left) is turned off.

4   Click the down arrow next to **Line Style** icon (third icon from the left) and click style you prefer.

206

5 Click the down arrow next to **Line Width** icon (fourth icon from the left) and click width you prefer.

6 Click **Border Color** icon (fifth icon from the left) and choose colour you prefer.

7 Click down the arrow next to the **Borders** icon (last icon on the right) and click the borders you would like to set (see below).

 Applies a border around the outside and of your selection.

 All borders – applies inside outside borders.

 Top border.

 Left border.

 Inside horizontal border.

 Inside borders.

 No borders.

 Bottom border.

 Right border.

 Inside vertical borders.

 Apply diagonal borders top left right to bottom right through the cells in your selection.

 Apply diagonal borders top to bottom left through the cells in your selection.

 Inserts a grey decorative border wherever your cursor is.

Shading

Tables, like paragraphs, can have coloured shading applied to them as well as borders. If you have a complex table, you can make it easier to read by shading parts of it.

Shading Using The Menu

1 Select the part of the table you wish to colour in.

2 Click on the **Format** menu.

3 Click **Borders and Shading.**

4 Click the **Shading** tab.

207

5   Click on the colour you require from the grid

or

click **More Colors** if the colour you require is not found.

6   Click **OK.**

Using The Toolbar

1   Select the part of the table you wish to colour in.

2   If it's not displayed already, click the **Tables and Borders** icon to display the *Tables and Borders* toolbar.

3   Make sure the **Pencil** icon is turned off.

4   Click the down arrow next to the **Shading** icon.

5   Click on the colour you require

or

click **More Fill Colors** if the colour you require is not found.

Merging And Splitting Cells

Got too many cells in your table? Merge some together. Need more cells? Split some up. Let's have a look.

Merging Cells Together

Look at the table below.

This is a heading, but the cell is not merged		

It would look better if the heading in the first cell was spread all across the top of the table, which means merging the cells. Just select the cells you wish to merge (in this case the top three cells), and click the **Merge Cells** icon on the *Tables and Borders* toolbar.

Or, once you've selected the cells, click on the **Table** menu and then click on **Merge Cells.**

This is a heading, but now the cell **is** merged		

Splitting Cells

You can split cells to create extra columns where needed, or split up cells which have been merged. Look at this table:

Age				Gender		Department		
16–20	21–25	36–30	31–40	Male	Female	Finance	Sales	Admin

Originally there were three cells in the bottom row. They have been split up to show the different categories. To split up a cell, select the cell(s) you want to split, and click the **Split Cells** icon

on the **Tables and Borders** toolbar. Type in the number of columns and/or rows you need, and click **OK.**

Splitting A Table

If you wish to create two, or more, separate tables out of one, you can split the table up. Place your cursor in the row below where you require a split, click on the **Table** menu, and click on **Split Table.**

Table AutoFormat

AutoFormat is a quick way of making your table look good. You can choose from a list of fancy table styles, and Word will do all the hard work for you.

AutoFormatting A Table

1   Click inside the table you want to AutoFormat.

2   Click the **AutoFormat** icon on the *Tables and Borders* toolbar.

or

click on the **Table** menu.

Click **Table AutoFormat.**

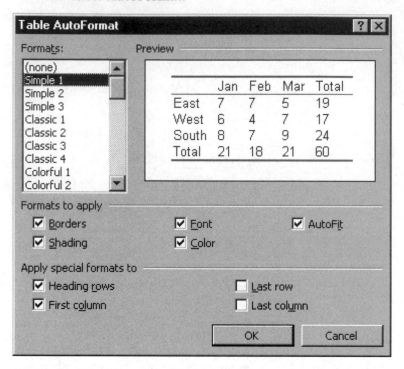

3   Click on the format you like in the list at the top left.

4   Click **OK**.

Changing The Formats To Apply

When applying the AutoFormat, click in box next to the format you require to add or remove the tick.

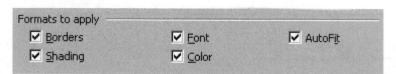

Borders   Adds or removes any printing borders around the table.

Shading   Adds or removes any shading to the cells in the table.

Font   Adds or removes any special font formatting, such as bold, to the text in the table.

Color   Changes colour to black and white or vice versa.

AutoFit   When ticked, this changes the column widths so that they are as wide as the text inside them.

Applying Special Formats

These boxes indicate where AutoFormat will place distinctive formatting for the headings or totals in your table. So if your headings are in the first column, make sure that *First column* is ticked. Click inside the box next to the special format required to add or remove the tick.

Apply special formats to
☑ Heading rows   ☐ Last row
☑ First column   ☐ Last column

Chapter 5

Graphics

Drawing Shapes

The Drawing Toolbar

The Drawing toolbar is what you will use to draw shapes, create fancy pictures, draw lines, create text boxes, do 3-D effects, and much more. If it is not displayed:

1   Click on the **View** menu.

2   Click on **Toolbars**.

3   Click on **Drawing**.

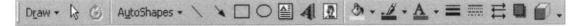

Drawing Circles And Squares

1   Click on the shape you require on the *Drawing* toolbar.

2   Release the mouse button.

3   Click and drag the shape on the page – the mouse pointer will look like a cross.

Drawing AutoShapes

1   Click on *AutoShapes* on the *Drawing* toolbar.

2   Click on the category you require, e.g. *Stars and Banners*.

3   Click on the shape you require.

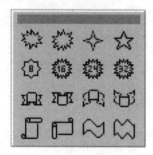

4   Click and drag to draw the shape on the page – the mouse will look like a cross.

Drawing Lines And Arrows

1   Click on the **Line** or **Arrow** icon on the *Drawing* toolbar.

2   Click and drag to draw the line or arrow on the page – the mouse will look like a cross.

Creating A Perfect Shape Or A Straight Line

If you want to create a perfectly square shape, or a perfectly round circle, just hold down the **Shift** key while you are drawing the shape.

214

Selecting A Shape

Click once on the shape until white boxes (called 'handles') appear around the edge. Click away from the shape to deselect it.

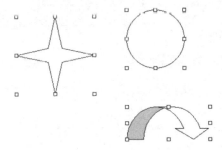

Selecting More Than One Shape

1   Click on the first shape you want to select.

2   Hold down the **Shift** key.

3   Click on any other shapes you want to select – handles will appear around all selected shapes.

Selecting More Than One Shape With The Select Objects Icon

1   Click on the **Select Objects** icon on the *Drawing* toolbar.

2   Position the mouse **underneath ALL** the shapes you wish to select and **to the left of ALL** the shapes you wish to select.

3   Click and drag over the shapes as if you were drawing a big box to cover them all – a dotted line will appear around them.

4   Release the mouse button – handles will appear around the selected shapes.

Deleting Shapes

1   Select the shape you wish to delete.

2   Press the **Delete** key.

215

Moving Shapes

1   Select the shape(s) you want to move.

2   Position your mouse pointer in the middle of the shape(s) – the mouse pointer will change to a four-headed arrow.

3   Click and drag the shape(s) to a new position.

Resizing Shapes

1   Select the shape(s) you want to resize.

2   Hover the mouse pointer over a handle – the pointer will change to a double-headed arrow.

3   Click and drag outwards to make the shape bigger

or

click and drag inwards to make the shape smaller.

Check This Out...

Which Handle Should I Resize From?

Handles at the corner of a selected shape will allow you to resize both the height and the width at the same time. Handles in the middle will allow you to stretch or squash the shape.

Changing The Shape Of An AutoShape

1   Select the AutoShape you require.

2   Position your mouse over the yellow diamond.

3   Click and drag to change the shape.

This will adjust the shape of the AutoShape – look at the two shapes below for an example. The first one is a normal shape. The second one has had the yellow diamond moved inwards.

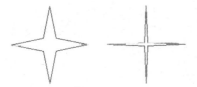

Formatting Shapes

Changing The Fill Colour Of Shapes

1 Select the shape(s) you want to change.

2 Click on the down arrow next to the **Fill Color** icon on the *Drawing* toolbar.

3 Click on the colour you require

or

click on **More Fill Colors** if the colour you require is not listed.

Getting A Choice Of Colours

You must click the down arrow next to the **Fill Color** icon to get a choice of colours. If you click the bucket image, the colour will change to whatever the fill colour is currently set to

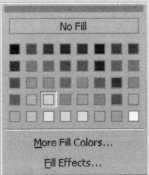

Formatting Lines

1   Select the line(s) you want to change.

2   Click on the line style icon you require (shown below).

➤ The first icon changes the thickness of lines.

➤ The second icon makes the lines dotted or dashed.

➤ The third icon makes the lines into arrows.

3   Click on the style you require.

Changing The Line Colour

1   Select the line(s) you want to change.

2   Click on the down arrow next to the **Line Color** icon on the *Drawing* toolbar.

3   Click on the colour you require

or

click on **More Line Colors** if the colour you require is not listed.

3-D Shapes

Take your lines and shapes into the third dimension with the 3-D tools – that sounds more exciting than it actually is, but hey, I'm doing my best here. It looks pretty cool, so who knows, you might even get a little bit excited about it. Look at the following shape – it's just one of the block arrows from the Basic Shapes AutoShapes, with a blue 3-D effect. Isn't it exciting? No? Okay, suit yourself.

Adding 3-D

1   Select the shape(s) you want to change.

2   Click on the **3-D** icon on the *Drawing* toolbar.

3   Click on the 3-D setting you require.

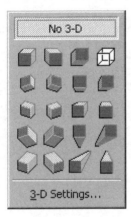

The 3-D Toolbar

1   Select the shape(s) you want to change.

2   Click on the **3-D** icon on the *Drawing* toolbar.

3   Click on **3D Settings** – the *3-D* toolbar will appear.

Here is what all those icons do, going from left to right:

➤ Removes the 3-D effect.

➤ Tilt down – rotates the shape forwards.

➤ Tilt up – rotates the shape backwards.

➤ Tilt left – rotates the shape left.

➤ Tilt right – rotates the shape right.

➤ Changes the depth of the 3-D effect.

➤ Changes the direction of the 3-D effect.

219

➤ Changes the lighting direction and/or brightness.

➤ Changes the surface texture.

➤ Changes the 3-D colour.

Adding Text To Shapes

Adding Text To Shapes

To add text to a shape, simply right click on it, click on **Add Text** from the little menu that pops up, and start typing. To format the text, just select it and format it as normal. Looks pretty fancy, doesn't it?

Drawing A Text Box

1 Click on the **Text Box** icon on the *Drawing* toolbar

ab|

2 Click and drag over the page to create the text box, as if you were drawing a normal box.

3 Type your text into the box.

Drawing Callouts

Callouts are used when you wish to label something on your page. Some of them can be used as speech bubbles, some for captions on pictures.

1 Click on **AutoShapes**.

2 Click on **Callouts**.

3 Click on the callout style you require.

4   Click and drag to create the callout.

Callouts Work The Same As Text Boxes

As soon as you draw a callout, a cursor will appear, ready for you to start typing.

Deleting Shapes That Contain Text

1   Click inside the shape – diagonal lines will appear around the border.

2   Click on the diagonal lines – dotted lines will replace the diagonal lines.

3   Press the **Delete** key.

What Is The Difference Between Diagonal Lines And Dotted Lines?

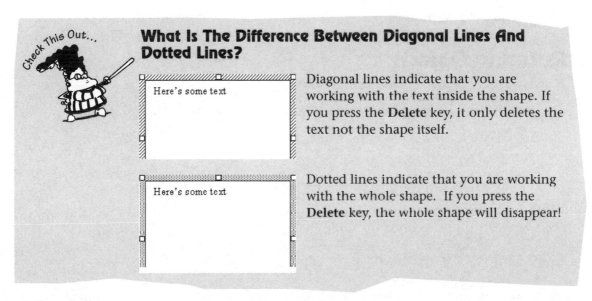

Diagonal lines indicate that you are working with the text inside the shape. If you press the **Delete** key, it only deletes the text not the shape itself.

Dotted lines indicate that you are working with the whole shape. If you press the **Delete** key, the whole shape will disappear!

221

Moving Shapes That Contain Text

Once you have added text to a shape, you cannot move it by dragging from the middle, instead you need to do this:

1　Click inside the shape until the diagonal lines appear around the border.

2　Click on the diagonal lines to make the dotted line appear around the border.

3　Position the mouse over the dotted line, NOT the handles.

4　Click and drag the shape to a new position.

Rotating And Ordering

Flipping Objects

1　Select the shape(s) you require.

2　Click **Draw**.

3　Click **Rotate** or **Flip**.

4　Click **Flip Horizontal**

or

click **Flip Vertical**.

Rotating Objects

1　Select the shape(s) you want to rotate.

2　Click on the **Free Rotate** icon – green circles will appear.

3　Hover the mouse over a green circle – the rotate symbol will appear.

4　Click and drag to turn the shape.

Or

1　Select the shape(s) to rotate.

2　Click **Draw**.

3   Click **Rotate** or **Flip**.

4   Click **Rotate Left**

or

click **Rotate Right**.

Or use the menu to rotate a shape more exactly.

1   Select the shape(s) to rotate.

2   Click on the **Format** menu.

3   Click **Object** or **AutoShape**.

4   Click on the **Size** tab.

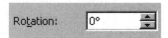

5   Change the rotation options as required – type in the angle you want to rotate by, or use the up and down arrows.

6   Click **OK**.

Changing The Ordering

If you have several objects on a page that are on top of each other, they form a kind of 'queue'. Whichever object you can see on top is at the front of the queue, and whichever object you can see underneath all the others, is at the back of the queue. In the diagram below there are three circles, and their number corresponds to their position in the queue:

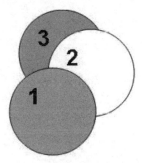

You can change this order using the **Send to back/Bring to front** commands, or the **Send backward/Bring forward** commands. Let's imagine that you decide to send the

1st circle to the back. The circle will go to the back of the queue, behind the other two circles:

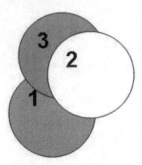

If, however, you sent the same circle backwards it would just go one stage behind in the queue, rather than all the way to the back. In other words, it would go behind the 2nd circle, but not behind the 3rd:

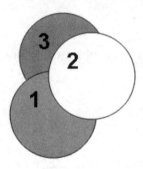

1   Select the object you wish to move.

2   Click **Draw**.

3   Click on **Order**.

4   Click **Send to Back**.

     or

     click **Bring to Front**

     or

     click **Send Backward**

     or

     click **Bring Forward**.

224

Adding Graphics

Inserting Pictures

1   Position the cursor where you would like to insert the picture.

2   Click the **Clip Art** icon on the *Drawing* toolbar

Or

1   Click on the **Insert** menu.

2   Click on the *Picture* sub-menu and click *Clip Art* – you will be taken to the Clip Art Gallery.

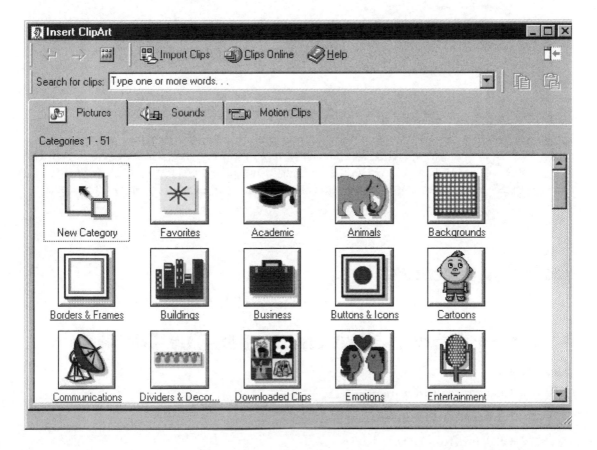

3   Click on the Category you require, e.g. *Buildings* – a list of pictures in that category will appear.

4   Click on the picture you require – you may have to navigate through the gallery to see more pictures (see page 227).

5   Click on the **Insert Clip** icon.

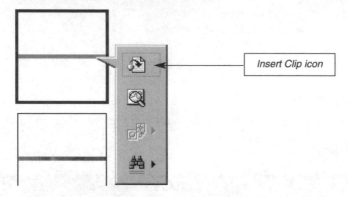

Insert Clip icon

6   Click on the X at the top right of the Clip Art Gallery to close it.

The Clip Art Gallery Does Not Close Itself Down

Once you have inserted your picture it will not appear to have gone in, and the Clip Art gallery will remain on the screen. In fact, your picture **has** gone in, you just need to close the gallery to see it. Click on the X at the top right of the Clip Art Gallery to close it – you will then be able to see the picture.

Deleting Pictures

Click on the picture you want to delete, and press the **Delete** key.

Inserting Pictures That Are Not In The Clip Art Gallery

1   Click on the **Insert** menu.

2   Click on the **Picture** submenu.

3   Click on **From File**.

4   Change the *Look in* box to the folder where your picture is saved.

5   Select the picture file you want to insert.

6   Click **Insert**.

Using The Clip Art Gallery

Navigating Around The Clip Art Gallery

The Clip Art Gallery can only show you a few pictures at a time. If you choose a category with hundreds of pictures in it, you will have to navigate through all of them.

➤   To move **forward** through the current category, scroll down to the bottom of the screen, and click on the **Keep Looking** icon.

Keep Looking

➤   To move **backwards** through the current category, click on the **Back** icon.

➤   To **return to the categories** screen, click on the **Categories** icon.

Searching For Pictures

1   Click into the *Search for clips* box.

2   Type one or more keywords to indicate the type of picture you want.

3   Press **Return**.

Previewing A Picture

1   Click on the picture you want to preview.

2   Click on the **Preview** icon (the second icon from the top).

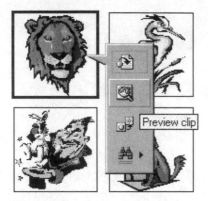

3   Click on the X at the top right of the *Preview* to close.

Finding Similar Pictures

1   Click on the picture you like.

2   Click on the **Find Similar Clips** icon (the bottom icon).

3   Click on **Artistic Style**

    or

    click on **Color & Shape**

    or

    click on a keyword – similar pictures will appear.

Adding Your Own Pictures To The Gallery

1 Click on **Import Clips**.

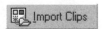

2 Change the *Look In* box to the folder where your picture is saved.

3 Click on the name of your picture.

4 Click on **Import**.

5 Type a description of the picture.

6 Click on the **Categories** tab and tick the categories that this picture will appear in.

7 Click on the **Keywords** tab.

8 Click on *New Keyword*, and type in a new keyword for your picture.

9 Repeat step 8 for other keywords.

10 Click **OK**.

Getting Extra Pictures From The Web

If you are connected to the Internet you can access even more pictures online.

1 Click on **Clips Online**.

2 Click **OK** to the dialog box that appears – your Internet browser will open, and you will be taken to Microsoft's Clip Art site.

3   Enter your search options on the left-hand side (see above).

4   Click on **Go**.

5   Click on the arrows to move through the pictures.

6   Click on the grey box under the picture you require – the image will download to your computer.

7   Click on the picture in the Clip Art gallery.

8   Remember to disconnect from the Internet if you are using a modem.

Changing The Text Wrapping

Clip Art Which Is In Line With The Text

➤ When you first insert a picture it is **in line** with the text. In other words, it is just like a piece of text itself.

➤ If you want to move it, you move it just as you would a piece of text using cut and paste, or drag and drop.

➤ An in-line picture can**not** be put anywhere on the page – only where there is text.

Clip Art Which Floats Over The Text

If you want the freedom to move the picture anywhere on the page you have to change its text wrapping, so that it floats over the text.

1   Select the picture.

2   Click on the **Format** menu.

3   Click on **Picture**.

4   Click on the **Layout** tab.

230

5   Click on a different wrapping style.

Or, if the *Picture* toolbar is displayed:

1   Select the picture.

2   Click on the **Text Wrapping** Icon.

3   Click on the text wrapping style you require (any except **In line with text**).

Selecting, Moving And Resizing Pictures

Selecting

Select the picture as you would select anything else – click once on the picture. When a picture is selected, handles will appear around the edge (black handles for in-line pictures, white handles for pictures that are floating over the text). To deselect the picture, just click away from it.

Moving

A picture which is in-line with the text can only be moved in the same way as text. It cannot go anywhere on the page. To move it, click into the middle of the picture, then click and drag to a new location. A fuzzy grey cursor will show you where you are going. To move a picture that is floating over the top of text, click into the middle of it, and drag it to a new location. The mouse pointer should look like a four-headed arrow when you are moving it.

Resizing

1   Select the picture you want to resize.

2   Position the mouse over a handle – the mouse pointer will change to a double-headed arrow.

3   Click and drag outwards to make the picture bigger

    or

    click and drag inwards to make the picture smaller.

231

Keeping The Picture In Proportion

If you drag from a corner handle then the picture will stay in proportion. If you drag from a middle handle you will stretch or squash the picture.

Deleting A Picture

Select the picture you want to delete, and press the **Delete** key.

Customizing Clip Art

Displaying The Picture Toolbar

Select a picture, and the *Picture* toolbar should display automatically. If not, then click on the **View** menu, click on the **Toolbars** sub-menu, and click on **Picture**. The next sections explain what each icon does, going from left to right on the *Picture* toolbar.

Insert Picture

This icon simply lets you insert a picture – click on it, and browse your hard disk for a picture that you would like to insert.

Image Control

This icon lets you make an image greyscale, black and white, or watermark. Select the picture, click on the **Image Control** icon, and then click on the style you require.

The Order In Which You Change The Image Control Makes A Difference

Changing from Automatic to black and white, for example, gives a black and white image BUT, changing from watermark to black and white creates a white silhouette or makes the image disappear completely!

Contrast And Brightness

These work just like the controls on a TV set. The first two icons increase and decrease contrast, the second two increase and decrease brightness. Select the picture, and then click on the particular icon you require to change the contrast or brightness.

Cropping

This allows you to cut the edges off a picture.

1   Select the picture.

2   Click on the **Crop** icon.

3   Position the mouse pointer over a handle – the pointer will change to the crop sign.

4   Click and drag inwards to cut off an edge.

Line Style

This icon lets you apply borders to your picture.

Borders Can Only Be Used If Your Picture Is Floating Over Text!

If it is an in-line picture, then you cannot use borders.

1　Select the picture.

2　Click on the **Line Style** icon.

3　Click on the style of border you require.

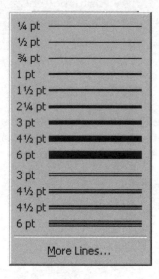

or

click on **More Lines.**

4　Change the line options as required.

5　Click **OK.**

How Do I Remove Borders?

Follow Steps 1 to 3 above, clicking on the *More Lines* option. In the Line section, click on the drop-down arrow next to *Color*, and choose *No Line.*

Text Wrapping

This icon lets you change the way text wraps around the picture.

1　Select the picture.

2　Click on the **Text Wrapping** icon.

3　Click on the text wrapping you require.

Format Picture

This icon brings up the *Format Picture* dialog box, so that you can change the text wrapping, colours, lines, size, position, etc.

Set Transparent Colour

A transparent colour is one that you can see through to the text or images underneath. You might want to be able to see through part of a picture, or make the background invisible.

The Set Transparent Colour Option Is Not Always Available

It will only work on bitmap pictures that are not already transparent, and on some, but not all, Clip Art.

1   Select the picture.

2   Click on the **Set Transparent Color** icon.

3   Position the mouse pointer over the area you want to make transparent.

4   Click the left mouse button once.

You Can Only Make One Colour Transparent

If you have scanned in photographs, the **Set Transparent Color** option will often be available, but it will not appear to work. This is because photographs are made up of hundreds of colours. Even an area which appears to be one colour, such as a blue sky, will usually be made up of many different shades of colour.

Reset Picture

This icon lets you return a picture to its original size, colour and position. Just select the picture, and click on the icon.

Chapter 6

Templates

Templates

What Are Templates?

All documents are based on a template. Every time you create a new document you are actually using a template that decides the basic format of that document, for example:

- ➤ The size of the margins.
- ➤ Which font you will use.
- ➤ What headers and footers you will have.
- ➤ Which toolbars you will see.
- ➤ Which AutoTexts you have access to.
- ➤ Whether any text appears before you have started typing (e.g. the headings in a fax or memo).

The template that you are probably used to using is the **Normal template**. Whenever you click on the **New Blank Document** icon, Word brings you a copy of the Normal template to start typing on. That's why the margins, the fonts, and the toolbars are already set for you.

There are other templates which come with Word for creating letters, memos and faxes, etc. You can also create your own for work or personal use.

The Difference Between Templates And Documents

➤ **Templates are standard:** they contain all the things that don't change. For example, a template for a memo will usually contain headings such as From and To and they will be formatted correctly. Templates end in the extension .dot.

➤ **Documents are based on templates:** whenever you create a new document it is based on a template. Word brings you a copy of the template to start typing on. Documents end in the extension .doc.

Using Word's Templates

1   Click on the **File** menu.

2   Click on **New**.

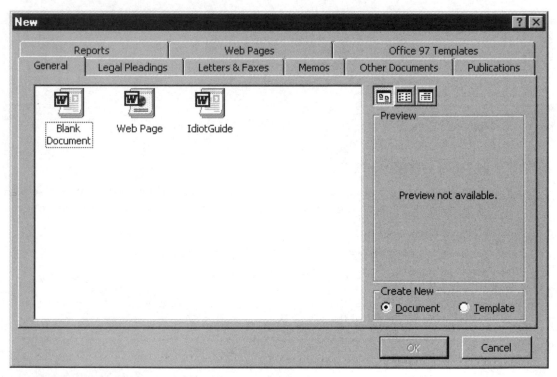

3   Click on the tab you require from the top.

4   Click on the template you wish to use.

5   Click **OK**.

You Can Preview Templates Before You Choose Them

If you click once on the template you wish to see, a preview will appear on the right of the box.

Creating A New Template

You Can Start With An Existing Template!

When you create a new template, it will always be based on an existing template. This may be just a blank document (based on the Normal template) or you can choose another template that is closer to what you need.

1   Click on the **File** menu.

2   Click on **New**.

3   Click on the template you would like to base your new template on.

4   Click in the circle next to *Template*.

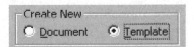

5   Click **OK**.

6   Add any text or formatting that you require on your template.

7   Save the template – **do not change the folder Word saves it in!**

Or

1   Create a new document as normal.

2   Add any text or formatting that you require on your template.

3   Click on the **File** menu.

4   Click **Save**.

5   Click the down arrow next to *Save as type*.

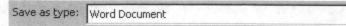

Save as type: | Word Document | ▼

6   Choose *Document Template*.

7   Click **Save – do not change the folder which Word saves it into!**

Remember – The Template Only Contains Standard Text!

Any text you add to the template will appear whenever you create a new document based on it – so be careful only to add standard information.

How Do I Know I Have Created A Template?

Word will display the text template in the title bar at the top of the screen.

Creating Documents Based On Your New Template

1   Click on the **File** menu.

2   Click on **New**.

3   Click on the **General** tab (if you are not there already).

4   Click on your template.

5   Click **OK**.

How Do I Know That I Have Created A Document?

Word will display the text document in the title bar at the top of the screen.

240

Where Are Templates Stored?

➤ Word 2000 stores **your** templates in a special folder:

C:\Windows\Application Data\Microsoft\Templates

➤ Templates that come with the program are usually stored in:

C:\Program Files\Microsoft Office\Templates\1033

However it will depend on how your version of Office 2000 has been installed. If you cannot find the templates here, then find out from the person who installed Office where they put them on your machine.

Editing A Template

If You Have Made A Mistake On Your Template ...

You cannot get back to it by going to **File** and **New**, because File and New will **always** create something **new**. It won't allow you to go back to your original template and edit it.

1   Click on open icon.

2   Change the *Look in* box to the location where your template is stored.

3   Click on the template you wish to edit.

4   Click on **Open**.

5   Make your changes to the template.

6   Save and close the template.

Or, if you have created your template recently:

1   Click on the **File** menu.

2   Click on your template from the list of recently used documents at the bottom.

3   Make your changes to the template.

4   Save and close the template.

Chapter 7

File Management

Advanced Saving

Creating A Copy Of A Document Using Save As

If you need to quickly make a copy of a file you are working on, use the Save As tool. You might want to make a copy if you are testing something, and want to make sure that your original document is safe in case anything goes wrong.

1   Click on the **File** menu.

2   Click on **Save As**.

3   If required, type a new name for the document.

4   If required, change the folder to save the document into.

5   Click on **Save**.

Creating Folders While Saving

1   Click on the **File** menu.

2   Click on **Save As**.

3   Change the *Save in* box to the folder or drive you wish to create the new folder in, e.g. if you click on (*C:*) the new folder will be created on the (C:) drive.

4   Click on the **New Folder** icon.

5   Type in a name for your folder.

6   Press **Return**.

Saving As A Different Format

Word documents can be saved in various different formats. Which one you choose depends on what you want to do with the file.

> ➤ **RTF** (Rich text format) will allow the file to be opened in programs other than Word.

> ➤ **Web Page** i.e. HTML (Hyper-text markup language), will allow the file to be seen on the World Wide Web (see below).

> ➤ **Word 97** and **Word 6.0/95** will allow the file to be opened in previous versions of Word.

1   Click on the **File** menu.

2   Click **Save As**.

3   Click the drop-down arrow to the right of the *Save as type* box.

4   Click on the file type you require.

5   Click **Save**.

Saving A Document As A Web Page

This will save your file in HTML format, suitable for viewing on the Web.

1   Open the document you wish to save as a Web page.

2   Click on the **File** menu.

3   Click on **Save as Web Page**.

4   Type in the file name you require.

5   Change the folder to save into as required.

6   Click on **Save**.

244

Searching For Lost Files

Starting A Search In Word

1 Click on the **Open** icon.

2 Click on the **Tools** menu.

3 Click on **Find** – the *Find* box will appear.

Choosing The Drive To Look Through

1 Ensure that the folder or drive you wish to search through is shown at the bottom.

Look in: 　 Local Disk (C:)

2 Ensure that *Search subfolders* is ticked.

You Can Only Look Through One Drive At A Time!

You cannot look through every drive on your computer.

Ensure That 'Search Subfolders' Is Ticked

If you do not tick this box, then Word will not look inside any folders within the drive you have chosen. For example, if you have chosen to look through the C: drive, and you do not tick *Search subfolders*, then Word will not look in any of the folders or subfolders contained on the C: drive to find your document.

Adding Properties And Conditions

In order for Word to find your document, you must tell it as much as you can remember about it. This can include the following kinds of information:

➤ The file name.

➤ When you last worked on it.

➤ When you created it.

➤ Which program you created it in.

➤ How many pages it has.

➤ Any text it contains.

You can tell Word these things using the properties and conditions in the *Find* box.

1   Click on the drop-down arrow underneath *Property* and choose the property you require, e.g. *File name*.

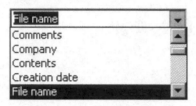

2   Click on the drop-down arrow underneath *Condition* and choose the condition you require, e.g. *includes*.

3   Click into the *Value* box (if available) and type the value you require, e.g. if the file name includes the word **minutes**, type **minutes** into the *Value* box.

4   Click on **Add to List**.

5   Repeat steps 1–4 for any other information you know about the file.

The conditions will be added to the list at the top of the window.

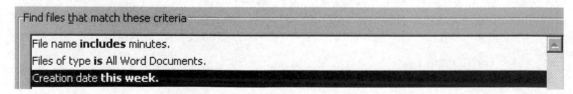

Performing The Search

1 Click on the **Find Now** button – Word will look for the document.

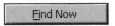

2 Double-click on the file you require from the results.

Name	Size	Type	Modified
My Pictures		Folder	12/06/02 10:41
Meeting Minutes test	19 KB	Microsoft Word ...	23/07/02 15:38
Old Excel Documents	1 KB	Shortcut	12/06/02 10:33

Is Word Looking For My Document?

It can take a while for Word to find your document. If you can't wait any longer, click **Cancel** to stop the search.

Changing The Search Conditions

If your first search does not find the file you were looking for, you can try changing the properties and conditions and have another go. As long as you don't close the *Open* box, Word will remember all the conditions you set for the last search.

1 Click on the **Tools** menu.

2 Click **Find**.

3 Click on a search condition to be removed.

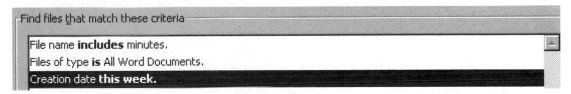

4 Click on **Delete**.

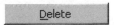

5 Repeat for any other search conditions to be removed.

6   Add any new search conditions to the list (see page 246).

7   Click **Find Now**.

Chapter 8

Importing Objects

Excel Worksheets In Word

What Is An Excel Worksheet?

An Excel worksheet lets you perform spreadsheet functions in Word without having to open Excel separately. For more about Excel, spreadsheets, and other great mysteries of life, see Module 4: *Spreadsheets*.

Creating Worksheets

1   Click on the **Insert Microsoft Excel Worksheet** button.

2   Click and drag over the number of cells you require.

3   Insert your data into the spreadsheet.

4   Click away from your spreadsheet, inside your Word document.

Editing A Worksheet

1 Double-click on your Excel Worksheet.

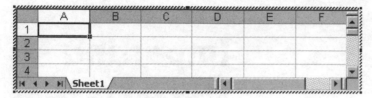

2 Click in the cell to edit and make your changes.

3 Press **Return**.

4 Click away from your spreadsheet, inside your Word document.

Importing Excel Worksheets

1 Click on the **Insert** menu.

2 Click on **Object**.

3 Click on the **Create from File** tab.

4 Click on **Browse**.

5 Locate the file you wish to insert and double-click on it.

6 To create a Linked Object, click on *Link to File* – to create an Embedded Object, Do **not** click on *Link to File*.

7 Click **OK**.

Check This Out...

Linked Or Embedded?

A linked object is one that will automatically update when the original file is changed. An embedded object is not linked – it will not update, and exists as a separate spreadsheet in its own right.

Deleting A Worksheet

1 Click outside of the worksheet, and then select it – white boxes (handles) will appear around the edge.

2 Press the **Delete** key.

250

Excel Charts In Word

A chart is a way of displaying numbers in a fancy way that is easy to understand. You can have bar charts, pie charts, and many other different types.

Importing Charts From Excel Into Word

1   Open the Excel spreadsheet containing the chart you wish to import.

2   Select the chart – black squares will appear around the whole chart border.

3   Click on the **Edit** menu.

4   Click **Copy**.

5   Go back to the Word document (click on the Word document on the taskbar).

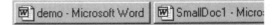

6   Place the cursor where you want the chart to appear.

7   Click on the **Edit** menu.

8   Click on **Paste Special**.

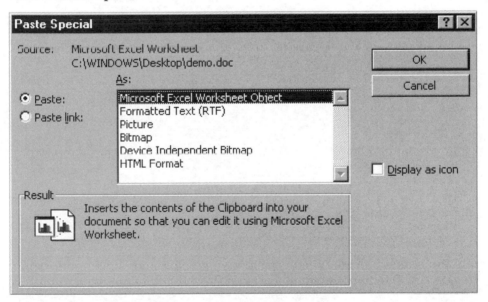

251

9   Click on *Microsoft Excel Chart Object.*

10 Click inside the circle next to *Paste link.*

11 Click **OK** – now, any changes made to the original Excel spreadsheet will also change the chart in Word.

Creating An Embedded Excel Chart

1   Click on the **Insert** menu.

2   Click on **Object**.

3   Click on the **Create New** tab.

4   Click on *Microsoft Excel Chart.*

5   Click **OK**.

6   To switch between the chart and the worksheet, click on the **Chart1** and **Sheet1** tabs.

Chart1 ⟋ Sheet1 ⟋

7   When you have finished entering your data, click outside of the chart.

Chapter 9

Mail Merge

Mail Merge

Mail Merge is used to send the same letter to lots of different people. Suppose you had 100 people you wanted to send your letter to – you can create the standard letter, and insert a special mail merge code for their name and address. Using a separate file containing all the names and addresses, Word will merge the letter with each name and address, printing out each one.

A Mail Merge always involves the following three steps:

> ➤ Creating the **Data Document** – which contains all the personal information that will change from letter to letter.

> ➤ Creating the **Main Document** – which is the letter you are sending.

> ➤ **Merging** the Data Document and the Main Document together into individual letters.

The Data Document

> ➤ The Data Document is laid out in a table.

> ➤ In the columns of the table are **fields**, or the types of information that will change from letter to letter. The **field names** are held in the first row.

➤ In the subsequent rows are the **records**, or the information that will show on each of the letters.

Name	Address	Salutation	Previous Course	Date Attended	
Mr Frederick Bloggs	10 High Street Lewisham London SE13 6HD	Mr Bloggs	Word Essentials	12/6/98	Field names are held in first row
Mrs Bianca Watford	16 Rosemary Avenue Clerkenwell London EC1R 4TD	Mrs Rowland	Access Intermediate	7/7/98	Records are held in subsequent rows
Mr Arthur Mitchell	22 Ladbroke Grove Notting Hill London W12 5JK	Mr Mitchell	Word Intermediate	1/4/98	

The Main Document

➤ The main document contains all the standard text which will not change between letters.

➤ At the point where information will change, a **merge field** has been inserted, to indicate to Word that it must find the required information in the data document.

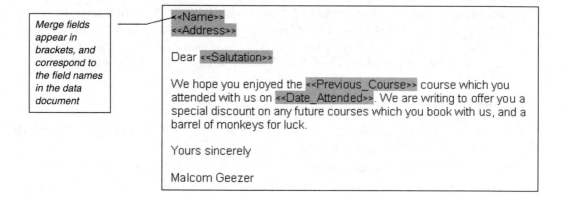

Merge fields appear in brackets, and correspond to the field names in the data document

<<Name>>
<<Address>>

Dear <<Salutation>>

We hope you enjoyed the <<Previous_Course>> course which you attended with us on <<Date_Attended>>. We are writing to offer you a special discount on any future courses which you book with us, and a barrel of monkeys for luck.

Yours sincerely

Malcom Geezer

Creating Your Data Document

How Will The Data Document Look?

The data document will be laid out in a table, with the field names in the top row.

Name	Address	Salutation	Previous Course	Date Attended
Mr Frederick Bloggs	10 High Street Lewisham London SE13 6HD	Mr Bloggs	Word Essentials	12/6/98
Mrs Bianca Watford	16 Rosemary Avenue Clerkenwell London EC1R 4TD	Mrs Watford	Access Intermediate	7/7/98
Mr Arthur Mitchell	22 Ladbroke Grove Notting Hill London W12 5JK	Mr Mitchell	Word Intermediate	1/4/98

Creating The Data Document

1   Create a new, blank document.

2   Create a table (see page 191)

> ➤ The number of columns = the number of fields.

> ➤ The number of rows = the number of records + 1 (for the field names).

3   Type the field names into the first row.

4   Type the records into the subsequent rows.

5   Save the data document.

6   Close the data document.

Check This Out...

How Should The Addresses Be Laid Out?

Enter the address as it will be laid out on the letter, with hard returns after each line.

Creating A Main Document

How Will The Main Document Look?

The main document will look exactly like a normal letter except at the points where information needs to be retrieved from the data document, where you will see merge fields.

Merge fields appear in brackets, and correspond to the field names in the data document

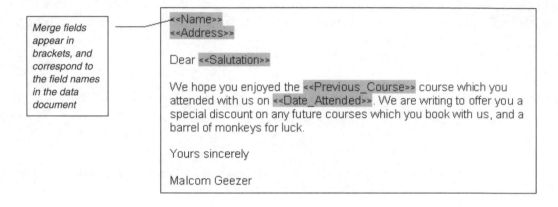

```
<<Name>>
<<Address>>

Dear <<Salutation>>

We hope you enjoyed the <<Previous_Course>> course which you
attended with us on <<Date_Attended>>. We are writing to offer you a
special discount on any future courses which you book with us, and a
barrel of monkeys for luck.

Yours sincerely

Malcom Geezer
```

Creating The Main Document

1   Create a new, blank document.

2   Type all of your standard text as normal.

3   Click on the **Tools** menu.

4   Click **Mail Merge**.

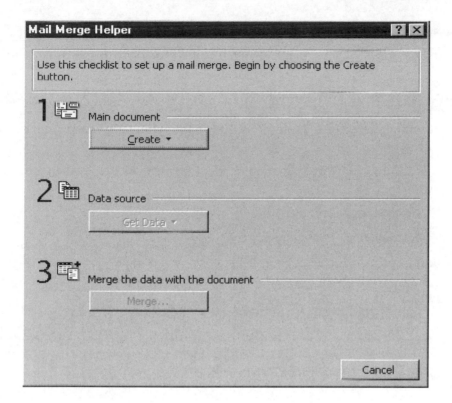

5   Click **Create**.

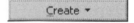

6   Click **Form Letters**.

7   Click **Active Window** from the dialog box that appears.

8   Click **Get Data**.

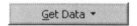

9   Click **Open Data Source**.

10 Change the *Look in* box to the folder where your data document is saved.

11 Select your data document.

12 Click **Open**.

13 Click **Edit Main Document** from the dialog box that appears.

Inserting Merge Fields Into Your Main Document

Once you have created your Main Document, a new toolbar will appear on your screen.

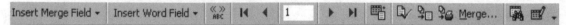

This is the *Mail Merge* toolbar. You can use it to insert your merge fields into the main document.

1 Position the cursor where you require your first merge field (e.g. the name or address).

2 Click **Insert Merge Field**.

3 Click on the name of field you require.

4 Repeat steps 1 to 3 until all your merge fields are inserted.

Remember To Include Spaces Around The Merge Fields

The letters will be laid out exactly the same as your main document. If there is no space between your merge fields and the standard text, then the words will run into each other!

Inserting The Date

1 Position cursor where you require the date.

2 Click on the **Insert** menu.

3 Click **Date and Time**.

4 Click style of date you require.

5 Click **OK**.

Carrying Out A Mail Merge

Previewing Before You Merge

Before you actually carry out the merge, you can preview it to see how your letters look. This often reveals small mistakes, and can save time later.

1   Make sure you are in the main document.

2   Click on the **View Merged Data** icon on the *Mail Merge* toolbar

3   Click on the **Record Navigation** icons to move through your letters.

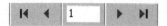

➤   The first icon on the left takes you to the first record.

➤   The second icon takes you to the previous record.

➤   The second icon from the right takes you to the next record.

➤   The last icon on the right takes you to the final record.

4   Click on the **View Merged Data** icon again when you have finished.

If there are mistakes in your main document, correct them now. If there are mistakes in your data document:

1   Click on the **Edit Data Source** icon.

2   Click **View Source**.

3   Make your changes to the table.

4   Click on the **Mail Merge Main Document** icon when you have finished.

or

save and close the data document.

Merging With The Document On Screen

When you are ready to merge, click on the **Merge to New Document** icon.

A new document containing your letter is created on screen. Each letter will start on a new page.

Printing Merged Documents

Click on the **Merge to Printer** icon.

Never Save A Merged Document!

Saving merged documents wastes space on your computer. As long as you have your main document and your data document, you can just do the merge again when you require the same letters.

Merging Selected Records

1   Click on the **Tools** menu.

2   Click **Mail Merge**.

3   Click **Merge**.

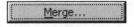

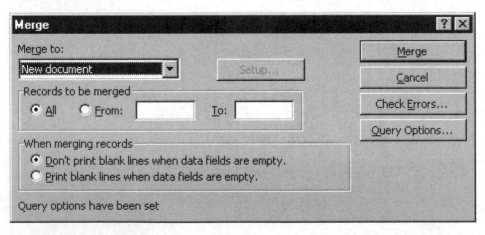

4   Click inside the circle next to *From*.

5   Type in the number of the first record you wish to merge.

6   Click in box next to *To*.

7   Type in the number of the last record you wish to merge.

8   Click **Merge**.

Mail Merge To Labels

Creating A Data Document For Labels

You can use the same data source for your labels as your letters, as long as it contains fields for the name and address! See page 258.

Creating The Main Document

1   Start a new document.

2   Click on the **Tools** menu.

3   Click **Mail Merge**.

4   Click **Create**.

5   Click **Mailing Labels**.

6   Click **Active Window** from dialog box which appears.

   or

   click **New Main Document** to start on a blank document.

7   Click **Get Data**.

8   Click **Open Data Source**.

9   Change the *Look in* box to point to the folder where your data document is saved.

10 Click **Open**.

11 Click **Set Up Main Document**.

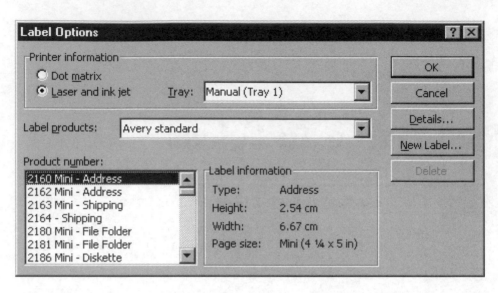

12 Click on the drop-down arrow at the end of the *Label products* box and change to your label manufacturer.

13 Click on the required product number.

14 Click **OK**.

15 Click **Insert Merge Field** to add your fields.

16 Click on the field you wish to insert – separate with normal punctuation as required (e.g hard return).

17 Click **OK**.

18 Click **Close**.

Carrying Out The Merge

Click on the **Merge to New Document** icon to create a new document containing your labels.

Or

Click on the **Merge to Printer** icon to print the labels.

Query Options In A Mail Merge

Sorting Records

1   Open your main document.

2   Click on the **Tools** menu.

3   Click **Mail Merge**.

4   Click **Query Options**.

5   Click on the **Sort Records** tab.

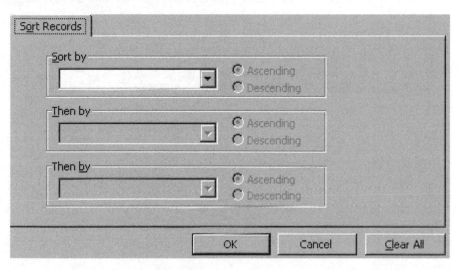

263

6 Click on the drop-down arrow underneath *Sort by*.

7 Click on the first field you wish to sort.

8 If required, click on the drop-down arrow under *Then by*.

9 Click on the second field you wish to sort.

10 Click **OK**.

11 Click **Merge**.

12 Click **Merge**.

Extracting Records To Merge

1 Open your main document.

2 Click on the **Tools** menu.

3 Click **Mail Merge**.

4 Click **Query Options**.

5 Click **Filter Records** tab.

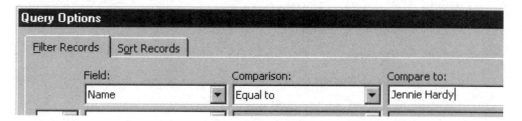

6 Click on the drop-down arrow underneath *Field*.

7 Click on the field you wish to extract from.

8 Click on the drop-down arrow underneath *Comparison*.

9 Click on the comparison required.

10 Click in the *Compare to* box.

11 Type in what you are looking for.

12 Click **OK**.

13 Click **Merge**.

14 Click **Merge**.

Extracting Records On More Than One Criteria

When you extract records on more than one criteria, you must specify whether you are using **AND** or **OR**. For example, suppose my two criteria are all staff who are **female** and work in the **Finance department**:

➤ **AND** will give you records which meet **BOTH** of your criteria. So I will get all the females who work in the Finance department.

➤ **OR** will give you records which meet **EITHER** of your criteria. So I will get all the females, and all the people who work in the Finance department.

Supposing you wanted to merge the records of people who work in Finance and are female, here is how you would do it:

1 Click on the **Tools** menu.

2 Click **Mail Merge**.

3 Click **Query Options**.

4 Click on the **Filter Records** tab.

5 Set fields and comparisons as required.

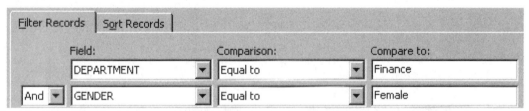

Filter Records	Sort Records				
	Field:		Comparison:		Compare to:
	DEPARTMENT	▼	Equal to	▼	Finance
And ▼	GENDER	▼	Equal to	▼	Female

6 Click **OK**.

7 Click **Merge**.

8 Click **Merge**.

If You Have Set Query Options Before

Click **Clear All** in the query options dialog box to clear all your previous settings.

Troubleshooting Mail Merge

Error Message 'Word Could Not Open Data As Data Or Header Source Because It Is A Mail Merge Main Document'

Somehow or other, the data document has become A Mail Merge main document. To fix this error;

1 Open the data document.

2 Click on the **Tools** menu.

3 Click **Mail Merge**.

4 Click **Create**.

5 Click on *Restore to normal Word document.*

6 Click **Yes**.

7 Click **Close**.

8 Save the data document.

9 Close the data document.

10 Try the Mail Merge again!

When I Click Insert Merge Field My Field Names Do Not Appear

1 Open the data document.

2 Make sure that the first row of the table contains the field names.

3 Make sure that there are no hard returns above your table.

4 Save the data document.

5 Close the data document.

6 Try the Mail Merge again!

Word Tells Me There Are No Field Delimiters In My Data Source

This means that there is text above the table. Word always expects to find the field names in a table at the very top of the document. If there is text or space above the table, you will get this error message. To fix this:

1   Open the data document.

2   Delete all spaces and text above the table.

3   Make sure that the table is at the very top of the document, and that the first row contains the field names.

4   Save the data document.

5   Close the data document.

6   Try the Mail Merge again!

Date And Time

Inserting The Date With The Menu

The date can be added in two ways:

➤   Fixed – this will always show the same date

➤   Automatically updating – the date changes automatically, so that it is always showing the current date.

1   Position the cursor where you require the date.

2   Click on the **Insert** menu.

3   Click **Date and Time**.

4   Choose the date format you require from the left-hand side.

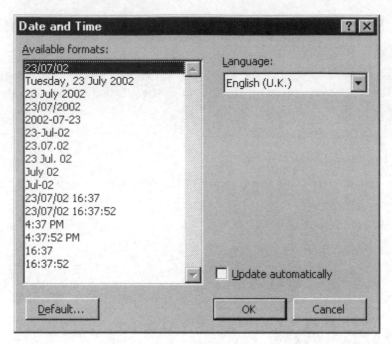

5   Tick the box next to *Update automatically* if you require the date to change in the future

or

untick the box next to *Update automatically* if you require the date to be fixed.

6   Click **OK**.

When You Insert An Automatically Updating Date It Becomes A Field

A field is a special piece of text in Word, which changes automatically. Another example would be page numbers, which change on every page. When you click on a field, it will usually become highlighted in grey.

Inserting The Date Or Time With The Keyboard

Press **Alt+Shift+D** to insert the date.

Press **Alt+Shift+T** to insert the time.

Deleting The Date If It Updates Automatically

If you have chosen to insert the date so that it updates automatically, you have actually inserted a field. Fields are not deleted in the same way as normal text – follow these steps to delete it:

1   Click and drag over the date so that it is selected.

2   Press the **Delete** key.

Or

1   Position your cursor next to the date.

2   Press the **Delete** key or **Backspace** twice.

Changing The Default Date Format

The default date format is the style of date that you use automatically. If you insert the date with the keyboard, you will always get the default format.

1   Click on the **Insert** menu.

2   Click **Date and Time**.

3   Click on the style of date you want to make the default.

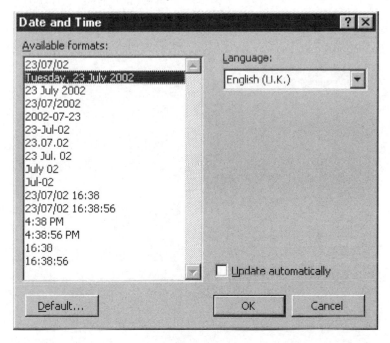

4   Click **Default**.

5 Click **Yes**.

6 Click **OK** if you wish to insert the date

or

click **Cancel** if you wish to leave the date and time box without inserting the date.

Module 4
Spreadsheets

Chapter 1

Getting Started

What Is Excel For?

Excel is a spreadsheet program. Spreadsheets are basically big tables that hold text and numbers. Calculations can then be performed on these numbers, to help you manage your accounts, work out sales figures, or calculate interest payments on loans. Excel can be used for:

➤ Formulae or calculations

➤ Storing information (as a database)

➤ Creating tables.

For Formulae (Calculations)

A very simple domestic budget using Excel can be seen on the next page.

For more information on formulae see page 299.

	A	B	C	D	E	F
1	Income	£1,200.00				
2						
3	**Outgoings**					
4	Rent	£ 250.00				
5	Food	£ 150.00				
6	Social	£ 85.00				
7	Gas	£ 30.00				
8	Electricity	£ 30.00				
9						
10	**Total Outgoings**	£ 545.00				
11						
12	Left Over	£ 655.00				
13						
14						
15						
16						

This cell contains a formula to add up the total outgoings

This cell contains a formula which takes the total outgoings away from the income, which gives you the left over amount

For Storing Information (As A Database)

The diagram below shows part of a database in Excel. The columns represent the fields in the database and the rows hold the records.

	B	C	D	E	F	G
1	**Surname**	**First Name**	**Sex**	**Date of Birth**	**Department**	**Number**
2	Jekyll	Abigail	Female	23-May-60	Design	1
3	Akinlotan	Abimbola	Female	12-Mar-58	Sales	5
4	Hyde	Alexander	Male	23-May-28	Finance	3
5	Richards	Anna	Female	27-Mar-68	Sales	6
6	Dalloway	Anne	Female	15-Jun-59	Personnel	8
7	Olivelle	Anthony	Male	21-Nov-67	Technology	5

Excel has a simple database facility that allows you to:

➤ Sort information into any order (e.g. by surname).

➤ Extract the information you wish to see (e.g. only the females).

For Creating Tables

Excel can also be used very much like word processing tables, i.e. for laying information out neatly in rows and columns. Spreadsheets can then be formatted to look quite nice!

	A	B	C	D
1	**Competitor**	**Current Share**	**Share in 2 years**	
2	Largest competitor	50%	30%	
3	Second competitor	25%	20%	
4	Third competitor	15%	10%	

274

Starting And Closing Excel

Starting Excel

1   Click on the **Start** button.

2   Click on the **Programs** sub-menu.

3   Click on **Microsoft Excel**.

Or, if you have a shortcut:

Double-click on the shortcut on the desktop, or click once on the shortcut on the toolbar.

Closing Excel

1   Click on the **File** menu.

2   Click on **Exit**.

Or

Click on the X at the top right-hand corner of the screen.

What Are Workbooks?

➤ Excel files are known as **workbooks**.

➤ Workbooks are made up of **sheets**, or **spreadsheets**.

The Excel 2000 Screen

What Are All The Bits Called?

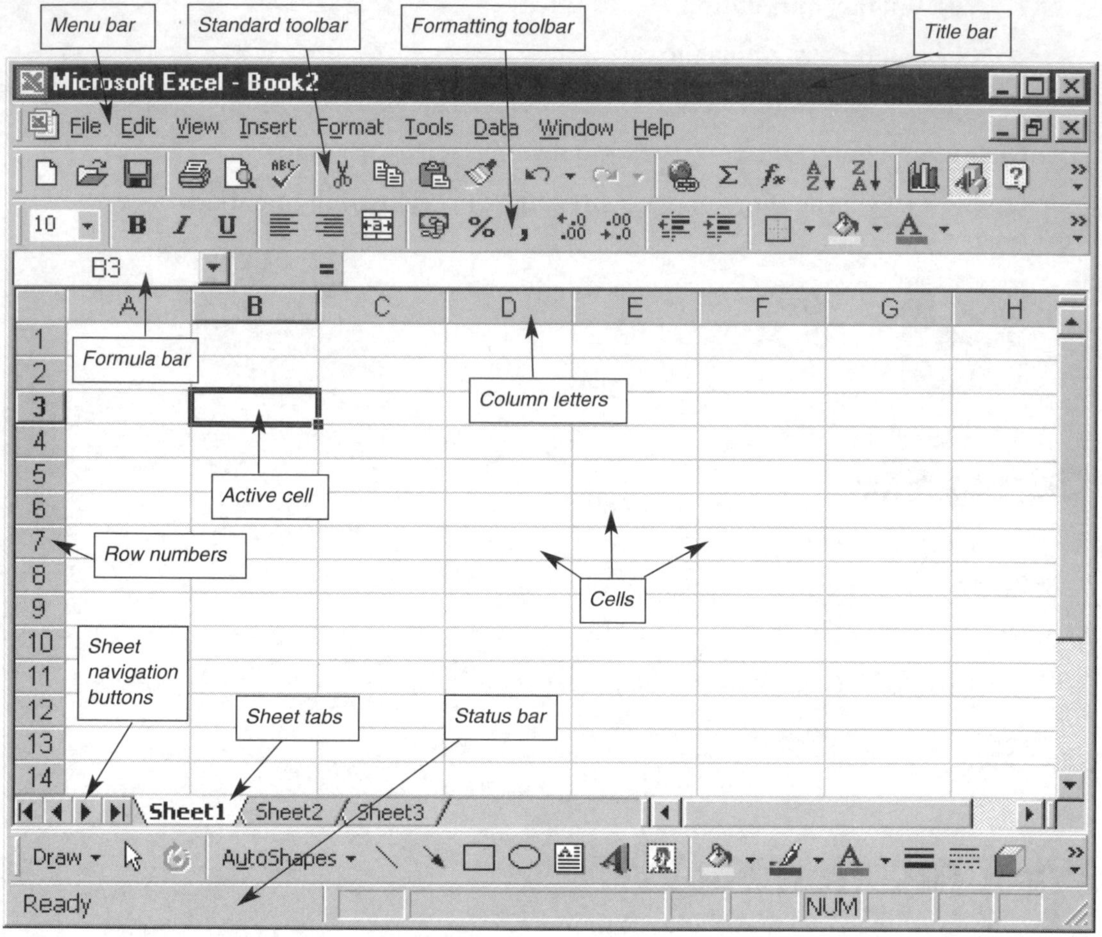
Menu bar
Standard toolbar
Formatting toolbar
Title bar
Microsoft Excel - Book2
File Edit View Insert Format Tools Data Window Help
B3
Formula bar
Column letters
Active cell
Row numbers
Cells
Sheet navigation buttons
Sheet tabs
Status bar
Sheet1 Sheet2 Sheet3
Draw AutoShapes
Ready
NUM

The Different Shapes Of The Mouse

As you progress through Excel you will see that the mouse changes shape all the time, depending on what action you are performing. It's very important that before you start to do anything, you check that your mouse looks correct. Use this page as a reference to remind you what the different mouse shapes mean.

	Where does my mouse pointer have to be?	**When would I use this icon?**
✛	*Big Plus Sign* Position your mouse pointer over the middle of a cell.	When you are selecting cells. (See page 289)
Monday	*Small Plus Sign* Position your mouse pointer over the the bottom right-hand corner of active cell.	When you are using AutoFill. (See page 306)
▹	*Pointer* Pointer your mouse pointer at the border of the active cell.	When you are moving or copying a range of cells. (See page 303)
I	*I-Bar* Click into the *Formula* bar, or double-click inside a cell.	When you are adding or deleting text from a cell. (See page 286)
✛	*Cross Arrow* Position your mouse pointer between two column letters or between two row numbers.	When you are resizing a row or column. (See page 339)
⚲	*Magnifying Glass* Position your mouse pointer over the spreadsheet in Print Preview.	When you want to zoom in or out of the print preview. (See page 326)
⤡	*Double Arrow* Select a picture or drawn shape and position the mouse over the boxes that appear.	When you are resizing a picture, chart or drawn shape. (See page 362)
⌛	*Egg Timer* Anywhere on the screen.	The mouse will change to an egg timer when Excel is busy. If you wait for a moment, it will disappear.

Saving Your Workbook

Saving Your Work For The First Time

1   Click on the **Save** icon.

2   Type in a name for your workbook (up to 255 characters).

3   Change the folder to save in, if required.

4   Click on **Save**.

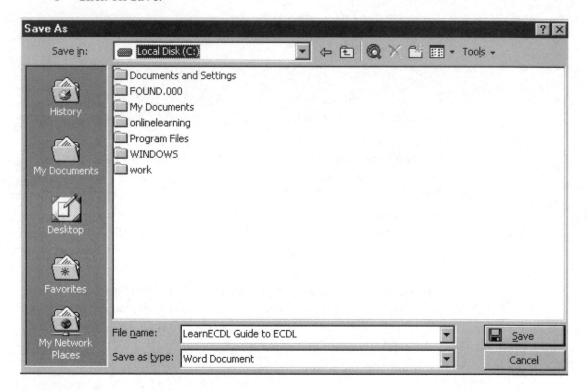

What Are Folders?

See *Module 2: Using The Computer And Managing Files.*

Saving Your Workbook After You Have Made Changes

Click on the **Save** icon to save your work after you have made changes. The file will be saved in the same place with the same name.

Check This Out...

Save Your Work Regularly!

Keep clicking on the **Save** icon as you are working to ensure that you do not lose your work!

Creating A Copy Using Save As

Using Save As will allow you to make a copy of your workbook with a different name and/or in a different location.

1   Click on the **File** menu.

2   Click on **Save As**.

3   Type in a new file name for the workbook if required.

4   Change the folder if required.

5   Click **Save**.

Changing The Default Folder

1   Click on the **Tools** menu.

2   Click on **Options**.

3   Click on the **General** tab.

4   Click inside the box next to Default file location (see below).

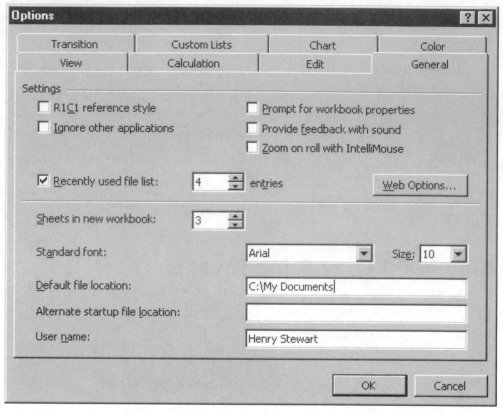

5   Type in the drive and folder you wish to save to, e.g. C:\work.

6   Click **OK**.

Closing And Opening Your Workbook

Opening Your Workbook

1   Click on the **Open** icon.

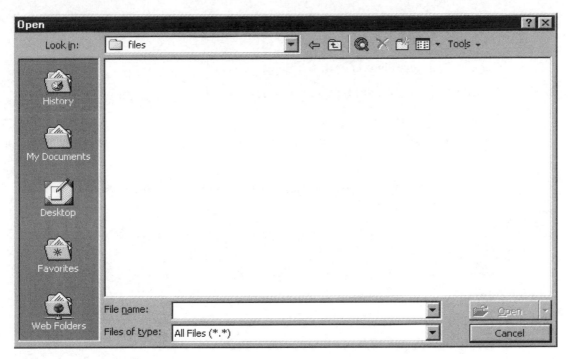

2   Change the folder Excel is looking in if required.

3   Click on the name of the workbook you wish to open, scrolling across if necessary.

4   Click on **Open**.

What Are Folders?

See *Module 2: Using The Computer And Managing Files*.

Multiple Workbooks

In Excel you can open more than one workbook at a time. If you find that you need to open another workbook, simply open it in the normal way (see previous section). You may wish to have more than one workbook open if you want to copy information from one workbook to the other.

If you know that you will want to use more than one workbook when you start, you can select all the workbooks that you will need from the *Open* dialog box, and then click on **Open**. From the *Open* dialog box:

1   Click on the first file you wish to open.

2   Hold down the **Ctrl** key on the keyboard.

3   Click on the next file you wish to open.

4   Continue clicking on all the files you wish to select.

5   Release the **Ctrl** key.

6   Click **Open** – all the selected files will be opened in separate windows.

How Can I Switch Between More Than One Open Workbook?

1   Click on the **Window** menu – a list of open workbooks can be seen at the bottom of the menu.

2   Click on the file you wish to switch to.

Switching Between Open Workbooks

1   Click on the **Window** menu – a list of open workbooks can be seen at the bottom of the menu.

2   Click on the file you wish to switch to.

Or

Click on the button on the taskbar for that workbook.

Closing Your Workbook

Click on the bottom X at the top right of the Excel screen (see below) – **not** the top one!

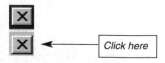

Click here

Or

1   Click on the **File** menu.

2   Click on **Close**.

What Happened? Excel Closed Completely!

You must have clicked the top X instead of the bottom one. Clicking the top one closes Excel completely, so make sure you only click the bottom X to close your workbook.

Creating A New Workbook

Creating A New Workbook

Click on the **New** icon.

Or

1   Click on the **File** menu.

2   Click on **New**.

3   Ensure you are on the **General** tab.

4   Click **Workbook**.

5   Click **OK**.

Changing The Zoom Control

What Is The Zoom Control?

This allows you to zoom out from your spreadsheet, so you can see more of it, or zoom in closer, so you can see fine details. It does not change the size of the spreadsheet when it prints out.

Changing The Zoom Control With The Icon

1   Click on the drop-down arrow next to the the *Zoom* box.

2 Click on the zoom level you require (the higher the percentage, the closer you get!).

Changing The Zoom Control With The Menu

1 Click on the **View** menu.

2 Click on **Zoom**.

3 Click in the circle next to the zoom you require

or

type in your required zoom in the *Custom* box (see below).

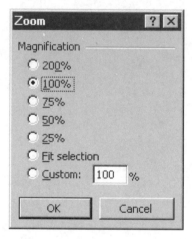

4 Click **OK**.

Moving Around A Spreadsheet

Moving Around With The Scroll Bars

There are two scroll bars around the spreadsheet: horizontal and vertical.

To move up and down, use the vertical scroll bar to the right of the spreadsheet:

➤ Click on the up arrow repeatedly to move up slowly.

➤ Click and hold the mouse button down on the up arrow to move up quickly.

➤ Click and drag the grey box to move quickly up or down.

➤ Click on the down arrow repeatedly to move down slowly.

➤ Click and hold the mouse button down on the down arrow to move down quickly.

To move left or right, use the horizontal scroll bar:

➤ Click on the left arrow repeatedly to move slowly to the left.

➤ Click and hold the mouse button down on the left arrow to move left quickly.

➤ Click and drag the grey box to move quickly left or right.

➤ Click on the right arrow repeatedly to move slowly to the right.

➤ Click and hold the mouse button down on the right arrow to move right quickly.

Moving With The Keyboard

Press this on the keyboard	You will move
Up arrow key	Up one cell
Down arrow key	Down one cell
Left arrow key	Left a cell
Right arrow key	Right a cell
Ctrl+right-arrow key	To the furthest right column of the current spreadsheet
Ctrl+left arrow key	To the furthest left column of the current spreadsheet
Ctrl+up arrow key	To the top row of the sheet
Ctrl+down arrow key	To the bottom row of the sheet
Home	To column A
Ctrl+Home	To cell A1
Ctrl+End	To the bottom right cell of the current spreadsheet
Page Up	The active cell up one screen
Page Down	The active cell down one screen

Moving Around With The Mouse

1   Position the mouse over the middle of the cell you wish to move to.

2   Click when your mouse looks like a big white cross.

To Move, Your Mouse Pointer Must Look Like A Big White Cross!

Toolbars

Hiding And Showing Toolbars

1   Click on the **View** menu.

2   Click on the **Toolbars** sub-menu.

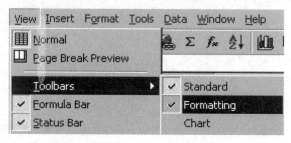

3   Click on the toolbar you wish to show or hide – the toolbar is ticked when on.

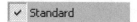

Entering Text And Numbers

What Happens When I Enter Text And Numbers?

➤ When you enter text or numbers into a cell, the state of the cell changes.

➤ When you have finished typing you must confirm that you have finished by pressing Enter or clicking on the green tick.

When you are not entering text	When you are entering text
You will see a thick border around the cell	You will see a thin border around the cell and a flashing cursor inside the cell.

There is no red cross or green tick on the *Formula* bar.

Any text that you type will appear on the *Formula* bar, along with a red cross and green tick.

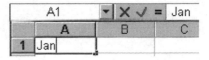

Entering Text

1   Click on the cell you want to enter text into.

2   Type the text you require.

3   Press **Enter**

    or

    click on the green tick – the text will appear on the left-hand side of the cell.

Entering Numbers

1   Click on the cell you want to enter a number into.

2   Type the number you require.

3   Press **Enter**

    or

    click on the green tick – the number will appear on the right-hand side of the cell.

Entering Dates

1   Click on the cell you want to enter a date into.

2   Type the date you require with slashes dividing date, month and year, e.g. 1/1/2000

3   Press **Enter**

    or

    click on the green tick – the date will appear on the right-hand side of the cell.

Always Enter Dates With Slashes

If you enter dates with dots, e.g. 1.1.2000, then Excel will see them as text rather than numbers. You will then be unable to perform calculations on the date. Performing calculations on dates is very common when you wish to calculate how many days there are between two dates.

Entering Percentages

1   Click on the cell you want to enter a percentage into.

2   Type the percentage you require, e.g. 10%.

3   Press **Enter**

   or

   click on the green tick – the percentage will appear on the right of the cell.

What Is The Difference Between Enter And The Green Tick?

➤ If you press **Enter**, you move down one cell after you have pressed it.

➤ If you click on the green tick, you remain in the same cell after you have clicked it.

Why Do Numbers Go On The Right?

When Excel puts data on the right it confirms that calculations can be performed on the data you have entered. Any data that appears on the left cannot be used in a calculation.

What If I Make a Mistake?

If you make a mistake, and you have not yet confirmed the entry by pressing **Return** or clicking the green tick:

Click on the red cross on the *Formula* bar.

Selecting Cells

To Select, Your Mouse Must Look Like A Big White Cross!

Why Select Cells?

If you want to work with just a part of your spreadsheet, you must select the part you wish to work with. The list below shows some of the situations in which you may need to select.

➤ When you are formatting part of the spreadsheet, e.g. making it bold, italic, changing the size.

➤ When you are copying or moving part of the spreadsheet.

➤ When you are adding or deleting rows and columns.

➤ When you are choosing the cells you wish to use in a calculation or formula.

➤ When you are printing part of your spreadsheet.

Selecting A Range Of Cells

1 Position the mouse over the middle of the cell, at the top left-hand corner of the area you wish to select.

2 Make sure your mouse looks like a big white cross.

3 Click and drag the mouse pointer over the cells you require.

What Do Cells Look Like When They Are Selected?

All the cells, apart from the first one you selected, will go black. The first cell remains white (this indicates the active cell of the selection).

12	GRANTS	40500	43760	53404
13	DONATIONS	34550	34500	30000
14	SALES	12000	2103	2300
15	OTHER	4055	3402	2344

289

Selecting Columns

Click on the grey column letter you require.

Or

Click and drag over the column letters to select several columns.

Selecting Rows

Click on the grey row number you require.

Or

Click and drag over the row numbers to select several rows.

Selecting the Whole Spreadsheet

Click on the grey square at the top left of the spreadsheet.

	A
1	

Selecting Cells Which Are Not Next To Each Other

1   Select the first range of cells you require.

2   Hold down **Control (Ctrl)** on the keyboard.

3   Select the second range of cells you require.

4   Release the mouse.

5   Release the **Ctrl** key.

Deselecting Cells

Click onto a cell outside of the selection.

Or, if you have selected the whole spreadsheet:

Click into the middle of the sheet.

Adding Numbers Up With AutoSum

What Is AutoSum?

AutoSum is a quick and easy way of adding up a list of figures.

Using AutoSum

1   Click on the cell where you would like to put the answer.

2   Click on the **AutoSum** icon – flashing lights will appear around the figures you are adding up.

3   The formula will appear in the cell (see below).

4   Press **Enter** or click on the green tick.

What Does The Sum Formula Mean?

When you use *AutoSum*, you will see a formula similar to the one shown below in the cell.

=SUM(A1:A6)

SUM means that Excel is going to add numbers up. The cell references in brackets show the range of cells which will be included in the addition. The last cell reference (A6 in the example above) should always be a blank cell (see next page).

Always Include A Blank Cell Between The Figures And The Answer

This ensures that if you need to add any more figures to the list you are adding up, the answer will update to include the new information. If you do not leave a blank line, you may end up with an incorrect answer.

What If AutoSum Has Put Flashing Lights Around The Wrong Figures?

1 Ensure that you can still see the flashing lights around the wrong figures (if you can't, click on the cell and click on the **AutoSum** icon again!).

2 Click and drag over the correct figures, remembering to include the blank cell.

3 Press **Enter** or click on the green tick.

What Is A Circular Reference?

A circular reference occurs when the cell which contains the formula is used in the formula. Excel can't give you the answer because the answer is part of the calculation. This can happen when you correct **AutoSum** after it has put flashing lights around the wrong figures, if you have selected the formula cell by mistake. You will see this error message after you confirm the formula.

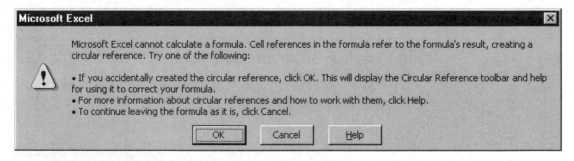

The diagram below shows an example of a spreadsheet with a circular reference.

To correct a circular reference:

1   Click on the cell which contains the formula.

2   Press the **Delete** key.

3   Enter the formula again, without including any reference to the cell which the formula is in!

Typing The Sum Function To Add Numbers Up

The Sum Function

Typing the Sum function gives you exactly the same result as using the **AutoSum** icon. It just means that you type in the formula yourself, rather than getting AutoSum to do it for you. This can save you having to correct AutoSum when it guesses at the wrong cells. Here's how:

1   Select the cell you want to put the answer into.

2   Type =**SUM.**

3   Type an open bracket, like this (.

4   Type in the first cell reference from the list you want to add up.

5   Type a colon, like this :.

6   Type the last cell reference from the list you want to add up (this should be a blank cell).

7   Type a closed bracket, like this).

8   Press **Enter** or click on the green tick.

So if you wanted to add up the cells from cell A2 to D6, you would type in =**SUM(A2:D6).**

Formulae

Formula / Formulae?

Formula is the term used for a calculation in a spreadsheet. The word **formulae** just means more than one formula. One formula, two formulae, three formulae, etc. You can say formulas if you prefer, but the correct word is formulae.

Types Of Calculation

There are four main types of calculation:

Type of calculation	What it is used for
Addition	For adding numbers together, e.g. finding totals.
Subtraction	For finding the difference between two numbers, e.g. subtracting expenses from income.
Multiplication	For multiplying two numbers together. This is commonly used in spreadsheets to find VAT and other percentages – if you see the word **of**, then you need a percentage multiplication: e.g. 20% **of** £100 is 20% multiplied by £100 $^3/_4$ **of** 200 is $^3/_4$ multiplied by 200.
Division	Used when you wish to divide an amount up by another number. For example, finding the amount per month for a loan would involve dividing the total amount of the loan by the number of months you need to repay it.

Addition is usually carried out by using AutoSum or typing the Sum function. If you need to do another sort of calculation, you will have to create a formula as detailed below.

Creating A Formula

1   Click on the cell where you require the answer.

2   Type the = sign.

3   Type the first cell reference you require

    or

    click on the first cell you require – flashing lines will appear around the cell, and the cell reference will be inserted.

4   Type in the mathematical symbol you require (see page 00).

5   Type the next cell reference you require – flashing lines will appear around the cell, and the cell reference will be inserted

or

click on the next cell you require.

6   Press **Enter**

or

click on the green tick to confirm the formula – the answer will appear in the cell, and the formula will appear on the *Formula* bar.

Always Use Cell References In Formulae – And Never Numbers!

Although formulae will still work if you use numbers instead of cell references, it is never advisable. Using cell references means that if the number contained in the cell should change, the formula will update to show the correct answer. So your spreadsheet is always correct!

Mathematical Symbols

➤ Press +   To perform an addition.

➤ Press -   To perform a subtraction.

➤ Press *   To perform a multiplication.

➤ Press /   To perform a division.

Use The Number Keypad!

The easiest way of typing the mathematical symbols is to use the keys around the number pad on the right-hand side of the keyboard. If they don't work, press the **Num Lock** key – the Num Lock light must be on to use these numbers.

Precedence Of Calculation

Calculations are not simply done from left to right, as you might expect. Below is the order in which all calculations are performed:

Priority	Symbol	Explanation
1	( )	Anything in brackets is done before anything outside the brackets is even considered.
2	^	Raises a number in order of magnitude: raises it to the power of something else, e.g. 3^3.
3	* /	Multiply and divide are on the same level. Whichever is the furthest left in the formula is done first.
4	+ -	Plus and minus are on the same level. Whichever is the furthest left is done first.

The acronym for this is **BODMAS**:

*B*rackets *O*rder *D*ivide *M*ultiply *A*dd *S*ubtract

Undo And Redo – A Licence To Make Mistakes

Undo allows you to cancel up to 16 of your previous actions if you have made a mistake. If you then decide that you hadn't really made a mistake after all, you can redo up to 16 things you have undone. But if you keep going backwards and forwards, you might go a bit mad.

Undoing Your Last Action

Click on the **Undo** button.

Or

Press **Ctrl+Z** on the keyboard.

Or

1   Click on the **Edit** menu.

2   Click on **Undo**.

Redoing Your Last Undo

Click on the **Redo** button.

Or

Press **Ctrl+Y** on the keyboard.

Or

1   Click on the **Edit** menu.

2   Click on **Redo**.

Undoing Up To 16 Actions

You Can't Select One Action To Undo

When you undo more than one action, you cannot pick out just one from the previous sixteen actions and undo that alone. In other words, if the action you want to undo was 5 actions ago, you must undo ALL 5 of your last actions.

1   Click on the down arrow next to **Undo** icon.

2   Locate the action(s) you want to undo, scrolling down if necessary.

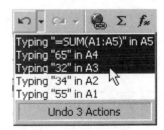

Click on the action you wish to undo from the list.

Redoing Up To 16 Actions

1   Click on the down arrow next to **Redo** icon.

2   Locate the action(s) you wish to redo from the list, scrolling down if necessary.

3   Click on the last action you want to redo.

Correcting Mistakes

Deleting The Contents Of A Cell

1   Click on the cell you wish to delete.

2   Press the **Delete** key.

Or

1   Click on the cell you wish to delete.

2   Click on the **Edit** menu.

3   Click **Clear**.

4   Click **Contents**.

Replacing The Contents Of A Cell

1   Click on the cell you wish to replace.

2   Type in the new text – the original contents will disappear.

Editing The Contents Of A Cell

There are three ways of editing the contents of a cell:

1   Double-click on the cell you wish to edit – a cursor will appear inside the cell.

2   Enter or amend the text.

3   Press **Enter** or click on the green tick.

Or

1   Click on the cell you wish to edit.

2   Press **F2** on the keyboard – a cursor will appear inside the cell.

3   Enter or amend the text.

4   Press **Enter** or click on the green tick.

Or

1   Click on the cell you wish to edit – the *Formula* bar will show the contents of the cell.

2   Click on the text on the *Formula* bar.

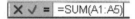

3   Enter or amend the text.

4   Press **Enter** or click on the green tick.

Entering Simple Formulae

The diagrams on the next page show an example formula being entered.

To work out the surplus, we need to do a calculation by taking away the expenditure from the salary. You can see this being entered on the left-hand side. On the right-hand side, you can see what happens after the formula has been entered.

COUNTIF	▼	✗ ✓ =	=B3-B12	
	A	**B**	**C**	
1	*Home Budget*			
2				
3	*Income*	£2,000.00		
4				
5	**Expenditure**			
6	Rent	£ 200.00		
7	Food	£ 150.00		
8	Social	£ 35.00		
9	Bills	£ 50.00		
10	Loan	£ 100.00		
11				
12	*Total*	£ 535.00		
13				
14	*Surplus*	=B3-B12		
15				

B14	▼	=	=B3-B12	
	A	**B**	**C**	
1	*Home Budget*			
2				
3	*Income*	£2,000.00		
4				
5	**Expenditure**			
6	Rent	£ 200.00		
7	Food	£ 150.00		
8	Social	£ 35.00		
9	Bills	£ 50.00		
10	Loan	£ 100.00		
11				
12	*Total*	£ 535.00		
13				
14	*Surplus*	£1,465.00		
15				

How Is The Formula Made Up?

➤ Formulae always start with an equals (=) sign – that's how Excel knows it's a formula.

➤ Cell references are used in the calculation instead of numbers. This means that if the number inside the cell changes, the answer to the formula will update!

➤ A mathematical symbol is used to denote the type of calculation.

Here is the formula from the example above which found us the surplus (or money left over).

Starts with the equals sign

The cell which contains the total expenditure

Cell which contains the income

The subtraction sign

Editing Formulae

What Do The Error Messages Mean?

When something goes wrong with a formula, Excel produces messages that attempt to describe what the problem is:

Error message	What it means
#DIV/0!	You have attempted to divide by zero – make sure all the cells being used in the formula have numbers in them.
#N/A!	Part of your formula is using a cell that does not have information in it, or the information is not yet available.
#NAME?	There is some text in the formula that does not mean anything to Excel. There may be a range name in the formula that Excel does not recognize.
#NULL!	Two areas do not intersect. You may have forgotten to include a comma between two ranges of cells.
#NUM!	You have used text instead of numbers whilst performing a function, or the result of the formula is too big or too small to be shown by Excel.
#REF!	One of the cells being used in the formula does not exist. It may have been deleted after you created the formula.
#VALUE!	A cell containing text has been used in the formula.

You may also see error messages about circular references (see pages 00–00).

Correcting Formulae

1   Select the cell containing the formula.

2   Click on the formula on the *Formula* bar.

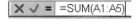

3   Amend the formula as required (see Check This Out below).

4   Press **Enter**

     or

     click on the green tick.

Amending The Formula

You can delete the parts of the formula you do not want with the **Delete** or **Backspace** keys on the keyboard. If you want to enter new cell references, you can either type them in, or click on the cells you require.

Chapter 2

Editing A Worksheet

Drag And Drop

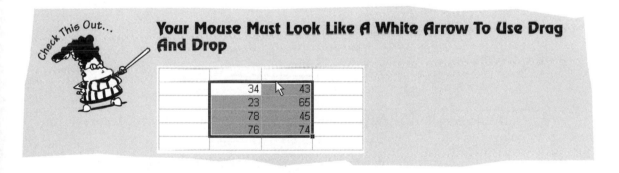

Check This Out...

Your Mouse Must Look Like A White Arrow To Use Drag And Drop

Moving Text With Drag And Drop

1 Select the cells you wish to move.

2 Position your mouse at the edge of the selection – the mouse pointer will change to a white arrow.

3 Click and drag to the new postion – a fuzzy grey line will show you where you are going.

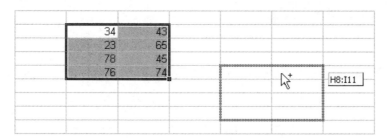

4   Release the mouse when you are in the correct place.

Copying Text With Drag And Drop

1   Select the cells you wish to copy.

2   Position your mouse at the edge of the selection – the mouse will change to a white arrow.

3   Hold down **Ctrl** on the keyboard – a plus sign will appear next to the white arrow.

4   Click and drag to the new position – a fuzzy grey line will show you where you are going.

5   Release the mouse button when you are in the correct place.

6   Release **Ctrl**.

Cut, Copy And Paste

The Clipboard

When you copy or cut anything it is temporarily stored on an area called the clipboard until you need it again. The clipboard can only hold one item at a time, and when you copy or cut a new item it will overwrite what was previously there.

Moving Data

1   Select the cells you wish to move.

2   Click on the **Cut** icon. The selection will have flashing lights around it, and will be moved to the Windows clipboard.

3   Select the cell you wish to move to. This cell will become the top left-hand corner of the cells you cut.

4   Click on the **Paste** icon.

Copying Data

1   Select the cells you wish to copy.

2   Click on the **Copy** icon. The selection will have flashing lights around it, and will be moved to the Windows clipboard.

3   Select the cell you wish to copy to. This cell will become the top left-hand corner of the cells you copied.

4   Click on the **Paste** icon.

You Can Copy More Than One Item Using The Windows Clipboard!

See the section called *Copying or Moving More Than One Thing* on page 167.

Using AutoFill To Copy Text And Formulae

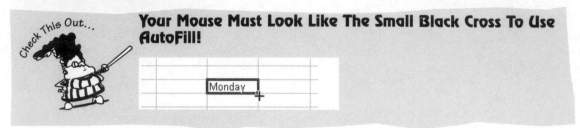

Your Mouse Must Look Like The Small Black Cross To Use AutoFill!

What Is AutoFill?

AutoFill is a quick way of entering standard information onto your spreadsheet, such as the months or days of the week. You can also use it to copy text or formulae very quickly.

Using AutoFill

1   Click on the cell(s) you wish to copy.

2   Position the mouse pointer over the small square at the bottom right-hand corner of the active cell – your mouse pointer will change to a small black cross.

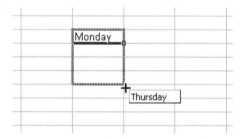

3   Click and drag over the cells you wish to copy to – a fuzzy grey line will appear around the cells, and labels will appear to show you what is being copied.

Make Sure Your Mouse Looks Like The Small Black Cross ...

before you click and drag, otherwise you might get some unexpected results! If you find that you have ended up selecting the cells, deselect and try again. If you find that you have ended up moving the cells somewhere else, click the **Undo** icon and try again.

Special Lists

Certain text works well with AutoFill, such as months, days or dates. Have a look at the examples below, which were all created using AutoFill:

January		Qtr 1		26/07/02
February		Qtr 2		27/07/02
March		Qtr 3		28/07/02
April		Qtr 4		29/07/02
May				30/07/02
June				31/07/02
Monday	Tuesday	Wednesday	Thursday	Friday

Starting The Sequence Off For AutoFill

Sometimes you may want to start off a sequence of numbers or dates for AutoFill, e.g. when you want to enter a list of dates that go from week to week, rather than day to day. To achieve this, you must first start the sequence for AutoFill.

1 Type in the first date or number you require.

2 Type the second date or number you require in the next cell, e.g.

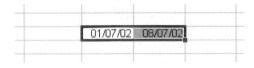

3 Select both of the cells.

4 AutoFill as normal.

	01/07/02	08/07/02	15/07/02	22/07/02	29/07/02	05/08/02

Creating Your Own Custom Lists

1 Click on the **Tools** menu.

2 Click on **Options**.

3 Click on **Custom Lists** tab.

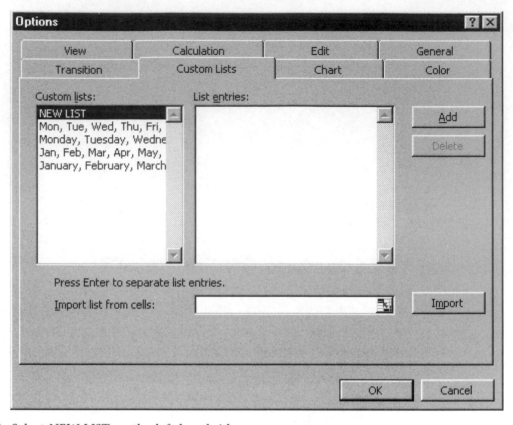

4 Select *NEW LIST* on the left-hand side.

5 Click in the box underneath *List entries*.

6 Type the first entry in your new list.

7 Press **Enter**.

8 Type the next entry in your list.

9 Repeat steps 7 and 8 until your list is finished.

10 Click **Add**.

11 Click **OK**.

Holding Down Ctrl When You AutoFill

If you hold down **Ctrl** when AutoFilling a number, Excel will go up by one number at a time, e.g. 1 2 3, rather than just giving you the same number again and again!

308

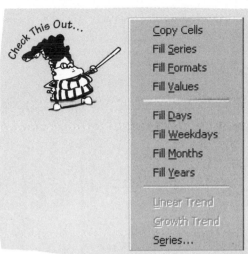

Copy Cells

Fill Series

Fill Formats

Fill Values

Fill Days

Fill Weekdays

Fill Months

Fill Years

Linear Trend

Growth Trend

Series...

Using The Right Mouse Button To AutoFill

Instead of dragging the AutoFill handle with the left mouse button, you can use the right. When you let go, you will be presented with a menu of options that you can pick from (such as creating a sequence of dates that go a month at a time).

Find And Replace

Using Find

1   Select the cells you wish to search, or click in any cell to search the entire sheet.

2   Click on the **Edit** menu.

3   Click on **Find**.

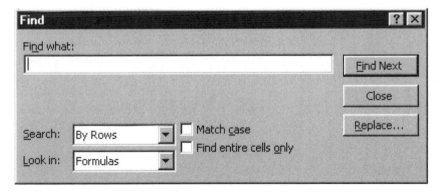

4   Type the text or number you are searching for into the white box.

5   Click **Find Next**.

6   Keep clicking **Find Next** until you have found what you are looking for.

7   Click **Close**.

Find And Replace

1 Select the cells you wish to search, or click in any cell to search the entire sheet.

2 Click on the **Edit** menu.

3 Click on **Replace**.

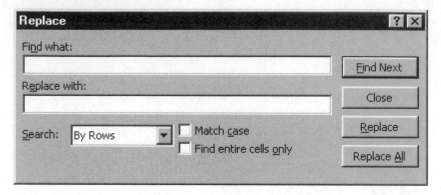

4 Type what you are searching for into the *Find what* box.

5 Type what you want to replace it with into the *Replace with* box.

6 Click **Find Next** and **Replace** to replace individual occurrences.

7 Keep clicking **Find Next** until you have found what you are looking for

or

click **Replace All** to replace all occurrences.

8 Click **Close**.

Checking The Spelling

1 Click on the **Tools** menu.

2 Click **Spelling**.

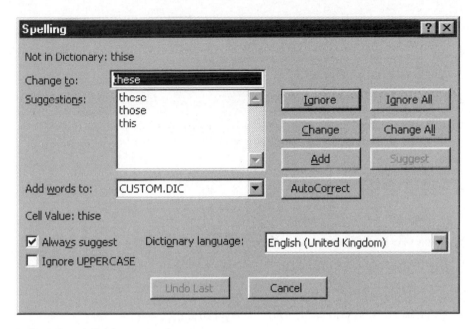

3   When Excel finds a mistake:

click **Ignore** to leave it alone

or

click **Ignore All** to leave all occurrences of this word alone

or

choose a suggested replacement, and click **Change** to correct the spelling

or

choose a suggested replacement, and click **Change All** to correct all the spellings.

4   Keep checking the spellings, or click **Cancel** to finish.

Symbols And Special Characters

Excel cannot insert symbols or special characters. However, you can copy and paste them in from Word or another program.

Inserting Symbols

1 Open Word or another application.

2 Click on the **Insert** menu.

3 Click **Symbol**.

4 Change the font if necessary and click on the symbol you want to insert – a magnified image will appear when you click on a symbol.

5 Click **Insert**.

6 Click on **Close**.

7 Select the symbol you have inserted.

8 Click on the **Edit** menu.

9 Click on **Copy**.

10 Switch back to Excel.

11 Click in the cell you want to put the symbol in.

12 Click on the **Edit** menu.

13 Click **Paste**.

14 Change the font of the cell to the Symbol font (or the font you chose when creating the symbol).

Check This Out...

You Can Also Add Symbols Using The Keyboard

1 Select the cell you wish to add a symbol to.

2 Change the font to Wingdings.

3 Press the shortcut key for the symbol you require.

To find out the shortcut key for the symbol you require:

1 Click on the **Start** menu.

2 Click **Programs**.

3 Click **Accessories**.

4 Click **System Tools**.

5 Click **Character Map**.

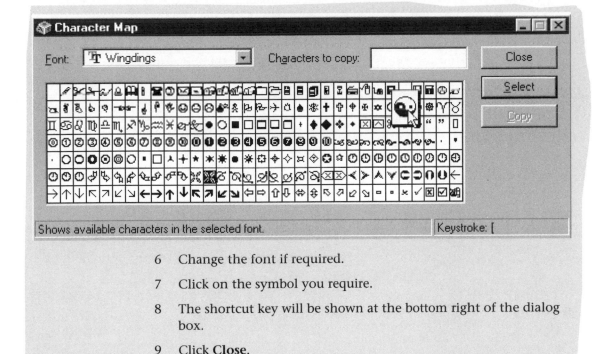

6   Change the font if required.

7   Click on the symbol you require.

8   The shortcut key will be shown at the bottom right of the dialog box.

9   Click **Close**.

You must have Character Map installed in order for this to work!

Sorting

Sorting is usually used to sort a database by one or more of its **fields**, e.g. name, date, cost, etc.

1   Click into any cell in the column you wish to sort (**do not** select the whole column).

2   Click on the **Sort Ascending** icon

or

click on the **Sort Descending** icon.

313

Why Can't I Select The Whole Column?

If you select a column before you sort, only the data in that column moves. The rest of the information on the spreadsheet stays still. If you are working with a database this can cause the information to become mismatched. Have a look at the spreadsheet below:

	A	B	C	D	E
1	Payroll Number	Title	Surname	First Name	Sex
2	5	Mr	Olivelle	Anthony	Male
3	23	Miss	Duck	Caroline	Female
4	19	Mr	Dodgson	Charles	Male
5	26	Mrs	Richards	Anna	Female

You want to sort this spreadsheet by order of sex. If you select column E before you sort (which contains the sex), look at what happens:

	A	B	C	D	E
1	Payroll Number	Title	Surname	First Name	Sex
2	5	Mr	Olivelle	Anthony	Female
3	23	Miss	Duck	Caroline	Female
4	19	Mr	Dodgson	Charles	Male
5	26	Mrs	Richards	Anna	Male

The information in column E gets sorted, but everything else stays in the same place – so Anthony Olivelle in row 2 is apparently female, and Anna Richards in row 5 is apparently male!

What Is The Difference Between Ascending And Descending?

If you are sorting	Ascending means	Descending means
Text	A to Z	Z to A
Numbers	Lowest to highest	Highest to lowest
Dates	Earliest to latest	Latest to earliest

Sorting By More Than One Column

Sometimes you may wish to sort by more than one bit of information. This tends to happen when you have a certain field which people can be *grouped* by, e.g. Department, Gender, etc., and you want to sort them within their groups. The spreadsheet below has been sorted by Department initially, and then within this, people have been sorted by their surname.

	A	B	C
1	**Department**	**Title**	**Surname**
2	Design	Dr	Jekyll
3	Design	Mr	Jospin
4	Design	Miss	Pullen
5	Design	Mrs	Robinson
6	Design	Ms	Sierra de la Guerra
7	Finance	Ms	Corwall
8	Finance	Mr	Hyde
9	Finance	Mrs	Minniver
10	Finance	Miss	Ross
11	Manufacture	Mr	Al Said
12	Manufacture	Miss	Duck
13	Manufacture	Ms	Hull
14	Manufacture	Mr	Scot
15	Manufacture	Mr	Sutherland
16	Manufacture	Dr	Zhivago

1 Click into any cell within the database you wish to sort.

2 Click on the **Data** menu.

3 Click **Sort** – the text in the spreadsheet will become highlighted.

4 Click the down arrow underneath *Sort by*.

5 Click on the field you wish to sort.

6 Click next to *Ascending* or *Descending* for the first field.

7 Click on the down arrow underneath *Then by*.

8 Click on the next field you wish to sort.

9 Click next to *Ascending* or *Descending* for the second field.

10 Enter sort information for a third field if required.

11 Click in the circle next to *Header row* if the fieldnames are held in the top row.

12 Click **OK**.

Inserting, Deleting, Moving And Copying Sheets

Excel files are called **workbooks**. Just like any book they contain several sheets, or pages. To begin with you will only have three, but you can have up to 255 sheets, or delete the ones that you don't need.

Why Have More Than One Sheet?

Imagine that you have to store information about your organization's budget over five years. If you try and put all this information onto one sheet it will become impossible to navigate and find things easily.

If, however, you set up similar sheets for each year, or even for each month, then it becomes a lot easier to find the information you are looking for.

Selecting Sheets

Click on the sheet tab you require – it will become white.

Sheet1

Moving Through The Book

1   Click on the **Sheet Navigation** buttons (see below).

Going from left to right:

➤   Go to the first sheet in the workbook.

➤   Go one sheet to the left.

➤   Go one sheet to the right.

➤   Go to the last sheet in the workbook.

2   Click on the sheet tab you require.

Inserting Sheets

1   Click on the sheet **to the right of** where you want the new sheet to appear.

2   Click on the **Insert** menu.

3   Click **Worksheet**.

Or

1   Right-click on the sheet tab **to the right of** where you want the new sheet to appear – a menu will appear.

2   Click **Insert**.

3   Click **Worksheet**.

4   Click **OK**.

Renaming Sheets

1   Double-click on top of the name on the sheet tab – it will go black.

Sheet1

2   Type in the new name.

3   Press **Enter**.

Or

1   Right-click on the sheet tab – a menu will appear.

2   Click **Rename** – it will go black.

317

3   Type the new name.

4   Press **Enter**.

Deleting Sheets

1   Click on the sheet tab you require.

2   Click on the **Edit** menu.

3   Click **Delete Sheet**.

4   Click **OK**.

Or

1   Right click on the sheet tab – a menu will appear.

2   Click **Delete**.

3   Click **OK**.

Copying Sheets

1   Click on the sheet tab you wish to copy.

2   Click on the **Edit** menu.

3   Click **Move or Copy sheet**.

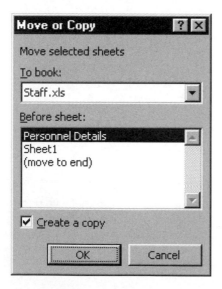

4   Click in the box next to *Create a copy* so that it is ticked.

5   Click on the sheet that you wish to place the copied sheet before

     or

     click (*move to end*).

6   Click **OK**.

Or

1   Click on the sheet tab you wish to copy.

2   Hold down the **Ctrl** key on the keyboard.

3   Click and drag the sheet to its new position.

Moving Sheets

1   Click on the sheet tab you wish to move.

2   Click on the **Edit** menu.

3   Click **Move or Copy sheet**.

4   Ensure that the *Create a copy* box is **not** ticked.

5   Click on the sheet you wish to move the sheet before

     or

     click on (*move to end*).

6   Click **OK**.

Or

Click and drag the sheet tab you require to its new location.

Chapter 3

Functions And Cell References

Using Absolute Cell References

What Are Absolute Cell References?

➤ Formulae usually use **relative cell references**. When you AutoFill a relative cell reference it adjusts as you move down or across (see the section on AutoFilling on page 306). This is, on the whole, what you need in order for your spreadsheet to make sense.

➤ Occasionally, however, you will want one of the cell references to stay the same when it is AutoFilled. A cell reference that does not adjust when it is AutoFilled is an **absolute cell reference**.

The spreadsheet below shows an absolute cell reference in action. Everyone's salary is due to increase by 10%. The first formula, to find Bloggs' new salary, has been created. We multiply his current salary (cell C4) by 10% (cell B1).

D4		▼	=	=C4*B1	
	B	**C**	**D**	**E**	
1	**10%**				
2					
3	*Name*	*Old Salary*	*Increase*		
4	Bloggs	£67,895.00	£6,789.50		
5	Richards	£15,678.00			
6	Dalloway	£26,748.00			
7	Olivelle	£20,000.00			
8	Duck	£12,500.00			
9					

However, everyone's salary is being increased by 10%. If we AutoFill the formula as it is, then the cell reference B1 will be adjusted to B2, then B3, etc., and we'll end up with some funny answers.

	B	C	D
1	**10%**		
2			
3	*Name*	*Old Salary*	*Increase*
4	Bloggs	£67,895.00	=C4*B1
5	Richards	£15,678.00	=C5*B2
6	Dalloway	£26,748.00	=C6*B3
7	Olivelle	£20,000.00	=C7*B4
8	Duck	£12,500.00	=C8*B5

AutoFill has adjusted the reference to the 10% in cell B1.

	B	C	D
1	**10%**		
2			
3	*Name*	*Old Salary*	*Increase*
4	Bloggs	£67,895.00	£6,789.50
5	Richards	£15,678.00	£ -
6	Dalloway	£26,748.00	#VALUE!
7	Olivelle	£20,000.00	#VALUE!
8	Duck	£12,500.00	#VALUE!

The answers don't make sense, because Excel has changed the B1 reference.

We actually need cell B1 to remain constant or **absolute** as it is AutoFilled down. In other words, we need to tell Excel that this is an **absolute cell reference**! The diagrams below show what happens when you make B1 absolute.

	B	C	D
1	**10%**		
2			
3	*Name*	*Old Salary*	*Increase*
4	Bloggs	£67,895.00	=C4*$B$1
5	Richards	£15,678.00	=C5*$B$2
6	Dalloway	£26,748.00	=C6*$B$3
7	Olivelle	£20,000.00	=C7*$B$4
8	Duck	£12,500.00	=C8*$B$5

B1 stays the same all the way down.

	B	C	D
1	**10%**		
2			
3	*Name*	*Old Salary*	*Increase*
4	Bloggs	£67,895.00	£6,789.50
5	Richards	£15,678.00	£1,567.80
6	Dalloway	£26,748.00	£2,674.80
7	Olivelle	£20,000.00	£2,000.00
8	Duck	£12,500.00	£1,250.00

Now the answers make sense!

Creating Absolute Cell References

1   Click on the cell where you require the answer.

2   Enter the formula as normal.

3   Position the cursor next to the cell reference which you need to make absolute.

4   Press **F4** on the keyboard – dollar signs will appear around the cell reference.

=C4*$B$1

5   Press **Enter** or click on the green tick.

6   AutoFill the formula as normal.

Existing Formulae Can Be Changed To Have Absolute Cell References

Just edit the contents of the cell (see page 298), and follow the instructions from step 3 above!

Not Sure Whether You Need An Absolute Cell Reference?

Absolute cell references are only needed when you want to AutoFill formulae. If you aren't sure, just AutoFill your formula and see if it works. If you find that you are getting strange answers, you may very well need an absolute cell reference.

Finding The Average

What Are Functions?

Some calculations can become a bit long-winded if you try to create them with straightforward formulae, such as finding the average of a group of numbers. Functions let you quickly perform complex calculations, like finding the average of a group of cells.

Finding The Average

1   Select the cell where you want to put the answer.

2   Type =.

3   Type **Average**.

4   Type an open bracket, like this (.

5   Type the first cell reference you require.

6   Type a colon, like this :.

7   Type the last cell reference you require – this should be a blank cell.

8   Type a closed bracket, like this).

9   Press **Enter**

or

click on the green tick.

e.g. = **AVERAGE(A1:A6)**

Chapter 4

Printing Workbooks

Print Preview And Printing A Worksheet

What Is Print Preview?

There are two views in Excel:

➤ **Normal View:** used for the majority of the time you are working with Excel.

➤ **Print Preview:** used to show you how the spreadsheet will print out.

Print Preview is especially important in Excel, as Normal View does not give you a clear indication of where your pages begin or end, or whether there is page numbering, etc.

Getting A Print Preview

Click on the **Print Preview** icon – a new toolbar will appear.

Or

1   Click on the **File** menu.

2   Click **Print Preview** – a new toolbar will appear.

Moving Between Pages In Print Preview

You can see how many pages will print out at the bottom left of the screen.

Click on **Next** or **Previous** to move through the pages.

Or

Use the scroll bar on the right of the screen.

Using The Zoom In Print Preview

1   Position the mouse pointer over the page – it will change to a magnifying glass.

2   Click once with the left mouse button – if you are zoomed out, you will zoom in, and if you are zoomed in, you will zoom out.

Or

Click on **Zoom**.

Printing From Print Preview

1   Click on the **Print** button.

2   Click **OK**.

Closing Print Preview

Click on the **Close** button.

Printing A Worksheet

Click on the **Print** icon.

326

Be Patient With Your Printer!

Sometimes it can take a while for your spreadsheet to print out, and it is tempting to click the **Print** icon again. If you do, you will get two copies!

Printing Ranges And More Than One Copy

Printing Selections

1 Select the cells you wish to print.

2 Click on the **File** menu.

3 Click **Print**.

4 Click in the circle next to *Selection* underneath *Print what*.

5 Click **OK**.

Printing More Than One Copy

1 Click on the **File** menu.

2 Click **Print**.

3 Change the number of copies to the number you require (see below).

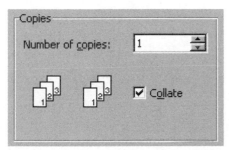

➤ Use the up and down arrows to change the number of copies, or click into the box and type in the number of copies you require.

➤ Tick *Collate* if you require the copies to come out in the page order 1, 2, 3, page 1, 2, 3, etc.

➤ Do not tick *Collate* if you require the copies to come out in the order page 1, page 1, page 2, page 2, etc.

4   Click **OK**.

Printing The Entire Workbook

1   Click on the **File** menu.

2   Click **Print**.

3   Click in the circle next to *Entire workbook* underneath *Print what*.

4   Click **OK**.

Changing The Page Setup

Opening The Page Setup

There are two ways of getting into Page Setup – through Print Preview, or from the Normal View. Going to Page Setup from Print Preview means that you can see how your changes have affected the spreadsheet. If you go from Normal View, you will not be able to see the changes.

From Print Preview:

Click on the **Setup** button.

From Normal view:

1   Click on the **File** menu.

2   Click **Page Setup**.

Changing The Margins

If you need to make a bit of extra room on your page, you might want to make the margins a bit smaller:

1 Bring up the *Page Setup* dialog box (see above).

2 Click on the **Margins** tab.

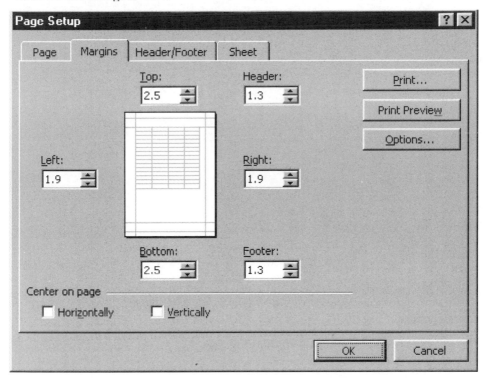

3 Type the margins you require into the boxes

or

use the up and down arrows next to the margin sizes.

Changing The Margins From Print Preview

1 Click on the **Margins** button.

2 Position your mouse pointer over the margin you wish to resize – the pointer will change to a cross arrow (the dotted lines represent the margins).

3   Click and drag the lines to change the margins.

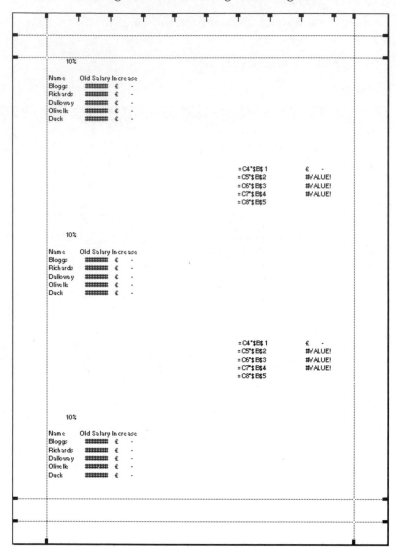

Centring The Spreadsheet On The Page

1   Bring up the *Page Setup* dialog box (see page 328).

2   Click on the **Margins** tab.

3   Click inside the box next to *Horizontally*, so that it is ticked.

4   Click inside the box next to *Vertically*, so that it is ticked.

330

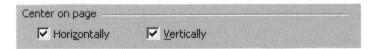

5   Click **OK**.

Changing The Orientation

1   Bring up the *Page Setup* dialog box (see page 328).

2   Click on the **Page** tab.

3   Click in the circle next to *Portrait* or *Landscape*.

4   Click **OK**.

Scaling The Size of a Spreadsheet

If your spreadsheet is too big to fit on the page, or it is too small to read, you can scale it up or down in size.

1   Bring up the *Page Setup* dialog box (see page 328).

2   Click on the **Page** tab.

3   Increase or decrease the percentage next to *Adjust to*.

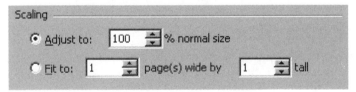

Or

If you want to fit the sheet onto one or more pages:

Click on *Fit to*.

Enter the number of pages you would like to adjust it to.

4   Click **OK**.

Printing The Gridlines

1   Bring up the *Page Setup* dialog box (see page 328).

2   Click on the **Sheet** tab.

3   Click in the box next to *Gridlines* so that it is ticked.

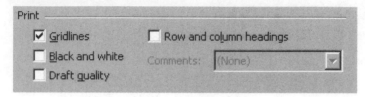

4   Click **OK**.

Changing The Page Order

1   Bring up the *Page Setup* dialog box (see page 328).

2   Click on the **Sheet** tab.

3   Choose the option you require underneath *Page order*.

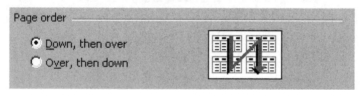

4   Click **OK**.

Changing The Paper Size

1   Bring up the *Page Setup* dialog box (see page 328).

2   Click on the **Page** tab.

3   Choose the paper size you require from the drop down list next to *Paper size*.

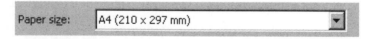

4   Click **OK**.

Using Help In Excel

Excel comes with an animated Office Assistant to help you if you get stuck. This works in exactly the same way as the assistant in Word – see the Office Assistant section in the Word module for more details.

Creating Headers And Footers

What Are Headers And Footers?

➤ Headers and footers contain information which appears at the top and bottom of every page of your spreadsheet when it is printed.

➤ They usually include things like the date, the name of the file, your organization name, page numbers, etc.

➤ You can only see headers and footers in *Print Preview*.

Creating Headers And Footers

1   Bring up the *Page Setup* dialog box (see page 328).

2   Click on the **Header/Footer** tab.

3   Click on the drop-down arrow underneath *Header*.

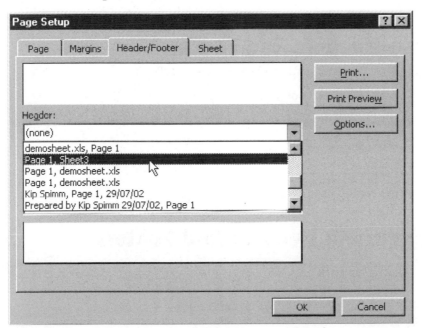

4   Click on the header you require.

5   Click on the drop-down arrow underneath *Footer*.

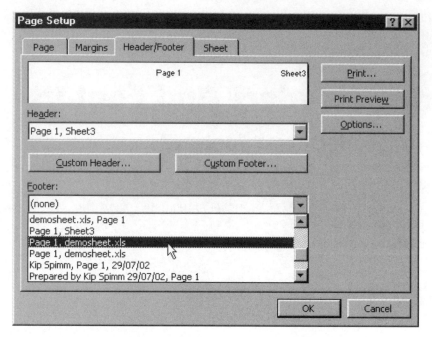

6   Click on the footer you require.

7   Click **OK**.

Removing Headers And Footers

1   Bring up the *Page Setup* dialog box (see page 328).

2   Click on the **Header/Footer** tab.

3   Click on the drop down arrow underneath *Header* or underneath *Footer*.

4   Scroll to the top of the list.

5   Click (*none*).

6   Click **OK**.

Creating Custom Headers And Footers

If you want a bit more flexibility, you will need to customize your headers and footers.

1   Bring up the *Page Setup* dialog box (see page 328).

2   Click on the **Header/Footer** tab.

3   Click **Custom Header**.

or

click **Custom Footer**.

4   Click into the section you require.

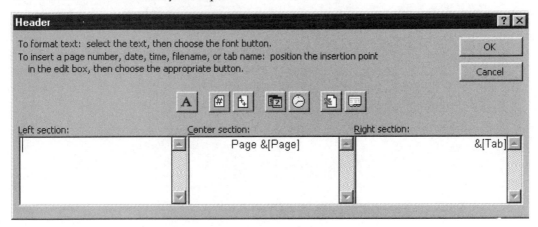

5   Enter the text you require

or

click on one of the icons shown to enter text (see below).

6   Click **OK**.

7   Click **OK**.

Going from left to right, here is what the icons mean:

➤ Change the font.
➤ Insert the page number.
➤ Insert the number of pages.
➤ Insert the date.
➤ Insert the time.
➤ Insert the file name.
➤ Insert the sheet name.

335

What Do The Codes Mean?

When you enter information from the toolbar, such as the date, you will see a code rather than the actual information, e.g. &[PAGES] for number of pages, and &[TAB] for the name of the sheet.

When you look at your spreadsheet in Print Preview, or print it out, however, the real information will appear!

Chapter 5

Formatting Worksheets

Inserting And Deleting Rows And Columns

Inserting A Row

1. Select the row **below** where you want a new one.

2. Click on the **Insert** menu.

3. Click **Rows** – a new row will be inserted above the selection.

Or

1. Select the row **below** where you want a new one.

2. Press **Ctrl** and + on the keyboard.

	A	B
1	Fishcakes	
2	Monkeysuits	
3	Stoat polishers	
4	Cheese wobblers	
5	Egg spanners	
6	Chicken dancers	
7		

	A	B
1	Fishcakes	
2	Monkeysuits	
3	Stoat polishers	
4	Cheese wobblers	
5		
6	Egg spanners	
7	Chicken dancers	

If you select row 5 ...   *... a new row is inserted above row 5.*

Inserting A Column

1   Select the column to the **right** of where you want a new one.

2   Click on the **Insert** menu.

3   Click **Columns** – a new column will be inserted to the left of the selection.

Or

1   Select the column to the **right** of where you want a new one.

2   Press **Ctrl** and **+** on the keyboard.

	A	B	C
1	Fishcakes	5	
2	Monkeysuits	10	
3	Stoat polishers	15	
4	Cheese wobblers	20	
5	Egg spanners	25	
6	Chicken dancers	30	

	A	B	C
1	Fishcakes		5
2	Monkeysuits		10
3	Stoat polishers		15
4	Cheese wobblers		20
5	Egg spanners		25
6	Chicken dancers		30

If you select column B ...   *... a new column is inserted to the left of column B.*

Inserting Several Rows And Columns

If you want to insert several rows or columns, you can do them all at once. Let's look at how you would insert six rows:

1   Select six rows **below** where you want the six new ones.

2   Click on the **Insert** menu.

3   Click **Rows** – six new rows will be inserted above the selection.

Or

1   Select six rows **below** where you want the six new ones.

2   Press **Ctrl** and **+** on the keyboard.

Inserting columns works the same way – select six columns to the right of where you want the new ones, click on the **Insert** menu, and click **Column** (or select the columns and use **Ctrl** and **+**).

Deleting Rows And Columns

1   Select the row(s) or column(s) you wish to delete.

2   Click on the **Edit** menu.

3   Click **Delete**.

Or

1   Select the row(s) or column(s) you wish to delete.

2   Press **Ctrl** and – on the keyboard.

Pressing Delete On The Keyboard Doesn't Work!

This will only delete any text that the row or column contains, rather than the row or column itself.

Resizing Rows And Columns

To Resize Columns Or Rows ...

Your mouse must look like the cross arrow. You can only see this if you position your mouse on the grey line between column letters or row numbers.

Resizing Rows And Columns

1   Position your mouse on the grey line to the right of the column letter you wish to resize

or

position your mouse on the grey line below the row number you wish to resize.

2   Click and drag to the size you require.

If You Make A Column Too Narrow For The Text It Contains ...

You will see hash signs (#) inside the cells. If you make the column a bit wider, you'll be able to read the text clearly again.

Using AutoFit

AutoFit will make a column or row just big enough for the information it contains.

1   Position your mouse on the grey line to the right of the column letter you wish to resize

or

position your mouse on the grey line below the row number you wish to resize.

2   Double-click.

Resizing Several Rows Or Columns At Once

1   Select the rows or columns you wish to resize.

2   Place your mouse on the grey line at the right-hand edge of the selected columns

or

place your mouse on the grey line underneath the selected rows.

3   Click and drag to the required size – all columns and rows will become that size.

Resizing All The Columns And Rows

1   Select the whole of the spreadsheet (see page 290).

2   Resize column *A* to the desired size

and/or

resize row *1* to the desired size.

3   Click in the middle of the spreadsheet to deselect.

Changing The Font And Font Size

What Is Formatting?

Formatting is changing the appearance of your spreadsheet, either to give emphasis to important parts, or to make it easier to read.

Common types of formatting are: **bold**, *italic*, underline, font (or typeface), size, borders and shading .

Applying Bold

1   Select the cell(s) you wish to make bold.

2   Click on the **Bold** icon – the **Bold** icon will look 'pushed in'.

Applying Italic

1   Select the cell(s) you wish to make italic.

2   Click on the **Italic** icon – the **Italic** icon will look 'pushed in'.

Applying Underline

1   Select the cell(s) you wish to underline.

2   Click on the **Underline** icon – the **Underline** icon will look 'pushed in'.

Removing Bold, Italic Or Underline

1   Select the cell(s) you wish to remove bold, italic or underline from.

2   Click on the **Bold**, **Italic** or **Underline** icon to remove it.

Changing The Font Size

1   Select the cell(s) you wish to change.

2   Click on the drop-down arrow in the *Font Size* box.

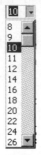

3   Click on the size you require – you may need to scroll through the sizes.

Or

1   Select the cell(s) you wish to change.

2   Click inside the *Font Size* box – the font size number will go blue.

3   Type in the size you require.

4   Press **Enter**.

Changing The Font

1   Select the cell(s) you wish to change.

2   Click on the drop-down arrow next to the *Font* box.

3   Click on the font you require – you may need to scroll through the fonts.

Or

1   Select the cell(s) you wish to change.

2   Click inside the *Font* box – the Font name will go blue.

3   Type in the name of the font you require.

4   Press **Enter**.

Changing The Font Colour

1   Select the cell(s) you wish to change.

2   Click on the drop-down arrow next to the **Font Color** icon.

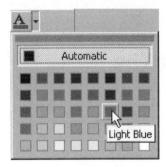

3   Click on the colour you require.

4   Deselect the cells – the colour may look strange until you deselect.

Changing The Number Format

What Are Number Formats?

When you enter numbers they are usually unformatted. They may, however, represent money or a percentage. In order to make them look like what they represent, you can apply a number format to them. Common number formats include:

➤ Currency
➤ Percentage
➤ Commas
➤ Dates
➤ Displaying negative numbers in red.

343

Applying Number Formats

1   Select the cell(s) you wish to change.

2   Click on the number format you require (see below).

Going from left to right, here is what each icon means:

➤ Currency

➤ Percentage

➤ Commas

➤ Increase decimal places

➤ Decrease decimal places.

Changing Number Formats With The Menu

Changing number formats with the menu gives you a much greater choice of formats.

1   Select the cell(s) you wish to change.

2   Click on the **Format** menu.

3   Click **Cells**.

4   Click on the **Number** tab.

5   Click on the category you require from the left-hand side.

6   Click on the style you require on the right – each category has different options, e.g. date.

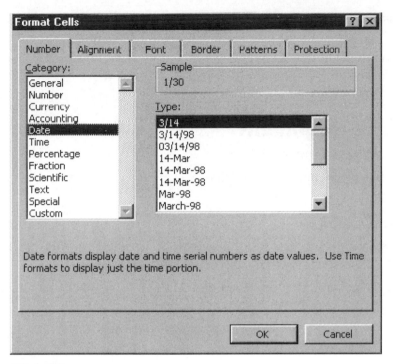

7   Click **OK**.

Removing Number Formats

1   Select the cell(s) you wish to remove number formats from.

2   Click on the **Edit** menu.

3   Click on the **Clear** sub-menu.

4   Click **Formats**.

Changing The Alignment

What Is Alignment?

Alignment refers to the position of data inside the cell. There are three main types in Excel:

➤ **Left** (usually for text)

➤ **Right** (usually for numbers)

➤ **Centre** (usually for headings)

Changing The Alignment

1   Select the cell(s) you wish to change.

2   Click on the alignment icon you require.

Merge And Center

Centre align will only centre text inside a column. Sometimes, however, you may require a heading to be centred in the middle of several cells.

1   Select the cell containing the text, and the cells you wish to put it in the middle of.

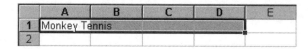

2   Click on the **Merge and Center** icon.

The cells have been merged together, and the heading is now centred.

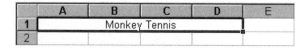

Removing Merge And Center

1   Select the cell that has been merged.

2   Click on the **Format** menu.

3   Click **Cells**.

4   Click on the **Alignment** tab.

5   Remove the tick next to *Merge cells*.

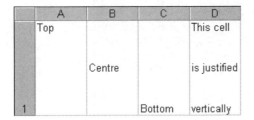

Vertical Alignment

If you have tall rows, you may wish to change the vertical alignment (top, centre, bottom, justify) rather than the horizontal (left, centre, right). Look at these cells:

	A	B	C	D
	Top			This cell
		Centre		is justified
1			Bottom	vertically

They have been aligned vertically. Cell A1 has the text at the top, B1 has it in the centre, and C1 has it at the bottom. Cell D1 is vertically justified, which means that the text is spaced out so that it touches the top and bottom of the cell.

1   Select the cell(s) you want to change.

2   Click on the **Format** menu.

3   Click **Cells**.

4   Click on the **Alignment** tab.

5   Click on the drop-down arrow under the *Vertical* box.

6   Click on the alignment you require.

7   Click **OK**.

Applying Borders

What Are Borders?

The lines that you can see around the cells in your spreadsheet don't necessarily print out. They are known as **gridlines**. If you want lines to print out, or you need to add decorative lines to your spreadsheet, then you can use **borders** to format it.

Applying Borders With The Icon

1   Select the cell(s) you wish to apply a border to.

2   Click on the arrow next to the **Borders** icon.

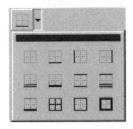

3 Click on the border style you require.

4 Deselect the cells – you can't see the border if the cells are still selected!

Drag The Border Styles Off The Toolbar

If you are applying a lot of borders, you can display the border choices permanently. Click the border arrow and then drag the border styles down using the grey bar at the top. It will become a mini toolbar.

Careful Which Cells You Select!

Sometimes you have to think carefully about which cells to select. Imagine that you want to add a double line above the selection of cells shown below.

10	Loan	£ 100.00	
11			
12	*Total*	**£ 535.00**	
13			
14	*Surplus*	£1,465.00	
15			

There is no option for adding a double line above, only one for adding a double line below:

However, if you select the cells in row 11 above the total, you can apply a double line below those. This has the same effect as applying a double line to the top of the cells containing the total.

10	Loan	£ 100.00	
11			
12	*Total*	£ 535.00	
13			
14	*Surplus*	£1,465.00	
15			

349

Applying Borders With The Menu

1   Select the cell(s) you wish to apply a border to.

2   Click on the **Format** menu.

3   Click **Cells**.

4   Click on the **Border** tab.

5   Click on the line style you require from the right-hand side.

6   Click on the drop-down arrow underneath *Color* and click on a different colour, if required.

7   Click on the **Border** icons to set the borders you require.

8   Click **OK**.

Removing Borders

1   Select the cells you wish to remove the borders from.

2   Click on the arrow next to the **Borders** icon.

3   Click on the *No Border* style.

Rotating Text

Rotating Text

You can use rotation if you want text to appear diagonally or vertically inside a cell. You can also use it if your monitor is crooked, although it's better just to get it fixed.

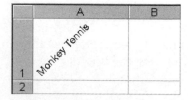

1   Select the cell(s) you wish to rotate.

2   Click on the **Format** menu.

3   Click **Cells**.

4   Click on the **Alignment** tab.

5   Change the rotation using the *Orientation* section.

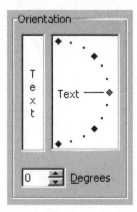

➤ Click on the vertical text in the first white box to make the text vertical.

➤ Click and drag the line in the second white box to change the angle of the text.

➤ Use the up or down arrows next to the *Degrees* box to change the angle, or type in the angle you want.

6   Click **OK**.

Chapter 6

Charts

Creating Charts

Creating a chart makes it easier to compare and contrast the figures in a spreadsheet.
Charts are also sometimes called graphs.

Which Chart Should I Use?

Area chart

Use this when you want to emphasise change over time.

 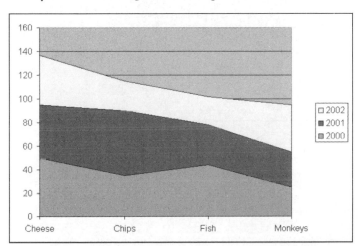

3-D surface

A surface chart is a bit like a 3-D map. Colours and patterns show areas that are in the same range of values.

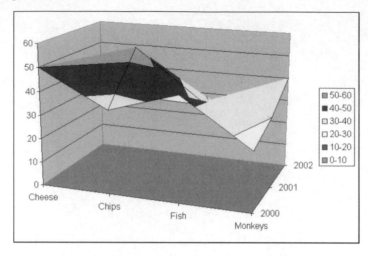

Bar chart

A bar chart simply compares values with each other, by displaying them as lines, or 'bars'.

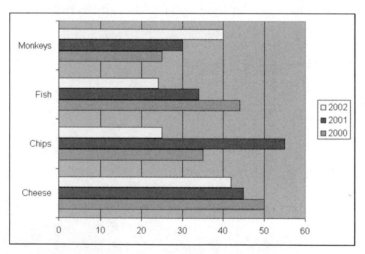

Radar chart

In this chart, each type of information has its own line radiating out from the centre. The further the line comes out from the centre, the higher the value.

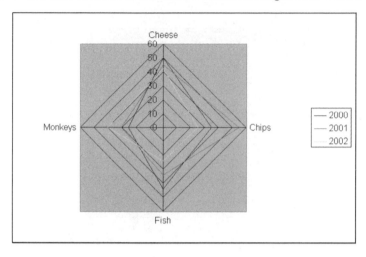

Column chart

A column chart is the same as a bar chart, except the bars are vertical instead of horizontal.

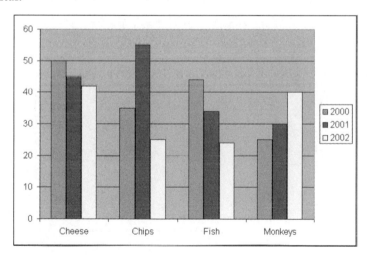

Bubble chart

A bubble chart shows three sets of variables, represented by the two axes and the size of the bubble. The bigger the bubble, the higher the value.

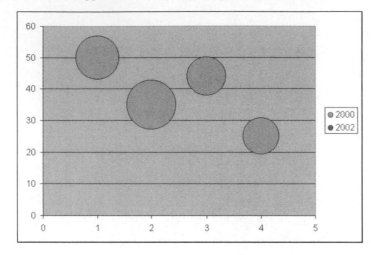

Line chart

A line chart is useful for comparing overlapping figures.

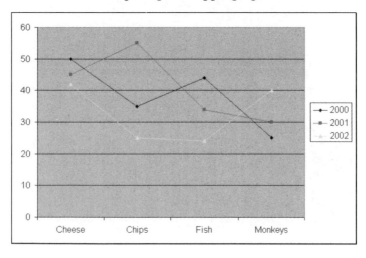

356

Scatter graph

A scatter graph is useful for comparing data with the average or estimated values. This type of chart is usually used for displaying scientific data.

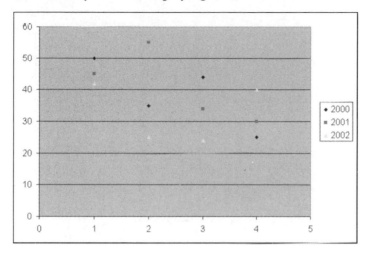

Pie chart

A pie chart is useful for showing one set of figures clearly.

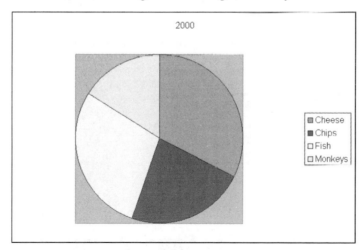

Doughnut chart

A doughnut chart is similar to a pie chart, but it can show more than one set of figures – each ring of the doughnut represents a set of figures.

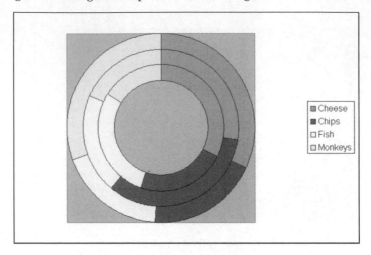

Creating Charts With The Keyboard

1 Select the cells you wish to chart – include labels and figures, but do **not** select whole rows or columns.

In this example, the types of product are selected, as are the years, and the numbers themselves:

	2000	2001	2002
Cheese	50	45	42
Chips	35	55	25
Fish	44	34	24
Monkeys	25	30	40

2 Press **F11** to create the chart.

Creating Charts With The Chart Wizard

1 Select the cells to be charted – include labels and figures, but do **not** select whole columns and rows.

358

2   Click on the **Chart Wizard** icon

3   In step 1 of the wizard, choose the chart type you require.

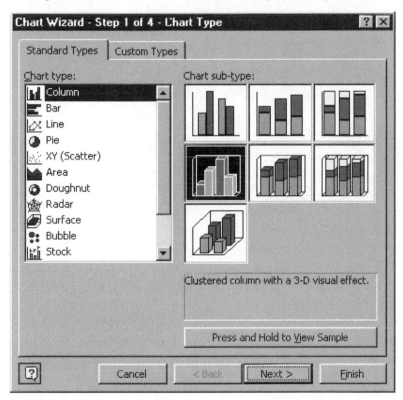

Choose a chart type from the list on the left, then choose a chart format from the examples shown on the right. To see an example of the chart you have selected, click and hold down the mouse button on the **Press and hold to view sample** button.

4   Click on **Next**.

5   In step 2 of the wizard, check that the cells you selected have produced the expected chart.

359

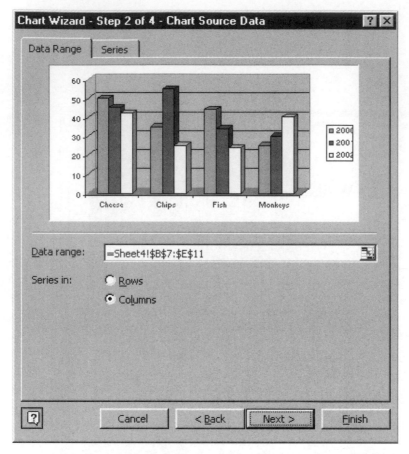

➤ The large area at the top shows you how your chart will look.

➤ The *Data range* box shows you what cells you have selected.

➤ Change the *Series in* section to decide whether the chart uses the rows or columns from your cells.

6 Click on **Next**.

7 In step 3 of the wizard, change the chart options if required (see below).

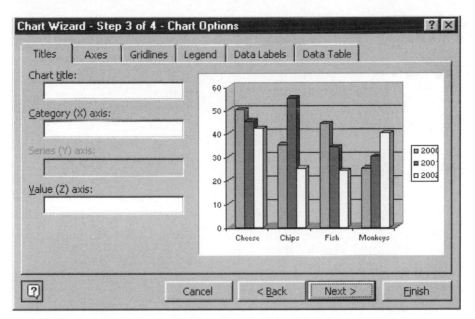

➤ Click on the **Titles** tab to add titles to the axes or to the whole chart.

➤ Click on the **Axes** tab to change the scale of the axes.

➤ Click on the **Gridlines** tab to choose whether to show major or minor gridlines.

➤ Click on the **Legend** tab to decide the position of the legend (the chart key) on the chart.

➤ Click on the **Data Labels** tab to show values or percentages around the bars.

➤ Click on the **Data Table** tab to include a table of the figures you have charted.

8　Click on **Next**.

9　In step 4 of the wizard, decide whether you wish your chart to appear on a new sheet or as an object next to your figures.

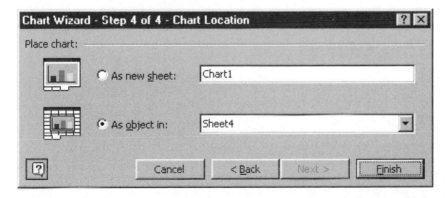

10　Click on **Finish**.

361

Moving, Resizing And Deleting Charts

This only applies to charts which have been created using the wizard, that are on a sheet as an object.

Moving Charts

1   Click on the white area of the chart to select it – black boxes will appear around the edge.

2   Click and drag from the middle of the chart to a new location – your mouse should look like a white arrow.

Resizing Charts

1   Click on the chart to select it – black boxes will appear around the edge.

2   Hover the mouse pointer over a box – your mouse pointer will change to a double-headed arrow.

3   Click and drag to make the chart larger or smaller.

Your Mouse Must Look Like A Double Headed Arrow To Resize A Chart!

Like this:

Deleting Charts

1   Click on the white area of the chart to select it – black boxes will appear around the edge.

2   Press the **Delete** key.

Formatting Charts

Selecting Parts Of A Pie Chart

Black Boxes Appear Around The Part Of The Chart That Is Selected!

Click on the part of the chart you wish to select (see below).

Or

Use the *Chart* toolbar (see page 374).

If You Want To Select One Piece Of Pie ...

You may have to click on it twice. When you first click, you will probably get the whole pie, but if you click again on the piece you want, you will get just that bit.

Selecting Parts Of A Bar Chart

Black Boxes Appear Around The Part Of The Chart That Is Selected!

Click on the part of the chart you wish to select.

Or

Use the *Chart* toolbar (see page 374).

Formatting Part Of A Chart

The instructions below describe how to format parts of charts in general. The options are different depending on which part you select.

1   Select the part of the chart you wish to change.

2   Click on the **Format** menu.

3   Click **Selected (name of part of chart you have selected)** – for example, if you have selected the bars, the option will be **Selected Data Series**.

4   Change the options as required.

Or

1   Select the part of the chart you wish to change.

2   Click **Format** icon on *Chart* toolbar (see page 374).

Formatting A Piece Of Pie

1   Select the piece of pie you wish to change.

2   Click on the **Format** menu.

3   Click **Selected Data Point**.

4   Change the options as required (see below).

364

If you want to change the borders and fill colour, see the section on changing the colours in a chart on page 371.

If you want to change the labels around a piece of pie, click on the **Data Labels** tab.

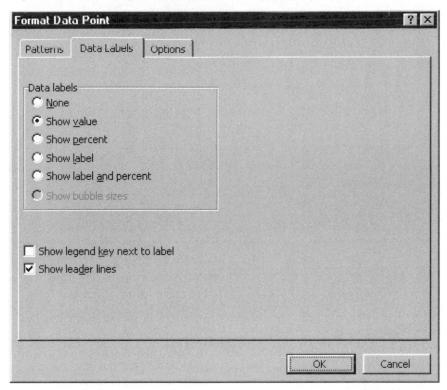

➤ Click in the circle next to the data label you wish to show.

➤ Click *Show legend key next to label* to label the piece of pie with its colour in the legend.

➤ Click *Show leader lines* to have a line from the label to the piece of pie.

To rotate the pie chart, click on the **Options** tab, and change the number inside the *Angle of first slice* box, or use the arrows to increase or decrease the angle.

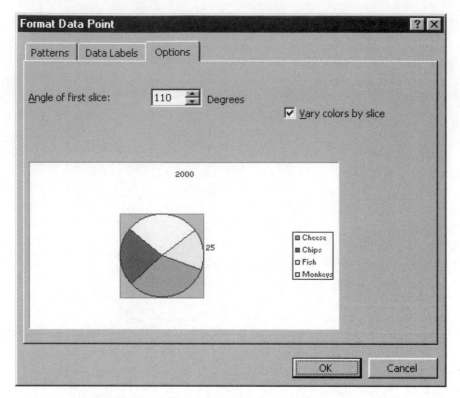

Formatting The Chart Background

1   Select the white chart background (or *Chart Area* fron the *Chart* toolbar).

2   Click on the **Format** menu.

3   Click **Selected Chart Area**.

4   Change the options as required (see below).

➤ If you want to change the borders and fill colour, see the section on page 371.

➤ If you want to change the font, see the section on page 372.

Formatting Axes

1   Select the axis you require.

2   Click on the **Format** menu.

3   Click **Selected Axis**.

4   Change the options as required (see pages 367–71).

Changing the Line Styles

You can change the type of lines that make up the axes, and the little tick marks that divide up the values. Click on the **Patterns** tab:

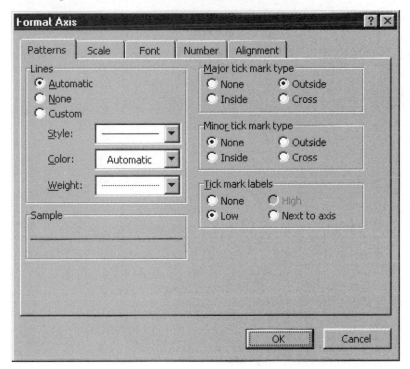

➤ Click in the circle next to the axis option you require – *Automatic* chooses them for you, *None* removes them, *Custom* lets you define your own.

➤ Click the drop-down arrows to change *Style*, *Color* or thickness (*Weight*) of the line.

➤ *Major* and *Minor tick marks* are the little dividing lines on the axis, like those on a ruler – the Major ones are the bigger ones, the Minor ones are the smaller ones.

➤ The *Tick mark label* is the text that runs along the axis, telling you what the values or the categories are.

Changing the Scale

The scale affects the distance between the numbers on the axes, and the size of your chart. For example, you might have numbers varying between 10 and 70, but you might want the chart to go up to 100, or only 80. The same chart is shown on the next page with a maximum of 60, then 100, to show the effect changing the scale can have.

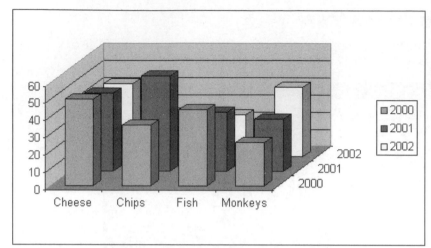

In this example, the chart axis goes to 60, which is just above the highest value.

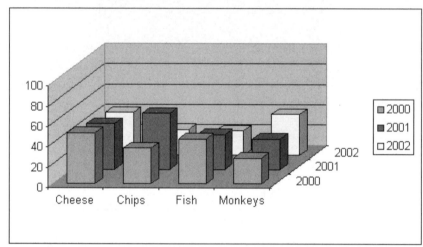

Here, the scale of the axis has been changed. It now goes up to 100, which makes the values look smaller.

Click on the **Scale** tab to change the scale – you will get different options depending on which axis you choose.

➤ *Minimum* and *Maximum*: the highest and lowest numbers you require on the axis.

➤ *Major* and *Minor*: the interval you require between the labels on the axis.

➤ *Floor (XY plane) Crosses at*: the number where you want the two axes to cross over – this is usually set to 0.

➤ *Number of categories between tick-mark labels*: the number of labels you require – entering a value of **1** will label every category.

➤ *Number of categories between tick marks*: the number of tick marks you require.

If you want to change the font, see the section on page 372.

368

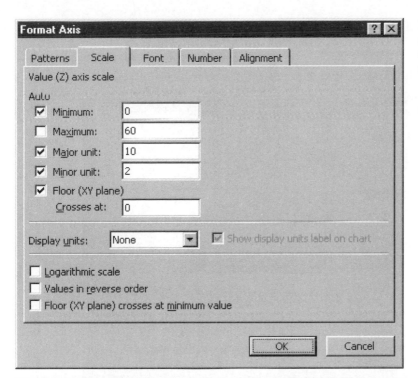

This shows the options you can change in a numbered axis.

This shows the options you can change in a text or other non-numbered axis.

Changing the Number Format

1   Click on the **Number** tab.

2   Click on the *Category* you require from the list on the left.

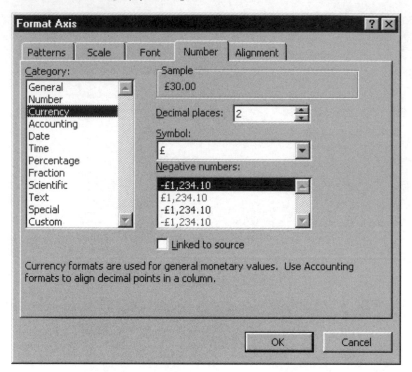

3   Change the options as required on right – there are different options for different
     categories.

For More Information About Number Formats

See the *Number Formats* section on page 343.

370

Changing the Alignment

Click on the **Alignment** tab.

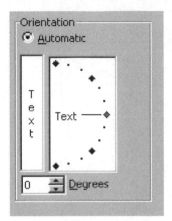

> ➤ Click on the vertical text in the white box on the left to make the text vertical.

> ➤ Click and drag the line in the white box on the right until you get the angle you want, or use the up and down arrows in the **Degrees** box to change it.

Changing The Colours In A Chart

1   Select the part of the chart you wish to change.

2   Click on the **Format** menu.

3   Click **Selected (name of part of selected chart)**.

4   Click on the **Patterns** tab.

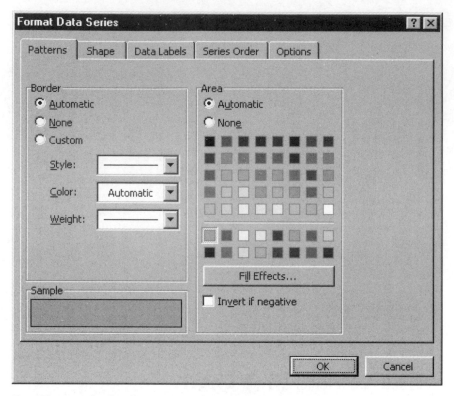

5   Change the border options from the *Border* section:

➤ *Automatic* chooses them for you, *None* removes them, *Custom* lets you define your own.

➤ For *Custom* borders, use the drop-down arrows to create them – *Style* lets you choose the type of line, *Color* changes the colour, and *Weight* changes the thickness.

6   Choose the colour in the *Area* section to change the fill colour – just click on the colour you like.

7   Click **OK**.

Changing The Fonts In A Chart

You can only change the font in a part of the chart that contains text – for example, you can't change the font on the background, because it doesn't have text to change. To change the font:

1   Select the part of the chart you wish to change.

2   Click on the **Format** menu.

3   Click **Selected (part of chart you wish to change)**.

4   Click on the **Font** tab:

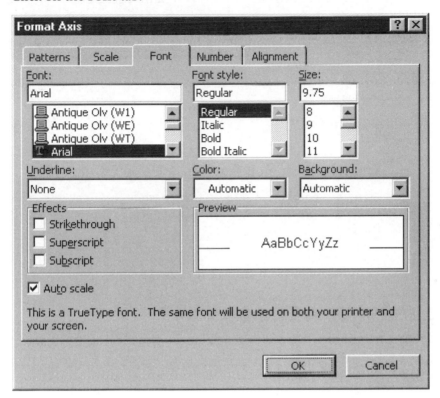

➤ *Font*: changes the font.

➤ *Font style*: changes the font style, i.e. bold, italic, etc.

➤ *Size*: changes the font size.

➤ *Underline*: changes the underline style – single, double, dottcd, etc.

➤ *Color*: changes the text colour.

➤ *Background*: decides whether the background of the text box is transparent (see-through) or opaque (not see-through).

➤ *Effects*: lets you apply special effects like ~~strikethrough~~, superscript, and subscript.

5   Make any changes you require.

6   Click **OK**.

Resizing Parts Of A Chart

Only certain parts of a chart can be resized. If you cannot get a double-headed arrow, then you cannot resize.

1   Select the part of the chart you wish to change – black boxes will appear around the selected part.

2   Position the mouse pointer over a black box – the mouse pointer will change to a double-headed arrow.

3   Click and drag to resize.

Check This Out...

Choose Which Box You Resize From Carefully!

Boxes at a corner will allow you to resize both the height and the width. Boxes that are not in the corners will allow you to resize the height or the width only.

Moving Parts Of A Chart

1   Select the part of the chart you wish to change – black boxes will appear around it.

2   Position the mouse pointer over a blank part in the middle – the mouse pointer will look like a white arrow.

3   Click and drag to move.

Using The Chart Toolbar

Displaying The Chart Toolbar

1   Click on the **View** menu.

2   Click **Toolbars** – any toolbars currently displayed will be ticked.

3   Click **Chart**.

Selecting With The Chart Toolbar

1   Click the drop-down arrow next to the *Chart Objects* box.

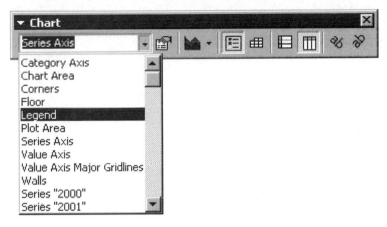

2   Click on the part you wish to select.

Formatting With The Chart Toolbar

1   Select the part of the chart you wish to format.

2   Click the **Format** icon on the *Chart* toolbar.

Changing The Chart Type

1   Select the white chart background.

2   Click on the drop-down arrow next to the **Chart Type** icon on the *Chart* toolbar.

375

3   Click on the chart type you prefer.

Show/Hide Legend

1   Select the white chart background.

2   Click on the **Legend** icon – this will show it if it's hidden, and hide it if it's shown.

Show/Hide Data Table

1   Select the white chart background.

2   Click on the **Data Table** icon – this will show it if it's hidden, and hide it if it's shown.

By Row And By Column

This lets you change the way Excel uses your data to create the chart – by row (left to right) or by column (top to bottom). If your chart looks the way you planned, then you probably don't need to use this.

1   Select the white chart background.

2   Click on the **By Row** icon.

or

click on the **By Column** icon.

Changing The Angle Of Text

1 Select the part of the chart with text in it – you cannot do this on a part that does not contain text.

2 Click on the **Angle Text Upward** icon.

or

click on the **Angle Text Downward** icon.

Changing Chart Options

Changing Chart Titles

1 Select the white chart background.

2 Click on the **Chart** menu.

3 Click **Chart Options**.

4 Click on the **Titles** tab.

5 Type in the titles you require.

6 Click **OK**.

Adding Data Labels

1 Select the white chart background.

2 Click on the **Chart** menu.

3 Click **Chart Options**.

4 Click on the **Data Labels** tab.

5 Click in the circle next to the type of data labels you would like to see.

6 Click **OK**.

Changing The Position Of The Legend

1 Select the white chart background.

2 Click on the **Chart** menu.

3 Click **Chart Options**.

4 Click on the **Legend** tab.

5 Click in the circle next to the position you require.

6 Click **OK**.

Chart Gridlines

1 Select the white chart background.

2 Click on the **Chart** menu.

3 Click **Chart Options**.

4 Click on the **Gridlines** tab.

5 Click in the boxes next to the gridlines you would like to see.

6 Click **OK**.

Printing Charts

Previewing A Chart

1 Select the white chart background.

2 Click on the **Print Preview** icon.

Printing A Chart On Its Own

1 Select the white chart background.

2 Click on the **Print** icon.

Printing A Chart With The Figures

To print a chart with the numbers next to it, do not select anything! First, move the chart next to the numbers, so that you can see both of them clearly. Then just deselect the chart by clicking on an empty cell, and click the **Print** icon.

Chapter 7

Other File Formats

Saving A Spreadsheet As A Web Page

Saving a spreadsheet as a web page allows you to put it up onto the World Wide Web. This is useful if you have some figures or a chart that you want to display on your Website.

1   Open the spreadsheet you wish to save as a web page.

2   If required, select the range of cells you wish to save.

3   Click on the **File** menu.

4   Click on **Save as Web Page**.

5   Use the arrow on the right of the *Save in* box to select a location to save to.

6   Click in the circle before *Entire Workbook*

    or

click in the circle before *Selection: Sheet*.

Save: ⦿ Entire **W**orkbook ○ **S**election: Sheet

What If I Only Want A Part Of My Worksheet As A Web Page?

Make sure you select the range of cells required in step 2. There will be a *Selection* option instead of the *Sheet* option in the *Save As* dialog box.

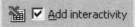

⦿ **S**election: $C$19:$F$25

Click into the circle before *Selection*.

Making The Sheet Interactive

If you tick the *Add interactivity* box, then people will be able to change figures on the web page as if it were a normal Excel spreadsheet!

☑ **A**dd interactivity

7   Type a file name into the *File name* box.

8   Click on **Save**.

Templates

What Are Templates?

A template is a design for a spreadsheet. Suppose you had lots of spreadsheets to create that all had the same headings and formulae – you could create a template with the headings and formulae you need, and then create new spreadsheets based on that template. When you create the new sheets, they will have all the headings and formulae you need, and all you have to do is fill in the new information.

If you find yourself creating a worksheet or a workbook that you need to use again and again you should consider using a template.

Templates are stored in a special template folder, and when you open one you are opening a copy of the original. This allows you to create as many new workbooks as you like based on just one model.

Using The Templates Supplied With Excel

Excel comes supplied with one main template which is the one that you open up each time you start a new workbook. This is called the Workbook template. To access the template:

1   Click on the **File** menu.

2   Click on **New**.

3   The *Template* dialog box opens.

4   Double-click *Workbook* – a new, blank workbook will open.

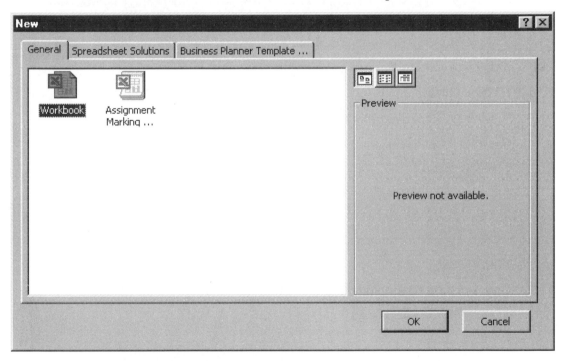

There are three tabs in the dialog box: the **General** tab, the **Spreadsheet Solutions** tab and the **Business Planner Template** tab.

Excel provides you with four other templates on the **Spreadsheet Solutions** tab to allow you to create invoices, expense statements and purchase orders. All you need to do is customize these templates. The **Business Planner Templates** are more complex templates, that let you create cash flow forecasts, profit and loss statements, balance sheets, and so on. Instructions are provided in each template.

When you open up the **Spreadsheet Solutions** templates supplied with Excel you will see a button which will allow you to customize the template by adding your own information. Just follow the on-screen tips and you will quickly have a fancy looking spreadsheet.

Creating A Template

1 Create your worksheet or workbook, inserting all the relevant formulae – you can use sample data to make sure that the formulae work, instead of leaving the number cells blank.

2 Format the headings as you require.

3 Insert any Clip Art or graphics such as logos.

4 Change any text alignment, column or row sizes, borders and shading, number formatting, etc.

5 Make sure to delete any sample data before you save your template.

6 When you have finished, click on the **File** menu.

7 Click on **Save As**.

8 Click on the drop-down arrow at the end of the *Save as type* box.

9 Click on *Template*.

Save as type: | Template (*.xlt)

10 Click in the *File name* box.

11 Type a name for your template.

12 Click **Save**.

When you wish to use your new template:

1 Click on the **File** menu.

2 Click on **New**.

3 Click on the **General** tab if necessary.

4 Double-click on the template you wish to use – a copy of your template will open.

Editing A Template

If you need to change something in a template, you will need to open the template itself so that you can modify it.

Microsoft Excel stores the templates you create in the Templates folder. To open this folder you need to navigate to:

C:\Windows\Application Data\Microsoft\Templates

Where Are My Templates?

When Microsoft Office was installed the templates may have been put in a different place! Ask the person who installed it.

1 Click on the **Open File** icon.

2 Change to the C: drive.

3 Double-click *Windows*.

4 Double-click on *Application Data*.

5 Double-click on *Microsoft*.

6 Double-click on *Templates*.

7 Double-click the template you wish to open.

8 Make the changes to your template.

9 Click the **Save** icon.

10 Close the template.

You may wish to open a document based on your modified template to see the changes.

Importing And Exporting To And From Word

Exporting Your Spreadsheet To Word

Suppose you need to write a report in Word, but the figures you need are all in Excel. How can you get them into your Word document? And how can you make sure that the figures are all up-to-date? What if you have to present the results, but your boss is being awkward, and wants you to make a quick change – while you're presenting it?

Don't panic – it's easy if you know how.

There are four ways to share data between different applications:

➤ Use Cut, Copy and Paste.

➤ Paste with a Link.

➤ Embed a document.

➤ Open a file in a different file format.

➤ *Copy* and *Paste* will put a picture of the data you wish to copy in your document.

➤ *Paste Link* will connect your document to the source file, and it will be updated when the source file changes.

➤ Embedding a document puts the document you wish to copy right into your application. The toolbars will change and you can edit your document where you are.

➤ Opening a file in a different format checks which file formats are supported by both applications.

To Paste A Picture Of Your Spreadsheet Into Word

1   Open Word.

2   Switch back to Excel using the taskbar.

3   Select the information you wish to copy.

4   Click on the **Edit** menu.

5   Click on **Copy**.

6   Switch to Word using the taskbar.

7   Move the cursor to the position you wish to insert your Excel spreadsheet.

8   Click on the **Edit** menu.

9   Click on **Paste** – a picture of your spreadsheet is pasted into the document.

To Paste Your Spreadsheet In Word With A Link

1   Open Word.

2   Switch back to Excel using the taskbar.

3   Select the information you wish to copy.

384

4   Click on the **Edit** menu.

5   Click on **Copy**.

6   Switch to Word using the taskbar.

7   Move the cursor to the position you wish to insert your Excel spreadsheet.

8   Click on the **Edit** menu.

9   Click on **Paste Special**.

10 Click inside the *Paste link* circle.

11 Select a format – Excel will usually choose the correct format.

12 Click in the box before *Float over text* – this will let you reposition the sheet anywhere on the page.

    or

    click in the box before *Display as icon* if you want to display the file as an icon – when you click on the icon, the file will open.

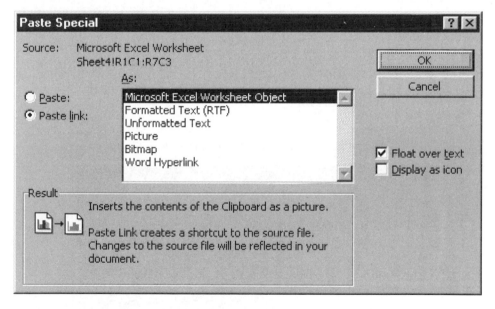

13 Click **OK**.

Your spreadsheet will be pasted into a Word document – any fields will be grey when you click on the inserted sheet, and will be updated when you change any information in Excel.

What Happens When I Change Information In Excel?

When you make any changes in Excel they will be reflected in the copy in your Word document. Give it a try – change one of the cells in the original Excel spreadsheet, and save it – then switch back to Word, and you'll see that the link has updated itself.

What Happens If The Original Spreadsheet Is Moved Or Renamed?

Your link will be lost! You may need to perform the copy and paste again.

To Embed Your Spreadsheet Into Word

1   Open Word.

2   Click on the **Insert** menu.

3   Click on **Object**.

4   Click on **Create from File**.

5   Enter the path and file name

    or

    click on **Browse** and choose the file from the *Open* dialog box.

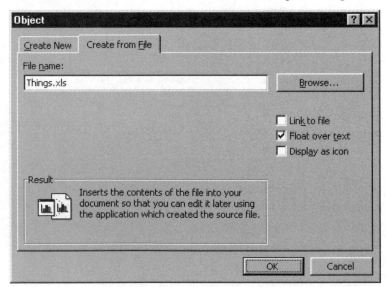

6   Click on *Link to file* to create an updating link if required.

7   Click in the box before *Float over text* if you want to reposition the sheet anywhere on the page

or

click on *Display as icon* to display the file as an icon.

8   Click **OK.**

Exporting An Excel Spreadsheet To Word

First save your Excel spreadsheet as a tab delimited text file:

1   Click on the **File** menu.

2   Click on **Save As.**

3   Click on the drop-down arrow next to the *Save as type* box, and choose *Text (Tab delimited).*

Save as type: | Text (Tab delimited) (*.txt) | ▼ |

What If My Workbook Has More Than One Sheet?

You will only be able to save the active sheet. Click *OK* to the message that appears.

4   Close the Excel file you have just saved (without saving it again).

Then import it into Word:

5   Switch to Word using the taskbar.

6   Click on the **Insert** menu.

7   Click on **File.**

8   Change the *Files of type* box to *Text Files.*

9   Locate the tab delimited text file you have just saved – the file will be displayed with a text icon.

Ex1.txt

10   Click on **OK** – your spreadsheet will be pasted into Word.

 **The Excel Information Is Pasted Into The Word Document Like A Table As Long As You Have Saved It As A Text (Tab Delimited) File.**

Copying Data From Word

1   Make sure that both Word and Excel are open.

2   Select the text you wish to copy.

3   Click on the **Edit** menu.

4   Click on **Copy**.

5   Switch to Excel by clicking on the button on the taskbar.

6   If required, select the cell you wish to paste into.

7   Click on the **Edit** menu.

8   Click on **Paste** – the text is pasted into Excel.

 ### It Doesn't Look The Same!

Some formatting may be lost when copying between Word and Excel. That's just the way these things work – but there's nothing stopping you from putting the formatting back in yourself.

Copying Linked Data From Word

1   Make sure both Word and Excel are open.

2   Select the text you wish to copy.

3   Click on the **Edit** menu.

4   Click on **Copy**.

5   Switch to Excel by clicking on the button on the taskbar.

6   If required, select the cell you wish to paste into.

7   Click on the **Edit** menu.

8   Click on **Paste Special**.

9   Click inside the circle next to *Paste link*.

10   Click **OK**.

Your Word document or selected text will now be pasted, and will automatically update itself. So any changes you make in the Word document will be reflected in Excel.

Double-Click To Edit The Text

You will be taken to the Word document automatically where you can make your changes.

Embedding A Word Document Into Excel

1   Open the worksheet where you wish to store the file.

2   Click on the **Insert** menu.

3   Click on **Object**.

4   Click on the **Create from File** tab.

5   Type in the path and file name.

   or

   click **Browse** and choose the document from the list.

6   Click **OK**.

Double-Click To Edit The Text

Rulers will appear around the text and you will be able to edit it as if you were in Word. Click away from the text when you have finished.

What Has Happened To The Toolbars?

When you paste link or embed a document, the toolbars of the host application change to reflect those of the document you are copying.

Importing A Word Document

1   Open the Word document.

2   Click on the **File** menu.

3   Click on **Save As**.

4   Click on the drop-down arrow next to the *Save as type* box, and choose *Text (Tab delimited)*.

5   Close the document.

6   Open the Excel spreadsheet into which you wish to import the Word document.

7   Click on the **File** menu.

8   Click on **Open**.

9   Click on the drop-down arrow next to the *Files of type* box.

10   Click on *All Files*.

11   Select the document you wish to import – it will look like a document icon.

12   Follow the wizard to import the document into Excel:

➤   Choose *Delimited* if you have saved the Word document as a tab delimited text file – this section shows you how to import one of these file types.

➤   Choose Fixed width if it is not tab delimited, but has the text layed out in columns.

➤   Look at the preview window at the bottom to see how the layout will appear.

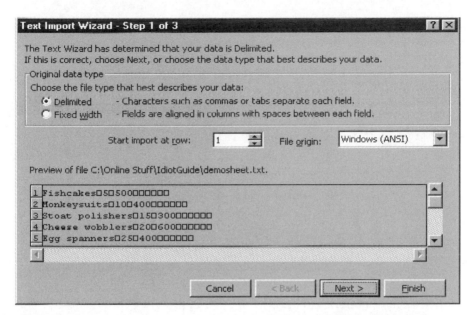

13 Click **Next** to continue.

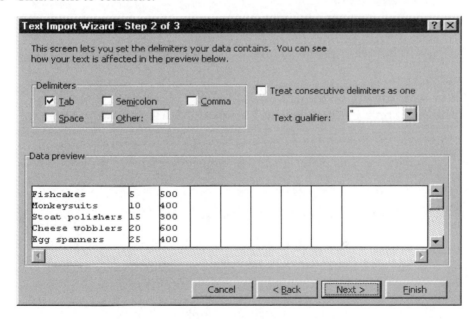

14 Because you have saved the file as a tab delimited text file, click in the box next to *Tab* to tell Excel what type of 'delimiters' (separators) you have used – if it is a different type, such as comma delimited, choose the appropriate option.

15 Click **Next** to continue.

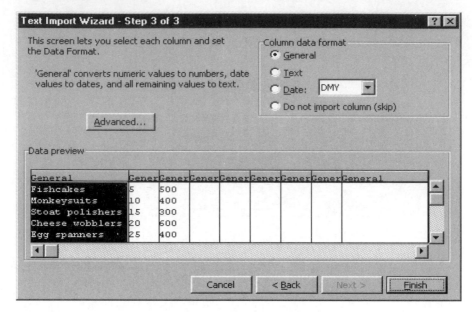

If necessary, you can set the data format for each column here – or you can wait until the information is in the spreadsheet. If you want to do it now:

1 Select each column in turn.

2 Choose the *Column data format* that you require.

3 Click **Finish** to import the data.

Your data is now entered into the Excel Spreadsheet.

It's All A Bit Cramped!

To make sure that it fits a bit better …

1 Select the columns that contain the data.

2 Click on the **Format** menu.

3 Click on **Column**.

4 Click on **AutoFit Selection**.

Other File Types

Older Versions Of Excel

To save a spreadsheet as an older version of Excel:

1   Click on the **File** menu.

2   Click on **Save As**.

3   Click on the drop-down arrow next to the *Save as type* box.

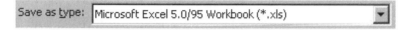

4   Click on the version of Excel you require (e.g. *Excel 50/95 Workbook*).

5   Click **Save**.

Other File Types

1   Click on the **File** menu.

2   Click on **Save As**.

3   Click on the drop-down arrow next to the *Save as type* box.

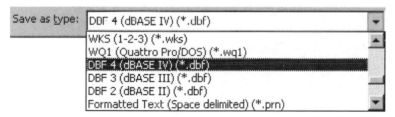

4   Click on the file format you require (*dBASE IV, Quattro, Text (Tab delimited)*, etc.).

5   Click **Save**.

393

Chapter 8

Quick Reference

What Do All The Icons Mean?

The Standard Toolbar

 Create a new, blank workbook.

 Open a workbook.

 Save the current workbook.

 Print one copy of the active sheet.

 Print preview the active sheet.

 Spell check.

 Cut the selected cells.

 Copy the selected cells.

 Paste.

 Format painter (not covered in ECDL).

 Undo.

 Redo.

Insert a hyperlink to another location (not covered in ECDL).

 AutoSum.

 Paste function (not covered in ECDL).

 Sort ascending.

 Sort descending.

 The Chart Wizard.

 Displays the *Drawing* toolbar (not covered in ECDL).

 Zoom control.

 The Office Assistant.

The Formatting Toolbar

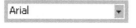 Changes the font.

 Changes the font size.

 Adds/removes bold.

 Adds/removes italics.

 Adds/removes underlining.

 Left-aligns the selected cells.

 Centre-aligns the selected cells.

 Right-aligns the selected cells.

 Merge and centre.

Applies the currency format.

Applies the percentage format.

Applies the comma format.

Increases the decimal places.

Decreases the decimal places.

Decreases the indent (not covered in ECDL).

Increases the indent (not covered in ECDL).

 Adds borders.

 Adds shading.

396

Changes the font colour.

Glossary

Absolute Cell References

If you want to copy a formula to another cell, but you want to prevent Excel from adjusting the cell references, make the cell references absolute. Absolute cell references are indicated by a dollar sign ($).

Active Cell

The cell border of the active cell is darker than the other cells, and shows you which cell you are currently working on.

AutoFill

This feature allows you to enter a series of numbers, dates or formulae.

AutoFormat

This will automatically format your table, for example adding borders, shading and bold.

AutoSum

Automatically adds up the figures in the cells above or to the left of the active cell. If necessary, you can choose which cells you want added up.

Cell

This is the basic building block of the Excel worksheet. A cell is formed by the intersection of the row and column gridlines. Each cell is identified by the letter of the column and the number of the row, e.g. *B7*.

Cell Range

A group of cells that are next to each other.

Cell References

These are the co-ordinates of the cell in the worksheet, e.g. *B7*.

Chart Sheet

This is a sheet in a workbook containing a chart. The chart sheet is updated when the worksheet data is changed.

Fill Handle

This is a solid black square in the right-hand corner of the active cell border. Using your mouse, grab the black square and drag it across to AutoFill your cells.

Formulae

Formulae are the basis of Excel. Formulae will do all the calculations that will normally be done by a calculator. You can use formulae to do simple calculations such as additions, subtractions, multiplication, division as well as statistical, financial and scientific calculations.

Formula Bar

This is the bar at the top of the Excel screen. It is used to enter and edit formulae and values. It also displays the formula in a particular cell.

Gridlines

These are the lines that you see in your spreadsheet. You can choose to print them, or leave them out.

Label

This is the text which usually appears next to the figures in a spreadsheet, and identifies what the figures mean.

Legends

A legend (also known as a key) is used in charts and graphs. Excel actually creates legends from the labels on the worksheet. The legends can be customized with borders, patterns and different fonts.

Mixed Cell References

In a formula there can be a combination of relative and absolute cell references. A mixed reference can look like this *$A1* or *A$1*. *$A1* refers to column *A* regardless of the position of the cell containing the formula.

Paste Function

This allows you to enter commonly used calculations quickly, such as finding the average, maximum or minimum of a group of numbers.

Relative Cell References

Relative cell references are used in formulae where you do not wish the reference to remain constant as the formula is AutoFilled. Relative cell references do not contain the $ that is found in absolute cell references.

Sheets

It is possible to insert, delete, rename, move and copy sheets in Excel. It can be a worksheet, a chart sheet, a module sheet or a dialogue sheet. A worksheet is the one used most often.

Worksheet

This is also called a spreadsheet. The worksheet is the primary document used in Excel. A worksheet is made up of cells in columns and rows, and is always part of a workbook.

Module 5
Databases

Chapter 1

Getting Started

Access

Access is a database program. That's all very well and good, but what is a database? Well, suppose you had a list made up of a lot of names and addresses – this is a simple database. Access is a bit cleverer than that, though. It lets you store names and addresses, sure, but you can create clever things called relational databases, that contain lots of little databases linked together. So you could have the names and addresses database, which is linked to an employment record database, which is linked to a holiday/sick day database, which is linked to a database that records the salaries – it's as complex or as simple as you want it to be.

Starting Access

1   Click on the **Start** button.

2   Click on the **Programs** sub-menu.

3   Click on **Microsoft Access**.

Or, if you have a shortcut on the desktop, double-click on the shortcut.

Access will open, and a box will appear offering you choices of what to open.

➤ The first option creates a new, blank database.

➤ The second option creates a new database using a wizard to guide you through it.

➤ The third option opens an existing database – you can choose from the list below which shows your recently used files, or click on *More Files* to browse your folders.

➤ Click **OK** to open or create a new database (depending on the option selected above.

➤ Click **Cancel** to close this box

You Can Click On Cancel!

Access is just trying to be helpful by offering you a choice of what you want to create or open. You can ignore this box by just clicking on **Cancel!**

Closing Access

1   Click on the **File** menu.

2   Click **Exit**.

Or

Click the top X at the top right of the Access window.

Opening, Saving And Closing A Database

Opening A Database

1   Click on the **File** menu.

2   Click **Open**

   or

   click on the **Open** icon.

3   If necessary, click on the drop-down arrow next to the *Look in* box to change the folder you are in.

4   Double-click on the database you require

   or

   click on the database you require.

   Click **Open**.

I Can't See My Database!

Check the folder you are looking in.

If you need to look in a different folder or drive:

1   Click on the drop-down arrow next to the *Look in* box.

2   Click on the folder or drive you wish to look in.

To look in a sub folder or folder in a drive:

1   Click on the folder or sub folder required.

2   Click on *Open*.

Closing A Database

1   Click on the **File** menu.

2   Click **Close**.

Or

Click the X at the top right of the database window.

Saving A Database

Databases are not saved in the same way as Word documents, or Excel spreadsheets, etc.

➤ When you create a new database it is automatically saved.

➤ When you add records to a database they are automatically saved.

➤ When you delete or modify the information in a database, your changes are automatically saved.

➤ It is only when you alter the design or structure of a database that you need to save your changes.

What Is A Database?

A database is a collection of information with the *information arranged in a structured way.* You have probably used paper databases to look information up, e.g. a telephone book, card index, or a filing system.

The Advantages Of Using Computerized Databases

If you have a lot of information to deal with, it is almost always better to use a computer rather than paper records. The main advantages are:

406

➤ You can sort your information into any order, e.g. a phone book on a computer could be arranged in order of postcode, name of the town, area code, etc.

➤ Finding people is much easier. Unlike a paper system, you are not reliant on one key piece of information, e.g. to find someone in a phone book you have to know their surname. If the phone book was on a computer, you could know their address, their first name, etc., and still use it to find them.

➤ You do not have to see all the information at once. The information that you wish to see can be extracted from the whole, e.g. all the people who live in London, all the people who are 3 months late in paying their bill, etc.

➤ Information can be cross-referenced, which would be impossible on paper, e.g. you may want to see everyone who lives in London and is also 3 months late with paying their bill.

➤ Updates are much easier on a computer. You can quickly delete or edit the information.

➤ Computers use less space than a large paper filing system.

Do You Need A Database?

Consider what you need a database for. Will it help you work more efficiently, or will the effort and time you put in outweigh the benefit of using it?

➤ **A Good Example**
If you have a list of clients on a database, you could search through and find those clients that meet a specific criteria. For example, those in Warwickshire, who have spent X amount on your product or service in the last year, but have not placed an order in the last three months. You could then send them a letter to see if they want to buy anything.

➤ **A Bad Example**
A list of suppliers who you only need to look up by name. A simple card file (or table in Word) may be quicker and a lot cheaper, if all the information is simply listed in alphabetical order and is only needed in that order.

The Parts Of An Access Database

The Database Window

When you first open a database you will see the database window. This is like the 'control centre' of the database – everything you create and use will be done from here. When the database is open, this window will also be open somewhere on the screen.

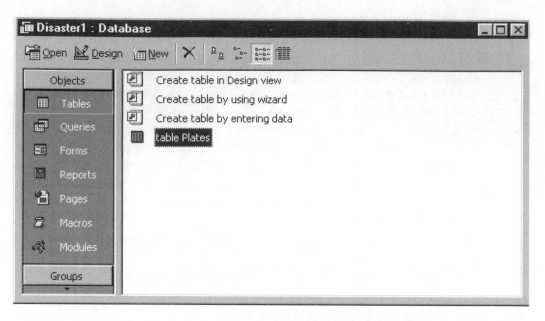

➤ The name of the database is shown on the title bar – in this case, 'Disaster1'.

➤ The *Objects* bar on the left shows you the seven possible parts of a database.

➤ At the moment you are looking at the tables – there is one table in this database, called 'Plates'.

What Do The Parts Of A Database Do?

The seven different parts all work together to make the whole database function. Each part has a specific role in the way the database works.

Tables

➤ Tables are where all the information in your database is stored.

➤ They are the first part to be created, and no other part can function until the tables are in place.

➤ You can use tables to input information.

➤ Tables also allow you to see lots of information at once.

➤ A database with one table is known as a flat-file database.

➤ Most databases have more than one table. These tables will be related to each other in some way, e.g. one table for employee details, and another table for the training they go on. This is known as a relational database.

Queries   ➤   Queries allow you to extract information from the tables. Tables contain all the information, but you may wish to take out a section from the whole, e.g. all the people who live in London, all the sales staff, etc.

                 ➤   You can think of queries as the 'questions' you ask of your tables.

                 ➤   Queries appear as 'mini' tables.

Forms   ➤   Forms are based on tables and contain the same information.

                 ➤   They are used to input information in a more user-friendly way than tables.

Reports   ➤   Reports are used to print information off from the database. They are based on the information found in tables or queries.

                 ➤   Reports can also be used to produce mailing labels.

Pages   ➤   Pages are used for adding, editing or viewing data on the Web. They are like tables, but published as Web pages.

Macros   ➤   Macros are used to speed up the way a database works, e.g. you could create a macro which automatically starts your database on a specific form.

Modules   ➤   Modules have the same function as macros. They allow you to write small programs which can run within Access to speed up your work.

Navigating Around The Database Window

To use different parts of the database, just click on the button you require from the *Objects* bar on the left. Objects of that type will appear to the right – so if you clicked on **Queries**, then all the Queries would appear on the right.

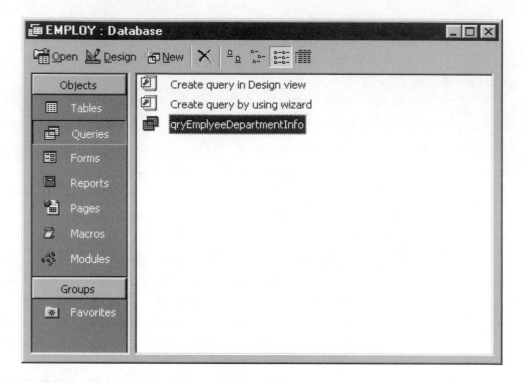

Opening A Database Object

1   Click on the button you require, e.g. **Tables**.

2   Double-click on the object you require.

Or

1   Click on the button you require, e.g. **Tables**.

2   Click on the object you require.

3   Click **Open**.

You Can End Up With Lots Of Windows Open!

When you open an object, it appears in a new window. The database window remains open behind the object window. If you open up more objects, you can end up with a lot of windows on your screen. Don't worry, this is perfectly natural. If you get worried, just close the windows you don't need – but don't close the main database window, or your whole database will close!

Closing A Database Object

1   Click on the **File** menu.

2   Click **Close**.

Or

Click the X at the top of the object window.

Using Tables

What Is A Table?

➤ Tables are the core of your database, and contain all the raw information. No other part of the database can function without tables.

➤ Some databases store all the information in one table. These are known as **flat-file** databases.

➤ More commonly, databases store the information in more than one table. These are known as **relational** databases. We will look at relationships in more detail later on.

Opening A Table

1   Click on the **Tables** button.

2   Click on the table you wish to open.

3   Click **Open**.

Or

1   Click the **Tables** button.

2   Double-click on the table you want to open.

Table Jargon

➤ Each table is made up of rows and columns.

➤ Each row holds one complete piece of information – a **record**. The picture below shows the record for Geoff Cohen.

EMPLOYEE ID	LASTNAME	FIRSTNAME	INITIAL	GENDER	DEPARTMENT	PHONE
5	Cohen	Geoff	A	Male	SALES	(217)555-4204

➤ Each column holds one piece of information per record – a **field**, e.g. last name, department, gender, etc. The field names are shown in grey at the top of the table.

EMPLOYEE ID	LASTNAME	FIRSTNAME	INITIAL	GENDER	DEPARTMENT	PHONE

➤ Each box of the table is a **cell** and contains one piece of information.

Moving Around A Table

To move around cells:

Click on the cell you require.

Or

Press the **Tab** key to move one cell to the right.

Or

Use the cursor keys to move around the cells.

To move around records:

Click on the record you require.

Or

Use the vertical scroll bar to move up and down the records.

Or

Use the record navigation buttons at the bottom left of the screen.

Going from left to right, here is what the navigation icons do:

➤ Move to the first record.

➤ Move to the previous record.

➤ Displays the current record (you can type in a record number and press *Return* to go to that record).

412

➤ Move to the next record.

➤ Move to the last record.

➤ The number to the right displays the total number of records – you cannot click on this.

To move around fields:

Click on the field you require.

Or

Use the horizontal scroll bar to move left and right around the fields.

Editing The Information In A Table

1   Move to the cell you wish to change.

2   Make any changes you require.

3   Click outside the record you are in – the changes are automatically saved.

To quickly change everything in the cell:

1   Position the mouse pointer at the bottom right of the cell – it will change to a big white cross.

2   Click the left mouse button once – the cell will be selected.

3   Type in the new information.

4   Click outside the record you are in – the changes are automatically saved.

When Are My Changes Saved?

As soon as you start typing, a pencil will appear to the left of the record.

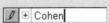

As long as you can see the pencil, the information is not saved. However, as soon as you move out of this record, the pencil will disappear, and your changes are saved automatically.

When I Edit The Information, A Drop-Down Arrow Appears ...

This means that you are working with a lookup field. If you click the drop-down arrow, you will get a choice of information which can go in this field, e.g. male or female for a gender field. This saves you time and helps to prevent mistakes.

I Can't Get Out Of The Record I'm Editing!

If you find yourself stuck in a record which Access won't let you get out of, press **Escape** (**Esc**) on the keyboard.

Entering New Records

1   Click on **New Record** icon.

2   Type in the new information.

3   Click outside the record when you have finished – the changes are saved automatically.

What Does AutoNumber Mean?

Somtimes you might find a field with the word AutoNumber in. You don't have to enter information into this field yourself, Access automatically adds a number for you.

Can I Add A New Record Anywhere In The Table?

No, only in the last row of the table.

	Peterson	John
*		

The asterisk (*) symbol shows you that this is the space for a new record.

Selecting Records

Click on the **Record Selector** to the left of the record – the mouse pointer will change to a black arrow

Or, if you would like to select several records:

1 Click on the **Record Selector** to the left of the first record and hold down the mouse button.

2 Drag over the other records you wish to select.

Can I Select Records That Are Not Next To Each Other?

No! Usually, if you select things, then you can use the **Ctrl** key to select items that are not next to each other. In an Access table, you can only select multiple records if they are next to each other.

Deleting Records

1 Select the record you wish to delete (using the **Record Selector** to the left of the record).

2 Press the **Delete** key

or

click the **Delete** icon.

When I Try To Delete, Access Says ...

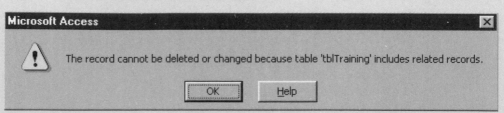

This means that you have a 'relational' database and your table is linked to another one. The person you are trying to delete has information about them in another table within this database. In order to delete them, you will have to go to the linked table first and delete them from there.

Why Doesn't The Autonumber Change When I Add A New Record?

If you delete a record, the AutoNumber goes with it! In other words, if you delete the record which has the number 49, then the number 49 will be deleted with it. The next record you create will be number 50. This is because AutoNumber is not used to count records, it is used to uniquely identify each record – this is very important when you are creating relational databases.

Changing The Look Of A Table

Selecting Columns

Click on the grey bar containing the field name – the mouse will change to a black, downward pointing arrow

⬇ PHONE

Or

Click and drag over several columns to select more than one.

Changing The Width Of Columns

1   Position the mouse pointer over the grey title area to the right of the column you wish to widen – the pointer will change to a double-headed arrow.

FIRSTNAME↔ INITIAL

416

2   Click and drag to widen the column

or

double-click – the column will resize automatically.

Moving Columns

1   Select the column you wish to move.

2   Position the mouse pointer in the middle of the grey title area – the pointer will change to a white arrow.

3   Click and drag the column to a new location – a thick vertical black line will indicate where the column is going.

Freezing Columns

When you scroll across the fields in a wide table, you lose sight of the first few fields. This can be annoying if the first fields contain information that you need to see while you look at the other columns, e.g. first name, last name. To get around this, you can 'freeze' columns so that they stay visible on the screen regardless of where you scroll to.

1   Select the column(s) you wish to freeze.

2   Click on the **Format** menu.

3   Click **Freeze Columns**.

The Columns I Froze Have Moved!

Any columns which you choose to freeze will jump to the start of the table.

Unfreezing Columns

1   Click on the **Format** menu.

2   Click **Unfreeze All Columns**.

417

Check This Out...

Why Have My Columns Not Returned To Their Original Position?

When you freeze a column it will jump to the start of the table, and will remain there until you move it, or until you close the table without saving your layout changes.

Hiding A Column

You can temporarily hide columns if you do not need to enter information into them.

1   Select the column(s) you wish to hide.

2   Click on the **Format** menu.

3   Click **Hide Columns**.

Showing A Column

Hidden columns can be shown again just as easily.

1   Click on the **Format** menu.

2   Click **Unhide Columns**.

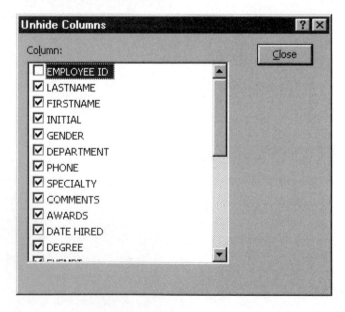

3   Click in the box(es) next to the column(s) you wish to show.

4   Click **Close**.

Saving The Layout Changes

If you change the way that your table looks, you do not have to save the changes you have made. When you close the table, Access will ask you if you want to save what you have done with the layout.

1   Click on the **File** menu.

2   Click **Close**

    or

    click the X at the top right of the table.

3   Click **Yes** if you would like to keep the layout you have

    or

    click **No** if you would like to return to the original layout.

Remember that Access automatically saves the information you have keyed in! When it asks you whether you want to save, it is only referring to the layout.

Finding And Sorting Records

Finding Records

Access tables allow you to find one record at a time in order to make amendments, delete, or view a certain record quickly. However, it will not extract records from the whole table, or allow you to search based on more than one piece of information – to do that you will need to use a query.

1   Click into the column you wish to search through, e.g. lastname, department.

2   Click **Find**.

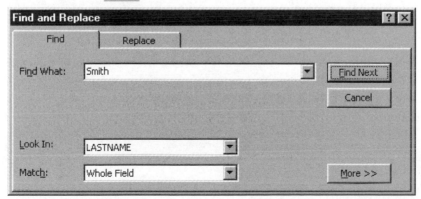

3   Type the data you wish to find next to *Find What*.

4   Click the drop-down arrow next to *Match* and choose the option you require –
imagine that you are searching for someone whose lastname is 'Smith', and you
have typed the word 'Smith' next to *Find What*. Here's what will happen with the
different match options:

➤ *Any Part of Field*: will find anything that contains the word 'Smith', e.g.
'Smithson', 'Taylor-Smith' and 'Smith' itself.

➤ *Whole Field:* will only find the word 'Smith' and nothing else.

➤ *Start of Field:* will find the word 'Smith' at the beginning of the text, e.g.
'Smithson', 'Smith', but not 'Taylor-Smith.

5   Click **Find Next** – the found record is highlighted in the table.

6   Click **Find Next** again to find the next record.

When Access has finished it will display a message to tell you it has finished (see
screenshot in next section).

7   Click **OK**.

8   Click **Cancel** to close the *Find and Replace* box.

Doing A More Specific Search

If you want to be very specific about what you are searching for, then you can turn on
more options.

1   Click into the column you want to search on.

2   Click on the **Find** button.

3   Type what you want to find in the *Find What* box.

4   Change the *Match* option if necessary.

5   Click on the *More* button.

6   Choose the *Option* you want:

420

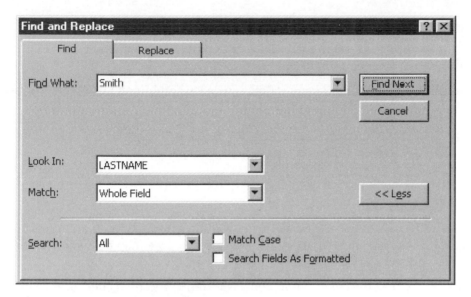

➤ *All:* will search the entire column.

➤ *Up:* will search only the records above where your cursor is in the column.

➤ *Down:* will search only the records below where your cursor is in the column.

7 Click **Find Next** (as before, click on **Find Next** again if required).

8 When Access has finished it will display this message;

9 Click **OK**.

10 Click **Cancel** to close the *Find and Replace* box.

Matching The Case In A Find

If you want Access to find only text that is in the same case as you type it (e.g. 'DATA' will only find 'DATA' and not 'data'):

Click in the *Match Case* box to turn this option on and off (it is on when ticked).

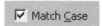

Searching For Text In A Particular Format

If you only want Access to find text that is in exactly the format you type it (e.g. in a particular date format of 02/02/00 and not 02-02-00):

Click in the *Search Fields As Formatted* box to turn this option on and off (it is on when ticked).

☑ Search Fields As Formatted

Sorting Records

You can sort records to make it easier to view or find information. In an Access table you can only sort on one field. If you want to sort on more than one you will need to use a query.

To sort records, click into the column you wish to sort, and then click on the **Sort** icon you require:

The first icon sorts in ascending order, the second sorts in descending order.

What Do Ascending And Descending Mean?

It depends on what you are sorting. Have a look at the list below to get an idea of how it works.

	Ascending	Descending
Text	A to Z	Z to A
Numbers	Smallest to biggest	Biggest to smallest
Dates	Earliest to latest	Latest to earliest

Blanks will appear at the top if you are sorting ascending, or at the bottom if you are sorting descending.

I Have A Field That Won't Sort!

Memo, OLE and Hyperlink fields do not sort (see the *Specifying Data Types* section on page 508 for more information on field types).

How Do I Save The Results Of My Sort?

Close the table and save the layout changes when you are prompted.

Printing Tables

Printing All Your Records

Click on the **Print** icon.

Printing A Selection Of Records

1   Select the records you wish to print.

2   Click on the **File** menu.

3   Click **Print**.

4   Click the circle next to *Selected Record(s)*.

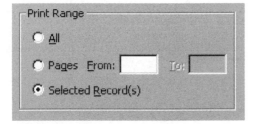

5   Click **OK**.

Print Preview

If you want to see the layout of what you are printing before you send it to the printer, click the **Print Preview** icon.

To close print preview, click on the **Close** button.

Zooming In And Out In Print Preview

To zoom in or out of the page:

Click on the page – the mouse pointer will look like a magnifying glass.

Moving Through The Pages

To see different pages in the preview window, use the navigation buttons:

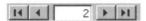

Going from left to right, here is what each button does:

➤ Goes to the first page.

➤ Goes to the previous page.

➤ Displays the current page – you can type in a page number and press **Return** to go to that page.

➤ Goes to the next page.

➤ Goes to the last page.

Changing The Number Of Pages Displayed In Print Preview

You can see one, two or multiple pages in the print preview window. To change the number of pages displayed:

Click on the **One Page** icon to see one page.

Or

Click on the **Two Pages** icon to see two pages.

Or

1 Click on the **Multiple Pages** icon.

2 Drag across the number of pages you wish to see (e.g. 2 × 3 Pages) – the boxes will be highlighted in blue.

3 Click once with the left mouse button.

Using Help In Access

Access 2000 comes with an animated Office Assistant to help you if you get stuck. This works in exactly the same way as the assistant in Word – see the Office Assistant section in the Word section for more details.

Toolbars

What Are Toolbars?

Toolbars are used to carry out commands in your software. They contain pictures called icons which you click on to carry out an action, e.g. the *Database* toolbar.

If you cannot see the toolbar you need, you will need to turn it on using the **View** menu.

Turning Toolbars On And Off

1   Click on the **View** menu.

2   Click on the **Toolbars** sub-menu.

3   Click on name of toolbar you wish to turn on or off – if it is on, it will be switched off, and if it is off, it will be switched on.

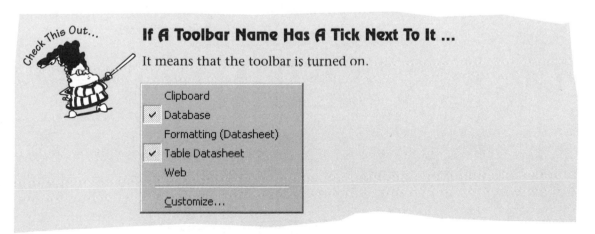

If A Toolbar Name Has A Tick Next To It ...

It means that the toolbar is turned on.

Chapter 2

Queries

Creating A Simple Query

What Is A Query?

Queries allow you to extract information from tables, e.g. all the women in the Sales department, all the staff who earn between £20,000 and £30,000, in alphabetical order.

Queries look exactly the same as tables – which is not surprising, as they are really the same thing – they just show you the information you have chosen to extract.

Queries also let you input information into the table, without having to see the whole table. If you input data into a query, it will automatically go into the table the query was based on.

Most of the time you will be producing **select queries**. These are queries that simply extract and display the information you asked for. There are other types of query which we will deal with in the *Advanced Queries* section.

Creating A Query

There are four main steps to creating a query:

1   Choosing the table you wish to extract information from.

2   Choosing the fields you wish to see in the query.

3   Running the query to see the result.

4   Saving the query (if required).

Step One: Choosing The Table

1   Click on the **Queries** button in the database window.

2   Double-click on *Create query in Design view* – the *Show Table* box will appear

📄   Create query in Design view

or

Click on **New**.

Click on **Design View**.

Click **OK** – the *Show Table* box will appear.

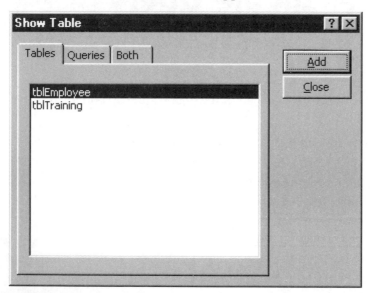

3   Double-click on the table you wish to use – the table will appear in the background.

4   Click **Close**.

I Didn't Add A Table Before I Clicked Close

Click on the **Show Table** icon to bring the box back!

I Added The Same Table More Than Once

It's very easy to double-click on the same table more than once, or forget to close the *Show Table* box. If you have added the same table twice, click on the second table

and press the **Delete** key!

Step Two: Choosing The Fields

You are now in the Design View of the query. It is here that you get to ask Access for the fields you wish to see.

Double-click on the field you wish to see from the list within the table – the field will jump to the query grid.

Or

Click and drag the field you require to the Field row in the query grid.

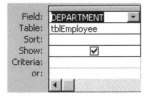

I Can't See All The Fields I've Added

If you add lots of fields to the query grid, you will need to use the horizontal scroll bar to see them all.

I've Added The Wrong Field

See page 512 for information on how to delete fields.

How Can I Add All The Fields At Once?

Double-click the * at the top of the list of fields.

Step Three: Running A Query

You are still in Design View, and this is the place where you ask Access for the information you wish to see. You now want to see the answer, and that's where running the query comes in. Running the query takes you out of Design View and into Datasheet View, where you can see the records that match what you've asked for:

Click on the **Run** icon.

Or

Click the **Datasheet View** icon.

What Is The Difference Between The Run Icon And The Datasheet View Icon?

At this stage – nothing! It's only when you get to more advanced queries that the difference will become clear.

Why Can I See 'expr' Next To Some Of My Fields?

You've probably added the same field more than once! You need to return to Design View and delete one of the fields – see page 512 for how to delete fields.

What Will Happen If I Change The Data I Can See In The Query?

The table will also change! Think of the query as the same as the table – you are just seeing less of it. So if you change the data in the query, the data in the table will change as well.

Saving A Query

1   Click on the **Save** icon.

2   Enter a name for the query.

3   Click **OK**.

Give Queries A Consistent Name

E.g. start the name off with the letters QRY, qry or Query. That way you will know that it's a query whenever you come across it.

Closing A Query

1   Click on the **File** menu.

2   Click **Close**.

Or

Click the X at the top right of the query.

Changing The View

What Are Views?

There are two views which you will need to use in a query:

➤ **Design View:** this is where you add the table and the fields that you wish to see in the query. You can think of it as the place where you ask Access what you want to see.

➤ **Datasheet View:** this is where you can see the answer. The Datasheet View looks just like the table.

You will also see another view available – **SQL View**. This shows how the query will look in SQL code. However, you will not need to use it unless you are interested in using code to program your database.

Switching To Design View

Click on the the **Design View** icon.

Switching To Datasheet View

Click on the **Datasheet View** icon.

Switching To SQL View

1   Click the drop-down arrow next to the view icon.

2   Click *SQL View*.

Editing A Query

You Must Be In Design View To Edit A Query!

Design View allows you to edit the question which you are asking Access. Datasheet View allows you to see the answer.

Selecting Fields In Design View

1   Position the mouse on the grey bar just above the field in the query grid – the pointer will change to a black, downward-pointing arrow.

2   Click once with the left mouse button.

Deleting Fields

1   Ensure that you are in the Design View.

2   Select the field you wish to delete.

3   Press the **Delete** key.

Moving Fields

1   Ensure that you are in the Design View.

2   Select the field you wish to move.

3   Position the mouse in the middle of the grey bar just above the field in the query grid.

4   Click and drag to a new position – a vertical black line will show where you are going.

Printing Queries

1   Open the query you wish to print.

2   Click on the **Print** icon.

To Obtain A Print Preview Of Your Query

Click on the **Print Preview** icon.

Adding Criteria To Queries

What Are Criteria?

So far you have created queries that have pulled out certain fields from the table. However, it is more likely that you will want to pull out certain records, e.g. all the **females**, all the people in the **Sales** department, all the people who earn **over £20,000**. The text in bold is known as criteria, and they can easily be added to a query.

Searching For Records On One Criteria

1 Create a new query as normal.

2 Add the fields you wish to see in Design View.

3 Type in the criteria you wish to use on the *Criteria* row, under the relevant field name – the criteria will get quotation marks around it when you click outside.

4 Run the query as normal.

E.g. finding females. The word 'female' is typed on the *Criteria* row under the *Gender* field.

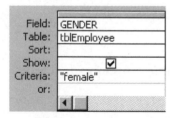

E.g. finding people in the Sales department. The word 'sales' is typed on the *Criteria* row under the *Department* field.

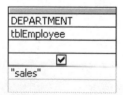

Check This Out...

Are Criteria Case Sensitive?

No, you can type in whatever case you like, as long as you spell it correctly!

434

Why Is My Query Not Showing Anything?

The biggest mistake with adding criteria is spelling the criteria incorrectly, or using a term which is not in the table. For example, let's say you want to find the females in this table.

		EMPLOYEE ID	LASTNAME	FIRSTNAME	INITIAL	GENDER
▶	⊞	5	Cohen	Geoff	A	Male
	⊞	9	Dean	Christine	W	Female
	⊞	12	Egan	Michelle	P	Female
	⊞	33	Orlando	John	S	Male
	⊞	21	Kaufman	Lisa	C	Female

If you type the word 'females' as your criteria, you won't find anybody, because the text in the table is 'female' without an 's' on the end!

It may also be that you have stray criteria left over from another time when you ran this query that is affecting your result.

Searching For Records Which Do NOT Meet A Criteria

You may want to find records which are **not** something, e.g. all the people who do **not** work in the Sales department.

1   Create a new query as normal.

2   Add the fields you wish to see in Design View.

3   Type the word **Not** in front of your criteria underneath the field you wish to find it in – your criteria will get quotation marks around it, once you click outside.

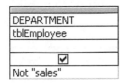

4   Run the query as normal.

Searching For Records Where Information Is Missing

You may have forgotten to add information in various fields when you were inputting them. Or you may have left certain information deliberately blank when you were inputting because you did not have the information to hand at the time. If you would like to find the blanks in a field:

1   Create your query as normal.

2   Add the fields you wish to see in Design View.

3   Type the word **NULL** into the *Criteria* row of the field you wish to find blanks in (this will change to 'Is Null' once you have clicked outside!).

This example will find people whose last name has been left blank:

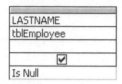

4   Run your query as normal.

Numbers, Dates And Wildcards

So far, the criteria you have added have not allowed you to make comparisons. You may want to find people who earn more or less than a certain figure, or people who started before or after a certain date. This section will show you how.

Using Numbers

Below are examples of criteria which can be added to make comparisons with numbers, e.g. greater than, less than, between, etc. In the examples below, the number 100 has been used to show you how it works:

What do you want to find?	This is what you type in the criteria row
Numbers greater than 100	>100
Numbers less than 100	<100
Numbers greater than or equal to 100	>=100
Numbers less than or equal to 100	<=100
Between 1 and 100	Between 1 and 100

When Using Numbers As Criteria

Just type the number – you do not have to include pound signs, percentage symbols, etc.

Using Dates

Below are examples of criteria which can be added to make comparisons with dates, e.g. before, after, between, etc. In the examples below, the date 1/1/2000 has been used to show you how it works.

What do you want to find?	This is what you type in the criteria row
Dates after 1/1/2000	>1/1/2000
Dates before 1/1/2000	<1/1/2000
Dates after or equal to 1/1/2000	>=1/1/2000
Dates before or equal to 1/1/2000	<=1/1/2000
Dates between 1/1/2000 and 31/12/2000	Between 1/1/2000 and 31/12/2000

Can I Type Dates With Full Stops?

No! Access won't let you, and you will get an error message. Always use slashes, like this: 1/1/2000.

Access Will Put Hashes (#) Around Your Dates!

In the same way as criteria has quotation marks when you click outside, dates will get hash marks (#) around them.

How Do I Remember Whether To Use Greater Than Or Less Than?

Imagine that Access takes the 1/1/2000 as 1. Every subsequent day goes up by an integer of one, so 2/1/2000 is 2, 3/1/2000 is 3, etc. The bigger the number the later the date. So if you want to find earlier dates it will be less than, and if you want to find later dates it will be greater than.

Using A Wildcard

Wildcards allow you to search for partial information in a field, e.g. finding words that start with a certain letter, finding words that end with a certain letter, finding dates that end in a certain year, etc. A wildcard is just an asterisk (*), and can be placed wherever there is blank information to be filled in. The table below shows examples of wildcards.

What do you want to find?	This is what you type in the criteria row
Words beginning with **Ke**	Ke*
Words ending in **son**	*son
Dates ending in the year 1984	*/*/84

Access Will Add The Word 'Like' And Quotation Marks Around Criteria With Wildcards!

In the same way that criteria get quotation marks around them when you click outside, wildcards will display this text.

Adding More Than One Criteria

What Are And And Or?

Often you will want to add more than one criteria, e.g. all the **females** who work in the **Sales** department, all the **males** who earn **under £20,000**, etc. If you have more than one criteria, you must specify whether the relationship between them is AND or OR:

➤ AND means you will find records which match **both** criteria e.g. only females who work in Sales; only males who earn over £20,000.

➤ OR means that you will find records which match **either** of the criteria e.g. all the females, and all the people who work in Sales; all the males, and all the people who earn over £20,000.

You Can't Have ANDs On The Same Field!

Female AND Male will not give you anybody, because no-one can be both female and male at the same time.

Ors Are Usually On The Same Field

Manchester OR London, will return all the records which are either Manchester or London. If you said London AND Manchester, you will not get anything because, you are asking Access to find you records which have both Manchester and London in the same field. You can't be in Manchester and London at the same time.

Using AND

1 Create your query as normal.

2 Add the fields you wish to see in Design View.

3 Type your first criteria onto the *Criteria* row under the relevant field.

4 Enter any other criteria on the same criteria row as the first and under the relevant field.

5 Run your query as normal.

The example below will show all the females in the Sales department.

GENDER	DEPARTMENT
tblEmployee	tblEmployee
☑	☑
"female"	"sales"

439

Using OR

1 Create your query as normal.

2 Add the fields you wish to see in Design View.

3 Type your first criteria onto the first *Criteria* row under the relevant field.

4 Type any additional criteria on a different *Criteria* row under the relevant field.

5 Run your query as normal.

The example below will show all the females, and all the people in the Sales department.

GENDER	DEPARTMENT
tblEmployee	tblEmployee
☑	☑
"female"	
	"sales"

Some Examples Of Queries With Multiple Criteria

This will find all the females in the Executive department who were hired after 1/1/80, i.e. Female AND executive AND after 1/1/80:

GENDER	DEPARTMENT	DATE HIRED
tblEmployee	tblEmployee	tblEmployee
☑	☑	☑
"female"	"executive"	>#01/01/80#

This will find all sales staff and all the executives, i.e. sales OR executive:

DEPARTMENT
tblEmployee
☑
"sales"
"executive"

This will find all the females who are executives and all the males who are salespeople, i.e. (Female AND executive) OR (male AND salesperson):

GENDER	DEPARTMENT
tblEmployee	tblEmployee
☑	☑
"female"	"executive"
"male"	"sales"

Sorting Queries

Sorting In Datasheet View

As well as choosing to see certain records, you can also change the order in which the information is displayed. To do this, you need to sort the query. You can sort in either Datasheet or Design View.

What's The Difference Between Sorting In Datasheet View And Sorting In Design View?

In Datasheet View you can only sort by one field.

In Design View you can sort on more than one field.

Sorting On One Field In Datasheet View

1   Click into the column you wish to sort.

2   Click on the sort button you require:

Sort ascending

or **Sort descending**.

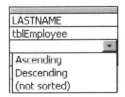

Sorting On One Field In Design View

1   Click into the sort row for the field you wish to sort.

LASTNAME
tblEmployee
▾
Ascending
Descending
(not sorted)

2   Click the drop-down arrow which appears.

3   Click *Ascending* or *Descending*.

4   Run your query as normal.

How Do I Remove The Sort Order?

This is done in the same way as sorting a field. Click the drop-down arrow in the sort box, and then click on (*not sorted*) to remove the sort order.

What Does Sorting On More Than One Field Mean?

Let's imagine that you wish to sort a query by the *Lastname* field. If lots of people have the same last name, then you would probably want to sort their first names within that, like the example below:

LASTNAME	FIRSTNAME
Pope	Jan
Rizzo	Ann
Rodan	Bill
Sanders	Kathy
Skye	Jim
Smith	Bob
Smith	Fred
Smith	Jane
Smith	Kim
Young	Sandy
Youngblood	Dick
Zambini	Rick

Imagine that you need to produce a list of the people who work in different departments. You could sort by the *Department* field first, and then within that sort by the person's lastname, like this:

DEPARTMENT	LASTNAME
EXECUTIVE	Anderson
EXECUTIVE	Barnett
EXECUTIVE	Beman
EXECUTIVE	Dean
EXECUTIVE	Dickerson
EXECUTIVE	Eivera
EXECUTIVE	Goreman
EXECUTIVE	Hamby
EXECUTIVE	Keegan
EXECUTIVE	Newman
EXECUTIVE	Zambini
SALES	Adams
SALES	Bicksby
SALES	Campbell
SALES	Cohen
SALES	Drasin
SALES	Drendon
SALES	Egan
SALES	Gilbert
SALES	Hart
SALES	Johnson
SALES	Kaufman
SALES	Keegan

Sorting On More Than One Field In Design View

The Field Which Is Your First Choice For Sorting Must Be To The Left!

In the query grid, the field which is your first choice for sorting must be on the left of any other fields you wish to sort.

E.g. Sorting by **department** and then by **lastname**.

This will not work, because the *Department* field is not to the left of *Lastname*.

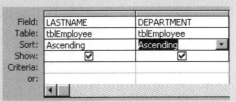

Field:	LASTNAME	DEPARTMENT
Table:	tblEmployee	tblEmployee
Sort:	Ascending	Ascending
Show:	☑	☑
Criteria:		
or:		

This will work, because the *Department* field is to the left of *Lastname*.

For information about moving fields in Design View, see the section about moving fields on page 433.

Field:	DEPARTMENT	LASTNAME
Table:	tblEmployee	tblEmployee
Sort:	Ascending	Ascending
Show:	☑	☑
Criteria:		
or:		

443

1 Ensure that the field which is your first choice for ordering is on the left.

2 Click into the *Sort* row for your first field.

3 Click the drop-down arrow.

4 Click *Ascending* or *Descending*.

5 Click into the *Sort* row for your second field.

6 Click *Ascending* or *Descending*.

7 Run your query as normal.

Showing/Hiding Fields

The Design View of a query also allows you to hide fields before you run it. This can be useful if you want to keep certain information confidential, e.g. salary.

1 Create your query as normal.

2 Add the fields you require in Design View.

3 Click the box on the *Show row* under the field you require. (A ticked box will show, a blank box will be hidden.)

In this example, the *Gender* field will show, but the *Salary* field will be hidden:

GENDER	SALARY
tblEmployee	tblEmployee
☑	☐

4 Run your query as normal.

Adding Filters

What Are Filters?

A filter is a way of filtering out the records you want to see, based on criteria which you set, e.g. all the people in the Sales department. It's a bit like using criteria in queries except quicker and easier, and that can't be bad.

Filters, however, can be applied to a table, a query or a form. When you apply them, Access will just show you the selected records you have chosen to see.

444

Filtering By Selection

1 Open the table, query or form you wish to filter.

2 Select the information which you would like to see from any record.

In the example below, you will get all the people in the Sales department.

EMPLOYEE ID	LASTNAME	FIRSTNAME	INITIAL	GENDER	DEPARTMENT
15	Adams	Nathan	K	Male	SALES

3 Click the **Filter By Selection** icon.

You can see whether records have been filtered by checking next to the navigation buttons. In the example below, the selected record has been filtered.

Record: |◄ ◄ | 1 | ► ►| ►* | of 32 (Filtered)

Do You Have To Select The Whole Field?

No! You can also select:

➤ The first part of the field, e.g. selecting
will filter all the records which begin with the letters 'And' such as Anderson, Andrews, etc.

LASTNAME
Anderson

➤ Any part of the field, e.g. selecting
will filter all the records which contain the letters 'der' anywhere within them such as Anderson, Sanderson, etc.

LASTNAME
Anderson

Can I Filter Records Which Have Been Filtered?

Yes! If you have more than one criteria which you would like to apply, you can apply another filter to the filtered records.

445

Excluding By Selection

This will allow you to filter records which do **not** meet the criteria you specify.

1   Open the table, query or form you wish to filter.

2   Select the information which you would **not** like to see from any record.

3   Right click over the selection – a menu will appear.

4   Click *Filter Excluding Selection*.

Removing Filters

Click on the **Remove Filter** icon.

Filtering By Form

Filter by Form allows you to do more complex filtering than Filter by Selection. It creates a form, which you use to fill out the criteria you require.

Using Filter By Form With More Than One Criteria

1   Open the table, query or form you wish to filter.

2   Click on the **Filter by Form** icon – a form will appear for you to fill in.

If you have used filters before, Access will remember the last thing you filtered and add this as your criteria.

3   Click into the field you wish to add criteria to.

4   Click the down arrow and choose the criteria you wish to add

or

type in the criteria you wish to add.

5   Click on the **Apply Filter** icon.

Using AND With Filter By Form

1   Open the table, query or form you wish to filter.

2   Click on the **Filter by Form** icon – a form will appear for you to fill in.

    If you have used filters before, Access will remember the last thing you filtered and add this as your criteria.

3   Enter the criteria you require underneath the appropriate fields – the example below will find all the females in the Sales department.

EMPLOYEE ID	LASTNAME	FIRSTNAME	INITIAL	GENDER	DEPARTMENT
					"SALES" ▾

4   Click on the **Apply Filter** icon.

Using OR With Filter By Form

1   Open the table, query or form you wish to filter.

2   Click on the **Filter by Form** icon – a form will appear for you to fill in – if you have used filters before, Access will remember the last thing you filtered and add this as your criteria.

3   Enter your first criteria underneath the appropriate field.

4   Click the **OR** tab at the bottom of the form.

5   Enter your next criteria underneath the appropriate field.

6   Repeat steps 4 and 5 if you have more criteria.

7   Click on the **Apply Filter** icon.

Check This Out...

You Can Use NULL And NOT In Filter By Form

If you would like to filter the blanks in a field, type the word **null** into the form underneath the relevant field.

If you would like to find records which do **not** meet the criteria you specify, type the word 'not' before the criteria, e.g. not Sales.

Saving A Filter As A Query

1   Click on the **Filter by Form** icon.

2   Enter your criteria as required.

3   Click on the **Save as Query** icon.

4   Enter a name for your query.

5   Click **OK**.

You can access your query from the queries in the Database window.

Deleting Criteria

1   Select the criteria you wish to delete.

2   Press the **Delete** key.

Chapter 3

Forms

Using Forms

What Are Forms?

Forms are based on tables or queries. They show the same information, but they look nicer. OK, they're more useful than that – you can use them to:

➤ Input data in a more user-friendly way than inputting data directly into a table or query.

➤ View individual records on the screen (rather than multiple records like a table or query).

➤ Input data into more than one table at once.

➤ Prevent users from having to access the tables in your database. The tables are the structure of your database, and if they are accidentally deleted, or their design is accidentally changed, it could ruin everything. Forms give people a way of inputting data without giving them access to the tables.

Opening A Form

1   Click on the **Forms** button.

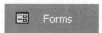

2   Click the form you wish to open.

3   Click **Open**.

Or

1   Click on the **Forms** button.

2   Double-click the form you wish to open.

Navigating Around Records

Click the required button at the bottom of the form.

Going from left to right, here is what the buttons do:

➤ Move to the first record.

➤ Move to the previous record.

➤ Move to the next record.

➤ Move to the last record.

Editing A Record

1   Go to the record you wish to edit.

2   Click on the field you wish to change.

3   Make your changes as required.

When Are My Changes Saved?

Just like in a table, as soon as you move onto another record the changes will be saved. So be careful!

Adding A New Record

Click on the **New Record** icon.

Changing The Orientation

1 Click on the **File** menu.

2 Click **Page Setup**.

3 Click on the **Page** tab.

4 Click in the circle next to *Landscape*

or

click in the circle next to *Portrait*.

5 Click **OK**.

Printing A Form

Click on the **Print** icon.

Closing A Form

Click the X on the form window.

You Will Not Be Asked To Save!

If you have only typed data in, Access will not ask you if you want to save the form.

Creating A Form Using The Form Wizard

Ways Of Creating A Form

There are seven ways of creating a form:

➤ **Design View:** will allow you to create the form completely from scratch with no help from Access whatsoever. This gives you more control, but can be scary.

➤ **Form Wizard:** will take you through a series of steps to help you create your form. This is much easier, but you don't have as much control.

➤ **AutoForm Columnar:** will instantly create a form where each record is shown on a different screen.

➤ **AutoForm Tabular:** will instantly create a form where several records are shown in tabular format.

➤ **AutoForm Datasheet:** will instantly create a form that looks the same as the table.

➤ **Chart Wizard:** will allow you to create a chart on a form.

➤ **Pivot Table Wizard:** will allow you to create a pivot table on a form.

Creating A Form Using The Form Wizard

1   Click on the **Forms** button.

2   Double-click on *Create form by using wizard*.

       📰   Create form by using wizard

or

click **New**.

Click *Form Wizard*.

Click **OK**.

3   Click the drop-down arrow under *Table/Queries*.

4   Click on the table to base your form on.

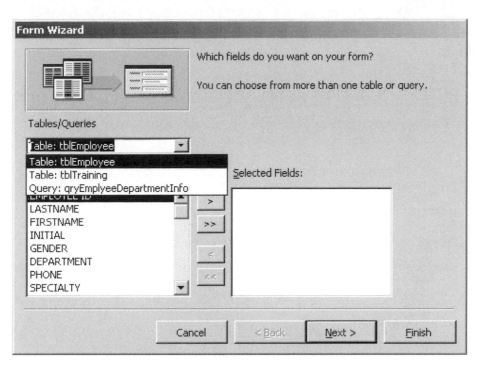

5   Double-click on the fields you wish to see on the form underneath *Available Fields* – they will jump over to the *Selected Fields* column.

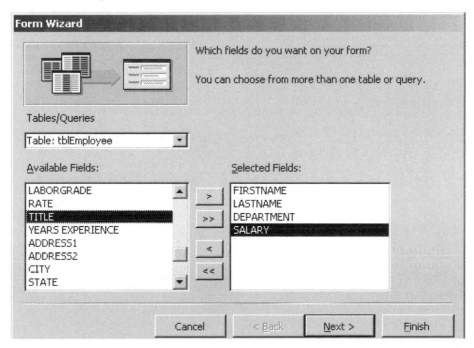

What If I Add The Wrong Field?

1   Click on the field you wish to remove underneath *Selected Fields*.

2   Click on the left-pointing arrow.

6   Click **Next**.

7   Click in the circle next to the layout you require.

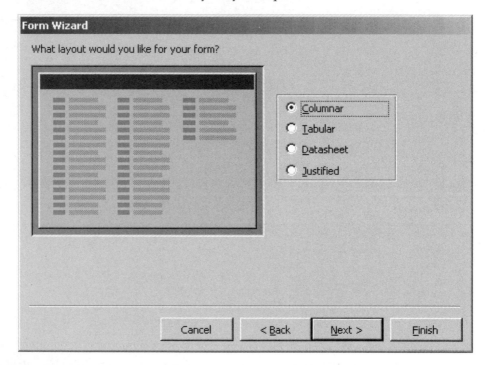

➤   *Columnar* will show you one record at a time on the screen.

➤   *Tabular* will show you multiple records at a time on the screen.

➤   *Datasheet* and *Justified* create a form with the same layout as the table.

8   Click **Next**.

9   Click on the style you require.

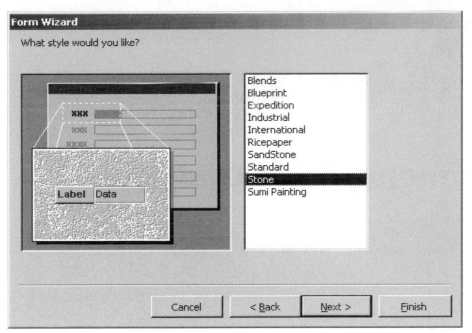

10 Click **Next**.

11 Type a name for your form – give your form a descriptive name, i.e. include the word 'Form' in the name.

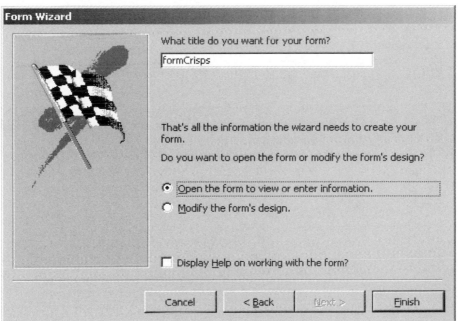

12 Click **Finish**.

When Is My Form Saved?

As soon as you click **Finish**!

Changing Form Design

The Views

There are three views to a form:

➤ **Form View:** where you can edit and view records.

➤ **Datasheet View:** where you can edit and view records in table format.

➤ **Design View:** where you can edit the way your form looks and works.

Changing The View

1   Click the drop-down arrow next to the **View** button.

2   Click on the view you require.

The View Button Looks Different Depending On Which View You Are In!

When you are in Form View it looks like this:

When you are in Design View it looks like this:

   However, it is always the first button on the toolbar.

The Elements Of A Form In Design View

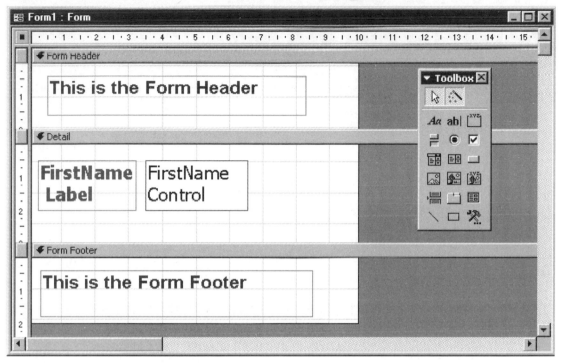

➤ The top box is the form header.

➤ The middle box is the *Detail* area:

Firstname Label – this looks the same in Design View as Form View, and tells you what type of field you are entering.

Firstname Control – this is where the actual information appears in Form View, e.g. Mark, Simon, etc., and is where you will type in the field information.

➤ The *Toolbox* is the floating toolbar with all your form buttons on.

➤ The bottom box is the *Form Footer*.

I Can't See The Toolbox!

Ensure that you are in Design View, and click on the **Toolbox** icon at the top of the screen.

The Parts Of A Form

What Are The Parts Of A Form?

There are three parts to a form:

➤ **Form Header:** often used for titles. This appears at the top of every page in the form.

➤ **Detail:** where all the data appears.

➤ **Form Footer:** often used for record numbers, etc. This appears at the bottom of every page in the form.

Selecting A Part

1 Ensure you are in Design View.

2 Click on the grey bar representing the part you require – the grey bar will go darker when it is selected.

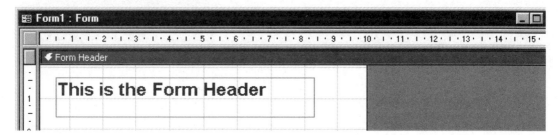

Resizing The Height

1 Ensure you are in Design View.

2 Position the mouse at the bottom border of the part you wish to resize, e.g. resizing the detail – the mouse pointer will change to a double-headed arrow.

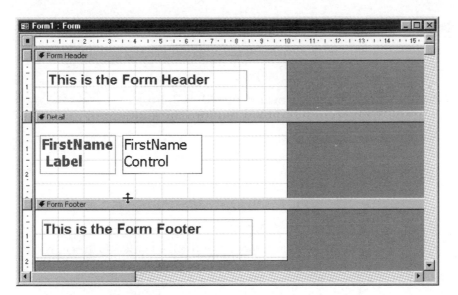

3 Click and drag to resize.

Resizing The Width

1 Ensure you are in Design View.

2 Position the mouse at the right-hand border of the part you wish to resize – the mouse pointer will change to a double-headed arrow.

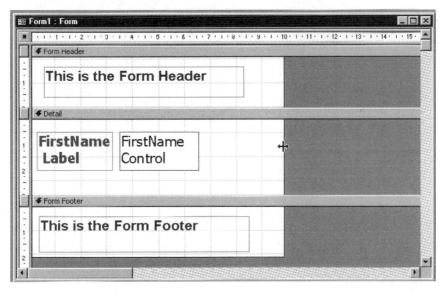

3 Click and drag to resize.

459

Changing The Colour Of A Part

1   Ensure you are in Design View.

2   Select the part you wish to change.

3   Click the drop-down arrow next to the **Fill Color** icon.

4   Click on the colour you require.

My Colour Hasn't Changed!

You probably have a picture in the background. To see the colour, you will need to remove the picture.

1   Double-click the **Select Form** button at the top left of the form to make the *Form Properties* box appear.

2   Click on the **Format** tab.

3   Scroll down the list of properties until you come to *Picture*.

Picture . . . .   C:\My Documents\ca

4   Delete the text inside the *Picture* box.

5   Click outside the *Picture* box – a message will appear.

6   Click **Yes**.

7   Click on the X to close the *Properties* box.

Controls And Labels

What Are Controls And Labels?

➤ A control is a box where data will appear in Form View.

➤ A label is a box that describes the control, and looks the same in Design View as it does in Form View.

GENDER   Female   ▼

How Can I Tell The Difference Between A Control And A Label?

In Design View, the control and label often look identical. It is up to you to switch back to Form View and check which box shows the actual data, and which just shows the label.

Selecting A Control Or Label

Ensure you are in Design View.

Click anywhere on the control.

Or

Click anywhere on the label.

Why Does It Look Like Both The Control And The Label Are Selected?

The control and its associated label are always linked. You will probably want to move them together, otherwise your control may lose its label.

Selecting Several Controls And Labels

1   Ensure you are in Design View.

2   Click on the first control/label you require.

3   Hold down **Shift** on the keyboard.

4   Click on the remaining control(s)/label(s) you require.

5   Release the **Shift** key.

What If I Accidentally Select A Control Or Label?

To remove something from a selection:

1   Hold down **Shift**.

2   Click on the control or label you want to remove from the selection.

Using The Ruler To Make A Selection

If your controls and labels are next to each other:

1   Ensure you are in Design View.

2   Click and drag down the ruler next to the controls/labels you wish to select.

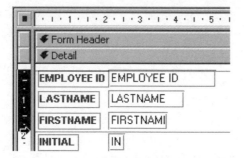

Moving A Control Or Label Separately

1   Ensure you are in Design View.

2   Select the control/label.

3   Position the mouse over the big box at the top left until the mouse pointer changes to a pointing hand.

4   Click and drag the control/label to a new position.

Moving A Control With Its Label

1   Ensure you are in Design View.

2   Select the control/label.

462

3   Position the mouse on the border of the selected control/label until the mouse
    pointer changes to an open hand.

4   Click and drag the control/label to a new position.

Resizing A Control Or Label

1   Ensure you are in Design View.

2   Select the control/label.

3   Hover your mouse pointer over a box until the mouse pointer changes to a
    double-headed arrow.

4   Click and drag the control/label to resize.

Making Labels And Controls The Same Size

1   Ensure you are in Design View.

2   Select the control(s)/label(s) you wish to change.

3   Click on the **Format** menu.

4   Click **Size**.

5   Click on the size option you require, e.g. *To Tallest* will make all the boxes the
    same height as the tallest.

Deleting A Control And Label

1   Ensure you are in Design View.

2   Select the control.

3   Press the **Delete** key.

Deleting A Label On Its Own

1   Ensure you are in Design View.

2   Select the label.

3   Press the **Delete** key.

Adding Descriptive Text

1 Ensure you are in Design View.

2 Ensure that you have enough space on your form for descriptive text.

3 Click on the **Label** button.

4 Click on the form where you require the text.

5 Start typing.

6 Press **Return**.

If You Cannot See The Toolbox Toolbar

Click on the **Toolbox** icon on the *Standard* toolbar.

Editing Text

You can only edit the text in labels. The text inside a control is just the name of the field where it gets its data from, and will show the actual data when you are in Form View.

1 Ensure you are in Design View.

2 Select the label.

3 Click in the middle of the label – a cursor will appear.

4 Edit the text as normal.

5 Press **Return**.

Adding A Field

When you start to use the form, you might realize that you have missed out a field that you needed, or you might delete a field by accident and want to get it back.

1 Ensure you are in Design View.

2 Ensure there is room for the field on the form.

3 Click on the **View** menu.

Click **Field List**

or

click on the **Field List** button.

4 Click and drag the field you require to the form.

Changing The Formatting

1 Ensure you are in Design View.

2 Select the control(s)/label(s).

3 Click the appropriate icon on the *Formatting* toolbar.

Going from left to right, here is what the icons do:

➤ Change the font.

➤ Change the font size.

➤ Add **Bold**, *Italic*, or <u>Underline</u>.

➤ Align to the left, centre, or right.

If You Increase The Size Of Text...

You may find that it no longer fits inside its box. This is really quick to solve – just double-click on one of the resizing boxes!

Changing The Borders And Colours

1 Ensure you are in Design View.

2 Select the control(s)/label(s).

3   Click the appropriate icon on the *Formatting* toolbar.

Going from left to right, here is what the icons do:

➤ Change the fill colour.

➤ Change the text colour.

➤ Change the border colour.

➤ Change the border thickness.

➤ Change the border style.

Alignment

You may need to line labels and controls up with each other – for example, the label and control below are slightly out of line:

1   Ensure you are in Design View.

2   Select the control(s)/label(s).

3   Click on the **Format** menu.

4   Click **Align**.

5   Click the alignment option you require – for example, 'left' will line the left edges of all the boxes up with whichever one is furthest left, 'top' will line the tops of all the boxes up with whichever one is furthest up.

Spacing

You may want to space labels and controls out evenly on the form – for example, the labels and controls below are all unevenly spaced.

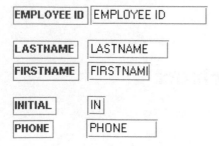

466

1 Ensure you are in Design View.

2 Select the control(s)/labels(s).

3 Click on the **Format** menu.

4 Click **Horizontal Spacing** if the boxes are unevenly spaced across the width of the form

   or

   click **Vertical Spacing** if the boxes are unevenly spaced along the length of the form.

5 Click on the option you require, e.g. *Make Equal*.

Size

You may want to adjust the size of your controls and labels so that they are all the same size.

1 Ensure you are in Design View.

2 Select the control(s)/label(s).

3 Click on the **Format** menu.

4 Click on **Size**.

5 Click the size option you require, e.g. *To Widest* will make the boxes the same size as the widest box in the selection.

AutoFormat

If you decide that you don't like the style of the form, you can make a new choice using AutoFormat.

1 Ensure you are in Design View.

2 Select the whole form by clicking the grey box at the top left of the form – a black box will appear when the form is selected.

3 Click on the **AutoFormat** button.

467

4 Click on a new format in the list.

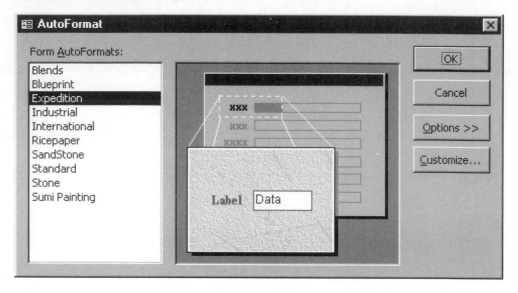

5 Click **OK**.

Tab Order

What Is The Tab Order?

When you input data in Form View, pressing the tab key should take you to the next field.

The tab order determines which field the tab key takes you to next in Form View. If you have moved controls around AFTER creating the form, the tab order may no longer correspond to the way people input data.

Resetting The Tab Order

This will automatically reset the tab order of the fields from left to right, row by row:

1 Ensure you are in Design View.

2 Click on the **View** menu.

3 Click **Tab Order**.

4 Click **AutoOrder**.

5 Click **OK**.

468

Customizing The Tab Order

This will allow you to choose the tab order you want.

1   Ensure you are in Design View.

2   Click on the **View** menu.

3   Click **Tab Order**.

4   Select the grey box to the left of the field you wish to move.

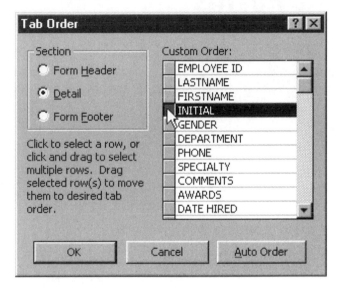

5   Click and drag the field to the position you require.

6   Repeat this process for any other fields you wish to move.

7   Click **OK**.

Saving Design Changes To A Form

Saving Changes

Access does not save your design changes automatically, you will have to do that yourself. To save the design changes:

Click **Save** icon.

Or

1   Close the form – Access will display a message.

2   Click **Yes** if you wish to save

or

click **No** to close the form without saving.

Creating AutoForms

What Is An AutoForm?

An AutoForm is a very quick and easy way of creating a form. You tell Access which table or query you wish to base the form on and it creates a form automatically.

However, you cannot choose the design of your form, and you must use all of the fields in the query or table.

Creating An AutoForm

1   Click on the **Forms** button.

2   Click **New**.

3   Click *AutoForm: Columnar.*

or

click *AutoForm: Tabular.*

or

click *AutoForm: Datasheet.*

4   Click on the drop-down arrow next to *Choose the table or query . . ..*

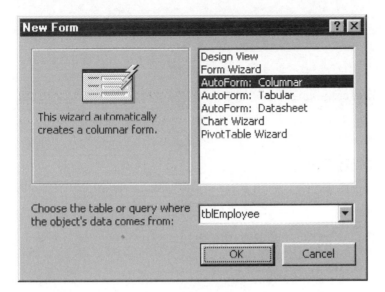

5   Click on the *Table* menu/query you require.

6   Click **OK** – the form will be created.

What Is The Difference Between Columnar, Tabular And Datasheet?

These refer to the layout of the form:

➤ Columnar means you will see one record on the screen at a time.

➤ Tabular means you will see more than one record on the screen at a time.

➤ Datasheet means your form will look the same as a table.

Adding Pictures

Inserting A Picture On A Form Or Report

1   Open the form or report you wish to change in Design View.

2   Select the part you wish to add a picture to.

3   Click on the **Insert** menu.

4   Click **Picture**.

471

5   Change the *Look in* box to the folder where your picture is saved.

Look in:

6   Click on the picture you require.

7   Click **OK**.

Moving A Picture

1   Ensure that you are in the Design View of the form or report.

2   Select the picture.

3   Position the mouse in the middle of the picture – the mouse pointer will look like an open hand.

4   Click and drag to a new position.

Changing The Size Of A Picture

I Can't Resize My Picture!

If you resize the picture as you would in Word, Excel, etc., you'll usually find that the frame which contains the picture changes, while the image itself remains the same size.

1   Ensure you are in the Design View of the form or report you wish to change.

2   Click on the picture you wish to change.

3   Click **Properties** – the *Properties* box will be displayed already if the icon is 'pushed in'.

4   Click on the **Format** tab.

5   Click into *Size Mode* box.

Size Mode . . . . Clip

472

6 Click on the drop-down arrow.

7 Click on **Zoom**.

8 Close the *Properties* box.

9 Resize the picture as normal.

How Do I Resize A Picture As Normal?

1 Select the picture – boxes will appear around the edge.

2 Position your mouse over a box – the mouse pointer will change to an arrow.

3 Click and drag to resize.

What Is The Difference Between Stretch And Zoom?

Stretch will make the picture fill the size of the box which it is in, regardless of whether it stays in proportion.

Zoom will make the picture fit inside the box it is in, and also keep it in proportion. However, it may not stretch to the sides of the box which it is in.

Adding A Picture As The Background Of A Form Or Report

1 Open the form or report you wish to change in Design View.

2 Click on the **Edit** menu.

Click **Select Report**

or

click **Select Form**.

473

3   Click on the **Properties** icon.

4   Click on the **Format** tab.

5   Click into *Picture* box.

6   Click on the icon next to the *Picture* box.

7   Change the *Look in* box to the folder where your picture is saved.

8   Click on the picture you require.

9   Click **OK**.

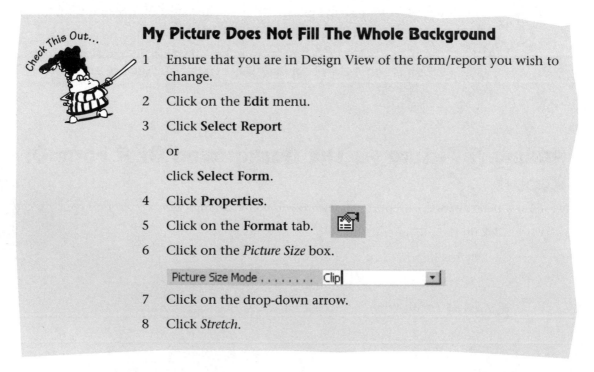

My Picture Does Not Fill The Whole Background

1   Ensure that you are in Design View of the form/report you wish to change.

2   Click on the **Edit** menu.

3   Click **Select Report**

or

click **Select Form**.

4   Click **Properties**.

5   Click on the **Format** tab.

6   Click on the *Picture Size* box.

7   Click on the drop-down arrow.

8   Click *Stretch*.

474

Adding A Picture To A Table

If you want each record to have a different picture on a form or report, you must create a field for it inside the table.

1   Create a new table and ensure that you are in Design View

    or

    open the table you wish to change in Design View.

2   Create a new field which will contain the picture.

3   Enter a name for the field.

4   Change the field's data type to OLE object.

Field Name	Data Type
▶ PHONE	OLE Object ▾

Inserting Pictures Into A Picture Field

This can only be done on a form, so ensure that you have created a form based on the table which contains the picture field.

1   Select the field you wish to add a picture to.

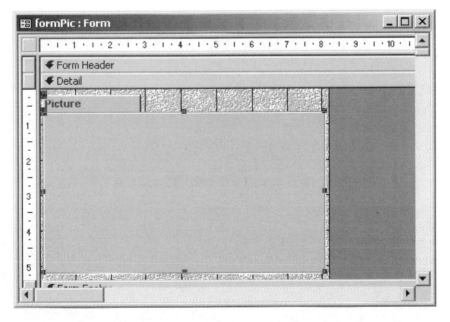

2   Click on the **Insert** menu.

3   Click **Object**.

4   Click in the circle next to *Create from File*.

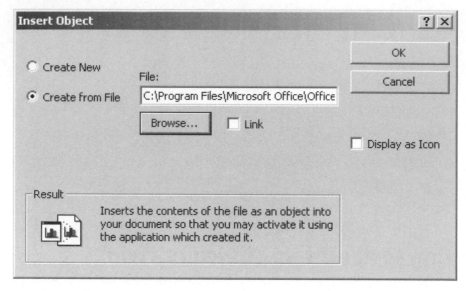

5   Click **Browse**.

6   Change the *Look in* box to the required drive and folder.

7   Click on the picture you require.

8   Click **OK**.

9   Click **OK**.

My Picture Doesn't Fit Into The Box!

Follow the instructions on page 472 – *Changing the Size of a Picture*.

Chapter 4

Reports

Using Reports

What Are Reports?

Reports are used to print off the information from your database in a presentable format. They are based on Tables or Queries. Base a report on a query if you only want to show certain records in your report, rather than every record in the tables. You can use reports to:

➤ Group information under key headings.

➤ Calculate totals and work out statistical information.

➤ Produce mailing labels.

Opening A Report

1   Click on the **Reports** button on the main database window (see pages 407–8).

2   Click on the report you wish to open.

3   Click **Open**.

Or

1   Click on the **Reports** button.

2   Double-click the report you wish to open.

Changing The Print Preview

When you open a report you will be taken to Print Preview. To change the way Print Preview looks, use the toolbar:

Going from left to right, here is what each icon means:

➤ Zooms in or out of the report.

➤ Shows one full page.

➤ Shows two full pages.

➤ Click this icon and drag over the grid to view multiple pages.

➤ Click the drop-down arrow to change the zoom level.

Moving Between The Pages

Click the navigation buttons at the bottom of the screen.

Going from left to right, here is what each icon means:

➤ Go to the first page.

➤ Go to the previous page.

➤ Displays the current page – you can type in a page number and press *Return* to go to that page.

➤ Go to the next page.

➤ Go to the last page.

Printing A Report

To print the whole report, just click once on the **Print** icon.

Printing A Selection Of Pages

1 Click on the **File** menu.

2 Click on **Print**.

3 Click in the circle before *Pages*.

4 Change the page numbers in the *From* and *To* boxes.

5 Click **OK**.

Closing A Report

Click on the X icon at the top of the report window.

Or

Click **Close**.

Creating Reports

The Ways Of Creating A Report

There are several different ways of creating a Report:

➤ **Design View:** will allow you to create the report from scratch with no help from Access.

➤ **Report Wizard:** will allow you to create a report with help from the Access Report Wizard. You can choose which fields you wish to see on the report.

➤ **AutoReport Columnar:** will create an instant report based on the query or table you specify, with each record laid out in a column. You cannot choose which fields you wish to see.

➤ **AutoReport Tabular:** will create an instant report based on the query or table you specify, with all the records laid out in tabular format. You cannot choose which fields you wish to see.

479

➤ **Chart Wizard:** will create a chart with help from the Chart Wizard.

➤ **Label Wizard:** will create mailing labels with help from the Label Wizard.

Creating A Report With The Report Wizard

1   Click on the **Reports** button.

2   Double-click **Create Report by Using Wizard**

or

click **New**,

click **Report Wizard**,

Click **OK**.

3   Click the drop-down arrow under *Tables/Queries*.

4   Click on the table or query you wish to base the report on.

5   Double-click the fields you wish to see on your report from underneath *Available Fields* – they will jump over to the *Selected Fields* column.

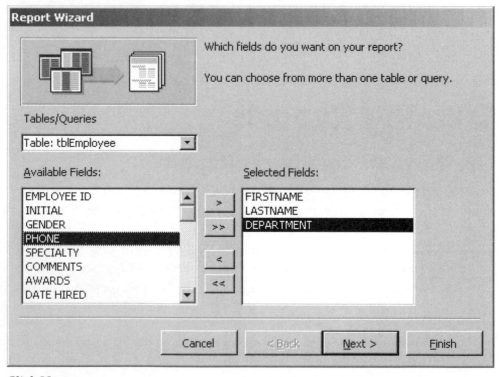

6   Click **Next**.

Next >

7   If required, double-click on the field(s) you wish to group by, e.g. *Department*.

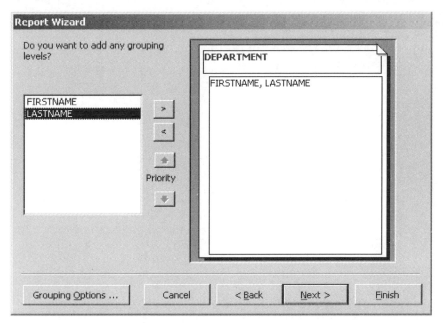

8   Click **Next**.

9   If required, click the drop-down arrow and click on the field you wish to sort by.

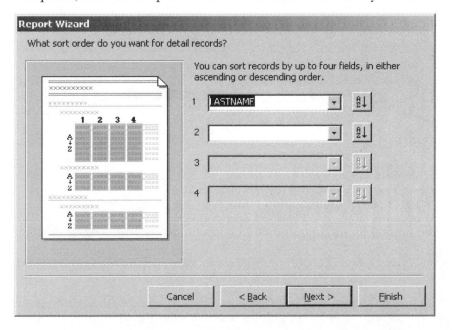

10 Click **Next**.

11 Click the circles next to the layout options you require for your report (the options will be slightly different if you are grouping by a field).

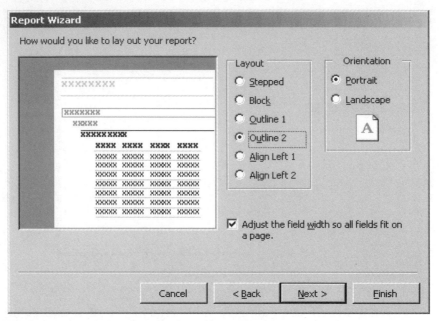

12 Click **Next**.

13 Click on the style you require for your report.

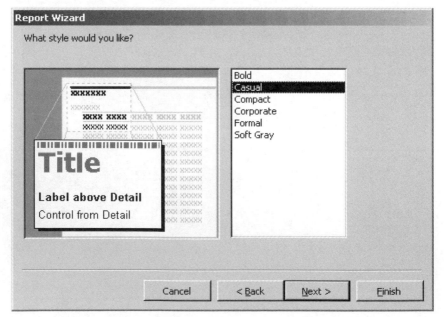

14 Click **Next**.

15 Type in a title for your report (this will appear as the title of the report).

16 Click **Finish**.

When Is My Report Saved?

As soon as you have typed a title and clicked on *Finish*, your report is saved.

Changing The Design Of A Report

What Are The Views?

There are three views to a report:

➤ **Print Preview:** where you can view the report as it will appear when printed.

➤ **Design View:** where you can change how the report is designed.

➤ *Layout View*: in which you can see the layout of your report with some sample information. You probably won't need to use this view very often.

Changing The View

1   Click the drop-down arrow next to the **View** button.

2   Click the view you require.

The View Button Will Look Different Depending On Which View You Are In!

When you are in Print Preview it looks like this:

When you are in Design View it looks like this:

However, it is always the first button on the toolbar.

The Parts Of A Report

What Are The Parts Of A Report In Design View?

➤ **Report Header:** which appears at the top of the report.

➤ **Page Header:** which appears at the top of every page in the report.

➤ **Detail:** which contains the actual records from the table.

➤ **Page Footer:** which appears at the bottom of every page in the report.

➤ **Report Footer:** which appears at the end of the report.

Sometimes reports can have extra headers and footers depending on whether information has been grouped. For example, in the report below the information has been grouped by department. The department field therefore appears in the 'department header'. Every time there is a new department, this header will appear.

reportFishcake

DEPARTMENT		
LASTNAME	**FIRSTNAME**	
	Dominique	
	Todd	
Collins	Sara	

DEPARTMENT	EXECUTIVE	
LASTNAME	**FIRSTNAME**	
Anderson	Debbie	
Anderson	Debbie	
Barnett	Lena	
Beman	Sandy	
Dean	Christine	

Selecting Parts

1   Ensure you are in Design View.

2   Click on the grey bar representing the part you require – the selected part will go a darker grey.

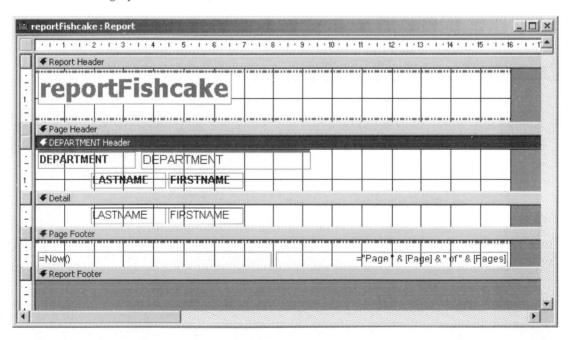

Resizing Height

1   Ensure you are in Design View.

2   Position the mouse at the bottom border of the part you wish to resize – the mouse pointer will change to a double-headed arrow.

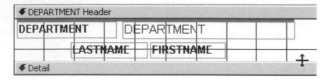

3   Click and drag to resize.

Resizing Width

1   Ensure you are in Design View.

2   Position the mouse at the right-hand border of the part you wish to resize – the mouse pointer will change to a double-headed arrow.

3   Click and drag to resize.

Deleting Headers And Footers

1   Ensure you are in Design View.

2   Click on the **View** menu.

3   Click **Page Header/Footer**

or

click **Report Header/Footer**. (They will be ticked in the menu when they are present in the report.)

Changing Labels And Controls On A Report

Changing Labels And Controls On A Report

Is exactly the same as changing them in the Design View of a form. If you would like to format these elements of the report, follow the instructions starting on page 460.

Adding Extras

Labels

If you want to add extra text to a report, you can add a label.

1   Ensure that the *Toolbox* toolbar is showing.

2   Click the **Label** icon.

3   Click on the report where you would like to add text.

4   Type your text.

The Toolbox Toolbar Is Not Showing!

Click the **Toolbox** icon on the *Standard* toolbar.

Editing The Text In Labels

1   Click on the label you wish to edit.

2   Click again on the label you wish to edit – a cursor will appear.

3   Edit the text as normal.

4   Press **Return**.

Adding The Date And Time

1 Ensure you are in Design View.

2 Click on the **Insert** menu.

3 Click **Date and Time**.

> ➤ If you require the date, tick the box next to *Include Date*, and click the circle next to the date format you require.

> ➤ If you require the time, tick the box next to *Include Time*, and click the circle next to the time format you require.

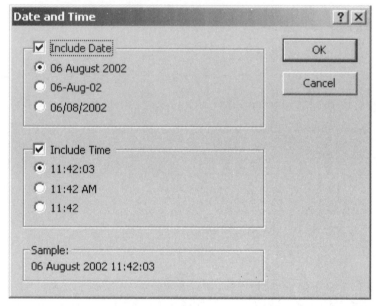

4 Change the options as required (see above).

5 Click **OK**.

6 Click and drag the date to its required location on the report – the mouse pointer will look like a hand.

Adding The Page Numbers

1 Ensure you are in Design View.

2 Click on the **Insert** menu.

3 Click **Page Numbers**.

> ➤ Click the circle next to the format you require.

➤ Click the circle next to the position you require.

➤ Click the drop-down arrow and choose the alignment you require.

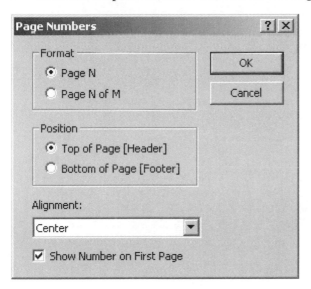

4   Click in the circle next to the page numbers option you require.

5   Click **OK**.

When You Are In Design View You Will See The Field Code!

You have to be in Print Preview to see the actual page number or date that you have added.

Adding Common Expressions Using A Text Box

You may want to add the date, or the page number onto your report. To do this you need to add a text box and enter an expression into it.

1   Ensure that you are in Design View.

2   Ensure that the *Toolbox* toolbar is showing.

3   Click on the **Text Box** icon.

ab|

4 Click on the report where you require the text box.

5 Click on the control (this will probably say 'unbound').

6 Click on the **Properties** icon.

7 Click on the **Data** tab.

8 Click into the *Control Source* box.

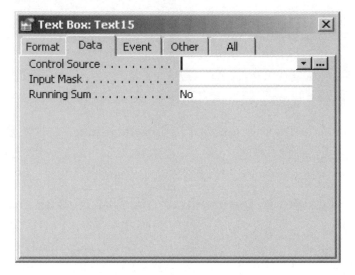

9 Click on the **Expression builder** symbol.

10 Double-click *Common Expressions* in the left column.

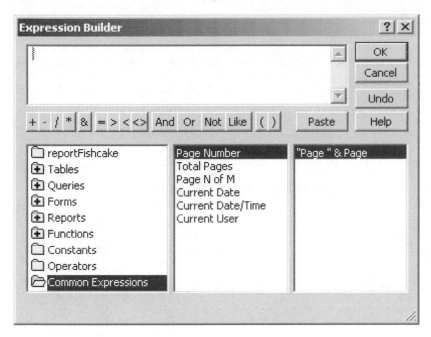

11 Double-click the expression you require, e.g. *Page Number*, *Total Pages*, etc.

12 Click **OK**.

13 Click on the X at the top right of the *Properties* box.

14 Switch to Print Preview to see the actual information.

Text Box Label

The text box will come with a label. You may wish to change the text in this box as it will probably say something like 'Text18'.

Mailing Labels

Creating Mailing Labels

Mailing labels are easy to create using Access. Like any report they must be based on a table or query.

It doesn't really matter whether you base them on a table or query as long as the name and address fields are included! However, if you want to produce mailing labels for a select number of records from the table (e.g. all the people who live in London), you will have to use a query.

1 Click on the **Reports** button on the main database window (see pages 407–8).

2 Click **New**.

3 Click **Label Wizard**.

4 Click the drop-down arrow next to *Choose the table or query ....*

5 Click on the table or query which contains the names and addresses.

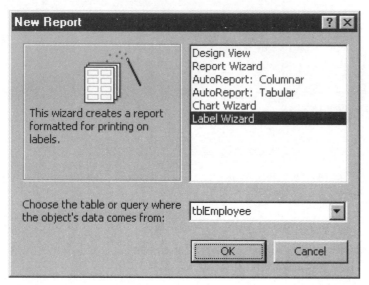

6 Click **OK**.

7 Choose the correct label size.

Product number:	Dimensions:	Number across:
28171	90.2 mm x 42.3 mm	2
28173	96.5 mm x 44.5 mm	2
28175	83.8 mm x 42.3 mm	2
28179	84.0 mm x 42.0 mm	2
28183	83.8 mm x 42.3 mm	2

What label size would you like?

8 Click **Next**.

9 Change the formatting options if required (see below).

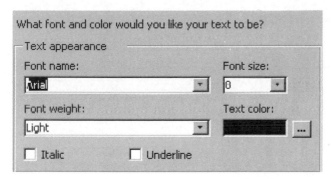

➤ Click the drop-down arrows to choose a different font, font size and font weight (thickness).

➤ Click on the button next to the *Text color* box to choose a different font colour.

➤ Click the *Italic* or *Underline* boxes to make the text *italic* or <u>underlined</u>.

Be Careful With The Font Size

If you make it too large it might not fit on the label!

10 Click **Next**.

11 Position your cursor where you require the field on the prototype label.

12 Double-click the field you require – the label should be set up in exactly the way you want it, i.e. with spaces between the fields and returns to separate the fields on each line.

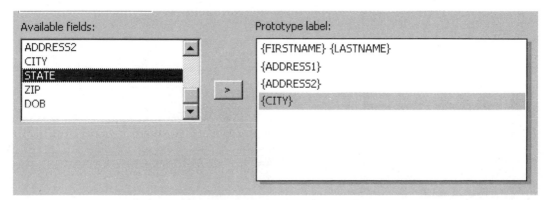

How Do I Delete It If I Add The Wrong Field?

Click and drag over the field you wish to delete, then press *Delete*!

13   Click **Next**.

14   Double-click a field to sort by, if required.

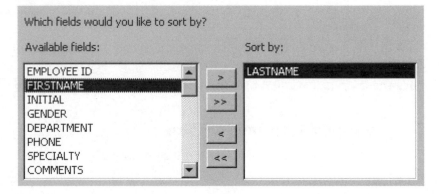

15   Click **Next**.

16   Type a name that clearly describes the labels, e.g. Staff Labels.

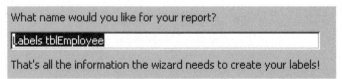

17   Click **Finish**.

Creating AutoReports

What Is An AutoReport?

An AutoReport is a quick and easy way of creating a report. You choose the table or query you wish Access to base the report on, and it creates it automatically.

The disadvantage of using AutoReport is that you cannot sort the records, or group them by a particular field. You also have to use all of the fields in the table or query you base the report on.

Creating An AutoReport

1   Click on the **Reports** button.

2   Click **New**.

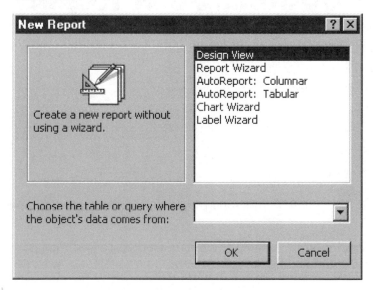

3   Click *AutoReport: Columnar*

    or

    click *AutoReport: Tabular*.

4   Click the drop-down arrow next to *Choose the table or query ....*

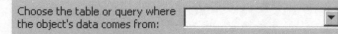

> Choose the table or query where
> the object's data comes from:

5   Click on the table/query you wish to base your report on.

6   Click **OK**.

What Is The Difference Between Columnar And Tabular?

This refers to the way your report is laid out:

➤ Columnar means that your records will appear with the field names running down the page.

➤ Tabular means that you records will appear with the field names running across the page.

Summary Options On A Report

What Are Summary Options?

You can use the report wizard to summarize number or currency fields on your report. They will allow you to produce:

➤ Totals

➤ Averages

➤ Maximum Number

➤ Minimum Number.

If your report is grouped, you can also obtain subtotals, sub-averages, etc. based on each group.

For example the report opposite has used Summary Options to find the total salary, the average salary, the maximum salary, and the minimum salary for each department.

The Summary Options for salary are shown at the bottom right of the report – the Sum, the Average, the Minimum and the Maximum.

496

DEPARTMENT	LASTNAME	FIRSTNAME	SALARY
EXECUTIVE			
		Dominique	20000
		Todd	20000
	Anderson	Debbie	12000
	Anderson	Debbie	12000
	Barrett	Lena	12250
	Beman	Sandy	35000
	Collins	Sara	20000
	Dean	Christine	14500
	Dickerson	Lori	49000
	Eivera	Harry	10500
	Goreman	Vicky	59000
	Hamby	Mary	11500
	Keegan	Marilyn	16500
	Newman	Robert	52000
	Zambini	Rick	79500

Sum £423,750.00
Avg £28,250.00
Min £10,500.00
Max £79,500.00

Creating Summary Options

1   Click on the **Reports** button.

2   Click **New**.

3   Click *Report Wizard*.

4   Click **OK**.

5   Click the drop-down arrow under *Tables/Queries*.

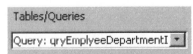

6   Click on the table or query you wish to base this report on.

7 Double-click the fields you wish to see on the report.

8 Click **Next**.

9 Double-click the field(s) you wish to group by if required. If you wish to create subtotals for a set of records, you will have to group by the field you wish to find subtotals for.

10 Click **Next**.

11 Choose the field(s) to sort by if required by clicking the drop-down arrow.

12 Click the **Summary Options** button.

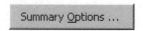

13 Tick the boxes next to the field summary values you require.

14 Choose the options you require underneath *Show*.

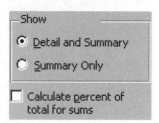

15 Click **OK**.

16 Click **Next**.

17 Choose the layout you require.

18 Click **Next**.

19 Click the style you require.

20 Click **Next**.

21 Type the title you require for your report.

22 Click **Finish**.

498

Chapter 5

Creating A Simple Database

Planning A Database

What Is The Purpose Of My Database?

Designing databases can be a complex business. The more time and thought you put into the planning stage, the more effective your database will be later.

To get an idea of what you will need, ask yourself the following questions:

➤ What do you want the database to do for you?

➤ What will other people need the database to do?

➤ Do you already use some paper forms in a manual system? If you do, this information could be valuable.

The Key Question – What Information Do I Want Out Of My Database?

Start working on paper first:

➤ List all of the information that you want to get out.

➤ Spend time ensuring that you have thought of everything.

Make Sure There Is A Separate Field For Each Piece Of Data You Wish To Sort Or Extract

For example, if you create a field called name that includes both the first name and the last name, you will not be able to sort it alphabetically by the last name. It will also be difficult to extract people whose last name is, for example, 'Smith'. When you create the query you will have to use wildcards.

Creating A New Database

Creating A New Database Without Wizards

1   Click on the **File** menu.

2   Click on **New**

or

click on the **New** icon.

3   Click on the **General** tab.

4   Select *Database*.

5   Click **OK**.

6   Change the folder to save the database in, if required, by clicking on the drop-down arrow next to the *Save in* box and choosing a new location.

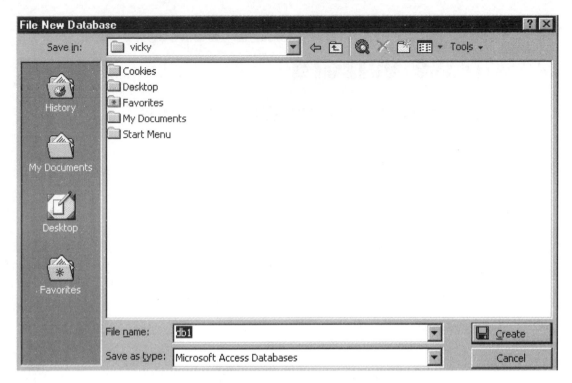

7   Type the file name for your database.

8   Click **Create** – the *Database* window will appear.

Why Do I Give The Filename And Choose The Folder First?

The database is created and saved first. Then the tables, queries, forms, etc., are added to the database. If you didn't save first, then Access would not be able to automatically save the data which you input into your database.

Creating A Database With The Database Wizard

Creating A New Database With Wizards

1　Click on the **File** menu.

2　Click on **New**

　or

　click on the **New** icon.

3　Click on the **Databases** tab.

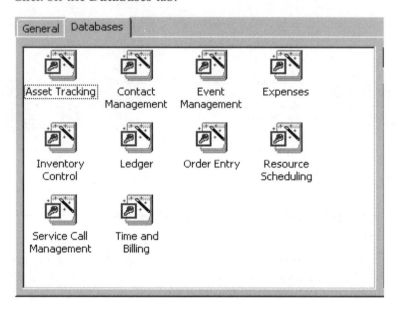

4　Click on the type of database you require, e.g. *Asset Tracking*.

5　Click **OK**.

6　Change the folder to save the database in, if required.

7　Type the file name for your database.

8　Click **Create** – the Wizard will start.

What Will My Database Store?

The first step of the wizard will tell you the type of information you will be able to store in the database.

The Asset Tracking database will store:

- Asset information
- Asset depreciation history
- Asset maintenance history
- Information about employees
- Department information
- Vendor information

9　Click on **Next** – the next step will show you the tables and fields in the database.

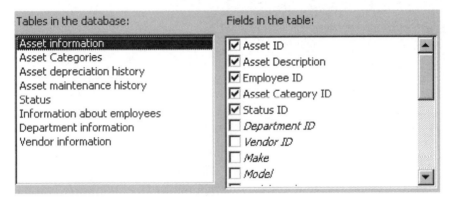

Tables in the database:

Asset information
Asset Categories
Asset depreciation history
Asset maintenance history
Status
Information about employees
Department information
Vendor information

Fields in the table:

☑ Asset ID
☑ Asset Description
☑ Employee ID
☑ Asset Category ID
☑ Status ID
☐ *Department ID*
☐ *Vendor ID*
☐ *Make*
☐ *Model*

10　Click in the box next to any fields you wish to add – they are ticked when included.

Why Can't I Remove Some Of The Fields?

If you try to click into a box to remove a field from a table you may see the following error message.

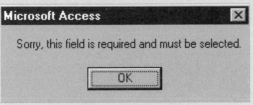

Microsoft Access   ✕

Sorry, this field is required and must be selected.

OK

This means that the field you have tried to remove is required in the table.

11 Click on **Next**.

503

12 Click on the style you would like your database to use for forms.

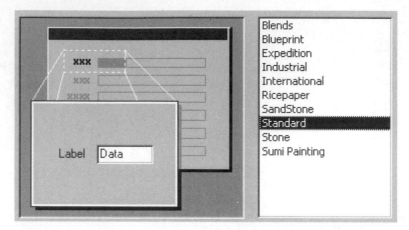

13 Click on **Next**.

14 Click on the style you would like your database to use for reports.

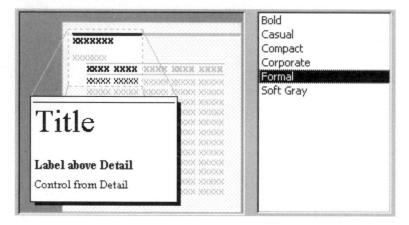

15 Click on **Next**.

16 Type a title for your database.

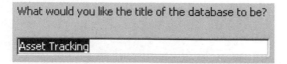

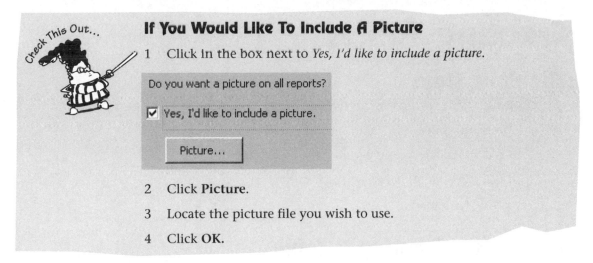

If You Would Like To Include A Picture

1   Click in the box next to *Yes, I'd like to include a picture.*

> Do you want a picture on all reports?
>
> ☑ Yes, I'd like to include a picture.
>
> [Picture...]

2   Click **Picture**.

3   Locate the picture file you wish to use.

4   Click **OK**.

17   Click on **Next**.

18   Click on **Finish** – Access will create your database after a few seconds.

Using The Switchboard

When Access creates your database using a wizard, you will find that you have a switchboard. This helps you to use the database, and helps to keep the data protected. Just click on the button next to the function you require.

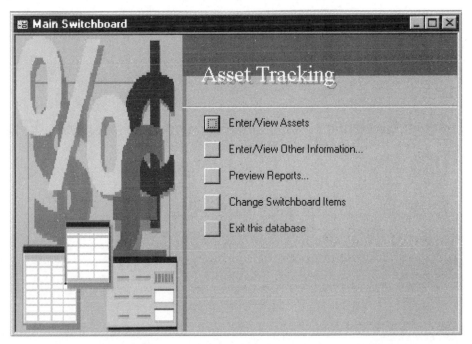

Creating Tables

The Four Steps

Creating a table without using a wizard has four main steps:

1 Creating a table.

2 Creating the fields and deciding the data types.

3 Deciding on a primary key field if needed.

4 Saving the table.

Step One – Creating A Table

1 Click on the **Tables** button.

2 Double-click on *Create table in Design View.*

            Create table in Design view

Or

1 Click **New**.

2 Click *Design View.*

3 Click **OK**.

Step Two – Creating The Fields And Deciding The Data Type

1 Click into the first row under *Field Name.*

	Field Name	Data Type	Description
▶			

2 Type in your first field name, e.g. **OrganisationID**.

506

3   Press **Tab**.

or

click into the *Data Type* column

4   If required, click the drop-down arrow and change the data type (see next section).

5   Press **Tab**.

or

click into the *Description* column.

6   If required, type in a description for this field (e.g. what the field is for).

Field Name	Data Type	Description
OrganisationID	AutoNumber	A number to identify the organisation
OrganisationName	Text	

Access Will Not Allow The Following Characters In Field Names

. (full-stop) ! (exclamation point)   [ ] (brackets)   ` (grave accent)

It Is Good Practice To Not Include Spaces In Field Names

Although you can use spaces in field names and it will not usually cause problems, it can cause conflicts if you use Visual Basic for Applications with Access.

Specifying Data Types

You must specify what data type each of the fields in your table should be.

Data Type	What does it store?	Example	Extra information
Text	Letters or numbers	Firstname Lastname	Holds up to 255 characters. Most of your fields will probably be text.
Memo	Letters or numbers	Comments	Holds up to 64,000 characters. It is usually used when you need to add a lot of text.
Number	Numbers	Number of staff	Holds numbers that you intend to sort numerically, or perform calculations on.
Date/Time	Dates and Times	Date hired Order date	Holds dates that you can then sort into date order and perform calculations on.
Currency	Monetary values	Salary	Formats numbers as currency and allows you to perform calculations on those numbers.
AutoNumber	A number which Access generates automatically for each record.	ID number	Used mostly as a primary key field, because the number will be unique for each record. Even if the record is deleted, the number goes with it.
Yes/No	A field which gives you the choice of 'yes' ' or 'no	Full-time	e.g.
OLE Object	OLE objects are generally graphics, e.g. photographs, logos	Logo Product preview	Holds up to 1 gigabyte (limited by disk space).

Hyperlink	Links to somewhere else that your computer has access to, e.g. a Word document, a Website	Company Website	When you click on the data in this field it will link you to somewhere else.
Lookup Wizard	A field that allows you to choose from a drop-down list	Gender Department	e.g. (see image)

Is A Phone Number A Number Data Type?

No! For phone numbers, part numbers, or numbers on which you don't intend to do calculations are **text**! If you make them numbers, you will not be able to have a '0' at the start of your phone numbers!

Step Three – The Primary Key

What Is The Primary Key?

➤ A special field that **uniquely** identifies each record in the table. In other words there is different information in that field for each record, e.g. id number, product code. You could not use something like 'lastname' as the primary key because some people are likely to have the same lastname. The primary key must be unique to each record.

➤ It is good practice to identify a primary key for each table, although you do not have to if you think you do not need one.

➤ If you are creating relationships then there **must** be a primary key in the table which is **one** side of the relationship.

1   Click into the field you want to become a primary key.

	Field Name
▶	OrganisationID

2   Click on the **Primary Key** icon – a Key will appear next to field.

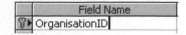

If You Do Not Create A Primary Key You Will Be Asked About It When You Save The Table!

See the next section for more details on this.

Saving The Table

You must save tables before you can input data into them.

1   Click on the **Save** button.

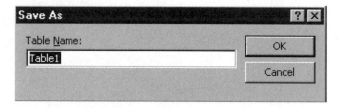

2   Type a name for the table, e.g. **Table Organizations** or **tblOrganizations**.

3   Click **OK**.

What Should I Call My Table?

When saving a table it is good practice to identify it as a table in the name, e.g. table organizations, table students, table employees. Most people would type tblOrganizations, tblStudents, or tblEmployees, for example.

If You Didn't Create A Primary Key ...

Access will ask you if you want to create one when saving.

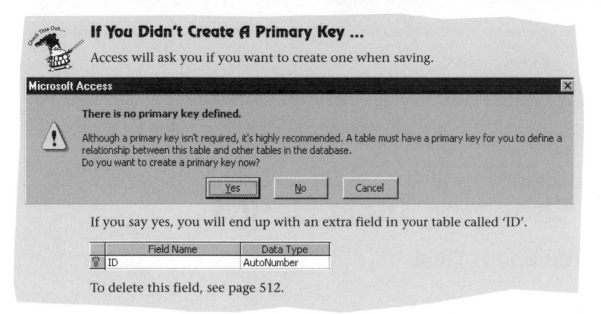

Microsoft Access ✕

There is no primary key defined.

Although a primary key isn't required, it's highly recommended. A table must have a primary key for you to define a relationship between this table and other tables in the database.
Do you want to create a primary key now?

[Yes]   [No]   [Cancel]

If you say yes, you will end up with an extra field in your table called 'ID'.

Field Name	Data Type
ID	AutoNumber

To delete this field, see page 512.

Changing The View Of A Table

What Are The Views Of A Table?

There are two views to a table:

➤ **Design View:** where you can add, edit or delete fields and change the way your table works.

➤ **Datasheet View:** where you can input data.

Changing The View

1   Click the drop-down arrow next to the **View** button.

2   Click on the view you require.

The View Icon Looks Different Depending On Which View You Are In!

When you are in Design View it will look like this:

When you are in Datasheet View it will look like this:

Changing Table Design

Editing A Field

1   Ensure you are in Design View.

2   Click into the field you wish to edit.

3   Make any changes you require.

4   Click **Save**, or Access will warn you to save when you leave Design View.

Access Tells Me That Some Data May Be Deleted

If you have already typed information into the field in Datasheet view, then editing the field may create changes that render the existing information invalid. For example, if you change the data type from text to number then Access will delete the contents of the fields. If this is okay, click **Yes**, if not, click **No**.

Deleting A Field

1   Ensure you are in Design View.

2   Click on the grey bar next to the field you wish to delete – it will become highlighted.

3   Press **Delete**.

4   Click **Yes**.

5   Click **Save**, or Access will warn you to save when you leave Design View.

512

You Will Be Warned Twice About Deleting The Primary Key!

If you delete the primary key, Access will not only warn you that you are deleting a field, but also that it is the primary key for the table.

Moving Fields

1   Ensure you are in Design View.

2   Click on the grey bar next to the field you wish to delete – it will become highlighted to indicate that it is selected.

3   Position the mouse pointer on the grey bar next to the field.

4   Click and drag the field to a new location.

5   Click **Save**, or Access will warn you to save when you leave Design View.

Field Properties

What Are Field Properties?

Field properties are a way of limiting the information which people can type into your table – useful if you want to try and minimize the possibility of mistakes. For example, you can use them to:

➤ Limit the number of characters allowed into a field, e.g. allowing only 8 characters for a postcode.

➤ Specify a default, or automatic value, e.g. 'London' in the town field, if most of your addresses are in London.

➤ Change the way that data appears, e.g. formatting a date which is typed in as **1/1/99** to appear as **01 January 1999**.

Setting Field Properties

You Can Change The Field Properties At Any Time, But ...

... if you change them after you have already input data to the table, you may lose some of the information. If existing data doesn't fit the new requirements, Access may just delete it.

1   Ensure you are in Design View of the table.

2   Click into the field you wish to set properties for.

▶	DATE HIRED|	Date/Time
	DEGREE	Text

3   Change the properties as required (see next sections).

General	Lookup	
Format		▼
Input Mask		
Caption		
Default Value		
Validation Rule		
Validation Text		
Required	No	
Indexed	No	

4   Click on the **Save** icon.

Field Properties Change Depending On The Data Type!

For example fields with a text data type will have different properties available than a field with a number date type, etc.

Changing Field Size

What does it mean? The maximum number of characters which people can input into a field (including spaces).

514

When am I likely to use it? For text fields where there is always a limited number of characters, e.g. postcode, phone number.

1   Click into the *Field Size* box.

Field Size	11

2   Change the number to the maximum number allowed for your field.

Changing Format

What does it mean? Changes the way in which the data appears.

When am I likely to use it? For dates or numbers which you wish to appear differently from the way they are input, e.g. numbers which you wish to become percentages, dates which you wish to become long dates, 01 Jan 1999.

1   Click in the *Format* box.

2   Click the drop-down arrow.

Format		▼
General Number	3456.789	
Currency	£3,456.79	
Euro	€3,456.79	
Fixed	3456.79	
Standard	3,456.79	
Percent	123.00%	
Scientific	3.46E+03	

3   Click on the format you require.

Setting An Input Mask

What does it mean? Forces the information which is input to appear in a certain way. The input mask determines how it should appear, for example an input mask of '0000' would force people to enter four numbers into the field.

When am I likely to use it? When there is a standard format for the field in question, e.g. National Insurance numbers, which are always 2 letters, followed by six numbers and then one letter.

1   Click into the Input **Mask** box.

2   Type in the input mask you require, e.g. LL000000L for a national insurance number.

Input Mask	LL000000L

515

These are the symbols you are most likely to use in your input mask:

___

0   Number which must be filled in.

9   Number which does not have to be filled in.

Number or space which does not have to be filled in and can include plus or minus signs.

L   Letter which must be filled in.

?   Letter which does not need to be filled in.

A   Letter or number which must be filled in.

a   Letter or number which does not need to be filled in.

&   Any character or space which must be filled in.

C   Any character or space which does not have to be filled in.

<   All characters which follow this will be converted to lower case (the symbol does not show when you input data).

>   All characters which follow this will be converted to upper case (the symbol does not show when you input data).

___

Adding A Caption

What does it mean? The text which appears at the top of the column in Datasheet view.

When am I likely to use it? When you want the text at the top of the column to be different from the actual field name.

1   Click into the *Caption* box.

2   Type the caption you require.

Caption	D.O.B

Changing The Default Value

What does it mean? Text which is already typed into the field before you start to input data (you can still type something else, though).

When am I likely to use it? When you often type the same data into a field, e.g. if most of your records contain 'London' in the address, you could change the default for town/city to 'London'.

1   Click into the *Default Value* box.

2   Type the default you require.

Default Value	"London"

Setting The Validation Rule And Validation Text

What does it mean? Setting a rule for the data which can be input into a field. The validation text is the error message which will be displayed if the rule is broken.

When am I likely to use it? One example would be a credit limit. Imagine that nobody can have a credit limit over £50,000. You can set the validation rule as <50000, which forces Access to only accept numbers which are less than 50,000.

1   Click into the *Validation Rule* box.

2   Enter the validation rule, e.g. <50000.

3   Click into the *Validation Text* box.

4   Type the error message you wish to appear if people break the rule, e.g. 'Enter a value of less than £50,000'.

Validation Rule	<50000
Validation Text	Enter a figure of less than £50,000

Making A Field Required

What does it mean? People must enter something into this field when they create a new record.

When am I likely to use it? When you have a field which you do not want to be left blank, e.g. organization name, phone number, etc.

1   Click into the *Required* box.

2   Click the drop-down arrow.

3   Select **Yes**.

Required	Yes

If you do not fill in a required field in Datasheet View, Access will display the following message:

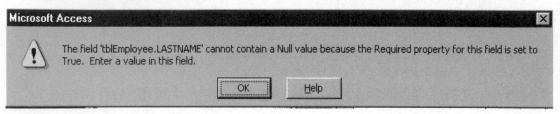

Allowing Zero Length

What does it mean? Allows you to leave a field blank on purpose.

When am I likely to use it? When you have a field which you know is to be left blank.

1   Click into the **Zero Length** box.

2   Click the drop-down arrow.

3   Click *Yes*.

Indexing A Field

What does it mean? Access keeps a sorted copy of this field in the background which speeds up sorting and grouping the data in this field.

When am I likely to use it? On fields which you are likely to sort often in a very large database.

1   Click into the *Indexed* box.

Indexed	No

2   Click *Yes (No Duplicates)* if this field is to be unique to each record, e.g. the primary key

or

click *Yes (Duplicated OK)* if this field will contain duplicates.

518

AutoNumber Property: New Values

What does it mean? The way in which AutoNumber generates the next number. Usually it goes up by one each time.

When am I likely to use it? When you do not want the AutoNumber to go up by one each time.

1 Click into the *New Values* box.

New Values	Increment

2 Click the drop-down arrow.

3 Click *Random*.

Number Property: Decimal

What does it mean? Determines how many decimal places are to appear to the right of the decimal point.

When am I likely to use it? When you need to specify a certain number of decimal points for a number field.

1 Click into the *Decimal Places* box.

Decimal Places	Auto

2 Click the drop-down arrow.

3 Click on the number of decimal places you require.

Text, Memo Or Hyperlink: Unicode Compression

What does it mean? Reduces the amount of space needed to store information in a text, memo or hyperlink field. It is on by default.

When am I likely to use it? If you want to minimize the amount of space needed to store that field.

1 Click into the *Unicode Compression* box.

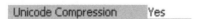

Unicode Compression	Yes

2 Click the drop-down arrow.

3 Click *Yes* or *No*.

Chapter 6

Quick Reference

The Flow Chart Of Database Design

Step One: Decide ...
- ➤ Decide what info do I want out?
- ➤ Work backwards, and decide what info you need to go in!

Step Two: Decide (On Paper)...
- ➤ What tables do you need?
- ➤ What fields do you need? Which ones should be lookups?

Step Three: Consult!
- ➤ It's crucial you take the time to talk to anyone who might use your database or need to take info from it!

Step Four: Create the Database
- ➤ Create a new database and name it.

Step Five: Create Tables

➤ Create your tables and your fields.
➤ Create lookups.

Step Six: Relationships

➤ Determine the relationships between your tables.
➤ Key in a few 'dummy' records.

Step Seven: Queries

➤ Create your most important queries (this will test whether you have put in everything that you need).

Step Eight: Forms And Reports

➤ Create your forms.
➤ Create your reports.

Step Nine: Test!

➤ Test your database again.
➤ Consult everyone and make sure that nothing has been missed!
➤ Delete the 'dummy' records and key in your real info.

Step Ten: Written Record

➤ Make a written record of the tables, fields, lookups and relationships in your database.

Module 6
Presentations

Chapter 1

Getting Started

What Is PowerPoint?

What Is It For?

PowerPoint is for producing presentations on:

- ➤ Acetates (overhead projector slides)
- ➤ 35mm slides
- ➤ Paper
- ➤ The computer screen
- ➤ The Internet.

Check This Out...

All Of These Are Created In Exactly The Same Way!

The only difference comes at the end when you wish to give the presentation. You could print onto acetate or paper, run the slide show on the screen, upload your presentation to the Internet, or send your presentation to a specialist shop to create 35mm slides.

It can also produce extra documents related to your presentation:

➤ Speaker's notes
➤ Audience handouts.

PowerPoint Jargon

Every presentation you produce is made up of slides. Slide is a generic term that can mean any of the types of presentation listed above.

A presentation

Slide One	Slide Two	Slide Three

Starting And Exiting PowerPoint

Starting PowerPoint

1   Click on the **Start** button.

2   Click on **Programs**.

3   Click **Microsoft PowerPoint**.

Or, if you have a shortcut on your desktop, double-click the shortcut.

Exiting PowerPoint

1   Click on the **File** menu.

2   Click **Exit**.

Or

Click on the X at the top right-hand corner of the screen.

The PowerPoint Screen In Normal View

Here is a picture of the PowerPoint screen in Normal view. The screen can look very different depending on which view you are in! (See page 541).

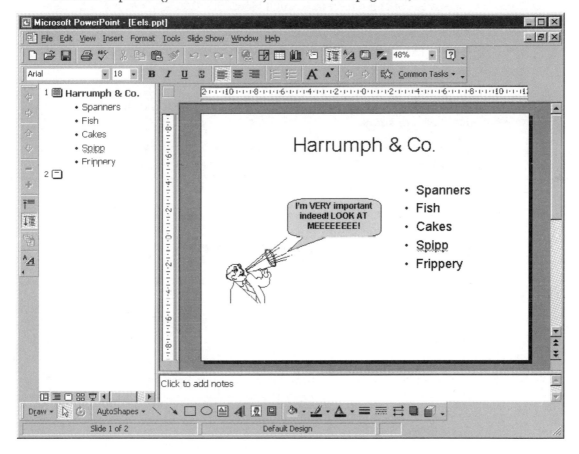

➤ The blue bar at the top is the title bar.

➤ Underneath that is the menu bar.

➤ Underneath that is the standard toolbar.

➤ Underneath that is the formatting toolbar.

➤ The large white bar on the left is the outline view area.

➤ The large area on the right is the slide view area.

➤ Just under that is the speaker's notes area.

➤ Under that is the drawing toolbar.

➤ Last, but not least, right at the bottom, is the status bar.

Adjusting The Areas Of The Screen

There are three areas of the screen in Normal view.

➤ Outline view area.

➤ Slide view area.

➤ Speaker's notes.

At different times in your work, you will want to concentrate on different areas. To make an area bigger or smaller:

1   Position your mouse at the edge of an area – the mouse pointer will change to a double-headed arrow.

2   Click and drag.

The Start Up Dialog Box

What Does It All Mean?

When you first start PowerPoint, you will see the *Start Up* dialog box. This is designed to help you get started with a new presentation, or open one that has already been created.

1   Click in the circle next to the option you require (see opposite).

2   Click **OK**.

➤ Click on *AutoContent Wizard* to use the AutoContent Wizard (see next section).

➤ Click on *Design Template* to create a new presentation based on a template.

➤ Click on *Blank presentation* to create a new, blank presentation.

➤ Click on *Open an existing presentation* to open a presentation you have already created.

You Do Not Have To Use The Dialog Box

The dialog box is there to help you. If you don't want to use it, just click on **Cancel** or press the **Escape** key (**Esc**) on the keyboard to go straight to into PowerPoint.

The AutoContent Wizard

The AutoContent Wizard will ask you questions on the subject matter of your presentation. It will then create a presentation, including text, based on the answers you give.

1 Select the answers you require.

2 Click on **Next** after you have answered.

3 Click on **Finish** at the end.

Design Template

A template is a pre-set design for your presentation. It will not add any text, but will put colours and graphics into the background of your slides.

1 Select the template you require, e.g. *Artsy*.

2 Click **OK** – the *New Slide* box will appear (see page 540).

What Is A Blank Presentation?

Exactly what it sounds like – this will produce a presentation with a white background and black text. It is up to you to jazz it up! If you choose this option, you will be taken to the *New Slide* box (see page 540).

Turning The Start Up Dialog Box Off

Once you are in PowerPoint you can turn the Start Up dialog box off, so that it doesn't appear when you start PowerPoint next time.

1 Click on the **Tools** menu.

2 Click **Options**.

3 Click on the **View** tab.

4 Click in the box next to *Startup Dialog*.

5 Click **OK**.

Creating A Presentation

Creating A Blank Presentation (White Background, Black Text)

1 Click on the **File** menu.

2 Click on **New**.

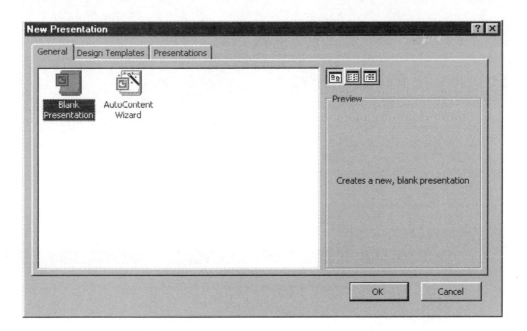

3 Click on *Blank Presentation*.

4 Click **OK.**

Or

Click on the **New Presentation** icon.

Should I Use The Menu Or The Icon?

The icon is the quickest way of creating a new presentation, but using the menu gives you access to PowerPoint's design templates, where you can choose colours and pictures for the backgrounds of your slides.

531

Saving A Presentation

Saving A Presentation

1   Click on the **Save** icon.

Or

Click on the **File** menu.

Click on **Save**.

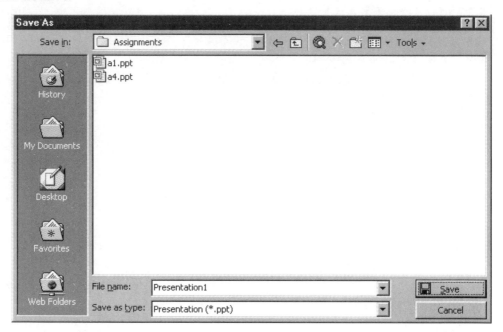

2   Type a file name (maximum of 255 characters) into the *File name* box.

3   Change the location in the *Save in* box if required, by clicking on the drop-down arrow next to it.

4   Click **Save**.

Saving A Presentation After You Have Made Changes

Just click on the **Save** icon – the previous version is overwritten.

Save Regularly!

Click on the **Save** icon at regular intervals when you are working. If you forget to save for a long time, you are in danger of losing your work if there is a power cut.

Opening And Closing A Presentation

Opening A Presentation

1   Click on the **Open** icon.

2   Click the drop-down arrow next to the *Look in* box, and go to the drive and folder where your file is saved.

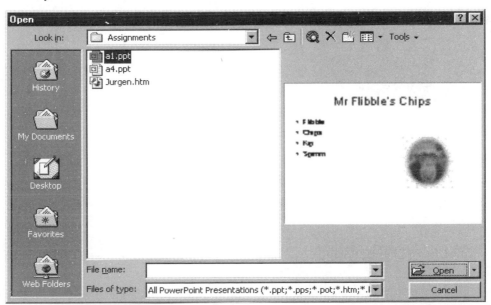

3   Click on the file/folder you require.

4   Click **Open**.

5   Repeat steps 3 and 4 until the file is opened.

Closing A Presentation

1   Click on the **File** menu.

2   Click **Close**.

Or

Click on the bottom X at the top-right hand corner of the screen.

Changing The Zoom Control

What Is The Zoom Control?

The zoom control allows you to zoom in and look at your presentation close up, or zoom out to look at your presentation from a distance.

Changing The Zoom With The Icon

1   Click the drop-down arrow next to the *Zoom* box.

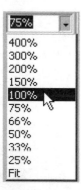

2   Click on the zoom level you require.

Changing The Zoom With The Menu

1   Click on the **View** menu.

2   Click **Zoom**.

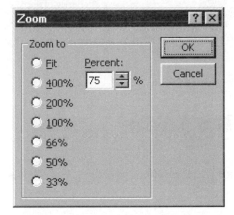

3   Click in the circle next to the zoom level you require.

or

click the up and down arrows next to the percent box.

4   Click **OK**.

Toolbars

You can choose which toolbars you want displayed according to what you are working on.

Displaying Toolbars

1   Click on the **View** menu.

2   Click on **Toolbars**.

3   Click on the name of the toolbar you want to display.

Hiding Toolbars

1   Click on the **View** menu.

2   Click on **Toolbars**.

3   Click on the name of the toolbar you want to hide.

Hidden Or Displayed?

You can tell which toolbars are currently displayed. The toolbars that are displayed have a tick next to them, the toolbars that are hidden do not. So if the toolbar you want is ticked, it is somewhere on the screen.

Moving Toolbars Around The Screen

If a toolbar is getting in the way:

1   Position the mouse on the blue part of the title bar.

2   Click and drag it to a new location.

Or

1   Position the mouse on the blue part of the title bar.

2   Double-click – the toolbar will stick to an edge of the screen.

If the title bar is not showing:

1   Position the mouse to the left of the toolbar.

2   Click and drag it to a new location.

Using Help In PowerPoint

PowerPoint comes with help files, just like all the other software packages. Press **F1** to call it up, and use it in the same way as you would any other help file.

Chapter 2

Basic Operations

Moving Around A Presentation

Where Am I?

Check the status bar at the bottom of the screen – it tells you what slide you are on, and how many slides you have.

Slide 1 of 2

Moving Around With The Scroll Bar

To move to the next slide, click the double-headed down arrows.

To move to the previous slide, click the double-headed up arrows.

Moving Around With The Keyboard

To move to the next slide, press **Page Down** (sometimes called PgDn).

To move to the previous slide, press **Page Up** (sometimes called PgUp).

To move to the first slide, press **Ctrl** and **Home**.

To move to the last slide, press **Ctrl** and **End**.

To Move To Individual Slides

Use the Slide Sorter view (see page 541).

Or

Click into the slide required in the Outline View area.

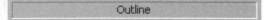

Adding Text To Slides

What Are Slide Layouts?

Every slide has a layout containing placeholders which you can enter text into. There are two layouts shown below:

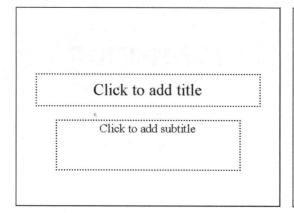

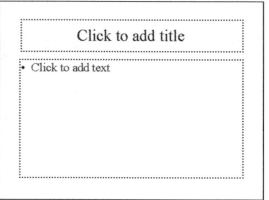

Title Slide Layout.

Bullet List Layout.

What Are Placeholders?

Every layout has placeholder for each item that you will put on your slides. These will always give instructions on how to add information.

 *Text Placeholder.*

 *Chart Placeholder.*

Clip Art Placeholder.

Media Clip Placeholder.

Adding Text To Placeholders

1   Click inside the placeholder you want to add text to – diagonal lines will appear around the edge.

2   Start typing!

3   Click outside the placeholder when you have finished.

PowerPoint Does The Formatting For You!

PowerPoint comes with pre-set formatting depending on the template you have chosen. Titles will be bigger, sub-titles and bulleted lists will be smaller. There will be different alignments and there will be different fonts.

You can change the formatting on individual slides, but you may lose consistency with the rest of the slides in the presentation. If you wish to change the formatting consistently use the master slides (see page 587).

Moving To The Next Placeholder With The Keyboard

Press **Esc**, then press **Tab**.

Creating Bulleted Lists

1   Click into the bulleted list placeholder.

2   Type your first point.

3   Press **Return** to start a new point.

539

Editing the Text Placeholders

1   Click inside the placeholder you want to change – diagonal lines will appear around the edge.

2   Make any changes you require.

Creating New Areas For Text

If the placeholders on your slide do not give you all the space you need for text, you can draw a text box.

1   Click on the **Text Box** icon on the drawing toolbar.

2   Position the mouse on the slide where you require extra text.

3   Click and drag the shape of the text box you require.

4   Start typing – text will wrap inside the box.

Creating New Slides

Creating New Slides

1   Move to the slide which will appear before the new one.

2   Click on the **New Slide** icon.

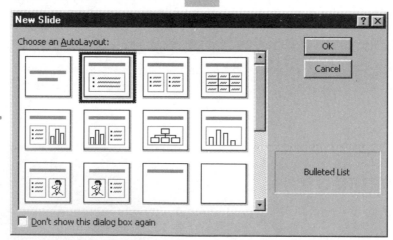

3   Click on the layout you require.

4   Click **OK**.

540

You Can Also Press Ctrl And M To Add A New Slide ...

Or click on *Common Tasks* and then click on *New Slide*.

Don't Create A New Presentation By Mistake!

Lots of people fall into the trap of creating new slides by clicking on the New icon, or by going to **File** and **New**. This won't just create a new slide, it will also create a new presentation – leaving all of your existing slides stranded. If you have done this, close down the new presentation, and you should end up back in the old one where you can add a new slide as normal.

Changing The Layout

If you wish to change the layout after you have created the slide:

1   Click on the **Format** menu.

2   Click on **Slide Layout**.

3   Click on the layout you require.

4   Click **Apply**.

The Different Views Of PowerPoint

Changing The View

1   Click on the **View** menu.

2   Click on the view you require.

Or

Click on the required icon from the bottom left of the screen.

541

Going from left to right, the icons will take you to a different view:

➤ Normal view

➤ Outline view

➤ Slide view

➤ Slide Sorter view

➤ Slide Show view (runs the slide show).

Normal View

Normal view is the one that you will work in most of the time. It offers you three different areas:

➤ Slide view area where you can see your slide.

➤ Outline view area where you can see all the text in your presentation.

➤ Speaker's notes area where you can write your own notes on the slides.

Each of these areas can be adjusted according to your preference. In normal view, you can:

➤ Add text

➤ Add pictures

➤ Create speaker's notes.

Outline View

Outline view allows you to work with the text. In this view, you can:

➤ Promote and demote text to create main points and sub points.

➤ Move text around.

➤ Create summary slides.

➤ Expand or collapse the detail of your presentation.

Slide View

Slide view shows you one slide at a time. You can:

➤ See individual slides in detail.

➤ Work with pictures.

➤ Work with diagrams.

Slide Sorter View

Slide Sorter view shows you all your slides as if they were laid out on a table. You cannot add text or pictures in Slide Sorter view, but you can:

➤ Change the order of slides.

➤ Delete slides.

➤ Add transition and animation effects (see pages 636–42).

Slide Show View

Slide Show view is used for giving an on-screen presentation. When you are finished creating your presentation, this is what you will use to present the show – or you can use it to make sure it works before standing up in front of 300 people.

Normal View

Getting To Normal View

This is the view that PowerPoint will open in. If you have changed views:

Click on the **Normal View** icon.

Or

Click on the **View** menu.

Click on **Normal**.

The Three Panes

Slide pane: in the Slide pane, you can see one slide at a time. You can:

➤ See individual slides in detail.

➤ Work with pictures.

➤ Work with diagrams.

Outline pane: use the Outline pane to work with the text in your presentation. You can:

➤ Promote and demote text to create main points and sub points.

➤ Move text around.

➤ Expand or collapse the detail of your presentation.

Notes pane: the Notes pane is for adding your speaker's notes to the slides.

Michael Caine: An acting legend, well known for his portrayal of Alfie in 'Alfie', Charlie in 'The Italian Job', and Peachy Carnahan in 'The Man Who Would Be King' (possibly his best role). He has absolutely nothing to do with PowerPoint, but his last name rhymes with 'pane', so I thought I'd mention him here to break up the monotony of all this talk of slides and panes. Now, back to work.

Switching Between Panes

Click into the required pane – the status bar will indicate where you are.

| Slide 1 of 2 | *Slide pane.* |

| Outline | *Outline pane.* |

| Slide Notes | *Notes pane.* |

How Do I Use Outline Pane?

Most of the things you can do in Outline view you can do in the Outline pane (see page 00–00).

Slide Sorter View

Getting To The Slide Sorter View

1   Click on the **View** menu.

2   Click **Slide Sorter**.

Or

Click on the **Slide Sorter View** icon.

Selecting Slides In Slide Sorter View

Click on the slide you require – a dark border will appear around the edge.

Or, if you would like to select several slides:

1   Click on the first slide you require.

2   Hold down the **Shift** key.

3   Click on the other slides you require.

Or, if you would like to select all of the slides:

Press **Ctrl+A**.

Moving Slides In Slide Sorter View

1   Select the slide you wish to move.

2   Click and drag to a new location – a vertical grey line indicates where your slide will be placed.

Deleting Slides In Slide Sorter View

1   Select the slide(s) you wish to delete.

2   Press **Delete**.

Creating A Summary Slide

The summary slide will lift the titles off any slides which you select, and turn them into a bulleted list, which you can use as an agenda or as a conclusion.

1   Select the slides you wish to appear in the summary.

2   Click on the **Summary Slide** icon.

Outline View

Getting To Outline View

Click on the **Outline View** icon.

You Can Also Use The Outline Pane In Normal View

When in Normal view you can see the Outline pane which allows you to do nearly everything that you can do in Outline view. You can resize this pane if you need more room (see page 528).

Understanding Outline View

Outline view shows you all the text in your presentation.

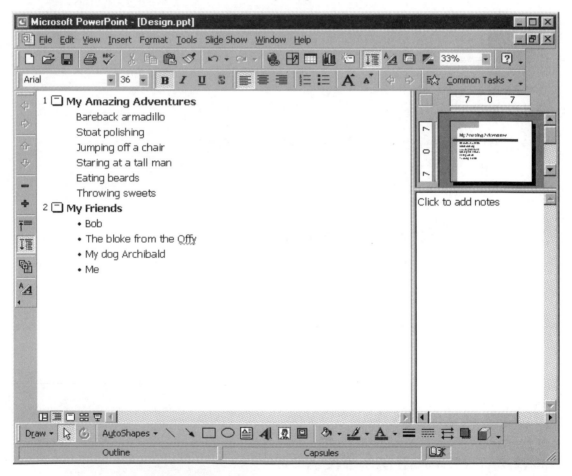

➤ The grey bar on the left is the *Outlining* toolbar.

➤ The main white area shows you a summary of your slides. The little slide icon indicates the start of a new slide.

➤ The top right area shows you a tiny preview of the selected slide.

➤ The bottom right area lets you add your own notes.

Displaying The Slide Miniature

The slide miniature will show you how the slide you are currently working on looks in Slide view. You can see it in other views and it will automatically appear at times, such as when you can't see the whole slide. If you can't see the slide miniature:

1 Click on the **View** menu.

2 Click **Slide Miniature**.

Displaying The Outlining Toolbar

The *Outlining* toolbar provides access to the commands available in Outline view. It is not always displayed. To turn it on or off:

1 Click on the **View** menu.

2 Click **Toolbars**.

3 Click **Outlining** – it is ticked when it is on.

Editing The Text

1 Click into the text to change.

2 Make any changes you require.

Adding New Points

1 Position the cursor at the end of the previous point.

2 Press the **Return** key – the new point will be at the same 'level' as the previous point.

Selecting A Slide

Click over the white box next to the slide you require – the mouse pointer will look like a four-headed arrow.

1

547

Selecting A Line

Click to the left of the line you require – the mouse pointer will look like a four-headed arrow.

Selecting Several Lines Or Slides

1   Select the first slide/line you require.

2   Hold down the **Shift** key.

3   Click on the last slide/line you require.

You Can Only Select Several Lines Or Slides If They Are Next To Each Other

So if you tried, for example, to select slide one and slide five, it wouldn't work. Sorry. It's a cruel world sometimes.

Select Everything

Press **Ctrl+A**.

Promote And Demote

Promoting and demoting changes the importance of the points on your slide. For instance, if you have a main point which you would like to become a sub point, you can demote it. If you have a main point, which you would like to become a new slide, you promote it. Have a look at the diagram below to see the different levels.

1 ⬚ New Slide 1
   • Main Point 1
   • Main Point 2
      • Sub-point 1
         • Sub-sub point 1
   • Main Point 3
      • Sub point 2
2 ⬚ New Slide 2

1   Click into the line you want to change

     or

select several lines you want to change.

2   Click on the **Promote** icon to increase its importance

or

click on the **Demote** icon to decrease its importance.

Moving Text A Short Distance

1   Click into the line you want to change

or

select several lines you want to change.

2   Click on the **Up** arrow to move up

or

click on the **Down** arrow to move down.

Moving Text A Long Distance

1   Select the line(s) to change – your mouse pointer must look like a four-headed arrow when you do this.

2   Don't release the mouse after selecting!

3   Click and drag the selection to its new position – a horizontal black line will show you where you are going.

Collapse And Expand All

This is useful if you do not want to see all the detail on your slides, or if you want to move slides around, without having to see all the detail they contain.

Click on the **Collapse All** icon – only slide titles will be shown.

Or

Click on the **Expand All** icon – all the text will be shown.

Collapse And Expand The Selection

1   Select the slide(s) you wish to collapse.

2   Click on the **Collapse** icon.

Or

1   Select the slide(s) you wish to expand.

2   Click on **Expand** icon.

Show/Hide Formatting

If you require more space on the screen to see the text, you can hide the formatting. To turn formatting on or off, click on the **Show/Hide Formatting** icon.

550

Page Setup

Changing The Size Of Slides For Different Presentations

1　Click on the **File** menu.

2　Click **Page Setup**.

3　Click the drop-down arrow underneath the **Slides sized for** box.

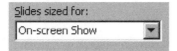

4　Click on the type of presentation you are creating.

5　Click **OK.**

Creating Custom Sized Slides

1　Click on the **File** menu.

2　Click **Page Setup**.

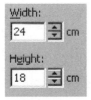

3　Change the width and height as required – click into the box and type a new number, or use the up and down arrows.

4　Click **OK.**

Changing The Orientation Of Your Slides, Outlines, Or Notes Pages

1　Click on the **File** menu.

2　Click **Page Setup**.

3　Click into the white circle next to the orientation you require.

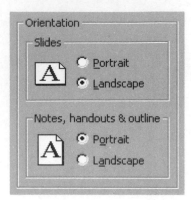

4   Click **OK**.

Can I Make Some Slides Portrait, And Some Slides Landscape?

Not in the same presentation. All the slides must be portrait or landscape

Printing Slides

Previewing In Greyscale

If you only have a black and white printer and would like to see what your presentation looks like in black and white before you print.

1   Click on the **Grayscale Preview** icon.

2   Click it again to return to colour.

Printing All The Slides

Click on the **Print** icon.

Print Options

1 Click on the **File** menu.

2 Click **Print**.

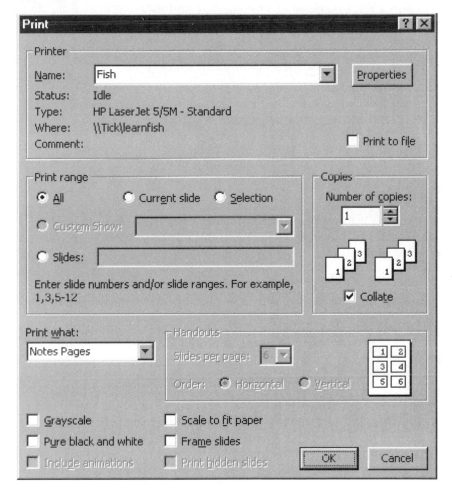

3 Change the *Print range* options as required:

➤ Click on *All* to print all slides, *Current slide* to print the slide you are on, or *Selection* to print whatever you have selected.

➤ Click on *Slides* and type in the slides you want to print – if you want to print slide 5, type in **5**, for slides 4 to 19, type **4-19**, for slide 3, slide 12 and slides 15 to 22, type **3,12,15-22**.

4 Change the *Copies* options as required – type in the number of copies you require, or use the up and down arrows.

5   Click the drop-down arrow by the *Print what* box and choose what you want to print, e.g. handouts, slides, etc.

6   Change any other options as required:

➤ *Grayscale* prints out in black and white and shades of grey, *Pure black and white* prints out in just black and white.

➤ *Scale to fit paper* reduces or enlarges the slide to fit the sheet of paper.

➤ *Frame slides* prints a border around the slides.

➤ *Collate* lets you change the order of pages – if you are not sure, leave it ticked. Ticked will print out a 3 page presentation in this order: 1, 2, 3, then 1, 2, 3. Unticked will print out in this order: 1, 1, 2, 2, 3, 3.

7   Click **OK**.

Print To File

If your computer is not connected to a printer you can use the *Print to file* feature. This takes all the information which a printer needs from your presentation and stores it in a file which can be opened on any machine – even if PowerPoint is not installed!

1   Click on the **File** menu.

2   Click **Print**.

3   Tick the box marked *Print to file*.

4   Click **OK**.

5   Type in a file name.

6   Change the *Save in* box to the folder where you wish to save the printer file.

7   Click **OK**.

Printing Handouts

You can print out handouts for your audience to write their notes on. They will include miniatures of the slides in your presentation.

1   Click on the **File** menu.

2   Click on **Print**.

3   Click the drop-down arrow under *Print what.*

4   Click on *Handouts*.

5   Click the drop-down arrow next to *Slides per page* and click on the number you require.

6   Choose the order you require.

7   Click **OK**.

Printing Speaker's Notes Or Outline View

If you would just like the outline text of your presentation (as it appears in the outline page), or you would like to print out the notes you have typed in the notes pane:

1   Click on the **File** menu.

2   Click **Print**.

3   Click the drop-down arrow underneath the *Print what* box.

4   Click on the option you require.

5   Click **OK**.

Selecting Text And Placeholders

Why Select?

➤ To format text or placeholders.

➤ To move text or placeholders.

➤ To resize placeholders.

➤ To delete placeholders.

Unless you select beforehand, PowerPoint does not know what you are trying to work with!

Working With Text Inside A Placeholder

1   Click inside the placeholder you want to change – diagonal lines will appear.

2   Make your changes to the text.

Selecting The Whole Of A Placeholder

1   Click inside the placeholder you want to change – diagonal lines appear.

2   Click on the diagonal lines – dotted lines appear.

3   Make your changes to the placeholder.

Selecting Text

1   Click inside the placeholder you want to change – diagonal lines will appear.

2   Click and drag over the text you require – the text will go white, with a black background.

3   Make any change to your text.

Deselecting Text Or Placeholders

Click outside the placeholder into any blank space – the text will go back to normal.

Moving, Resizing And Deleting Placeholders

Moving Placeholders

1   Select the whole placeholder – dotted lines appear around the edge.

2   Position the mouse over the dotted line – mouse pointer will change to a four-headed arrow.

3   Click and drag to a new location.

Resizing Placeholders

1   Select the whole placeholder, making sure that dotted lines appear around the edge – if they are diagonal lines, click on them once to make them dotted.

2   Position the mouse over a resizing handle – it will change to a double-headed arrow.

3   Click and drag to resize – dragging from a corner will resize the box proportionally, and dragging from a middle handle will stretch or squash the shape of the box.

Deleting Placeholders

1   Select the whole placeholder – dotted lines will appear around the edge.

2   Press **Delete**.

Formatting Placeholders

Formatting Colours And Lines

If you want to change the colours or lines around your placeholder, you need to bring up the Format AutoShapes box.

To bring up the Format AutoShape box:

1   Select the placeholder you wish to change.

2   Click on the **Format** menu.

3 Click **Placeholder**.

4 Click on the **Colors and Lines** tab.

To change the colour of the placeholder:

1 Click the drop-down arrow next to the *Color* box under *Fill*.

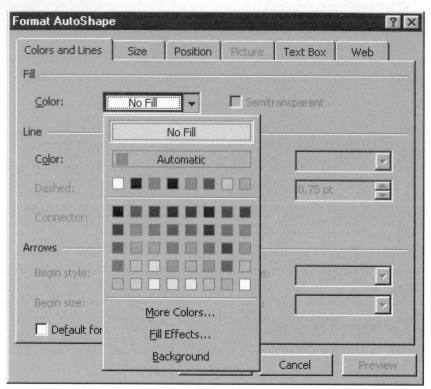

2 Click on the colour you require

or

click *More Colors*.

Click on the **Standard** tab.

Click on the colour you require.

Click **OK**.

To change the colour of the lines around the placeholder:

1 Click the drop-down arrow next to the *Color* box under *Line*.

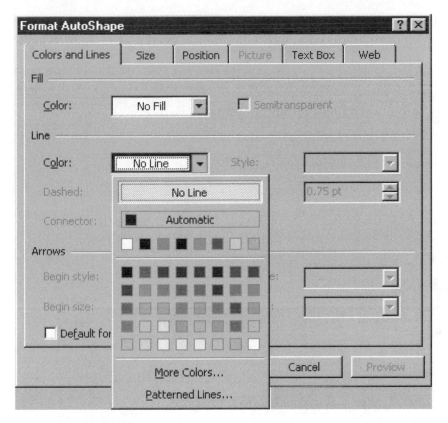

2   Click on the line colour you require

Or

click *More Colors*.

Click on the **Standard** tab.

Click colour you require.

Click **OK**.

To change the style of the lines around the placeholder:

1   Click the drop-down arrow next to the *Color* box under *Line*.

2   Choose a colour for your line (see above).

559

3   Click the drop-down arrows next to *Dashed* or *Style*.

4   Click on the style you require.

5   Click the up and down arrows next to *Weight* to change the thickness of the line.

Setting The Text Anchor Point

1   Select the placeholder.

2   Click on the **Format** menu.

3   Click **Placeholder**.

4   Click on the **Text Box** tab.

5   Click on the drop-down arrow to the right of *Text anchor point*.

6   Select a position for your text.

7   Click **OK.**

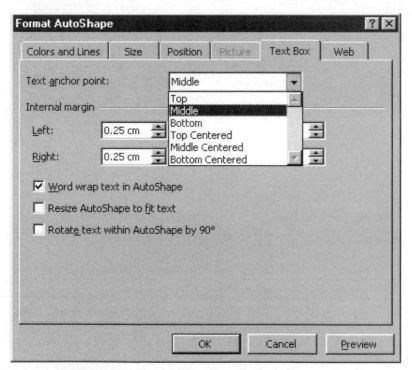

Moving And Copying Text

The Clipboard

When you copy or cut anything it is temporarily stored on an area called the Windows Clipboard until you need it again. The Windows Clipboard can only hold one item at a time. When you copy or cut a new item it will overwrite what was previously there.

In Office 2000 there is a special clipboard called the Office Clipboard. It looks like a toolbar, and you can see it if you try to copy more than one item at a time. The Office Clipboard can hold up to 12 items.

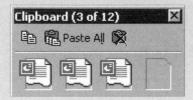

Moving Text Using The Icons

1   Select the text you would like to move.

2   Click on the **Cut** icon – the text is moved to the Windows Clipboard.

3   Position the cursor in the place you would like to move the text to.

4   Click on the **Paste** icon.

Copying Text Using The Icons

1   Select the text you would like to copy.

2   Click on **Copy** icon – the text is copied to the Windows Clipboard.

3   Position the cursor in the place you would like to copy the text to.

4   Click on the **Paste** icon.

Moving Text Using The Menu

1   Select the text you want to move.

2   Click on the **Edit** menu.

3   Click on **Cut**.

4   Click where you want to put your text.

5   Click on the **Edit** menu.

6   Click on **Paste** – the text will have moved to the new location.

Copying Text Using The Menu

1   Select the text you want to move.

2   Click on the **Edit** menu.

3   Click on **Copy**.

4   Click where you want to put your text.

5   Click on the **Edit** menu.

6   Click on **Paste** – the text will be in both the new and the original location.

Copying Or Moving More Than One Thing

PowerPoint 2000 gives you the option of putting lots of things on the clipboard, so that you can copy many separate pieces of text at once.

1   Select the first piece of text you wish to cut or copy.

2   Click **Cut** or **Copy** – the text is sent to the Office Clipboard.

3   Select the second piece of text you wish to cut or copy.

4   Click **Cut** or **Copy** – the text is sent to the Office Clipboard, and a new toolbar will appear.

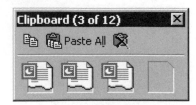

5   Continue cutting and/or copying up to 12 times.

6   Position the cursor where you would like to paste the text.

7   Click the icon for the text you would like to paste.

Or

Click on **Paste All** to paste everything – hover your mouse pointer over the icon to see which piece of text it is.

To display the Office Clipboard without copying anything.

1   Click on the **View** menu.

2   Click on **Toolbars**.

3   Click on **Clipboard**.

When you have finished using it, just click on the X in the top-right corner to hide it.

Eventually The Clipboard Will Get Full Up

Once you have cut or copied 12 items the clipboard will get full. Click on the **Clear Clipboard** icon to empty it.

Chapter 3

Formatting Slides

Changing The Appearance Of Text

Use The Master Slides For Consistent Formatting!

If you wish to change all the slides in your presentation, go to a master slide (see the section starting on page 587 for more on master slides).

Making Text Bold, Italic, Underlined Or Shadowed

1   Select the text or placeholder you want to change.

2   Click on the icon you require (shown below) – it will look pushed in when clicked.

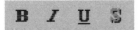

Going from left to right, here is what each icon does:

➤   **Bold**

➤   *Italic*

➤ Underline

➤ Shadow.

To remove any of these effects, just click the icon again – it will no longer look pushed in.

Changing The Fonts

1   Select the text or placeholder to change.

2   Click the drop-down arrow next to the *Font* box.

3   Click on the font you require – use the scroll bar to see more fonts if necessary.

Changing The Size Of Text

1   Select the text or placeholder to change.

2   Click the drop-down arrow next to the *Font Size* box.

3   Click on the size you require – use the scroll bar to see more sizes if necessary

Or

1   Select the text or placeholder to change.

2   Click on the **Increase** or **Decrease Font Size** icons – the big A increases the size, the small A decreases it.

Special Text Effects

1   Select the text or placeholder you wish to change.

2   Click on the **Format** menu.

3   Click **Font**.

4   Click to put a tick in the box next to the effect you require.

5   Click **OK**.

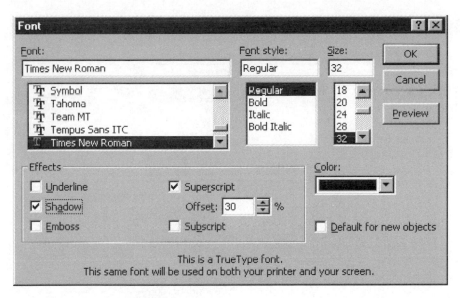

Examples of special text effects:

Embossed, superscript, subscript, Shadow.

Changing Font Colour

1 Select the text or placeholder you wish to change.

2 Click on the **Format** menu.

3 Click **Font**.

4 Click on the drop-down arrow next to *Color*.

5 Click on the colour you require

or

click on *More Colors*.

Click on the **Standard** tab.

Click on the colour you require.

6 Click **OK**.

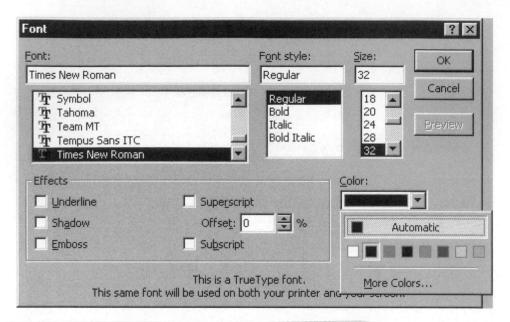

My Text Doesn't Look The Right Colour

The text will not look right until you deselect it. If it is still selected, it will look very wrong indeed.

Replacing Fonts

If there is a font in your presentation that you don't like, you can quickly change all instances of it to something else:

1   Click on the **Format** menu.

2   Click **Replace Fonts**.

3   Click the drop-down arrow underneath *Replace*.

4   Click on the font you wish to replace.

5   Click on the drop-down arrow underneath *With*.

6   Click on the font you wish to replace with.

7   Click **Replace**.

Changing Case

This is a quick and easy way to change the case of your text, and save retyping. There are five case options:

➤ This is sentence case.

➤ this is lowercase.

➤ THIS IS UPPERCASE.

➤ This Is Title Case.

➤ tHIS iS tOGGLE cASE.

1 Select the text you want to change.

2 Click on the **Format** menu.

3 Click **Change Case** – the *Change Case* dialog box will appear (see below).

4 Click in the circle to the left of the option you want.

5 Click **OK**.

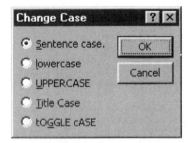

Title Case

In titles it is customary not to capitalize prepositions – e.g. **and**, **or**, **but**, **to**, etc. However, sometimes you can choose not to follow this rule, either for effect or to follow an established style (like we did in this book!).

Changing Line Spacing

1 Select the text or placeholder you want to change.

2 Click on the **Format** menu.

3 Click **Line Spacing**.

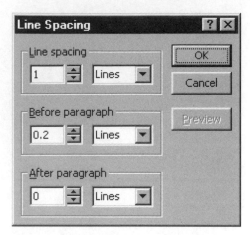

4   Change the options as required:

➤ *Line spacing*: the amount of space between the lines.

➤ *Before paragraph*: the amount of space between the paragraphs.

➤ *After paragraph*: the amount of space after the paragraphs.

5   Click **OK**.

Bullets And Numbering

Use The Master Slides For Consistent Formatting!

If you wish to change the bullets for all the slides in your presentation, go to a master slide (see the sections on master slides, starting on page 587).

Changing The Style Of Bullet Points

1   Select the text or placeholder you want to change.

2   Click on the **Format** menu.

3   Click **Bullets and Numbering**.

4   If necessary, click on the **Bulleted** tab.

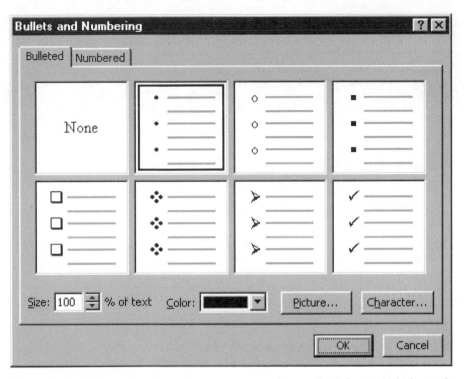

5   If required, click on the drop-down arrow underneath *Color* and click on the colour you require.

6   If required, click into the box underneath *Size* and choose the size you require.

7   Click on the bullet style you require.

8   Click **OK**.

Choosing Another Character

If you don't like any of the bullet styles, go to the *Bullets and Numbering* dialog box, and then:

1   Click on **Character**.

2   If required, click the drop-down arrow underneath *Bullets from* and choose the font you require.

3   Click on the symbol you require.

4   Click **OK**.

571

Click On A Symbol To Magnify It

If you click on one of the bullet styles in the box, it will become magnified. You can then use the cursor keys to move around the different styles

Removing Bullets

1   Select the paragraph you want to remove bullets from.

2   Click on the **Bullets** icon to remove bullets.

Logos

Use The Master Slides For Consistent Formatting!

If you wish to add the logo to all the individual slides in your presentation, add it to a master slide. If you add it on individual slides, you cannot guarantee that it will be the same size, or in the same position on every one. (See the sections on master slides, starting on page 587).

Adding A Logo

1   Click on the **Insert** menu.

2   Click on the **Picture** sub-menu.

3   Click **From File**.

4   Change the *Look in* box to the folder where your logo is saved.

5   Click on your logo's file name.

6   Click **Insert**.

Moving The Logo

1   Select the logo by clicking into the middle of it.

2   Click and drag it to a new location.

Resizing The Logo

1   Click on the logo – white boxes will appear around the edge.

2   Hover the mouse over a white box at a corner – the mouse pointer will change to a double-headed black arrow.

3   Click and drag outwards to make the logo bigger, or click and drag inwards to make the logo smaller.

Adding Transparent Colour To The Logo

If your logo has a background you may find that it clashes with the background of your slide. You can set the background colour to transparent so that it blends in better:

1   Select the logo – the *Picture* toolbar should appear.

2   Click on the **Set Transparent Color** icon – the mouse pointer will change to a pen shape.

3   Click on the background of your logo.

Aligning And Indenting Text

Use The Master Slides For Consistent Formatting!

If you wish to change all the slides in your presentation, go to a master slide (see the sections on master slides, starting on page 587).

Changing The Alignment

Changing the alignment changes the position of the text inside the placeholder. Text can either be aligned to the left of the placeholder, in the centre of the placeholder, or to the right of the placeholder.

1   Select the text or placeholder to change.

2   Click on the alignment option you require – the first icon aligns the text to the left, the next one centres it, and the last one aligns it to the right.

Changing The Indentation

You can change the indentation to alter the position of text and bullets inside a placeholder.

1   Click into the paragraph you want to change

or

select several paragraphs that you want to change.

2   Drag the required indent marker on the ruler:

➤   Drag a top triangle to move bullets.

➤   Drag a bottom triangle to move text.

➤   Drag a square to move the bullet and text together.

What Are The Indent Markers?

Each top triangle will line up to a bullet. Each bottom triangle will line up to text.

Displaying The Ruler

1   Click on the **View** menu.

2   Click **Ruler**.

Changing Tabs

What Are Tabs?

Tabs are used for lining up text against tab stops on the slide. To begin with, there are pre-set **tab stops** across the slide. If you press the tab key on the keyboard, the cursor jumps to the next available tab stop, and you can then type text which will line up to that tab. Pre-set tab stops are shown as grey lines underneath the ruler.

You can also set your own tabs, which appear as symbols on the ruler. There are four different types:

Left tab (left edge of the text lines up to the tab stop).

Centre tab (text is centred around the tab stop).

Right tab (right edge of the text lines up to the tab stop).

Decimal tab (this is used for figures with decimal points, so that the decimal points line up underneath each other).

The diagram on page 576 shows tabs in action. Tab stops are shown on the ruler, and the text lines up to them.

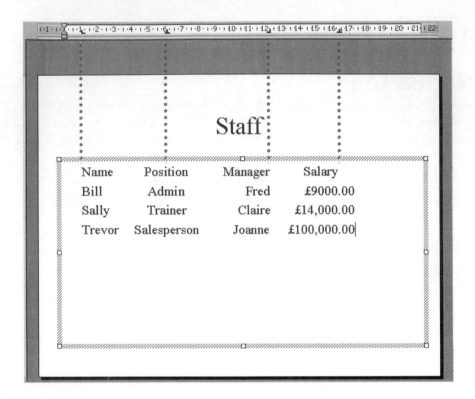

Setting Tabs

1   Click inside the placeholder you want to add tabs to – diagonal lines will appear around the edge.

2   Change the tab type selector to the type of tab you require – click on the *Tab* box at the top left of the ruler until it displays the tab type you want.

3   Click on the ruler where you require the tab – the tab symbol will appear on the ruler.

Using Tabs

1   Press the **Tab** key on the keyboard until the cursor lines up with the tab stop you require.

2   Press the **Return** or **Enter** key to create a new line – the tab stops will still be in place.

576

Moving Tabs

1   Click into the placeholder which contains the tab.

2   Position the mouse over the tab symbol on the ruler.

3   Click and drag it to a new position.

Changing The Tab Type

1   Click into the placeholder which contains the tab.

2   Position the mouse over the tab symbol on the ruler.

3   Click and drag it down off the ruler – the text will go a bit wobbly.

4   Set the new type of tab in the same position.

Deleting Tabs

1   Click into the placeholder which contains the tab.

2   Position the mouse over the tab symbol on the ruler.

3   Click and drag it off the ruler.

Changing The Background

Changing The Colour Of The Background

1   If you are in Slide Sorter view, select at least one slide.

2   Click on the **Format** menu.

3   Click **Background**.

4 Click the drop-down arrow underneath the preview.

5 Click on a colour from those pictured (these are from the current colour scheme)

or

click on *More Colors*.

Click on a colour from the **Standard** tab.

Click **OK**.

6 Click on **Apply to All** to change all the slides

or

click on **Apply** to change selected slides.

Adding A Fill Effect To The Background

1 Click on the **Format** menu.

2 Click **Background**.

3 Click the drop-down arrow underneath the preview to change the background.

4 Click **Fill Effects**.

5 Make your changes in the *Fill Effects* box (see following sections).

6 Click **OK**.

7 Click **Apply to All** to change all the slides

or

click **Apply** to change selected slides.

Changing The Gradient Fill Effect

1 From the *Fill Effects* dialog box, click on the **Gradient** tab

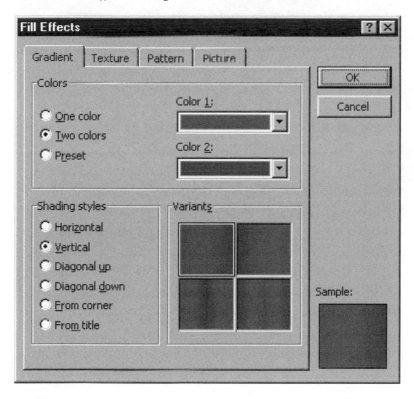

2 Under *Colors*, click the circle next to the colour setting you require:

➤ *One color*: goes from dark to light.

➤ *Two colors*: goes from one colour into another.

➤ *Preset*: shows you a list of preset shading settings which you can choose from.

3 Under *Shading styles*, click in the circle next to the style you require – this will change the direction in which your colours shade into each other.

4 Click on the variant you require under *Variants* – this is the final pattern shape.

5 Click **OK**.

Changing The Texture Fill Effect

1   From the *Fill Effects* dialog box, click on the **Texture** tab.

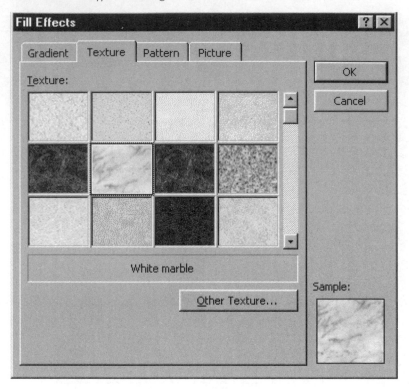

2   Click on the texture you require – scroll down to see more if required.

3   Click **OK**.

Changing The Pattern Fill Effect

Changing to a pattern fill effect can sometimes make your text to difficult to read, but sometimes it can make a slide look quite nice.

1   From the *Fill Effects* dialog box, click on the **Pattern** tab.

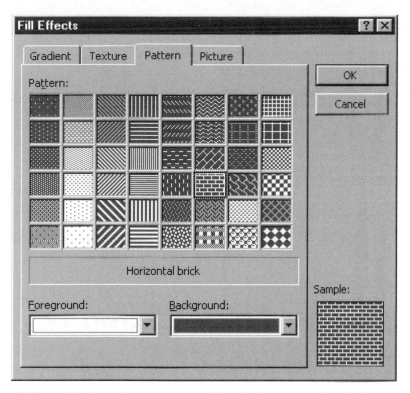

2 Click on the drop-down arrow underneath *Foreground* and change it to a different colour if required.

3 Click on the down arrow underneath *Background* and change it to a different colour if required.

4 Click on the pattern you require from the ones shown under *Patterns*.

5 Click **OK**.

Changing The Picture Fill Effect

If you want to add a picture or photograph to the background of your slides:

1 From the *Fill Effects* dialog box, click on the **Picture** tab.

2 Click **Select Picture**.

3 Change the *Look in* box to the folder where your picture is saved.

4 Click on the name of the picture.

5 Click **Insert**.

6 Click **OK**.

581

Omitting Background Graphics

If you have chosen a design template for your slides, it may have a graphic in the background which can sometimes get in the way. To prevent background graphics from showing:

1   Select the slide(s) you wish to change.

2   Click on the **Format** menu.

3   Click **Background**.

4   Tick the *Omit background graphics from master* box.

☑ Omit background graphics from master

5   Click on **Apply to All** to change all the slides or click on **Apply** to change the selected slides.

Changing The Colour Scheme

Changing The Colour Scheme

1   If you are in Slide Sorter view, select at least one slide.

2   Click on the **Format** menu.

3   Click **Slide Color Scheme**.

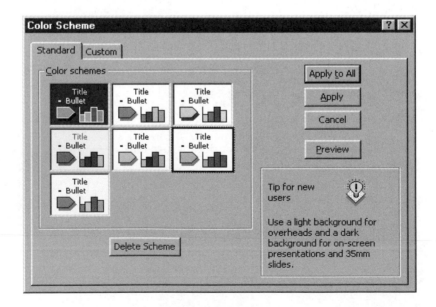

4   Click on the colour scheme you require.

5   Click **Apply to All** to change all the slides

or

click **Apply** to change selected slides

What Do Those Diagrams Mean?

➤ *Title of Slide*: title text colour.

➤ ●: bullet colour.

➤ *Bullet text*: bullet text colour.

➤ The background of the diagram shows you the background colour.

➤ The mini chart shows you how your charts will appear.

➤ The other shape (the sideways house) shows you how any drawn shapes will appear.

Customizing The Colour Scheme

1   Click on the **Format** menu.

2   Click **Slide Color Scheme**.

Color Scheme   ? ✕

Standard | **Custom**

Scheme colors

- Background
- Text and lines
- Shadows
- Title text
- Fills
- Accent
- Accent and hyperlink
- Accent and followed hyperlink

Change Color...

Add As Standard Scheme

Apply to All

Apply

Cancel

Preview

Title of Slide
- Bullet text

3   Click on the **Custom** tab.

4   Click on the coloured box representing the part of the scheme you wish to change.

5   Click **Change Color**.

6   Click on the **Standard** tab.

7   Click on the colour you require.

8   Click **OK**.

9   Click **Apply to All** to change all the slides

     or

     click **Apply** to change selected slides.

Check This Out...

Make The Background A Different Colour From The Other Elements!

Otherwise you may not be able to see the other elements, for example if you chose a white background and white text you would not be able to read the text.

Check This Out...

What Does Accent Mean?

Accent refers to things like bullet points, colours of graphics in the background, etc.

Adding A Standard Scheme

1 Create a customized colour scheme as above.

2 Click **Add as Standard Scheme** – the new scheme will now appear on the **Standard** tab.

Chapter 4

Masters And Templates

Using The Master Slides

What Are The Master Slides?

The master slides are there to save you time and give consistency to your presentation. When you make a change on a master, it changes all the slides. You can use them to:

➤ Change the fonts

➤ Change the bullet style

➤ Change the position of placeholders

➤ Change the graphics in the background of your slides

➤ Add a logo to the background

➤ Change the position of slide numbering, the date or footer information.

This saves you a lot of time and effort in keeping your presentation consistent.

Why Use A Master Slide?

Whatever you do on a master slide will affect everything consistently...

Change the slide master . . . . All your slides will change accordingly

Change the title master . . . . All your title slides will change

Change the handout master ...... All your handouts will change

Change the notes master .... All your speaker's notes pages will change

The Slide Master

Which Slide Does The Slide Master Affect?

Anything you do on the slide master will affect every slide, except those with the title slide layout.

There are two exceptions to this rule:

1   If you change the fonts on the slide master, ALL the slides in the presentation change.

2   If you have used the blank presentation template, you will not have access to a title master, and anything you do on the slide master will affect ALL the slides in the presentation.

Getting To The Slide Master

1   Click on the **View** menu.

2   Click **Master**.

3   Click **Slide Master**.

Or

1   Select a slide which does not have the title slide layout.

2   Hold down the **Shift** key.

3   Click on the **Slide View** icon.

The Slide Master

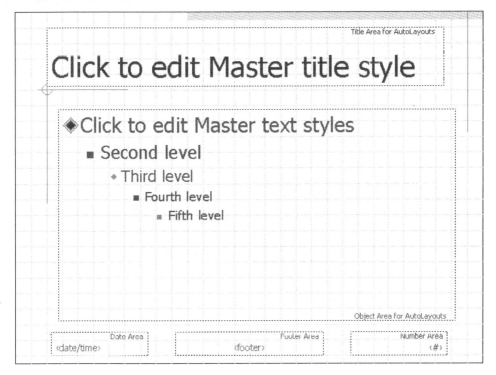

Master title style: How all your titles will look.

Master text style: How all your main points will look.

Second level, *Third level*, etc.: How all your sub-points will look.

The date and time will appear on the bottom left if you have added them.

The footer will appear on the bottom centre if you have added one.

The page/slide number will appear on the bottom right if you have added them.

You can also add any template graphics – these will appear on every slide.

You Can Ignore The Date Area, Footer Area And Number Area If You Have Not Added These To Your Slides.

To find out how to add information to these areas see page 657.

Closing The Slide Master

1   Click on the **View** menu.

2   Click on the view you wish to return to.

Or

Click on a slide view icon from the bottom left of the screen.

Or

Click **Close** on the *Master* toolbar.

Making Changes To The Slide Master

You can change the Slide Master just like you would change a normal slide.

To change the appearance of text . . . . See page 565.

To change the bullet style . . . . See page 570.

To add a logo . . . . See page 572.

To move the date, footer, or slide number . . See page 657.

To move or resize placeholders . . . . See page 557.

The Title Master

Which Slide Does The Title Master Affect?

Anything you do on the Title Master will affect every slide which has the Title Slide layout.

The Title Master is not available if you have used the blank presentation template. If you have a more complicated template, you can make the title slides look different from the other slides in the presentation, which will give them more emphasis.

Getting To The Title Master

1   Click on the **View** menu.

2   Click **Master**.

3   Click **Title Master**.

Or

1   Select any slide which has the title slide layout.

2   Hold down the **Shift** key.

3   Click on the **Slide View** icon.

The Title Master

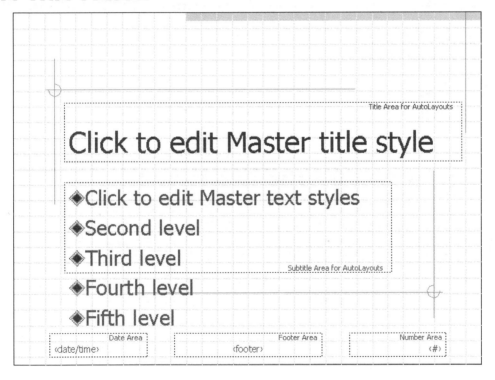

This works in the same way as the Slide Master, but everything you do here will change any slide based on the Title Slide layout.

591

You Can Ignore The Date Area, Footer Area And Number Area If You Have Not Added These To Your Slides.

To find out how to add information to these areas, see page 657.

Closing The Title Master

1   Click on the **View** menu.

2   Click on the view you wish to return to.

Or

Click on a slide view icon from the bottom of the screen.

Or

Click **Close** on the *Master* toolbar.

Making Changes On The Title Master

You can change the Title Master just like you would change a normal slide.

To change the appearance of text . . . . See page 565.

To add a logo . . . . See page 572.

To move the date, footer, or slide number . See page 657.

To move or resize placeholders . . . . See page 557.

The Handout Master

What Does The Handout Master Affect?

Anything you do on the handout master will affect your audience handouts.

Getting To The Handout Master

1   Click on the **View** menu.

2   Click **Master**.

3   Click **Handout Master**.

The Handout Master

Click on the handout you require from the *Handout Master* toolbar.

*Going from left to right, here is what each icon means:

➤ Two slides per page

➤ Three slides per page

➤ Four slides per page

➤ Six slides per page

➤ Nine slides per page

➤ Outline.

Closing The Handout Master

1   Click on the **View** menu.

2   Click on the view you wish to return to.

Or

Click on a slide view icon from the bottom of the screen.

Or

Click **Close** on the *Master* toolbar.

Making Changes On The Handout Master

You can change the Handout Master just like you would change a normal slide.

To change the appearance of text . . . . See page 565.

To add a logo . . . . See page 572.

To move the date, footer, or slide number . . See page 657.

The Notes Master

What Does The Notes Master Affect?

Anything you do on the notes master will affect your speaker's notes (see page 601).

Getting To The Notes Master

1   Click on the **View** menu.

2   Click **Master**.

3   Click **Notes Master**.

The Notes Master

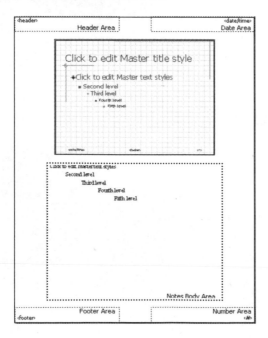

- ➤ If you added headers or footers, they will appear at the top left and bottom left.
- ➤ The miniature slide in the top half of the page can be moved or resized.
- ➤ The notes area in the bottom half of the page can also be moved or resized.
- ➤ The text in the notes area shows how your main and sub points will look on your notes.

Closing The Notes Master

1   Click on the **View** menu.

2   Click on the view you wish to return to.

Or

Click on a slide view icon from the bottom of the screen.

Or

Click **Close** on the *Master* toolbar.

Making Changes On The Notes Master

You can change the Notes Master just like you would change a normal slide.

To change the appearance of text . . . . See page 565.

To add a logo . . . . See page 572.

To move the date, footer, or slide number . . See page 657.

To move or resize placeholders . . . . See page 557.

Applying A Template

What Are Design Templates?

Design templates are pre-set formats that add graphics, colours and fonts consistently onto all the slides in your presentation. The design template will decide how the following elements look:

➤ Fonts and formatting.

➤ Bullet points.

➤ Background graphics.

The design template you are currently using will appear on the status bar at the bottom right of the screen.

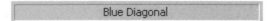

Applying A Design Template

1 Click on the **Format** menu.

2 Click on **Apply Design Template**.

3 Click on the template you require, e.g. *Blueprint* – a preview will appear.

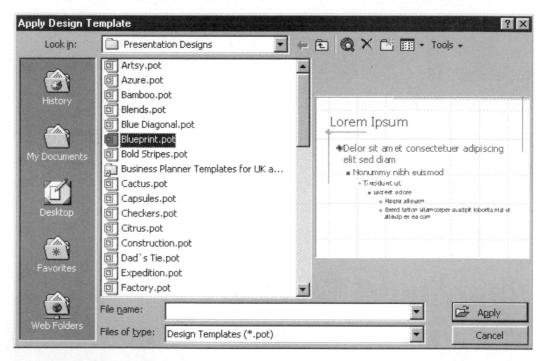

4 Click **Apply**.

Creating From A Template

Creating A Presentation Based On A Design Template

Rather than applying a design template after you have started your presentation, you can specify which one you want when creating a new presentation.

1　Click on the **File** menu.

2　Click **New**.

3　Click on the **Design Templates** tab.

4　Click on the template design you require, e.g. *Dad's Tie*.

5　Click **OK** – you will be taken to the *New Slide* dialog box.

Creating A Presentation With A Presentations Template

PowerPoint has lots of templates which already have slides and text added to them. You can then just fill your own text in.

1　Click on the **File** menu.

2　Click **New**.

3　Click on the **Presentations** tab.

4　Click on the presentations template you require, e.g. *Company Meeting*.

5　Click **OK** – a standard presentation will be created.

Creating Your Own Template

What Is A Template?

All PowerPoint presentations are based on a template. There are design templates which add colours and graphics to your presentation, and there are presentation templates which already have slides and text added. Creating your own template is easy. You just create a normal presentation and then add slides and change the design to suit your needs. You can then save it as a template.

To change the design:

➤ Change the colour scheme.

➤ Change the background.

➤ Change the Master Slides.

To add standard slides:

➤ Just create slides as normal (see page 540)!

The template is the standard on which your presentations are based. So don't add anything unique – just add the common elements that all presentations based on this template are going to need.

Creating A Template

1 Start a new, blank presentation.

2 Change the colour scheme as required (see page 582).

3 Change the background as required (see page 573).

4 Change the master slides as required (see pages 587–92).

5 Add any standard slides you require.

6 Click the **Save** icon.

7 Type in a name for your template.

8 Click the drop-down arrow next to the *Save as type* box.

9 Select *Design Template*.

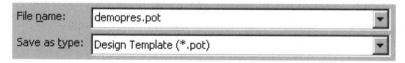

10 Ensure the *Save in* box shows the Templates folder.

11 Click **Save**.

Creating A New Presentation Using Your Template

1 Click on the **File** menu.

2 Click **New**.

3   Click on the **General** tab.

4   Click on your template.

5   Click **OK**.

Applying Your Template To An Existing Presentation

1   Click on the **Format** menu.

2   Click on **Apply Design Template**.

3   Click on your template (you might need to change the *Look in* box to the correct folder).

4   Click **OK**.

I Can't See Any Of The Standard Slides I Added!

If you apply your template to a presentation that already exists, only the design is applied. Any standard slides you created are ignored.

Editing Your Template

1   Click on the **File** menu.

2   Click **Open**.

3   In the *Files of type* box, click on the drop-down arrow and choose *Design Templates*.

4   Click on your template.

5   Click **Open**.

6   Make any changes you require.

7   Close and save the template.

Chapter 5

Speaker's Notes

Creating Speaker's Notes

Speaker's Notes are notes that you can type on to the bottom of your slides. They won't show up on a normal slide show, but are designed to be printed out. That way, when you are presenting the slide show, you can glance at your notes and see what this particular slide is supposed to be about. You can type your notes in Normal view in the Notes pane. Resize this pane if you need more room (see page 528).

Getting To The Notes Pane

1   Click on the **View** menu.

2   Click **Normal**.

3   Click into the Notes pane.

Or

1   Click on the **Normal** icon at the bottom left of the screen.

2   Click into the Notes pane.

Adding Notes

1   Use the scroll bar to move to the slide you wish to add notes to.

2   Click into the Notes pane.

3   Start typing.

Changing The Zoom Control

If the text isn't big enough for you to clearly see what you are typing you can increase the zoom on the notes pane.

1   Click into the Notes pane.

2   Click the drop-down arrow next to the zoom control.

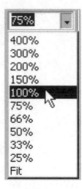

3   Click on a higher percentage.

Printing Speaker's Notes

Speaker's Notes will not appear on the slides when you give a presentation. To use your notes print them:

1   Click on the **File** menu.

2   Click **Print**.

3   Click the drop-down arrow next to *Print what*.

4   Select *Notes Pages*.

5   Click **OK**.

602

Chapter 6

Graphs And Charts

Creating A Chart

Creating Charts

1   Create a new slide.

2   Click on the *Chart layout*.

3   Click **OK**.

4   Double-click the chart area – you will be taken to Microsoft Graph (see the next section).

Or

1   Go to the slide you wish to add a chart to in Slide View.

2   Click on the **Chart** icon – you will be taken to Microsoft Graph (see the next section).

My Chart Has Got In The Way Of Everything Else!

When you add a chart with the icon it will go right in the middle of the slide. You will then have to move and resize it yourself (see page 607).

Or

1   Go to the slide you wish to add a chart to in Slide View.

2   Click on the **Insert** menu.

3   Click **Chart** – you will be taken to Microsoft Graph (see next section).

Microsoft Graph

What Is Microsoft Graph?

➤ Microsoft Graph is a separate program that comes free with PowerPoint.

➤ When you insert a chart, PowerPoint opens up Microsoft Graph.

➤ It is in this program, rather than PowerPoint, that you create and edit your chart.

➤ When you are in Microsoft Graph you will see a new toolbar and a datasheet on the screen, and your chart will have a thick diagonal line border around it (see below).

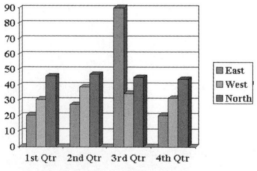

Chart selected in Microsoft Graph.

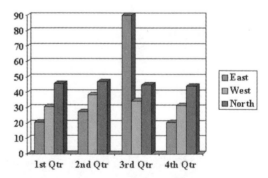

Chart selected in PowerPoint.

Switching From Microsoft Graph To PowerPoint

Once you have finished your chart, you will need to come out of Microsoft Graph and go back to PowerPoint:

Click outside the diagonal lines around the chart to go back to PowerPoint.

Switching From PowerPoint To Microsoft Graph

If you need to edit your chart, you will have to return to Microsoft Graph. Just double-click in the middle of the chart to go back to Microsoft Graph.

The Datasheet

The datasheet contains the text and figures that your chart is based on. When you create a new chart, PowerPoint inserts dummy text and figures to help you get an idea of what to do.

Deleting Information From The Datasheet

You must delete the dummy information using the following method, otherwise stray bits tend to crop up where they are not wanted.

1   Click the grey box in the top left corner to select the whole datasheet.

Presentation6 - Datasheet		A	B	C	D	E
		1st Qtr	2nd Qtr	3rd Qtr	4th Qtr	
1	East	20.4	27.4	90	20.4	
2	West	30.6	38.6	34.6	31.6	
3	North	45.9	46.9	45	43.9	
4						

2   Press **Delete**.

Moving Around The Datasheet

Press the cursor keys on the keyboard to move around the cells

or

click on to the cell you require

or

press the **Tab** key to move one cell to the right

or

press **Enter** key to move down one cell.

Adding Information Into The Datasheet

The information you wish to chart should be typed into the datasheet.

➤ Labels across the top must start directly underneath 'A'.

➤ Labels down the left-hand side must start directly next to '1'.

1 Click into the cell where you wish to start typing.

2 Start typing.

Microsoft Graph will 'build' the chart in the background.

The First Row And The First Column Are 'Frozen'

The headings for the figures in your datasheet are always held in the first row and the first column. These two areas remain on the screen if you scroll across or down. This can sometimes make it look as if you have lost some of the figures you have typed. However, if you scroll back to the left or back up towards the top, they should reappear.

Resizing The Datasheet

1 Position the mouse at a corner of the datasheet – the mouse pointer will change to a double-headed black arrow.

2 Click and drag to resize the datasheet.

Show/Hide The Datasheet

Click on the **Show/Hide datasheet** icon.

Or

1 Click on the **View** menu.

606

2   Click **Datasheet**.

You can also close the datasheet to hide it – just click on the X at the top right of the datasheet.

Moving, Resizing And Deleting A Chart

You Must Be In PowerPoint!

In order to move, resize or delete the chart on the slide, you must be in PowerPoint and not Microsoft Graph.

Moving The Chart

1   Select the chart – white boxes will appear around the edge.

2   Position the mouse pointer in the middle of the chart.

3   Click and drag it to a new location.

Resizing The Chart

1   Select the chart – white boxes will appear around the edge.

2   Position the mouse over a white box.

3   Click and drag to increase or decrease the size.

Deleting The Chart

1   Select the chart – white boxes will appear around the edge.

2   Press **Delete**.

Working With Charts

To Select Parts Of A Graph You Must Be In Microsoft Graph!

Once you are in a chart, they work in exactly the same way as charts in Excel. See the Chart section starting on page 353.

Creating An Organization Chart

What Is An Organization Chart?

An organization chart is used to create hierarchical charts which display the structure of an organization.

Adding An Organization Chart Using The Slide Layout

1   Create a new slide.

2   Choose *Organization Chart* layout.

3   Click **OK**.

4   Double-click the organization chart placeholder – you will be taken to Microsoft Organization Chart (see next section).

Or

1   Select the slide you wish to add an organization chart to.

2   Click on the **Insert** menu.

3   Click on **Object**.

4   Click on **MS Organization Chart 2.0**.

5   Click **OK** – you will be taken to Microsoft Organization Chart (see next section).

Microsoft Organization Chart 2.0

What Is It?

➤ Microsoft Organization chart is a separate program that comes free with PowerPoint.

➤ When you insert an organization chart, PowerPoint opens up this program.

➤ It is in this program, rather than PowerPoint, that you create and edit your chart.

➤ When you are in Organization Chart, a new window will appear on your screen and a new toolbar will appear within that window.

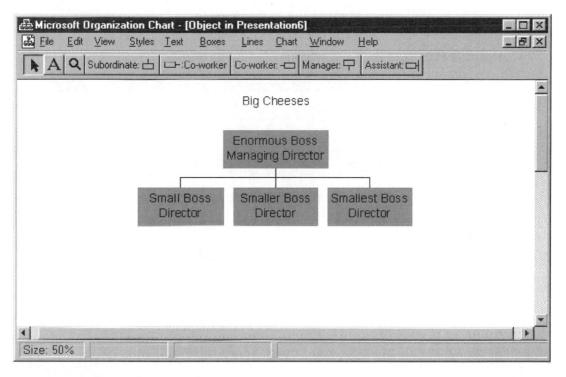

In Microsoft Organization Chart.

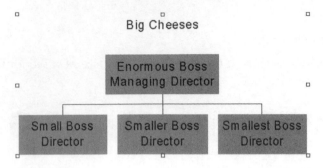

In PowerPoint.

Switching From Microsoft Organization Chart To PowerPoint

Once you have finished your chart you will need to come out of Microsoft Organization Chart and go back into PowerPoint. When you are in Microsoft Organization Chart:

1   Click on the **File** menu.

2   Click on **Exit** and **Return to (Name of Presentation)**.

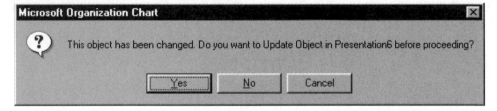

3   Click **Yes** if you wish to save the changes you have made to your organization chart.

Switching From PowerPoint To Microsoft Organization Chart

If you need to edit your organization chart, you will have to return to Microsoft Organization Chart. To do this, double-click in the middle of the organization chart.

610

Selecting In Microsoft Organization Chart

Selecting Boxes

1 Make sure that the selection tool is turned on – if it is not, click on it once (it will look 'pushed in').

2 Click on the box you require.

Selecting Several Boxes

1 Select the first box you require.

2 Hold down **Shift**.

3 Click on any other boxes you require – the boxes will go black.

Selecting Specific Workers

1 Click on the **Edit** menu.

2 Click on **Select**.

3 Click on the workers you wish to select.

Selecting Levels

1 Click on the **Edit** menu.

2 Click on **Select Levels**.

3 Type in the levels you wish to select.

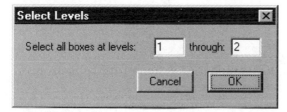

4 Click **OK**.

Selecting Lines

Click on the line you require.

Or, to select several lines.

1   Click on the first line you require.

2   Hold down the **Shift** key.

3   Click on any other lines you require.

Working With Organization Charts

Adding Information To A Box

When You First Go Into A New Organization Chart

The first box is highlighted, ready for you to type in the name. You do not have to click anywhere – just type!

1   Click into the box you wish to add information to.

2   Type in the name.

3   Press **Enter** on the keyboard.

4   Type in the job title.

5   Press **Enter** and type comments if required.

6   Click outside the box when you have finished

or

click into the next box you wish to add text to.

Amending Existing Text

1   Click twice on the box you wish to change.

2   Edit the text as normal.

You Must Click Twice On The Box!

If you click once, the whole box will be highlighted and you will overwrite all of the text it contains.

Adding Extra Boxes

1   Click on the type of worker you wish to add from the toolbar.

| Subordinate: | ⊏⊐:Co-worker | Co-worker: -⊏⊐ | Manager: ⊓ | Assistant: ⊏⊐⊦ |

2   Click on the box you wish to add the new worker to.

3   Type the name and job title for the new box.

Adding A Chart Title To An Organization Chart

1   Click on *Chart Title* above the chart.

2   Delete the words *Chart Title*.

3   Type in your own title.

Deleting Boxes

1   Select the box(es) you wish to delete.

2   Press **Delete**.

Moving Boxes

1   Click and drag from the middle of the box required.

2   Move the box over the box you wish to add it to.

3   Release the mouse.

Changing The Zoom Control

Click on the **Zoom Control** icon.

613

Or

1   Click on the **View** menu.

2   Click on the zoom level you require.

Formatting Organization Charts

Changing The Font

1   Select the text or box(es) you wish to change.

2   Click on **Text**.

3   Click on **Font**.

4   Change the font as required.

5   Click **OK**.

Changing The Style Of Chart

1   Select the box(es) you wish to change.

2   Click on **Style**.

3   Click on the style you require.

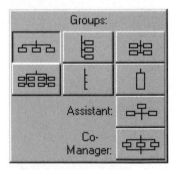

Changing The Box Colour

1   Select the box(es) you wish to change.

2   Click on **Boxes**.

3   Click on **Color**.

4   Click on the colour you require.

5   Click **OK**.

Adding Shadow

1   Select the box(es) you wish to change.

2   Click on **Boxes**.

3   Click on **Shadow**.

4   Click on the shadow style you require.

Changing The Box Borders

1   Select the box(es) you wish to change.

2   Click on **Boxes**.

3   Click on **Border Style**, **Border Color** or **Border Line Style**.

4   Click on the format you require.

Changing The Lines

1   Select the line(s) you wish to change.

2   Click on **Line**.

3   Click on **Thickness**, **Style** or **Color**.

4   Click on the format you require.

Changing The Background Colour

1   Click on the **Chart** menu.

2   Click on **Background Color**.

3   Click on the colour you require.

4   Click **OK**.

Drawing Extra Lines And Boxes

1   Click on the **View** menu.

2   Click on **Show Draw Tools** – extra icons will appear (shown below).

3   Click on the icon you require.

4   Click and drag to draw the shape.

Lines Must Be Drawn Between Existing Boxes

You cannot draw lines anywhere on the organization chart, they must go between two of the boxes.

Adding Extra Text

1   Click on the text icon.

2   Click on the organization chart where you would like to add text.

3   Type your text.

Chapter 7

Drawing Toolbar

Using The Drawing Toolbar

Displaying The Drawing Toolbar

You can use the *Drawing* toolbar to draw shapes and diagrams on your slide. When displayed, it is usually at the bottom of the PowerPoint screen. If it is not already displayed:

1   Click on the **View** menu.

2   Click **Toolbars**.

3   Click **Drawing** – if there is a tick next to it, it is already turned on.

Drawing Shapes

The *Drawing* toolbar works in exactly the same way as it does in Word. See the section on drawing shapes starting on page 213.

Chapter 8

Clip Art And Pictures

Adding Pictures To Slides

Inserting Pictures With The Slide Layout

1   If necessary, create a new slide.

2   Choose a layout with a placeholder for Clip Art.

3   Double-click the placeholder for Clip Art – you will be taken to the Clip Art gallery (see the section later in this chapter).

Or

1   Move to the slide you wish to add a picture to in Slide View.

2   Click on the **Clip Art** icon on the drawing toolbar – you will be taken to the Clip Art gallery (see the section later in this chapter).

Or

1   Move to the slide you wish to add a picture to in Slide View.

2   Click on the **Insert** menu.

3   Click **Picture**.

4   Click **Clip Art** – you will be taken to the Clip Art gallery (see the section later in this chapter).

Inserting Pictures That Are Not In The Clip Art Gallery

If you wish to insert a picture file that is not part of the Clip Art gallery, such as a logo or a scanned image:

Inserting a Picture From File.

1   Move to the slide you wish to add a picture to in Slide View.

2   Click on the **Insert** menu.

3   Click **Picture**.

4   Click **From File**.

5   Change the **Look in** box to the folder where your picture is saved.

6   Click on your picture file.

7   Click **Insert**.

Inserting a Picture From Scanner:

1   Move to the slide you wish to add a picture to in Slide View.

2   Click on the **Insert** menu.

3   Click **Picture**.

4   Click **From Scanner or Camera** – you will be taken to your scanning software.

5   Scan the picture as normal.

Inserting A Picture From The Clip Art Gallery

The Clip Art Gallery works in exactly the same way as the one in Word. See the section starting on page 227.

Working With Pictures

Once you have inserted Clip Art or pictures in PowerPoint, they work in exactly the same way as they do in Word. See the section starting on page 231.

There are two slight differences in PowerPoint:

If You Inserted The Clip Art Using The Placeholder, And Then Delete The Clip Art

You will still see the placeholder when your Clip Art is deleted. This will not print, and it will not show during an on-screen show. To get rid of it, change the layout, delete the placeholder or add a different piece of Clip Art.

Recolouring

This is a feature in PowerPoint that lets you change particular colours in a piece of Clip Art. You must have the *Picture* toolbar displayed to use this (click on the **View** menu, click on **Toolbars**, click on **Picture**).

1   Select the picture.

2   Click on the **Recolor Picture** icon.

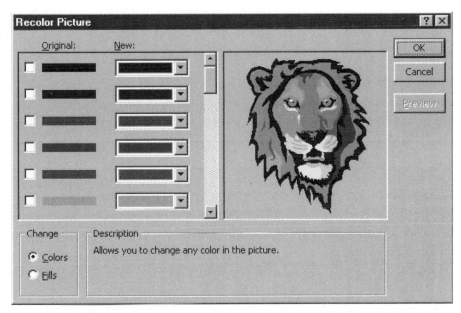

3   In the *Change* section, choose *Colors* to display the colours, and *Fills* to display the line colours.

4   Find the colour you wish to change from the list underneath *Original*.

5   Click the drop-down arrow underneath *New* next to the colour you wish to change.

6   Click on a new colour.

Or

Click *More Colors* if the colour you require isn't listed.

7   Click **OK**.

Chapter 9

Checking A Presentation

Spell Checking

Checking Spelling

1   Click on the **Spelling** icon – PowerPoint will highlight the first spelling error.

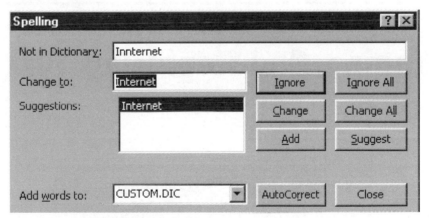

2   Click on the option you require (see next section).

3   Click **OK** when the check is finished.

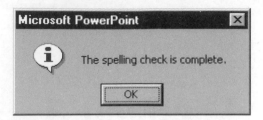

What Do All The Options Mean?

Option	What it does
Ignore	Ignores this error and moves on to the next one.
Ignore All	Ignores all instances of this error and moves onto the next error.
Change	Changes this error to the highlighted word next to *Suggestions*.
Change All	Change all instances of this error to the highlighted word next to *Suggestions*.
Add	Adds the word to the dictionary.
Suggest	Suggests the correct spelling of the error.
AutoCorrect	Adds the error to the AutoCorrect list so that it is automatically corrected to the highlighted suggestion in the future.
Close	Closes the spell-checker.

Finding And Replacing Text

Using Find

1   Click on the **Edit** menu.

2   Click **Find**.

3   Type in the word you wish to find into the box underneath *Find what*.

4   Tick the *Match case* box if you wish to match the case of the word e.g. 'CAPITAL' will find 'CAPITAL', but not 'capital'.

5   Tick *Find whole words only* if you wish to find the word on its own e.g. 'Look' will find 'Look', but not 'looking', 'looked', 'looks'.

6   Click **Find Next** – the word is highlighted on the slide.

7   Keep clicking **Find Next** to find all the instances.

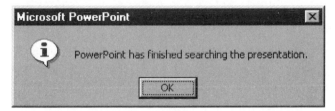

8   Click **OK**.

I Can't See The Highlighted Word In The Background!

Quite often, the *Find* box gets in the way of seeing the highlighted word.

Move it by clicking on its blue title bar and dragging it out of the way.

Using Find And Replace

1   Click on the **Edit** menu.

2   Click **Replace**.

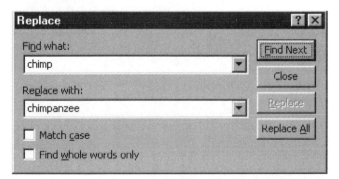

3   Type the word you wish to find into the box underneath *Find what*.

4   Type the word you wish to replace it with into the box underneath *Replace with*.

5   Click **Replace All** to replace all instances of the word

or

click **Find Next** – the first instance of the word is highlighted.

Click **Replace**.

Be Careful With Replace All!

If you use *Replace All* then you won't be able to check where PowerPoint is replacing words. Only use it if you are confident it will do the right thing!

Chapter 10

Importing

Importing Text From Word

Importing Text From Word

If you have text in a Word document that is very similar to the text you want in a presentation, you can get PowerPoint to import it.

1   Open the presentation you wish to import into.

2   If necessary, move to the slide which will appear **before** the imported information.

3   Click on the **Insert** menu.

4   Click **Slides from Outline**.

5   Click the drop-down arrow at the end of the *Look in* box.

6   Click on the folder where the Word document is saved.

7   Click on the Word document to select it.

8   Click **Insert** – new slides will appear in your presentation.

My Slides Look A Bit Funny!

PowerPoint guesses how you want to import the text from Word, based on how the document is formatted. It takes clues from headings, indented text and lists inside the document. Sometimes it can produce some strange results! If it doesn't look quite right, you'll have to format it to make it look right.

Importing Slides From Another Presentation

Inserting Slides from Other Presentations

If you have created slides which you wish to use in several presentations, it's easy to import them.

1   Open the presentation you wish to import into.

2   Move to the slide which will appear **before** the imported slide.

3   Click on the **Insert** menu.

4   Click **Slides from File**.

5   Click **Browse**.

6   Change the *Look in* box to the folder where the presentation you are importing from is saved.

7   Click on the name of the presentation you are importing from.

8   Click **Open**.

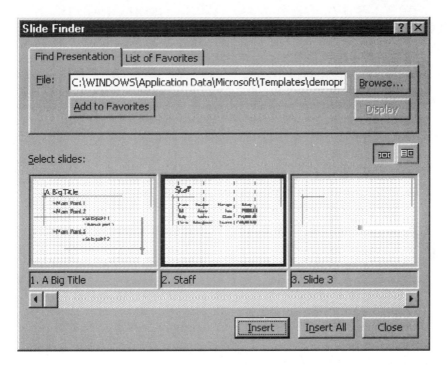

9 Change the display if required by clicking on the two icons just above the *Select slides* box – the first one shows previews of the slides, the second shows a summary list.

10 Click on the slide you wish to insert.

11 Click **Insert**.

or

click **Insert All** to insert all the slides – the box will remain on the screen, allowing you to insert other slides.

12 Click **Close**.

Inserted Slides Take On The Template Of The Current Presentation

Any slides which you insert may not look the same when they are put into the current presentation. They will follow the template of the presentation they are put into.

Copying Slides Using Slide Sorter View

1 Switch to Slide Sorter View.

2 Click on the slide you wish to copy.

3 Click on the **Copy** icon.

4 If required, open the presentation you wish to copy to.

5 Select the slide which will appear **before** the slide you wish to copy.

6 Click on the **Paste** icon.

Importing Charts

Importing A Chart From A File

1 Ensure you are in Microsoft Graph (see page 604).

2 Click on the **Import File** icon.

3 Change the *Look in* box to the folder where your file is saved.

4 Click on the file you wish to import.

5 Click **Open**.

6   Click on the sheet you require.

7   If required, click in the circle next to *Range* and type in the range name you require.

8   Tick *Overwrite existing cells* to remove all current data from the datasheet.

9   Click **OK**.

Creating A Chart Using Microsoft Excel
Getting Started

1   Create a slide with an object placeholder.

2   Double-click the object placeholder – the *Insert Object* box will appear (see next section).

Or

1   Click on the **Insert** menu.

2   Click **Object** – the *Insert Object* box will appear (see next section).

Insert Object Box

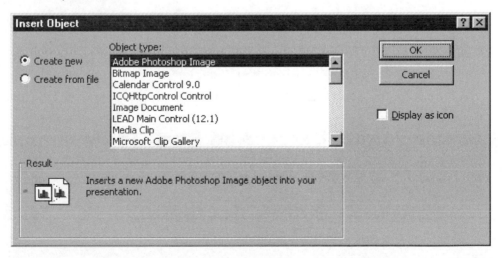

3   Ensure that *Create new* is selected on the left-hand side.

4   Click Microsoft Excel Chart from the *Object type* list underneath (you may have to scroll down).

5   Click **OK** – you will be taken into Microsoft Excel.

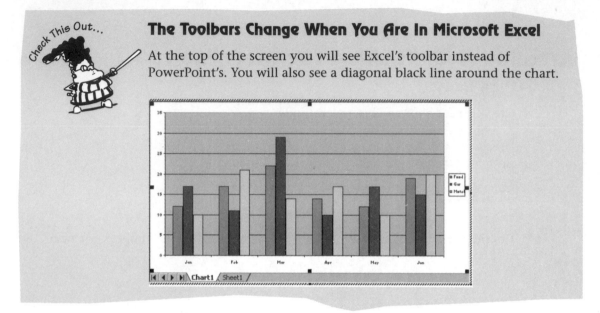

The Toolbars Change When You Are In Microsoft Excel

At the top of the screen you will see Excel's toolbar instead of PowerPoint's. You will also see a diagonal black line around the chart.

Adding Information For The Chart...

1   Click on the **Sheet1** tab in the chart.

\ Chart1 \ **Sheet1** /

2   Increase the zoom control if necessary to see the figures (see page 533).

3   Change the information given to fit your data.

4   Click on the **Chart1** tab when you have finished – the chart will have updated.

Switching Out Of Excel And Back To Powerpoint

Click anywhere outside the chart.

Switching from PowerPoint Back to Excel.

Double-click on the chart.

Chapter 11

On-Screen Shows

Using The Slide Show View

This is it, your big moment. You've slaved away creating a fancy presentation, you've checked it twice, plugged in the big projector, set up the screen, and the audience are sitting there patiently, waiting for you to impress them. It's time to run the slide show ...

Running Your Slide Show

1   Click on the **View** menu.

2   Click **Slide Show**.

Or

1   Click **Slide Show**.

2   Click **View Show**.

Or, if you want to start your show from any slide in the presentation:

1   Select the slide you wish to start from.

2   Click on the **Slide Show View** icon at the bottom left of the screen.

Using Slide Show Options

1   Click on the upward pointing arrow at the bottom left of the slide

or

right-click on the slide.

2   Click on the option you require from the menu.

Going To The Next Slide In Slide Show View

Click the mouse on a blank part of the slide.

Or

Press the right cursor key.

Going To The Previous Slide In Slide Show View

Press the left cursor key

Or

1   Bring up the slide show options (see above).

2   Click **Previous**.

Going To Any Slide In Slide Show View

1   Bring up the slide show options.

2   Click **Go**.

3   Click **By Title**.

Click on the slide you wish to go to

or

click **Slide Navigator**.

Click on the slide you wish to go to.

Click **Go To**.

Closing Slide Show View Before The Show Is Over

Press **Escape** on the keyboard.

Or

1   Bring up the slide show options.

2   Click **End Show**.

Drawing On Your Slides In Slide Show View

If you wish to underline points, or circle parts of your slide, you can change the mouse to a pencil and draw while you are in slide show view.

1   Bring up the slide show options.

2   Click **Pointer Options**.

3   Click **Pen** – the mouse pointer will change to a pen.

4   Click and drag to draw on the slide.

Or

1   Press **Ctrl+P** – the mouse pointer will change to a pen.

2   Click and drag to draw on the slide.

Drawing Straight Lines

Hold down the **shift** key when you click and drag, and your line will be straight.

How Do I Delete What I've Drawn?

What you draw with the pen is not permanent. Once you have moved to the next slide, whatever you have drawn is erased. Or you can press E on the keyboard to erase it straight away.

Turning The Pen Off In Slide Show View

1   Bring up the slide show options.

2   Click **Pointer Options**.

3   Click **Arrow** – the mouse pointer will look like an arrow.

Or

Press **Ctrl+A** – the mouse pointer will look like an arrow.

Changing The Pen Colour In Slide Show View

1   Bring up the slide show options.

2   Click **Pointer Options**.

3   Click **Pen Colour**.

4   Click on the colour you require.

Hiding The Mouse In Slide Show View

1   Bring up the slide show options (see page 634).

2   Click **Pointer Options**.

3   Click **Hidden**.

To turn the mouse back on:

1   Right click the mouse.

2   Click **Pointer Options**.

3   Click **Arrow**.

Adding Slide Transitions

What Are Slide Transitions?

This refers to the way slides come onto the screen during an on-screen show.

Creating Slide Transitions In Slide Sorter View

1   Select the slide you wish to change (see page 545).

2   Click the drop-down arrow next to the *Slide Transition* box.

No Transition

3   Click on the transition you require – scroll down to see more transitions if necessary

or

click *No Transition* at the top of the list, to remove the transition effect.

Using The Slide Transition Dialog Box

1   Click on the **Slide Show** menu.

2   Click **Slide Transition**

or

click on the **Slide Transition** icon in Slide Sorter view.

3   Click on the drop-down arrow underneath *Effect*.

4   Click on the effect you require.

5   Click in the circle next to the speed you require – *Slow*, *Medium* or *Fast*.

6   Tick the box you require underneath *Advance* – *On mouse click* will go to the next slide when you press the mouse button, *Automatically after* will go to the next slide after a set number of seconds, which you type into the box underneath.

7   Click the drop-down arrow underneath *Sound*.

8   Click on a sound effect if required.

9   Click **Apply** to apply to the current slide

or

click **Apply to All** to change all the slides.

Adding Animation To Slides

What Are Animation Effects?

Animation effects can be applied to any object on your slide, such as text or a picture. Once it is animated it will 'fly' onto the screen. This can be useful for long bulleted lists. Each point can fly in separately, so that your audience does not have to concentrate on the whole list at once.

Creating Animation Effects In Slide Sorter View

This will only affect objects which are in a placeholder, i.e. they must be part of the slide's original layout.

1   Select the slide(s) you wish to change (see page 545).

2   Click the drop-down arrow next to the *Animation* box.

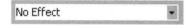

3   Click on the animation you require – scroll down to see more animations

or

click *No Effect* at the top of the list to remove the animation from the slide.

Preset Animation

This will only affect objects which are in a placeholder, i.e. they must be part of the slide's original layout. Preset animation will add animation and sometimes sound to your slides.

1   Select the slide(s) you wish to change in Slide Sorter view (see page 545).

2   Click **Slide Show**.

3   Click **Preset Animation**.

Click the animation effect you require

or

click *Off* at the top of the list to remove preset animation from the slide.

Getting To The Custom Animation Dialog Box

If you wish to do more complicated animations, for example with sound, then you can use custom animation.

1   Switch to Slide View or Normal View.

2   Go to the slide you wish to animate.

3   Click **Slide Show**.

4   Click **Custom Animation**.

Animating An Object

From the *Custom Animation* dialog box:

1   Tick the box for the object you wish to animate (see below).

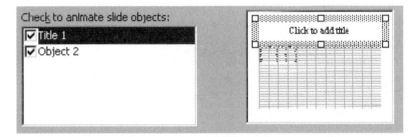

2   Click on the **Order & Timing** tab.

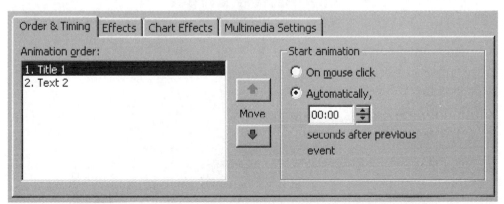

3   Click the object you wish to animate in the box under *Animation order.*

4   Click next to *On mouse click* to animate the object when you click the mouse

or

click next to *Automatically* and click the up and down arrows to change the
number of seconds to wait before animating.

Changing The Order Of Animation

If you have several objects being animated on the same slide and you wish to change
the order in which they are animated:

1   Click on the **Order & Timing** tab in the *Custom Animation* dialog box.

2   Click the object you wish to change the order of animation for.

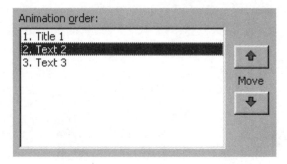

3   Click on the up arrow to move it up in the order of animation

or

click the drop-down arrow to move it down in the order of animation.

Choosing The Animation Effect

From the *Custom Animation* dialog box:

1   Click on the object you wish to change from the list (see below).

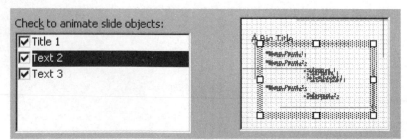

640

2   Click on the **Effects** tab.

3   Click the drop-down arrow underneath *Entry animation and sound*.

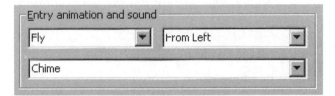

4   Click on the effect you require.

5   Click the drop-down arrow to the right (see above).

6   Click on the type and direction of animation you want – this may be unavailable for some animation effects.

7   Click on the drop-down arrow next to *Sound*.

8   Click on the sound you require.

9   Click **OK**.

Introduce Text Options

The Introduce Text options change the way that the text comes onto the screen. From the *Custom Animation* dialog box:

1   Select the text object you wish to change from the list.

2   Click on the **Effects** tab.

3   Click the drop-down arrow underneath *Introduce text*.

4   Click the option you require (all at once, word by word, or letter by letter).

5   Click the drop-down arrow next to *Grouped by*.

641

6   Click the option you require (whether main and sub-points come on together or separately).

7   If required, tick the box next to *In reverse order* (brings the last point on first, etc.).

8   Click **OK**.

After Animation Options

The After Animation Options allow you to hide or dim objects once they have been animated.

1   Once you have chosen an animation, select the object you require from the list underneath *Click to animate slide objects*.

2   Click on the **Effects** tab.

3   Click the drop-down arrow underneath *After animation*.

4   Click on a colour to dim the object to once it has been animated

or

click *More Colors* if the colour you require is not listed

or

click *Hide after Animation*

or

click *Hide on next mouse click*.

Previewing Your Animation

When you have made your changes, you can preview them before closing the *Custom Animation* dialog box.

From the *Custom Animation* dialog box:

Click **Preview** – the slide miniature will move to show you your animation.

Rehearsing Timings For An On-Screen Show

Rehearsing The Timings

1   Click on the **Slide Show** menu.

2   Click **Rehearse Timings** – PowerPoint is now recording you!

3   Run the slide show, clicking the mouse in keeping with the times you require, i.e. show a slide, make your speech, click to go to the next slide.

Or

1   Switch to Slide Sorter view.

2   Click on the **Rehearse Timings** icon.

3   Run the slide show, clicking the mouse in keeping with the times you require.

Once the slide show is finished, you will see a message:

4   Click **Yes** if you are happy with the timing.

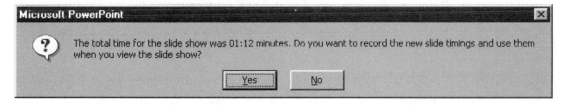

Microsoft PowerPoint

? The total time for the slide show was 01:12 minutes. Do you want to record the new slide timings and use them when you view the slide show?

Yes   No

The Rehearsal Box Will Appear When You Are Rehearsing The Timings

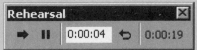

Going from left to right, the icons mean:

➤ Go to the next slide.

➤ Pause the rehearsal (click again to continue).

➤ Time the current slide has taken so far (4 seconds in this case).

➤ Repeat the current slide from the beginning.

➤ Time the presentation has taken so far (19 seconds in this case).

The Presentation Will Now Run Itself!

When you run slide show view now, PowerPoint will use the timings you just recorded. If you are not happy with the timings, you can record them again.

Changing The Advance Slides Option

If you would like to advance the slides using the mouse click again, you will have to change the set up show options.

1 Click on the **Slide Show** menu.

2 Click **Set Up Show**.

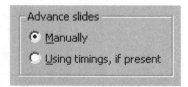

3 Click the circle next to *Manually*.

4 Click **OK**.

Changing The Show Type

1   Click on the **Slide Show** menu.

2   Click **Set Up Show**.

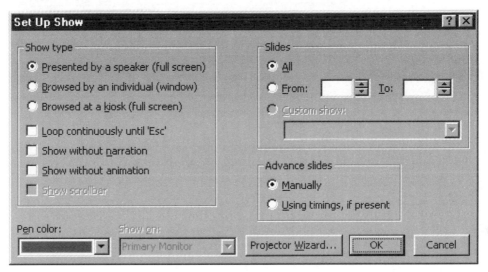

3   Change the options as required (see above and below).

4   Click **OK**.

Option	What it does
Presented by a speaker (full screen)	This shows the slides on the screen without any means for an audience to move from one slide to another.
Presented by an individual (window)	This shows the presentation in a window on the screen, and provides icons to move around the slides.
Browsed at a kiosk (full screen)	Shows the slides on the screen without any access to slide show options or means to move from one slide to another. To use this option you must have recorded timings, otherwise you will not be able to move through the slides!
Loop continuously until 'ESC'	Shows the presentation again and again, until someone presses **Escape** on the keyboard!
Show without narration	If you have recorded narration to go with your presentation, you can choose to include it or not.
Show without animation	If you have added animation effects to your slides, then you can choose whether or not to include them.

645

Slides (All, From, To, etc.)   Change these boxes if you wish to show all of the slides, or just some of the slides – *From* 3 *To* 9, etc.

Hiding Slides

Hiding Slides

1   Select the slide(s) you wish to hide.

2   Click on the **Slide Show** menu.

3   Click **Hide Slide** – the slide is hidden in slide show view, and a cross will appear through the slide number in Slide Sorter view.

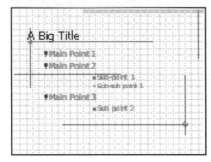

To unhide slides:

1   Select the slide(s) you wish to unhide.

2   Click on the **Slide Show** menu.

3   Click **Hide Slide** – the cross will be removed from the slide number in Slide Sorter view.

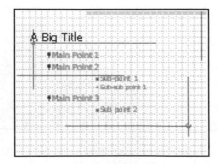

1

646

Chapter 12

File
Management

Advanced Saving

Creating A Copy Of A Presentation Using Save As

1   Click on the **File** menu.

2   Click on **Save As**.

3   If required, type in a new name for the presentation.

4   If required, click on the drop-down arrow next to the *Look in* box to change the folder you want to save the presentation into.

5   Click on **Save**.

Creating Folders

1   Click on the **File** menu.

2   Click on **Save As**.

3   Change the *Save in* box to the folder or drive you wish to be the parent of the new folder, e.g. if you click on (C:) the new folder will be created on the (C:) drive.

4   Click on the **New Folder** icon

5   Type in a name for your folder.

6   Press **Enter**.

Saving As A Different Format

When you save your presentation it is saved in the default format for PowerPoint 2000. In other words, the computer knows that it came from PowerPoint 2000 and it will only open it if you have PowerPoint 2000 on your computer. However, you may want to use your presentation to do something different – in which case you will need to save it in a different format. Below are some examples of the different versions you might use.

➤ As an earlier version of PowerPoint, so that the presentation can be opened in earlier versions.

➤ As a format that will be compatible across different programs/software e.g. text file or RTF (Rich Text Format). In PowerPoint this will mean saving the text you can see in outline view only.

➤ As HTML for the World Wide Web (see page 649).

➤ As a template to reuse the format again (see page 597).

➤ As an image file, e.g. WMF (Windows Metafile) or GIF (Graphics Interchange Format). This will enable you save a slide as an image. You will not be able to edit the slide once you have saved in this format, although you can edit the original slide and re-save it.

Saving As A Different Software Version

1   Click on the **File** menu.

2   Click *Save As*.

3   Click on the drop-down arrow to the right of the *Save as type* box.

4   Scroll down to see all the options if necessary.

5   Choose the version you want e.g. PowerPoint 95.

6   Type a new name into the *File name* box if required.

7   Click **Save**.

Downward Compatibility

As a general rule, newer versions of software will enable you to open older versions, but **not** vice versa. For example PowerPoint 2000 will open a PowerPoint 7 presentation, but you cannot open a PowerPoint 2000 presentation in PowerPoint 7. In the same way, the newer version will let you save as the older version, but not vice versa.

Keep It Simple

Certain types of formatting are not supported when saving as an older version and will be lost. If you know you will be taking your presentation to an older version, try not to use complex formatting not available in the earlier versions.

Saving For The Internet

Saving As A Web Page

You can save a presentation in a format that can be viewed using a Web browser. When saved in this way, you or other people can edit it over the Internet.

1 Click on the **File** menu.

2 Click **Save as Web Page**.

3 Type a name for the file.

4 If required, click on the drop-down menu next to *Save in* to change the folder you want to save the presentation in.

5 Click on **Change Title**.

6 Type in the title you wish to be diplayed in the title bar of the Web browser.

7 Click **OK**.

8 Click **Save**.

Why Publish As A Web Page?

➤ You can view the presentation when you are away from your computer.

➤ You can do the presentation anywhere, without having to take it with you.

➤ You can make presentations in places without PowerPoint software.

➤ You can use presentations to publicise yourself on the Web.

Publishing As A Web Page

1 Click on the **File** menu.

2 Click **Save as Web Page**.

3 Change the filename and folder to save in if required.

4 Click on **Publish**.

5 Click in the circle before *Complete presentation*

or

click in the circle before *Slide number* and enter the slide numbers you wish to start and end on – type a number into the box, or use the up and down arrows.

6 Click in the Box before *Display speaker notes* (if required).

7 This will be shown when the box is ticked.

8 Click in a circle under *Browser support* to choose browsers that can be used to view the web page.

9 Click on **Change** to change the title (if required).

10 Check the file name and path is correct by looking in the *File name* box – if you need to change it, click **Browse** and choose the location and file name.

11 If required, tick the box next to *Open published Web page in browser* – this will open the saved web page in an Internet browser so you can see if it works properly.

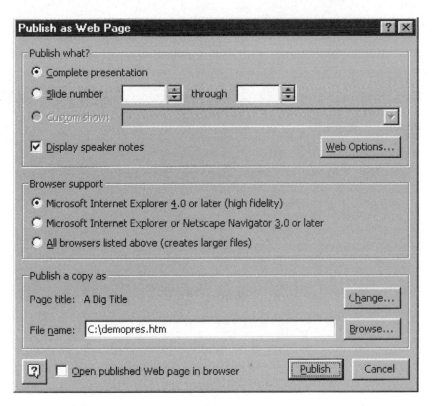

12 Click on **Publish**.

Filename And Path ...

If you have already saved the presentation it will keep the same file name and location (path). You can type a new name and location for your file if you wish.

Searching For Lost Files

Starting A Search

1 Click on the **Open** icon.

2 Click on the **Tools** menu.

3 Click on **Find** – the *Find* box will appear.

Choosing The Drive To Look Through

1   Ensure that the folder or drive you wish to search through is shown at the bottom.

Look in: C:\   ▼   ☑ Search subfolders

2   Ensure that *Search subfolders* is ticked.

You Can Only Look Through One Drive At A Time!

You cannot look through every drive on your computer. Sorry. But hey, if life was perfect, it would be really boring, wouldn't it?

Ensure That 'Search Subfolders' Is Ticked

If you do not tick this box, then PowerPoint will not look inside any folders within the drive you have chosen, e.g. if you have chosen to look through the C: drive, and you do not tick *Search subfolders*, then PowerPoint will not open any of the folders and sub-folders contained on the C: drive to find your presentation.

Adding Properties And Conditions

In order for PowerPoint to find your presentation, you must tell it as much as you can remember about it. This can include the following kinds of information:

➤ Its file name

➤ When you last worked on it

➤ When you created it

➤ Which program you created it in

➤ How many slides it has

➤ Any text it contains.

You can tell PowerPoint these things using properties and conditions in the *Find* box.

1   Click the drop-down arrow underneath *Property* and choose the property you require, e.g. *File name*.

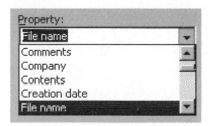

2 Click the drop-down arrow underneath *Condition* and choose the condition you require, e.g. *includes*.

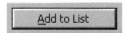

3 Click into the *Value* box and type the value you require, e.g. file name includes 'show'.

4 Click on **Add to List**.

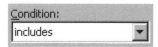

5 Repeat steps 1–4 for any other information you know about the file.

The conditions will be added to the list at the top of the window.

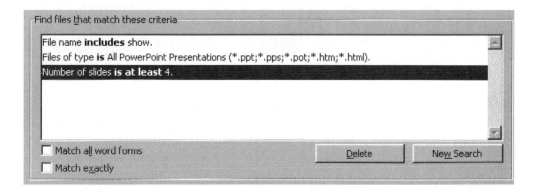

Performing The Search

1   Click on **Find Now** – PowerPoint will look for the document.

2   Double-click on the file you require from the results.

Is Powerpoint Looking For My Presentation?

It can take a while for PowerPoint to find your presentation. If you can't wait any longer, click **Cancel** to stop the search.

Changing The Search Conditions

If your first search does not find the file you were looking for, you can try changing the properties and conditions, then have another go. As long as you don't close the *Open* box, PowerPoint will remember all the conditions you set for the last search.

1   Click on the **Tools** menu.

2   Click **Find**.

3   Click on a search condition to be removed.

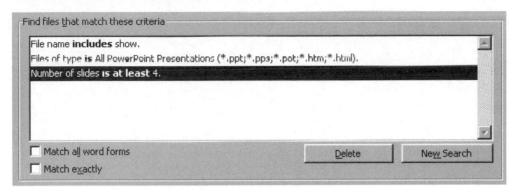

4   Click on **Delete**.

5   Repeat for any other search conditions to be removed.

6   Add any new search conditions to the list (see page 652).

7   Click **Find Now**.

Chapter 13

Headers And Footers

What Are Headers And Footers For?

Headers and Footers can be used display information such as page numbers, the date, and other information that you want repeated on every slide or page. On slides, you can only have footers, and not headers. Footers appear at the bottom of the slides so they are less conspicuous during presentations. Headers and footers can appear at the top and bottom of every page for notes and handouts.

Check This Out...

Headers And Footers Are Stored On The Master Slides

If you wish to make changes to headers and footers, go to the Slide Master or Title Master (see pages 587–92).

Adding Footers To Your Slides

1 Click on the **View** menu.

2 Click **Header and Footer**.

3   Click on the **Slide** tab (if you are not there already).

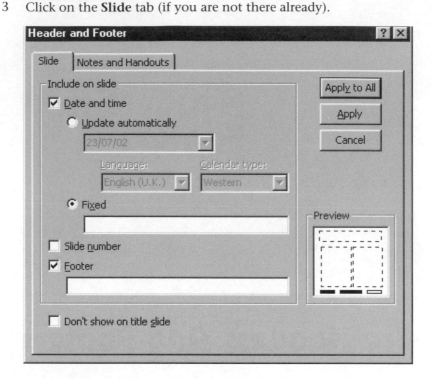

4   Tick the *Date and time* box if required.

5   If required, choose *Update automatically* to have the date updated when each time you open or print the presentation, and click on the drop-down arrow to choose a data format

or

type in a fixed date underneath *Fixed*.

6   Tick the *Slide number* box if required.

7   If required, tick the *Footer* box, and type your footer information into the white box.

8   Click **Apply to All** to change all the slides

or

click **Apply** to change selected slides.

Where Will My Footers Appear?

The black boxes with the thick outlines in the *Preview* box will show you where your footers will appear.

Adding Header And Footer Information To Your Notes And Handouts

1   Click on the **View** menu.

2   Click **Header and Footer**.

3   Click on the **Notes and Handouts** tab (if you are not there already).

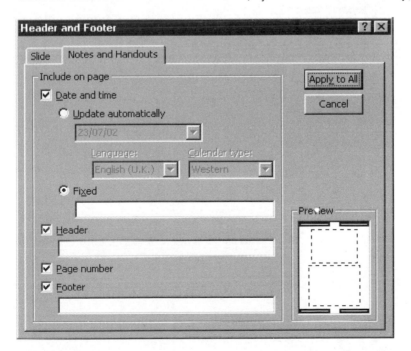

4 Tick the *Date and time* box if required.

5 If required, choose *Update automatically* to have the date updated each time you open or print the presentation, and click on the drop-down arrow to choose a data format

or

type in a fixed date underneath *Fixed*.

6 Tick the *Slide number* box if required.

7 If required, tick the *Footer* box, and type your footer information into the white box.

8 If required, tick the *Header* box, and type your header information into the white box.

9 Tick the *Page number* box if required.

10 Click **Apply to All** to change all the slides.

Where Will My Headers And Footers Appear?

The black boxes with the thick outlines in the *Preview* box will show you where your headers and footers will appear.

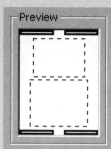

Module 7
Internet And E-mail

Chapter 1

Introduction To The Internet

What Is The Internet?

What Is The Internet?

➤ The Internet is a network of computers connected to each other through the telephone system.

➤ It is not intangible, but a physical structure that connects computers together.

The Main Parts Of The Internet

The Internet has two main parts:

➤ The World Wide Web (WWW)

➤ E-mail.

What Is The World Wide Web?

Here are just some of the things you can do over the World Wide Web.

➤ **Read pages of Information**
People throughout the world have produced Web pages on their computers. Other people can then read that information if they are also connected to the Internet.

➤ **E-commerce**
You can shop for goods over the World Wide Web. Things like books and last-minute flight deals are available.

➤ **Download software**
You can download files from the Web onto your computer. All sorts of stuff is available from games, to pictures, to trial versions of new software. Once they are downloaded, they can be used on your computer.

➤ **Chat**
Some Web pages allow you to chat with other people who are connected to the Internet at the same time as you. You can type messages to each other which appear on the screen immediately.

What Is E-mail?

➤ E-mail is a way of sending and receiving messages over the Internet.

➤ It is cheaper and faster than the traditional postal system.

➤ E-mail also allows you access to **Usenet**, otherwise known as **Newsgroups**. This is a bit like a collection of notice boards which you can send e-mails to. They are then posted up where other people can read them and reply. There are newsgroups on virtually every topic you can think of.

Chapter 2

Getting Started On The Web

Internet Explorer Screen

The Screen

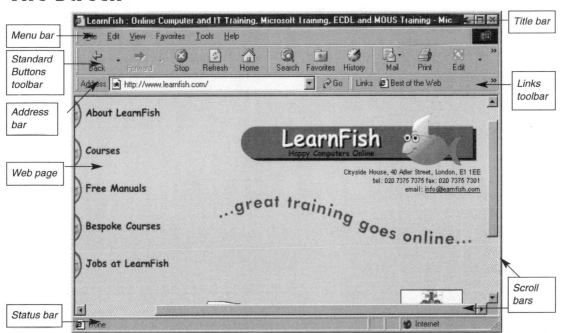

Part of the Screen	What Does It Do?
Title bar	Tells you the title of the web page you are looking at.
Menu bar	Gives you access to the commands available in Internet Explorer. All commands are grouped under one of the menus.
Standard Buttons toolbar	The icons on the *Standard* toolbar provide a quick way of carrying out standard commands.
Links toolbar	The icons on the Links toolbar provide a quick way of accessing Web pages you frequently visit.
Scroll bars	The vertical scroll bar allows you move through a long Web page, whilst the horizontal scroll bar allows you to move across a wide Web page.
Address bar	Can be used to enter the address of a Website you want to visit. Will also display the address of a Website you are currently viewing.
Status bar	Displays messages, such as the progress on connecting to a Website. The right-hand side will indicate the security settings for the Web page you are looking at.

Using Help In Internet Explorer

Internet Explorer comes with help files, just like all the other software packages. Press **F1** to call it up, and use it in the same way as you would any other help file.

You can also get help over the internet. Make sure you are connected to the Internet, then click on the **Help** menu, and click on **Tour** – you will be taken through Microsoft's tour of Internet Explorer.

Customizing The Screen
Seeing The Full Screen

Press **F11**

Or

1   Click on the **View** menu.

2   Click on **Full Screen**.

To Return To Normal View

Click on **Restore** at the top right of the screen – it's the second icon from the right, and looks like two little boxes.

Switching Toolbars On And Off

1 Click on the **View** menu.

2 Click on **Toolbars** – a list will appear.

3 Click on the toolbar you would like to turn on or off – a tick appears before toolbars that are switched on.

Switching The Status Bar On And Off

1 Click on the **View** menu.

2 Click on **Status Bar**.

Font Sizes

1 Click on the **View** menu.

2 Click on **Text Size** – a list will appear.

3 Click on the size you require.

Font Options

1 Click on the **Tools** menu.

2 Click on **Internet Options**.

3 Click on the **General** tab.

4 Click on **Fonts**.

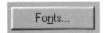

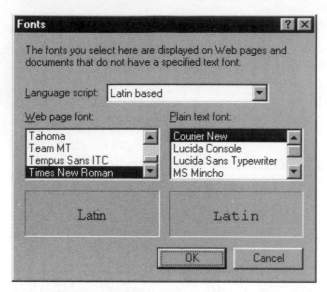

5   Select the fonts you require – choose a font from the *Web page font* list to choose
    the fonts you want to see on Web pages, and the *Plain text font* list for plain text
    fonts

6   Click **OK**.

7   Click **OK**.

Changing The Colours

1   Click on the **Tools** menu.

2   Click on **Internet Options**.

3   Click on **General** tab.

4   Click on **Colors**.

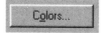

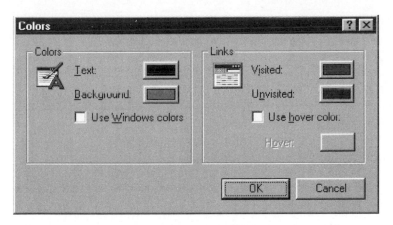

5   Remove the tick next to *Use Windows colors* so that you can change the text and background colours.

6   Click on the box showing the colour you wish to change.

7   Click on the colour you require from the palette.

8   Click **OK**.

9   Click **OK**.

The Toolbars

The Standard Buttons Toolbar

This toolbar gives you quick access to some of the standard commands available from the menus.

Going from left to right, here is what each icon does:

➤ Goes back to the previous page.

➤ Goes forward to the next page (you cannot use this unless you have gone back at least one page).

➤ Stops the page loading.

➤ Refreshes the page, or loads it again.

➤ Goes to the Home page.

➤ Uses Microsoft's search facility.

➤ Displays the Favorites list (a list of sites you have bookmarked).

➤ Displays the History list (sites you have recently visited).

➤ Lets you read or send e-mail.

➤ Prints the current page.

➤ Lets you edit the page with another piece of software.

➤ Lets you link up to a discussion server.

The Address Bar

This toolbar is used to enter the address of Websites you want to visit. You can also use it to revisit Websites (see page 674).

The Radio Toolbar

You can use this toolbar to listen to radio stations anywhere in the world. Click on the **Radio Stations** button, and choose a station.

What Is The Links Toolbar?

The *Links* toolbar contains shortcuts to sites that are selected by Internet Explorer. You can also add your own sites onto the bar for quick access.

Moving A Toolbar

1   Move the mouse to the beginning of the toolbar before the name of the toolbar where there is a grey line – the mouse pointer will change to a four-headed arrow.

2   Click and drag the *Links* bar to the position required.

Customizing The Toolbars

1   Click on the **View** menu.

2   Click on **Toolbars**.

3   Click on **Customize**.

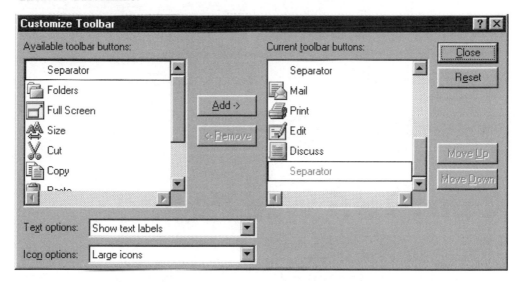

4   Make any changes you require:

> ➤ In the *Available toolbar buttons* list on the left, click on the icon you would like to see on the toolbar, then click on *Add*.

> ➤ In the *Current toolbar buttons* list on the right, click on the icon you would like to remove from the toolbar and then click on *Remove*.

> ➤ Click the drop-down arrow next to *Text options* to change how text is displayed on the toolbar.

> ➤ Click the drop-down arrow next to *Icon options* to change the size of the icons.

> ➤ In the *Current toolbar buttons* list on the right, click on an icon you would like to move, then click on *Move Up* or *Move Down* to change its position on the toolbar.

> ➤ Click on **Reset** to restore the original toolbar.

5   Click on **Close**.

Using The Links Bar

Click on the link you would like to go to, e.g. *Best of the Web*.

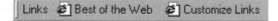

671

Create Your Own Links Button

1   Go to the page which you would like to turn into a link.

2   Click and drag the icon next to the address, until it is on the toolbar – then release the mouse button.

Delete A Links Button

1   Right click on the link you wish to delete – a new menu will appear.

2   Click on **Delete**.

Rearrange The Links Toolbar

Click and drag a button to a new location.

Going To A Web Page

Typing In The URL

If you know the URL (the Website address) of a Web page it is easy to get to:

1   Click into the *Address* bar – the existing URL will go blue.

2   Delete any existing address.

3   Type the address you require, e.g. **www.idiotsguides.com**

4   Press **Enter** – Internet Explorer will eventually load the page

or

click on **Go**.

Watch The Symbol At The Top Right

At the top right-hand corner of the screen you will see the Internet Explorer icon:

 If you can see this turning around, then Internet Explorer is busy down-loading your Web page. If it has stopped doing anything, then you may need to request your page again by clicking the **Refresh** button.

How Much Longer Do I Have To Wait?

If you check the status bar at the bottom left of the screen, you will often see an indicator of how much has been downloaded already.

When it is finished it will say *Done*.

Done

Error Messages

You may get error messages after you request the page. This can be for several reasons: the page may no longer exist, one of the servers that you need may be broken, or too many people may be trying to get the same page as you.

If you do get an error, wait for a while and then try again.

What If I Don't Know The Address?

If you don't know the address, you can guess it (see page 677) or use a search engine (see page 681).

AutoComplete

If you have typed in an address before, you will probably find that Internet Explorer will finish typing it for you before you have reached the end. This is AutoComplete in action. If you would like to stop Internet Explorer doing this:

1 Click on the **Tools** menu.

2 Click on **Internet Options**.

3 Click on the **Content** tab.

4 Click on *AutoComplete*.

5 Click in the box next to Web addresses so that it is **not** ticked.

☐ Web addresses

Matches In The Address Bar

If you have typed in an address before but do not have AutoComplete on, a list will probably appear as you begin to type. Just click on the site you want to visit to save time.

Accessing A Web Address You Have Already Visited

To return to an address that you have typed in recently:

1   Click the drop-down arrow at the end of the *Address* bar.

2   Click on the address you require.

Browsing The World Wide Web

The Home Page

➤ When you first connect to a site you will see its home page.

➤ This is like the front cover of a magazine which welcomes you in and gives you an idea of what you can expect to find inside.

➤ The Home page will usually contain links to other pages in the site.

This is Happy Computer's home page, which contains lots of links to other pages in the site.

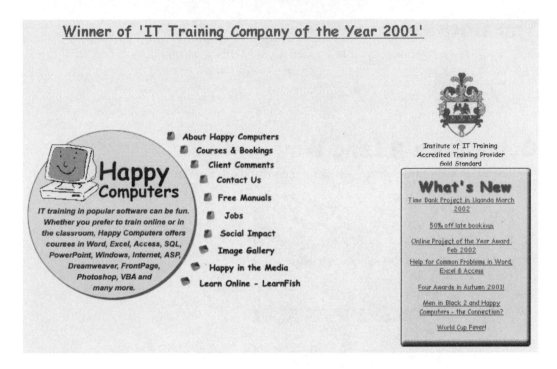

Links are usually underlined text (usually blue), or pictures – the mouse pointer will turn into a pointing hand when you hover it over a link. Use the scroll bar to see more of the page if necessary.

How Can I Tell Where The Links Are?

There are two sorts of links:

➤ **Hypertext Links:** underlined text, often coloured blue.

➤ **Hypermedia Links:** pictures that link you to somewhere else.

When you pass your mouse over a link it will look like a pointing hand.

Using A Link

1 Position the mouse over the hyperlink you require.

2 Click when the mouse looks like a hand – the page you are linking to will open.

675

The Back Button

To go back over pages you have seen already this session, click on the **Back** button.

Going Back A Long Way

1   Click the drop-down arrow next to the **Back** button.

2   Click on the site you require.

The Forward Button

To go forward again, once you have been back, click on the **Forward** button.

Going Forward A Long Way

1   Click the drop-down arrow next to the **Forward** button.

2   Click on the site you require.

The Home Button

The **Home** button takes you to your default home page. By default, this is usually Microsoft's site, or the shop you bought your PC from, but you can set it to whatever you want (see page 695). Click on the **Home** button to go to the home page.

The Stop Button

The **Stop** button stops a page downloading. Click on it if:

➤ A page is taking a long time to appear on the screen.

➤ You think you might have typed in the wrong address.

➤ Internet Explorer is going somewhere you don't want it to!

The Refresh Button

The **Refresh** button tells Internet Explorer to go and download the Web page you are looking at from the server. Click on it if:

➤ Internet Explorer hasn't finished downloading the page and seems to have stopped doing anything.

➤ You think the page may have changed since you downloaded it the first time.

The Structure Of A Web Address

When To Guess Web Addresses

Accessing a Web page is easy if you know the address. If you don't know it, it is sometimes useful to try guessing. You'll be surprised how often this is quicker and less frustrating than using a search engine to find it!

Part	Hypertext Transfer Protocol, World Wide Web	Domain Name	Org. Type	Country
Example	http://www.	happy.	co.	uk
What it means	This lets the browser know that you want to visit a Website	This is the domain name – it indicates the name of the organization	Identifies the type of organization. In this example, a commercial company	Identifies the country the site is registered in

The Prefix: http://www.

➤ Most Web addresses have this at the start.

➤ Some large companies, like Microsoft, seem to have managed to drop the www part.

The Domain Names

➤ This identifies the organization that owns the site, e.g. BBC, Channel 4, etc.

➤ The only difficulty is that organizations can abbreviate their names. At Happy Computers, the domain name is 'Happy', but it could just as easily have been 'HappyComputers', 'Happy-Computers', or 'Happyc'.

Organization Type

On UK sites the domain name is followed by a code that helps people identify what sort of organization it is. The most common are:

Abbreviation	Stands for	Examples
co.	Company	Commercial, profit making
org.	Non-profit organization	Charities, Unions, Trusts
ac.	Academic institutions	Universities, Colleges, Schools
gov.	Government	Government, Councils, Parliament Sites, Heritage Sites

Countries

Code	Country
uk	United Kingdom
de	Germany
fr	France
es	Spain

The Large Exception – The USA

The only big exceptions to the location and organizational info above, are sites registered in the United States.

➤ American sites do NOT need a country code at the end.

➤ There are different organizational codes (see below).

Abbreviation	Stands for
.com	Commercial organization in the US
.org	Non-profit organization in the US
.edu	Academic institution in the US

Tips For Guessing Sites

➤ Because it is cheaper to register in the US, some organizations which you would expect to have a .co.uk address actually end in .com, e.g. www.channel4.com – it's therefore worth trying .com if you can't find it with .co.uk

➤ It's always a good idea to guess the address of a site. If, however, after a few tries you still haven't found it, give up and use a search engine (see page 681).

Typing A Web Address Quickly

If you type in a domain name and then press **Ctrl** and **Enter**, Internet Explorer will automatically add the http://www at the start and a .com at the end.

Chapter 3

Using Search Engines

Introduction To Search Engines

What Are Search Engines?

Search Engines are ordinary Websites with huge databases tagged onto them. The databases contain information about Web pages and Websites on the WWW. If you wanted to find pages about monkeys, or cheese, you could use a search engine to find them, instead of trying to guess some bizarre, complicated address.

Using Search Engines – Keywords

➤ All search engines have a search box similar to the one shown below.

	Search

➤ To find information, you click into the search box and type in **keywords** to describe what you are looking for. So, if you wanted to find information on Shakespeare's tragedies you might type something like this:

Shakespeare tragedy	Search

➤ The search engine will then search its database looking for all the Web pages which contain those two words.

➤ Any sites which have both of the words, or have a high occurrence of either of the words will be listed near the top of your results. However, you may also get sites that have got the word 'tragedy' in them, but have nothing to do with Shakespeare, and nothing to do with drama either!

Using Search Engines – Categories

Some search engines also let you search by categories of information. Below is an example of Google's categories:

Arts & Humanities
Literature, Theatre, Photography...

Business & Economy
B2B, Shopping, Investments, Property...

Computers & Internet
Internet, Reviews, Software, Games...

Education
UK, Ireland, Universities...

Entertainment
Humour, Movies, Music, Picks...

Government
UK, Ireland, Politics, Law...

Health
Medicine, Drugs, Diseases, Fitness...

News & Media
Full Coverage, Weather, TV...

Recreation & Sport
Sport, Hobbies, Travel, Motoring...

Reference
Maps, Dictionaries, Phone Numbers...

Regional
UK, Ireland, Countries, Regions...

Science
Animals, Geography, Engineering...

Social Science
Economics, Languages, Psychology...

Society & Culture
People, Food & Drink, Royalty, Families...

How Many Search Engines Are On The Web?

➤ There are hundreds of search engines on the Web, and they all have different sites in their database.

➤ Because they are all different, it is **always** worth using more than one to find the information you are after.

The Three Types Of Search Engine

➤ Computer-Generated Search Engines

➤ Human Search Engines

➤ Hybrid Search Engines.

682

Computer-Generated Search Engines

For example WebCrawler.

➤ These search engines use computers to browse the Web which then add sites to the database.

➤ **Advantages**
Contains a huge number of sites.

➤ **Disadvantages**
Not categorized by humans, but by machine, so the results can be strange.
You are forced into using keywords to search for things.
You cannot look through categories of information.

Human Search Engines

For example Yahoo!

➤ Humans compile these search engines. People send the URL of their site to the search engine. The site is then reviewed, and a human categorizes the site and decides its search terms.

➤ **Advantages**
Results are more relevant.
You can look through categories of information to find what you need.

➤ **Disadvantages**
Because humans compile the search engine it takes longer for Websites to be registered.
It is often difficult to get your site registered quickly.
Contains fewer sites.

Hybrid Search Engines

For example AltaVista, HotBot, Excite.

➤ These search engines use a combination of humans and computers to compile their databases.

➤ **Advantages**
Can search by keywords and by categories.
Contains a huge number of sites.

➤ **Disadvantages**
Often hybrid search engines are not as thorough in categorizing Websites as the human search engines. They may only choose to include those which they find appealing, and you cannot guarantee that they have tried to review as many sites as possible.

Search Engine Tips

➤ **None of the search engines have information about everything on the Web**
A new Website is created every four seconds – there are literally millions of sites online and the number is growing. No single search engine has information on all of them.

➤ **Search engines do not follow the same rules**
If you search for the same thing in two different search engines, you won't always get the same results. Different search engines categorize Websites in different ways.

➤ **Use more than one search engine for the best results**
If you can't find what you need from one search engine – try another! They all have different Websites in their databases and just because one does not give you the information you need, doesn't mean that another won't provide it either.

➤ **Sometimes you will get hundreds of Websites back in your results**
It can be daunting when you search for a topic and find that you then have a million Websites to look through, but it is worthwhile remembering two things.

➤ Search engines always rank your results – the ones at the top will be the most relevant, whereas the ones at the bottom of the results may not have much relevance at all.

➤ Even though search engines may tell you that they have found a million pages, you will usually only be able to access the first 200 or so.

➤ **You can narrow your search with expressions**
For more information see page 691.

Going Directly To Search Engines

Some Common Search Engines

You can just type in the URL of a search engine to use it.

Often you will find that search engines give you predominately American sites, so there is often a UK version that will let you search for UK sites.

Search Engine Name	Global version	UK version
Google	www.google.com	www.google.co.uk
Yahoo!	www.yahoo.com	www.yahoo.co.uk
Excite	www.excite.com	
AltaVista	www.altavista.com	www.altavista.co.uk
Lycos		www.lycos.co.uk
Hotbot	www.hotbot.com	
InfoSeek	www.infoseek.com	
Northern Light	www.northernlight.com	

Getting To A Search Engine

1   Click into the *Address* bar.

2   Type in the address of the search engine, e.g. **www.google.co.uk**

3   Press **Enter**

    or

    click on the **Go** button.

Using Google

Getting To Google UK

1   Type **www.google.co.uk** into the *Address* bar.

2   Press **Enter**

    or

    click on the **Go** button.

Searching Through Google's Categories

Google provides categories of information to search through, rather than you having to type in keywords.

From Google's home page:

1   Click on *Directory.*

> Directory

2   Click on the category you require, e.g. *Games.*

Arts	**Home**	**Regional**
Movies, Music, Television,...	Consumers, Homeowners, Family,...	Asia, Europe, North America,...
Business	**Kids and Teens**	**Science**
Industries, Finance, Jobs,...	Computers, Entertainment, School,...	Biology, Psychology, Physics,...
Computers	**News**	**Shopping**
Hardware, Internet, Software,...	Media, Newspapers, Current Events,...	Autos, Clothing, Gifts,...
Games	**Recreation**	**Society**
Board, Roleplaying, Video,...	Food, Outdoors, Travel,...	Issues, People, Religion,...
Health	**Reference**	**Sports**
Alternative, Fitness, Medicine,...	Education, Libraries, Maps,...	Basketball, Football, Soccer,...

World
Deutsch, Español, Français, Italiano, Japanese, Korean, Nederlands, Polska, Svenska, ...

3   Click on a sub-category or Web page.

Games

> **Categories**

Board Games (3723)	Game Design (195)	Puzzles (488)
Card Games (1234)	Game Studies (67)	Resources (82)
Coin-Op (788)	Hand-Eye Coordination (49)	Retailers (3076)
Collecting (68)	Hand Games (32)	**Roleplaying** (5218)
Computer Games (1731)	**Internet** (6453)	Shopping (976)
Console Games (2856)	Investing Games (36)	Tile Games (69)
Consumer Information (111)	Miniatures (613)	Trading Cards (658)
Conventions (152)	MUDs (1617)	**Video Games** (40117)
Developers and Publishers (2560)	Paper and Pencil (29)	Web Hosting (16)
Dice Games (116)	Party Games (139)	Women in Gaming (34)
Fantasy Sports (856)	Play-By-Mail (135)	Wordplay (183)
Fortune Telling (85)	Play Groups (83)	Yard and Deck Games (61)
Gambling (3220)		

Related Categories:
Recreation (123291)
Sports (114937)

686

Limiting The Search To UK Sites

➤ The Web is monopolized by American sites that often make it difficult to find information about the UK.

➤ Google is at an advantage here by allowing you to search just for sites that are registered in the UK.

1 Type your keywords into the *Search* box.

2 Click in the circle next to the part you wish to search in.

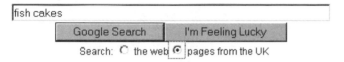

3 Click on **Search**.

Advanced Search Options

If you want to narrow your search further:

1 Click on *Advanced Search*

• Advanced Search

2 Type your keywords into one of the search boxes, depending on what you want to find.

Find results	with **all** of the words	
	with the **exact phrase**	
	with **at least one** of the words	fish cakes
	without the words	

Or

Search news stories by typing into the *News Search* box.

News Search (BETA)

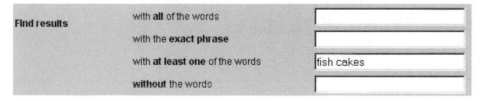

3 Choose any further options you require (see next page).

Language	Return pages written in	English ▼
File Format	Only ▼ return results of the file format	any format ▼
Date	Return web pages updated in the	past 6 months ▼
Occurrences	Return results where my terms occur	in the text of the page ▼
Domain	Only ▼ return results from the site or domain	
SafeSearch	⦿ No filtering ○ Filter using SafeSearch	*e.g. google.com, .org More info*

4   Click on **Google Search**.

How Did Google Find My Results?

➤ Google is indexed by a 'web crawler'. This is a machine that crawls the Web looking for new sites, which are then added to Google's database. A lot of sites are indexed, but Google then ranks them according to how many people link to them. This gives it much more accuracy than some sites.

➤ Google searches for pages that have **all** of your words on them.

➤ It then sorts them according to their relevancy in each specific area.

➤ Pages which more people have linked to will be listed nearer the top.

➤ Web pages whose title matches one of your keywords will appear higher in the list than those who have the word in the middle of the page or in the address.

Using AltaVista

Getting To AltaVista UK

1   Type **www.altavista.co.uk** into the *Address* bar.

2   Press **Enter**

or

click on the **Go** button.

Performing A Basic Keyword Search

1   Type your question into the *Search* box.

2   If necessary, click the drop-down arrow next to the language box and choose the language you would like displayed.

3   Click in the circle next to where you want to search – *UK* or *Worldwide*.

4   Click **Search**.

688

Use A Natural Question, Rather Than Just Words

AltaVista has a huge database with millions of sites. The more words you specify the more relevant your results will be, so using a natural question such as 'How many centimetres are there in an inch?' will tend to produce better results.

Searching For Images, Video And Audio

Click on one of the tabs to search for something other than Web pages.

Searching For Images, Audio And Video

1   Click the tab for *Images, MP3/Audio,* or *Video Clips*, depending on what you want to search for.

2   Type your keywords into the *Search* box.

3   Click on **Search**.

Seeing More Web Pages

1   Scroll to the bottom.

2   Click on the results page you would like to see, (the most relevant sites are on the left).

Searching For Keywords In A Specific Place

➤ AltaVista has the facility to find a word in a specific place in the Website, e.g. in the URL or in the title of the page.

➤ This can be useful for giving you more relevant sites (and fewer results!).

The table below shows a list of the terms you can use:

Term	Example	What it does
domain:	domain.com domain.uk	➤ Finds sites in a certain domain. ➤ **domain.com** will only find commercial sites. ➤ **domain.uk** will only find UK sites.
image:	image.dogs image:plants	➤ Finds an image with a certain file name. ➤ **image:dogs** will find sites with an image called 'dogs'. ➤ **image:plants** will find sites with an image called 'plants'.
link:	link:www.bbc.co.uk link:www.channel4.com	➤ Finds sites with a link to the URL you specify. ➤ **link:www.bbc.co.uk** will find sites with a link to the BBC's Website.
text:	text:mercedes text:shakespeare	➤ Finds sites which include the text you. specify – regardless of where it is on the page. ➤ **text:mercedes** will find sites with the word 'mercedes' anywhere on the page.
title:	title:shakespeare title:dogs	➤ Finds sites which include the text you specify in their title (this appears on the *Title* bar when you view the page). ➤ Finds sites which include the text you **title:shakespeare** will find sites with the word 'shakespeare' in the title.
url:	url:dogs url:shakespeare	➤ Finds sites which include the text you specify in their URL. ➤ **url:shakespeare** will find sites with the word 'shakespeare' in the URL.

How Did AltaVista Find My Results?

➤ AltaVista uses humans to index some of its Websites, like Google, but without the human link ranking. But because the work is done by machine and not man, it can sometimes give strange results!

690

➤ AltaVista can sometimes give many hundreds or thousands of results. However, they are ranked according to relevance. Those at the top of the list are much more likely to be what you are looking for.

➤ Each Web page gets a grade according to:

  ➤ how many of your search terms it contains;

  ➤ whereabouts search terms are in the page (e.g. in the title or in the domain name);

  ➤ how close search terms are to each other.

  The better the site scores in terms of these, the higher in will appear in the results list.

➤ Any sites which repeat a word over and over are ranked negatively as they are probably created by people who have needlessly repeated a common search term in order to get their site to show often in results pages.

Find Out About Search Engines!

In this manual we have looked at Google and AltaVista in detail. There are others though, so don't feel that these are the only ones you can use.

All search engines have a help facility – use it! It is the only way to understand how the search engine works, and how to get the best results when you use it.

Narrowing Your Search

These Tips Will Work In Most Search Engines ... But Not All!

Google and AltaVista support the tips given below. However, it is worth checking the help section of your chosen search engine to make sure.

Working With Phrases

Use quotes if you are searching for phrases or names. The quotes ensure that the search engine looks for that exact phrase.

691

| William Shakespeare | Search | | "William Shakespeare" | Search |

This will find sites that have the words William and Shakespeare but not necessarily together

This narrows the search to finding sites which have the phrase "William Shakespeare" in them

Using Plus (+)

Use a plus sign before a word if that word MUST BE INCLUDED in the Web pages found.

| Shakespeare sonnets | Search | | +Shakespeare sonnets | Search |

This will usually find all pages that have the words Shakespeare and Sonnets in them somewhere.

Putting a plus next to Shakespeare here, ensures that the sites found MUST include the word Shakespeare.

Google Does Not Need Plus Signs

Google automatically includes every word you type in, effectively adding a plus sign itself. Unless you use a common word like **the'**, in which case it will be excluded – if you want to include it in the search, then you'll need to put a plus sign in front of it.

Using Minus (–)

Use a minus sign before a word if that word MUST NOT BE INCLUDED in the Web pages found.

| -Shakespeare sonnets | Search |

This will find sites that include the word sonnets, but not if they're by Shakespeare.

Using A Combination

Any combination of the above can be used to really narrow your search down.

| +"Shakespeare plays" -sonnets | Search |

This will find sites that include the phrase "Shakespeare plays" and would reject those that include the word "sonnets".

Case-Sensitive

Most search engines are not case-sensitive, but to be on the safe side, stick to the following rules:

> ➤ **All lower case**: gives you anything containing that word, e.g. **boots** will find you information about the footwear, the shop, and anything else that contains the word boots.

> ➤ **Capitals at the start**: gives you sites containing that word when it occurs with a capital at the start, e.g. **Boots** should find you less about the shoes and more about the shop.

Use More Words!

If you only type one word you are likely to get thousands of pages back. The more specific you are the more specific your results will be!

Avoid Generic Terms

Think carefully about the words you use and try to make them as specific as possible. Have a look at the examples below.

Generic Term	More Specific
Car	Mini Cooper, Mercedes, BMW
Sports	Football, Tennis
Music	Pop, Rock, Dance, Classical

For More Information About Which Search Engines Support These Tips

See 'Search Engine Support' on page 770.

Chapter 4

Viewing And Saving Web Pages

Your Favourite Web Pages

Changing Your Home Page

If you find a site that you really like or find particularly useful, you may want to set it as your home page. This is the page that Internet Explorer will open with.

1   Click on the **Tools** menu.

2   Click on **Internet** *Options*.

3   Click on the **General** tab.

4   Click in the *Address* box in the *Home page* area.

5   Type the address of the page you wish to set as your home page.

6   Click **OK**.

What Are Favourites?

When you find a useful site, you will often want to return to it regularly. If you make it a favourite, then going back is easy!

Creating a Favourite

1   Go to the page which you would like to make a favourite.

2   Click on the **Favorites** menu.

3   Click on **Add to Favorites**.

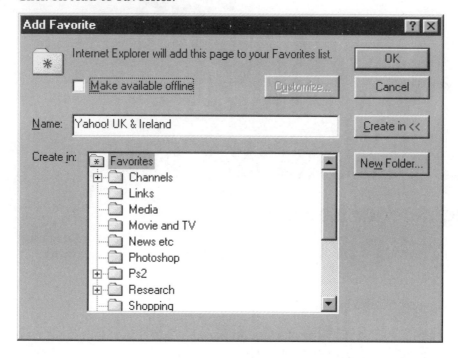

4   Give your favourite page a name if required – type it into the *Name* box.

5   Click **OK**.

Adding A Favourite To A Folder

1   Go the page which you would like to make a favourite.

2   Click on the **Favorites** menu.

3   Click on **Add to Favorites**.

4   Give your favourite page a name if required.

5   Click on **Create in**.

6   Double-click on the folder you wish to add the page to

or

click on **New Folder** to create a new folder to put your page in.

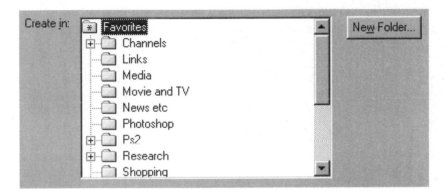

7   Click **OK**.

Accessing One Of Your Favourites

1   Click on the **Favorites** button – a list of favourites appears on the left.

2   If necessary, click on the folder you wish to open.

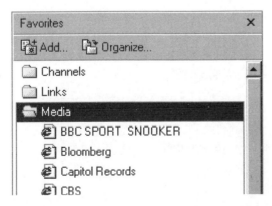

3   Click on the page you wish to go to.

4   Click on the **Favorites** button again to remove the list.

Deleting Favourites

1   Click on the **Favorites** button.

2   Right click on the site you wish to delete – a new menu will appear.

3   Click on **Delete**.

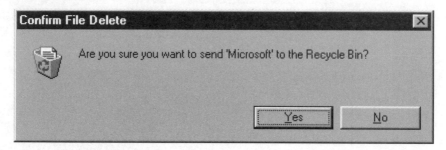

4   Click **Yes** to delete the page.

Creating Folders In Favourites

You can move favourites to different folders, rename, name, or create new folders at any time.

1   Click on the **Favorites** menu.

2   Click on **Organize Favorites**.

3   Click on **Create Folder**.

4   Type in a name for your folder.

5   Press **Enter**.

6   Click **Close**.

Renaming Folders Or Favourites

1   Click on the **Favorites** menu.

2   Click on **Organize Favorites**.

3   Click on the folder or page you wish to rename.

4   Click on **Rename**.

5   Type in a new name.

6   Press **Enter**.

7   Click **Close**.

Moving Favourites

1   Click on the **Favorites** menu.

2   Click on **Organize Favorites**.

3   Select the page or folder you wish to move.

4   Click on **Move to Folder**.

5   Click on the folder you would like to move into – if a folder has a plus sign next to it, click on the plus sign to see the subfolders.

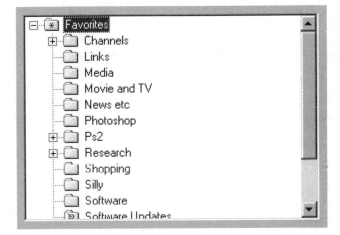

6   Click **OK**.

7   Click **Close**.

Saving Web Pages

Check This Out...

Saving The Page Saves Money!

If you save the page to your hard disk then you can look at it later on without having to connect to the Internet. If you are using a dial-up modem from home, then you will find this useful.

Saving To The Hard Disk

1   Go to the page you wish to save.

2   Click on the **File menu**.

3   Click on **Save As**.

4   Change the *Save in* box to the folder you wish to save in.

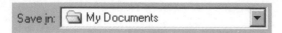

5   Type a file name for your page, if required

6   Click **Save**.

Why Do Extra Folders Appear When I Save A Page?

Often when you save, you will end up with extra folders as well as the file. These are usually to hold any graphics that come with the Web page. If you do not want to see the graphics, you can delete them.

Opening A Saved File

1   Click on the **File** menu.

2   Click on **Open**.

3   Click on **Browse**.

4   Change the *Look in* box to the folder where your file is saved.

5   Double-click on the file you wish to open.

6   Click **OK**.

My Address Bar Doesn't Have A Web Address!

Your *Address* bar will now have the pathname of the file you have just opened. AutoComplete won't work and neither will some of the buttons (e.g. **Back**). Type in a Web address or click on **Home** to return to the Web.

Editing A Web Page

If you prefer you can edit the Web page – just click on the **Edit** icon, your Web page will open (in Word, or FrontPage, or whatever your browser decides is the default editing program).

The Web Page Won't Go Into Word!

Sometimes Web designers add security to their site that will prevent you from seeing it in Word.

Images

Images Take A Long Time To Download!

If you stop your computer from downloading images off the Web, then you will massively speed up the download process. This can cut the cost of your phone bills dramatically.

Removing Images

1   Click on the **Tools** menu.

2   Click on **Internet Options**.

3   Click on the **Advanced** tab.

4   Scroll down until you see the *Multimedia* options.

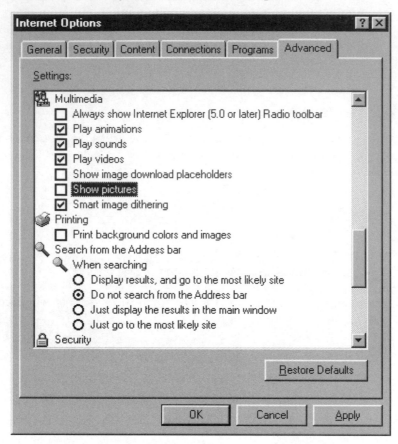

5   Remove the tick next to *Show pictures*.

6   Click **OK.**

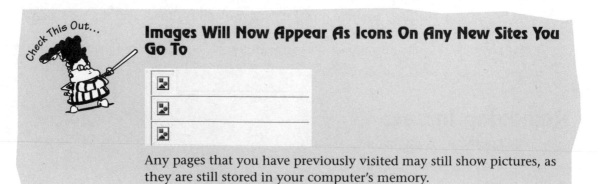

Check This Out...

Images Will Now Appear As Icons On Any New Sites You Go To

Any pages that you have previously visited may still show pictures, as they are still stored in your computer's memory.

Seeing Images Temporarily

If a Web page is not making sense without its images, you can turn them back on temporarily.

1   Right click on the picture you would like to see.

2   Click on **Show Picture**.

Switching Images Back On

1   Click on the **Tools** menu.

2   Click on **Internet Options**.

3   Click on the **Advanced** tab.

4   Scroll down to the *Multimedia* options.

5   Click in the box next to *Show pictures* so that it is ticked.

6   Click **OK**.

Chapter 5

Printing

Printing

Printing A Page

Click on the **Print** icon.

Printing Certain Pages

A Web page may not necessarily be just one sheet of A4. To print only certain pages:

1 Click on the **File** menu.

2 Click on **Print**.

3 Type in the pages required in the *Pages* boxes.

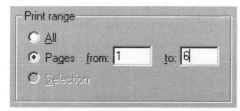

Printing More Than One Copy

1 Click on the **File** menu.

2 Click on **Print**.

3 Change the number of copies to the number you require (see below).

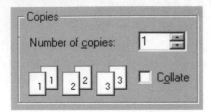

➤ Use the up and down arrows to change the number of copies, or click into the box and type in the number of copies you require.

➤ Tick *Collate* if you require the copies to come out in the order page 1, 2, 3, page 1, 2, 3, etc.

➤ Do not tick *Collate* if you require the copies to come out in the order page 1, page 1, page 2, page 2, etc.

4 Click **OK**.

Printing All Linked Documents

1 Click on the **File** menu.

2 Click on **Print**.

3 Click next to *Print all linked documents* so that it is ticked.

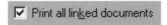

4 Click **OK**.

Printing A Table Of Links

This is useful if you want to see how many links there are from the page you are looking at.

1 Click on the **File** menu.

2 Click on **Print**.

3 Click next to *Print table of links* so that it is ticked.

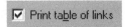 Print table of links

4   Click **OK**.

Printing Frames

Sometimes you may not want to print the Web page as it appears on the screen, but just a selection of it. You can do this if the page is divided into separate sections, or frames. This page has at least two frames – see one in the middle with a scroll bar.

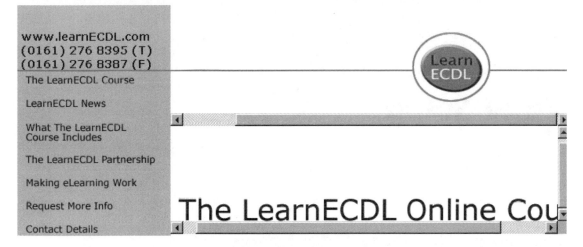

1   Click your cursor anywhere in the frame you wish to print (but not on a link!).

2   Click on the **File** menu.

3   Click on **Print**.

4   Click next to the option you require (see below).

5   Click **OK**.

How Can I Tell If A Page Has Frames?

Sometimes there will be scroll bars but more often the page will just have different sections that are separated by lines or that just look different. If the page doesn't use frames, the *Print frames* area in the *Print* dialog box will be greyed out.

Page Setup

You can change various things about the way that Internet Explorer prints your pages, such as whether the page has landscape or portrait orientation. Any options that you change will remain set for all the future pages that you print out, as well as the current Web page. You can change the page setup options as many times as you like.

Changing The Page Orientation

You can choose whether to have the page printed vertically (portrait) or horizontally (landscape). For example, a Web page might look better when printed landscape if it is wider than it is long.

1   Click on the **File** menu.

2   Click on **Page Setup**.

3   Click in the circle next to *Landscape*

    or

    click in the circle next to *Portrait*.

4   Click **OK.**

Changing The Margins

There are four margins on a printed page: top, bottom, left and right. Internet Explorer will set these for you automatically. You might want to increase these if you want more white space around the edge of the printed document.

1 Click on the **File** menu.

2 Click on **Page Setup**.

3 Click in the box for the margin you wish to change.

4 Change the margin to the amount you require.

5 Repeat steps 3 to 4 for any other margin you wish to change.

6 Click **OK**.

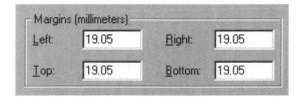

Margins (millimeters)

| Left: | 19.05 | Right: | 19.05 |
| Top: | 19.05 | Bottom: | 19.05 |

Check This Out...

Check The Unit Of Measurement

Look at the text next to *Margins* in the box to determine the unit of measurement being used. One inch is a lot bigger than one millimetre!

What Are Headers And Footers?

Headers and footers appear at the top and bottom of every page. They are usually used to display information such as page numbers, the title of the Web page, the date, etc.

Changing The Header And Footer

1 Click on the **File** menu.

2 Click on **Page Setup**.

3 Click in the *Header* box to change the header

or

click in the *Footer* box to change the footer.

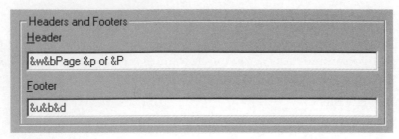

4   Type the required text or variables (see the next sections).

5   Click **OK.**

Adding Variable Information To A Header Or Footer

Some information that you want included in the headers and footers may change for different Web pages (such as the number of pages, the title of the page, the date, etc.). This variable information can be included by typing the appropriate character. The list below shows which characters to use:

Page title   &w

Page address (URL)   &u

Date in short format   &d

Date in long format   &D

Time   &t

Time in 24-hour format   &T

Current page number   &p

Total number of pages   &P

Formats For Date And Time

The formats used for date and time will vary depending on the regional settings of your computer.

710

Adding Text To A Header Or Footer

Any text that you require that does not change (such as your name) can be typed directly into the header or footer box.

Adding An Ampersand (&)

The ampersand is one of the characters used for specifying what variable information you want included. If you want to use an '&' in your header or footer, type && to let Explorer know this is what you want!

Using A Combination Of Text And Variables

You can use a combination of fixed text and variable information. For example you could prefix the page number with the word Page (i.e. **Page &p**).

Changing The Alignment Of Text

Text in the header and footer will automatically be aligned to the left of the page. You can change it to be centred on the page or aligned to the right.

1   Click on the **File** menu.

2   Click on **Page Setup**.

3   Type the text or variables required in the *Header* or *Footer* boxes.

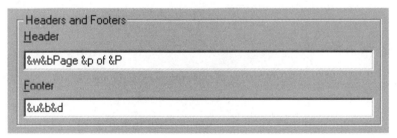

4   After the text or variable type **&b** to centre the text (e.g. &d&b)

    or

    after the text or variable type **&b&b** to align the text to the right (e.g. &d&b&b).

5   Click **OK**

Chapter 6

Getting Started With Outlook

Opening Outlook

Starting Outlook

1   Click on the **Start** button.

2   Click on **Programs**.

3   Click on **Microsoft Outlook**.

Or

From the desktop, double-click on the **Microsoft Outlook** icon.

Shutting Down Outlook

1   Click on the **File** menu.

2   Choose **Exit**.

Or

Click on the X on the top right of the title bar.

Outlook Screen

The Outlook Screen

The Outlook screen looks different depending on which component you are in. The picture below shows the Inbox screen in Outlook 2000.

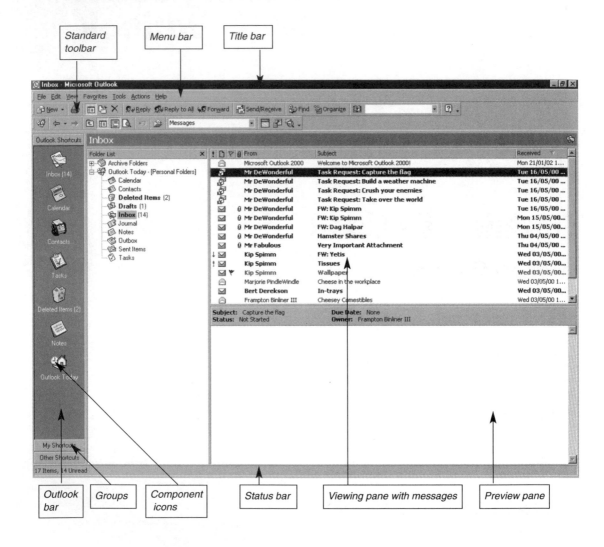

What Are The Components Of Outlook?

Outlook has several different components. Each component allows you to perform a different kind of task. This list below names the components and gives a brief description of what each one is for.

 **Outlook Today**

This is an introductory screen to Outlook. It shows you any appointments or events booked in your calendar for the coming week. It also shows you any tasks you have set for yourself, and whether you have e-mail messages waiting for you in your Inbox.

 Inbox

The Inbox stores the e-mails you receive.

 **Calendar**

The Calendar allows you to book out times for appointments, or meetings, just like a normal diary. You can also use the calendar to schedule meetings with other people.

 **Contacts**

This is just like an address book. It holds information about all the people you are in contact with.

 **Tasks**

A bit like a to-do list. Use it to keep track of all the things you need to do.

 **Notes**

Just like post-it notes. You can stick them to your computer screen as a reminder.

 **Deleted Items**

The same as the Recycle Bin in Windows. Use it to throw away any unwanted information.

Journal   This keeps track of all the programs and files you have opened in a day.

Displaying The Outlook Bar

The Outlook bar runs down the left-hand side of the screen and shows the components listed above. To turn it on or off.

1   Click on the **View** menu.

2   Click **Outlook Bar**.

Using Outlook Shortcuts

The easiest way of getting to the different components of Outlook is to use the Outlook Shortcuts group on the Outlook bar.

1   Ensure the Outlook bar is displayed (see previous section).

2   Click on the **Outlook Shortcuts** button.

> Outlook Shortcuts

3   Click the shortcut you require.

Opening The Inbox

What Is The Inbox?

The Inbox allows you to send and receive e-mails. The Inbox can be viewed from Outlook Shortcuts or the My Shortcuts bar. A list of the e-mails you have received is shown here. Outlook does not limit you to sending only text messages, you can also send pictures and other formatted files.

Opening The Inbox

Click on the **Inbox** icon on the Outlook bar.

Using Help In Outlook

Outlook comes with help files, just like all the other software packages. Press **F1** to call it up, and use it in the same way as you would any other help file.

Changing The View

You can customize the way your Inbox screen looks by changing your view, displaying folders and a preview pane, and showing or hiding toolbars.

Outlook Toolbars

Toolbars give you quick access to commands. There are three toolbars in Outlook: *Standard, Advanced* and *Web*.

Showing And Hiding Toolbars

1   Click on the **View** menu.

2   Click on **Toolbars**.

3   Click on toolbar you wish to see or hide.

Toolbars Are On When Ticked

If there is a tick next to the name of the toolbar in the **Toolbars** menu then it is on the screen. Toolbars are hidden when not ticked.

What Is The Preview Pane?

This is the default view for your Inbox. Your screen is split into two and you can view any message, read or unread, in your Inbox.

Showing The Preview Pane

Click on the **Preview Pane** icon on the *Advanced* toolbar.

Or

1   Click on the **View** menu.

2   Click on **Preview Pane**.

3   Select a message you want to preview.

Hiding The Preview Pane

Click on the **Preview Pane** icon on the *Advanced* toolbar.

Or

1   Click on the **View** menu.

2   Click on **Preview Pane**.

What Are Folders?

Folders are used to organize the messages you receive, send, save, and give you access to other components of Outlook. You can also create your own folders to store your messages.

Viewing Or Hiding The Folders List

Click on the **Folder List** icon.

Or

1   Click on the **View** menu.

2   Choose **Folder List**.

If the Folder List is displayed, then this will hide it – if it is hidden, then this will display it.

Changing Views

There are a number of different views that you can choose in Outlook. They determine what messages you see on your screen and how they are sorted.

1   Click on the drop-down arrow for the **Current View** icon on the *Advanced* toolbar.

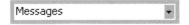

2   Select the required view.

View	What you see
Messages	Displays messages
Messages with AutoPreview	Displays messages in a list with the first 3 lines of the message showing
By Follow-up Flag	Displays messages in a list grouped by a message flag. Also shows the due date for the message flag
Last Seven Days	Displays messages that have arrived within the last 7 days
Flagged for Next Seven Days	Displays messages with a message flag for follow action due within the next 7 days
By Conversation Topic	Grouped by subject
By Sender	Grouped by Ssender
Unread Messages	Displays messages that are marked as unread

Sent To	Displays messages by the names of recipients
Message Timeline	Displays messages represented by icons arranged in chronological order by date sent

Chapter 7

Working With E-mail

Creating A Message

Creating An E-mail

1   Click **Inbox** from the Outlook bar (if you are not already there).

2   Click **New**.

3   Type in the address you wish to send to next to *To*, e.g. fredbloggs@fishface.com

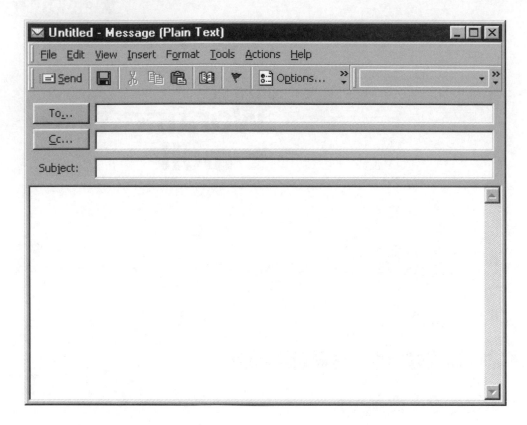

4   Type in any address(es) you wish to send a copy to next to *Cc* (Carbon copy).

5   Type in the subject next to *Subject*.

6   Type your message in the white space underneath.

Don't Forget The Subject!

The subject line appears in the recipient's Inbox before they open the
e-mail.

I Want To Send An E-mail To More Than One Person

Separate the addresses with a semi-colon, e.g. marymiggins@pies.com;
jobbo@spetetoot.com

Blind Copy

If you want to send a copy of your e-mail to someone, but don't want everybody else to know that they have been sent it, you can send a blind carbon copy (Bcc).

1   Create a new message.

2   Click on the **View** menu.

3   Click **Bcc Field** – a new box will appear under the *Cc* box.

4   Type in the address(es) next to the *Bcc*.

The Bcc Field Remains

You will still see the *Bcc* box for your future messages. To turn it off, click on the **View** menu and then click on **Bcc Field**.

Sending An E-mail

Click **Send**.

The message goes to Outbox if you are not connected to a network or the Internet. It is sent immediately if you are connected to a network or the Internet. Unless you are connected to a network, or the Internet, your message will go to the Outbox and will sit there until you do connect. To send your message from the Outbox:

Click on the **Send/Receive** icon.

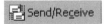

Saving A Message

If you start to type a message, and then don't send it, you can save it in your Drafts folder.

Click on the **Save** icon – the message is saved in the Drafts folder.

To get back to your message:

1   Click on the **View** menu.

2   Click **Folder List**.

3   Click **Drafts**.

4   Double-click on the message you require.

Flagging Mail Messages

You can indicate how urgent an e-mail is by flagging it. A symbol will appear next to the message in the recipient's inbox, so they can prioritize their mail.

1   Create your message as normal.

2   Click on the **Flag** icon.

3   Click the drop-down arrow next to *Flag to* and choose the subject for the flag.

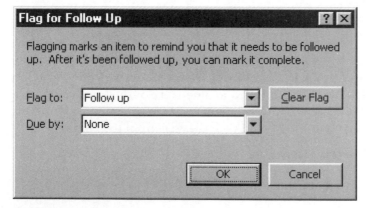

4   Click the drop-down arrow next to *Due by* and choose the response date for the e-mail.

5   Click **OK** – a flag message will appear above the e-mail.

Changing Message Options

This lets you change the way Outlook delivers the message, or link the message to contacts and categories.

1 Create the message as normal.

2 Click **Options**.

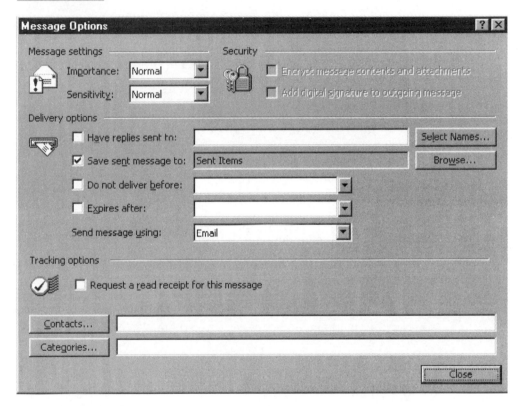

➤ Click the drop-down arrow next to *Importance* and choose the importance of the message.

➤ Click the drop-down arrow next to *Sensitivity* and choose the sensitivity of the message.

➤ In the *Have replies sent to* box, enter the address you wish replies to be sent to.

➤ Choose the folder you wish sent items to be stored in, by clicking the **Browse** button next to *Save sent message to*.

➤ In the *Do not deliver before* box, enter the date on which the message must be delivered.

725

➤ In the *Expires after* box, enter the date on which the message must be deleted.

➤ Click the *Request a read receipt for this message* box to receive an e-mail when the recipient has read the message.

➤ Click on the **Contacts** or **Categories** buttons to link the message to certain contacts or categories (see page 755)

3 Change the options as required (see above).

4 Click **Close**.

Making Your Message Important

You can let people know that your message is important – it will be marked with a red exclamation mark in the Outlook inbox.

1 Create the message as normal.

2 Click the **Importance: High** icon – the icon will appear 'pushed in' when you have clicked on it.

They Didn't Read My Important Message!

Just because you have flagged a message as important, it doesn't mean that Outlook will force the other person to read it! People will sometimes still ignore e-mails, no matter how many flags or red things you stick on them! If it's really really important, it might be better to phone them, or, better yet, meet them.

Receiving E-mail

Receiving An E-mail

If You Are Connected To A Network Or The Internet, You Do Not Have To Do Anything!

Your messages will just appear in your Inbox when they have arrived. As they are arriving, you should see a message at the bottom of the screen saying something like 'Receiving message 1 of 3'.

If you are not connected to the network or Internet, just click on the **Send/Receive** icon.

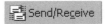

When you click it, a dialog box will appear:

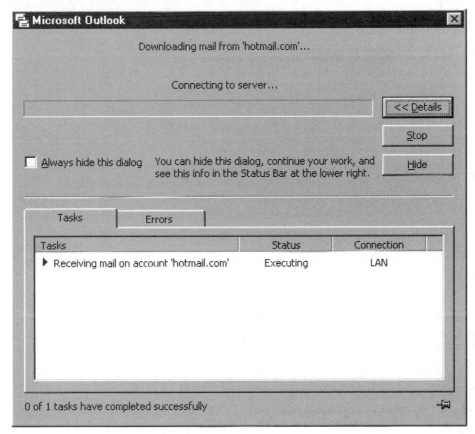

When this box disappears, Outlook has finished sending and receiving. If you don't have any new mail, then nobody has sent you any. Don't worry, you'll get some soon.

Reading Mail

How Do I Know If I Have Mail To Be Read?

There are several ways in which Outlook will indicate if there is new mail:

➤ The number of unread messages appears in brackets next to the **Inbox** icon.

Inbox (15)

➤ A closed envelope appears next to unread messages, and the text will appear in bold.

| ✉ | **Marjorie PindleWindle** | **Cheese in the workplace** |

➤ There is a message at the bottom left of the screen telling you how many unread messages you have.

19 Items, 17 Unread

To read your message, double-click on it. The message will open in a new window. Or you can click once on the message, and it will appear in the preview pane (see page 718).

How Do I Know If I've Read A Message?

Once a message has been read, the envelope will look as if it has been opened, and the text will no longer be in bold.

| ◁ | Marjorie PindleWindle | Cheese in the workplace |

Marking A Message As Unread

Once you have read a message you can make it look as though it still hasn't been read to draw your attention to it.

1   Click on the message in the Inbox.

2   Click on the **Edit** menu.

3   Click on **Mark as Unread**.

Closing An E-mail Message

1   Click the X on the title bar of the e-mail message (**not** the one on the Outlook bar!).

Or

1   Click on the **File** menu.

2   Click on **Close**.

Forwarding And Replying To E-Mail

Forwarding A Message

Sometimes you might want to send a message on to someone else – this is called forwarding.

1   Click on **Inbox** from the *Outlook* bar.

2   Select the message you wish to forward.

3   Click **Forward** – a new message window will appear.

4   Enter the e-mail address of the person you wish to forward the message to next to **To**.

5   Enter any text in the message area.

6   Send the message as normal.

Replying To An E-Mail

1   Select the message you want to reply to.

2   Click **Reply** – a new message window will appear.

3   The address will already be filled in, and the original text of the message will appear.

4   Type in your message.

5   Send the message as normal.

The Sender Gets Their Message Again!

When you reply to a message, your reply will include the text from the original message. See the two sections after the next one to learn how to delete this text, or how not to include it in the first place.

Replying To All The Recipients

If the message you are replying to was sent to more than one person originally, you can reply to all of them.

1   Select the message you want to reply to.

2   Click **Reply to All** – a new message window will appear.

3   The addresses will be filled in, and the original text of the message will appear.

4   Type in your new message.

5   Send the message as normal.

Deleting Text

You may want to delete some text when you are forwarding or replying, if you do not want the whole of the original message to be included.

1   Select the text you wish to delete.

2   Press **Delete** on the keyboard.

Not Including The Original Message

It's often useful to include the original message, so that the person you are replying to knows what they said to you in the first place. However, you can turn this feature off:

1   Click on the **Tools** menu.

2   Click **Options**.

3   Click on the **Preferences** tab.

4   Click *E-mail Options*.

5   Click the drop-down arrow underneath *When replying to a message*.

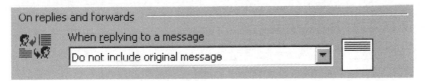

6   Click *Do not include original message*.

7   Click **OK**.

Sending And Receiving Attachments

An attachment is a file that you send with an e-mail. The attachment can be any sort of file – a Word document, an Excel spreadsheet, a film, a picture, etc.

Sending A Message With An Attachment

1   Create a new e-mail as normal.

2   Ensure that your cursor is flashing inside the message area – if not, click inside it.

3   Click on the **Attachment** icon.

4   Change the *Look in* box to the folder where the file you require is saved.

5   Click on the file you require.

6   Click **Insert** – the file will appear below the e-mail.

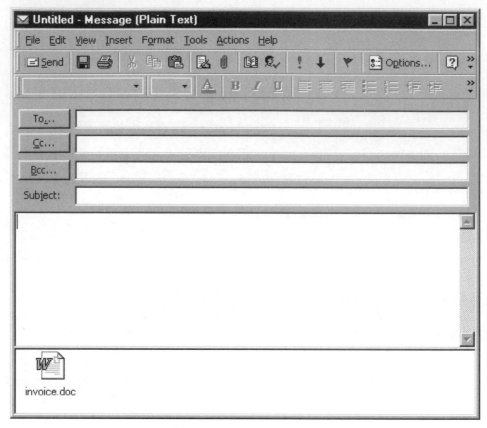

7   Click **Send**.

Receiving An Attachment

If your message has an attachment, you will see a paper clip symbol next to it in the Inbox.

✉   ◊ **Mr DeWonderful**   **Hamster Shares**

To open the attachment:

1   Double-click the e-mail you wish to open.

2   Double-click the attachment icon underneath the message.

3   If you are asked, click the circle next to *Open it*.

    or

click the circle next to *Save it to disk* if you wish to save the file onto your computer before you open it.

Or

1   Ensure the preview pane is displayed (see page 718).

2   Click on the e-mail that contains the attachment you wish to open.

3   Click on the **Attachment** icon at the top of the preview pane – it looks like a paperclip.

4   Click on the attachment you wish to open.

5   If you are asked, click the circle next to *Open it*

    or

    click the circle next to *Save it to disk* if you wish to save the file onto your computer before you open it.

I Can't Open My Attachment!

If the attachment was created in a program which you do not have on your machine, you may not be able to open it. For example, if someone sends you a Word 97 document and you have Word 6, you will not be able to open it. You must obtain the software, or ask the person who sent it to you to send it in a format which you can open.

Saving An Attachment

1   Select the message with the attachment.

2   Click on the **File** menu.

3   Choose **Save Attachments**.

4   Click on the attachment you want to save.

5   Click on the location where you wish to save the file.

6   Choose another name for the attachment if you want.

7   Click on **Save**.

A Quicker Way!

Open the message and right click the attachment icon and choose *Save As* from the shortcut menu. Specify where you want to save the attachment and give it a new name if you want to.

Beware – Viruses!

Be careful with attachments! If you are not sure that your attachment is completely virus free, check for viruses before opening the attachment. Most virus checkers will allow you to right click the attachment and scan it with the virus checking software. Do this even if it is from someone you trust – they could be infected without realizing!

Deleting An Attachment From An E-Mail Before Sending

If you attach the wrong file, it is easy to delete it.

1   Click on the attachment icon in the e-mail – it will become highlighted.

2   Press **Delete** on the keyboard.

Deleting An Attachment From An E-Mail In A Folder

You may want to delete an attachment from an e-mail in your Inbox or another folder. For instance, this might be to save space if you no longer need the attachment, but want to keep the message. Or, you may have already saved the attachment somewhere on your computer.

1   Open the e-mail with the attachment.

2   Click on the attachment icon in the e-mail – it will become highlighted.

3   Press **Delete** on the keyboard.

4   Click on the **File** menu.

5   Click **Save**.

6   Close the message.

Moving And Copying Text

Why Move And Copy Text?

If you have text that you need to repeat, there is no need to retype it – you can simply copy the text to anywhere in that e-mail, or into another e-mail. If you decide that the text needs to be somewhere other than where you have typed it, it is easy to move it as well.

You may also have text in another Windows file, such as a Word document, that you want to use in your e-mail. Moving or copying this text to e-mail will save you the effort of retyping it.

Moving Text In A New Message

1   Select the text you would like to move.

2   Click on the **Cut** icon – the text is moved to the Windows clipboard.

3   Position the cursor in the place you would like to move the text to.

4   Click on the **Paste** icon.

735

Copying Text In A New Message

1   Select the text you would like to copy.

2   Click on the **Copy** icon – the text is copied to the Windows clipboard.

3   Position the cursor in the place you would like to copy text to.

4   Click on the **Paste** icon.

The Cut Or Copied Text Remains On The Clipboard

If you click on **Paste** more than once, whatever was last cut or copied will appear again.

What Is the Windows Clipboard?

This is a temporary storage area within your computer. When you cut or copy text, the text is placed onto the clipboard ready for you to paste in somewhere else.

Switching Between A Message And The Inbox

Once you have opened a message (or created a new one), you can switch back to the Inbox without closing the e-mail. This is useful if you want to move or copy text, or just read something in another message. To go to the Inbox, click on the **Inbox** button on the taskbar.

To return to the message, click the button for the message on the taskbar.

Outlook Opens A New Window For Each Message

When you open a message, Outlook opens it in a new window with its own button on the taskbar. If you have several messages open, they will each have their own button on the taskbar. The subject of the message appears on the button so that you can tell them apart!

Opening More Than One Message

1   Open the first message.

2   Click on the **Inbox** button on the taskbar.

3   Open the second message.

4   Repeat steps 2 to 3 for any more messages you wish to open.

Switching Between Messages

You can have several messages open at the same time. If you have opened more than one message you can also switch between the open messages. Just click the button for the message on the taskbar to switch over to it.

Untitled Messages

If the message does not have a subject (for example a new message you have just created) it will be called **Untitled**.

Copying Text From A Message Into A New Message

1   Open the message you wish to copy text into.

2   Click on the **Inbox** button on the taskbar.

3   Open the message you wish to copy text from.

4   Select the text you would like to copy.

5   Click on the **Copy** icon.

6   Close the message.

7   Click the taskbar button for the message you wish to copy text to.

8   Position the cursor in the place you would like to copy the text to.

9   Click on the **Paste** icon.

Moving Text From A Message Into A New Message

1   Create a new message.

2   Click on the **Inbox** button on the taskbar.

3   Open the message you wish to move text from.

4   Click on the **Edit** menu.

5   Click **Edit Message**.

6   Select the text you would like to move.

7   Click on the **Edit** menu.

8   Click **Cut**.

9   Click on the **File** menu.

10   Click **Save**.

11   Close the message.

12   Click the taskbar button for the message you wish to move text to.

13   Position the cursor in the place you would like to move the text to.

14   Click on the **Paste** icon.

Editing A Message

If you cut text from an existing message, you will have to let Outlook know that you want to edit that message before it will let you. Remember to save the changes before you close it, or the text will still be in the message!

Copying Text From Word Into A New Message

1   Create a new message.

2   Open Word.

3   Open the document you are copying from.

4   Select the text you would like to copy.

5   Click on the **Copy** icon.

6   Click the taskbar button for the message you wish to copy text to.

7   Position the cursor where you would like to copy to.

8   Click on the **Paste** icon.

Signing Your E-mail

Creating Signatures

Signatures appear at the bottom of any messages you send, so that you don't have to keep typing in your details.

1   Click **Inbox** from the Outlook bar.

2   Click on the **Tools** menu.

3   Click **Options**.

4   Click on the **Mail Format** tab.

5   Click **Signature Picker**.

6   Click **New**.

7   Enter a name for your signature.

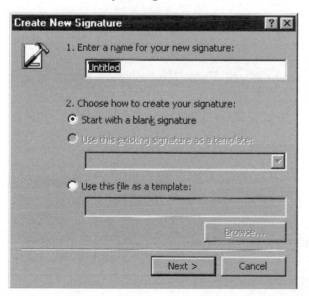

8 Click **Next**.

9 Type in the signature you require.

10 Click **Finish**.

11 Click **OK**.

You Can Create More Than One Signature

For example, you could have a formal and informal signature.

When You Create Your First Signature It Becomes The Default

Once you have created a signature, you will find that it appears at the bottom of all your e-mails. If you don't want this to happen, follow the instructions under *Changing the Default Signature* (the section after the next one).

Adding A Signature To A Message

1   Open the message you wish to add a signature to.

2   Position your cursor where you require the signature.

3   Click on the **Insert** menu.

4   Click **Signature**.

5   Click on the name of the signature you require.

Changing The Default Signature

The default signature appears automatically at the end of any new message you create.

1   Click on the **Tools** menu.

2   Click **Options**.

3   Click on the **Mail Format** tab.

4   Click the drop-down arrow next to *Use this Signature by default.*

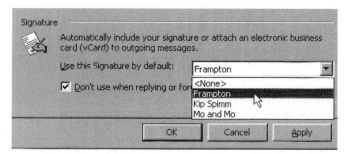

5   Click on the name of the signature you require

    or

    click *<None>* if you do not want a signature to appear automatically.

6   Click **OK**.

Editing Or Removing A Signature

1   Click on the **Tools** menu.

2   Click **Options**.

3   Click on the **Mail Format** tab.

4   Click **Signature Picker**.

5   Click on the name of the signature you wish to change.

6   Click **Remove**

    or

    click **Edit** to change the signature.

    Make any changes you require.

7   Click **OK.**

Checking Your Spelling

Spell Checking Messages

You can spell check any messages that you compose or you can set Outlook to automatically spell check every message before it is sent.

Spell Checking A Message

1   Click on the **Tools** menu.

2   Click on **Spelling** – the *Spelling* box will appear.

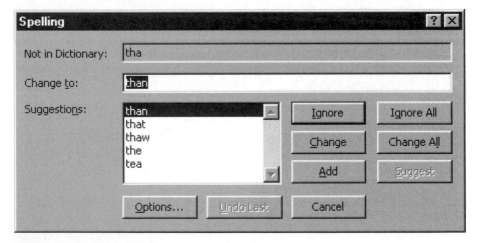

➤ The misspelling appears in the *Not in Dictionary* box.

➤ Click on the word you want to use from the list next to *Suggestions*.

➤ The *Change to* box shows you what the word will be changed to.

3   Click on the appropriate icon on the right-hand side.

4   Click **Cancel** to finish the spell check early.

How To Correct Your Mistakes With Spell Check

Problem	What you need to do
If the word is spelt correctly	Click on **Ignore**.
If the word is spelt correctly and occurs several times in the document	Click on **Ignore All**.
If the word is spelt correctly and is a word that you use very commonly, e.g. your name	Click on **Add**. This will add the word to the dictionary so that it is never seen as a misspelling again.
If the correct spelling is listed under suggestions	1 Click on the correct suggestion. 2 Click on **Change**.
If the correct spelling is listed under suggestions and the misspelling occurs commonly in the document	1 Click on the correct suggestion. 2 Click on **Change All**.
If the word is spelt incorrectly and the correct suggestion is not listed	1 Click into the **Change to** box. 2 Type the correct spelling. 3 Click on **Change**.

Setting The Automatic Spell Checker

You can set an automatic spell checker, so that every time you send a message Outlook will do a spell check before the message leaves.

1   Click on the **Tools** menu.

2   Choose **Options**.

3   Click on **Spelling**.

☑ Always check spelling before sending

4   Click in the box next to *Always check spelling before sending*

5   Click **OK**.

Chapter 8

Organizing Your E-mails

Organizing Your E-mails

E-mail Folders

E-mail is stored in several different folders within Outlook. The list below gives a brief description of what these folders do:

Folder	What it does
Inbox	Contains messages you have received
Drafts	Contains messages which you have written, but not yet sent
Outbox	Contains messages waiting to be sent over your network, or the Internet
Sent Items	Contains messages which you have sent

Displaying The Folder List

1   Click on the **View** menu.

2   Click **Folder List**.

Any folders shown in bold contain new messages.

Closing The Folder List

1   Click on the **View** menu.

2   Click **Folder List**.

Or

Click the X at the top right of the folder list.

Switching Between Folders

If the Folder List is displayed:

Click on the folder you require from the list – the contents are displayed on the right.

If the Folder List is not displayed:

1   Click on the grey title above the message list.

2   Click on the folder you require from the list – the contents are displayed on the right.

Creating Your Own Folders

1   Click on the **File** menu.

2   Click **New**

     or

click the drop-down arrow on the **New Mail Message** icon.

3 Click *Folder*.

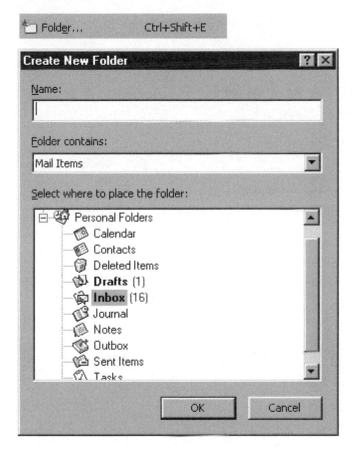

4 Type a name for your folder into the *Name* box.

5 Click on the drop-down arrow underneath *Folder contains*, and choose what the folder will be used for – usually you can leave it set at *Mail items*.

6 Click on the folder that will hold the folder you are creating, e.g. *Inbox*.

7 Click **OK**.

8 You may be asked if you want to create a shortcut – click **Yes** if you wish a shortcut to appear on the Outlook bar.

Moving E-Mails To A Folder

1   Click on the e-mail you wish to move.

2   Click on the **Edit** menu.

3   Click **Move to Folder**.

4   Click on the folder you want to move the e-mail to.

5   Click **OK**.

Copying E-Mails To A Folder

1   Click on the e-mail you want to copy.

2   Click on the **Edit** menu.

3   Click **Copy to Folder**.

4   Click on the folder you want to copy the e-mail to.

5   Click **OK**.

Sorting E-mails

1   Go to the folder you wish to sort.

2   Click on the **View** menu.

3   Click **Current View**.

4   Click on the element you would like to sort by, e.g. *By Message Flag*.

Or

1   Go to the folder you wish to sort.

2   Click on the **View** menu.

3   Click on **Current View**.

4   Click **Customize Current View**.

5   Click **Sort**.

6   Click the drop-down arrow underneath *Sort items by*.

7   Click on the criteria you want to sort by.

8   Click the circle next to *Ascending* or *Descending*.

9   If required, click the drop-down arrow underneath *Then by*, and choose something else to sort by.

10   Click **OK**.

11   Click **OK**.

Deleting E-mails

You can delete e-mail from any of your folders.

1   Click on the e-mail you wish to delete.

2   Press **Delete** – the e-mail is sent to the Deleted Items folder.

Deleted Items Folder

The Deleted Items folder stores all the messages that you have deleted. The number in brackets next to it indicates how many messages it contains.

 **Deleted Items** [2]

Opening The Deleted Items Folder

Click on the **Deleted Items folder** icon from the Outlook bar.

Or

Click on *Deleted Items* from the *Folders* list.

 **Deleted Items** [2]

Retrieving Messages From The Deleted Items Folder

Messages that have been deleted and are still stored in the Deleted Items folder can be retrieved by moving them to one of your folders.

1 Open the Deleted Items folder.

2 Click on the message you wish to retrieve.

3 Click on the **Edit** menu.

4 Click **Move to Folder**.

5 Click on the folder you wish to move the e-mail to.

6 Click **OK**.

Deleting Messages From The Deleted Items Folder

You can delete messages from Deleted Items manually, or you can set Outlook to delete them all every time you close Outlook.

To delete a message manually:

1 Click on the e-mail you wish to delete.

2 Press **Delete**.

Emptying The Deleted Items Folder Automatically

To empty the deleted items folder when you close Outlook:

1 Click on the **Tools** menu.

2 Click **Options**.

3 Click on the **Other** tab.

4 Click the box next to *Empty the Deleted Items folder upon exiting* – the box will become ticked.

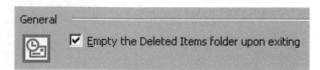

Finding Messages

Finding Messages In Your Inbox

1   Click on **Inbox** from the Outlook bar.

2   Click **Find** – a new pane will appear at the top of the Outlook screen.

3   Type in words to search for in the box next to *Look for*.

4   Remove the tick next to next to *Search all text in the message* if you only want to search the *From*, *Subject*, and *Received* information.

5   Click **Find Now** – any found messages are displayed.

6   Double-click on a message to open it.

To start a new search, or to display all your messages again:

Click *Clear Search*.

● Clear Search

To close the Find pane:

Click on the **Find** icon again.

Finding Messages Based On Words They Contain

1   Click **Inbox** from the Outlook bar.

2   Click on the **Tools** menu.

3   Click **Advanced Find**.

4   Click on the **Messages** tab.

5   Enter the words you wish to find in the box next to *Search for the word(s)*.

6   Click the drop-down arrow next to *In*, and choose the area you wish to find the words in.

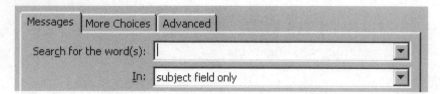

7   Click **Find Now** – any found messages appear at the bottom.

8   Double-click a message to open it.

Finding Messages Based On The From And To Lines

1   Click **Inbox** from the Outlook bar.

2   Click on the **Tools** menu.

3   Click **Advanced Find**.

4   Click on the **Messages** tab.

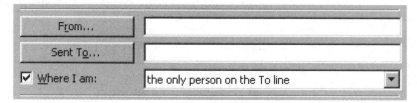

5   Enter the person the message is from in the box next to *From*
or

enter the person the message was sent to in the box next to *Sent To*

or

tick the *Where I am* box to find your own address.

Click the drop-down arrow next to *Where I am* and choose the option you require.

6   Click **Find Now** – any found messages appear at the bottom.

7   Double-click on a message to open it.

Finding Messages Based On Time

1   Click on **Inbox** from the Outlook bar.

2   Click on the **Tools** menu.

3   Click **Advanced Find**.

4   Click on the **Messages** tab.

5   Click the drop-down arrow next to the *Time* box.

6   Click the time you wish to search, e.g. received, sent, etc.

7   Click the drop-down arrow next to *anytime*.

8   Click on the specific time you wish to find, e.g. yesterday, today, etc.

9   Click **Find Now** – any found messages appear at the bottom.

10 Double-click the message to open it.

Finding Messages Based On Status

1   Click **Inbox** from the Outlook bar.

2   Click on the **Tools** menu.

3   Click **Advanced Find**.

4   Click on the **More Choices** tab.

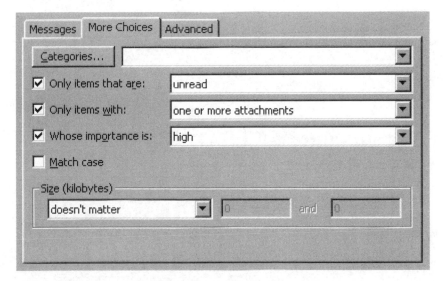

5   If required, tick the box next to *Only items that are*, and choose the appropriate option from the drop-down list.

6   If required, tick the box next to *Only items with*, and choose the appropriate option from the drop-down list.

7   If required, tick the box next to *Whose importance is*, and choose the appropriate option from the drop-down list.

8   If required, tick the box next to *Match case*.

9   If required, click the down arrow underneath *Size*, and choose the appropriate option from the drop-down list.

10   Click **Find Now** – any found messages appear at the bottom.

11   Double-click on a message to open it.

You Can Use A Combination Of Any Of These To Find Messages

For instance, if you wanted to find messages which contained the word 'happy' and were unread, you could enter both of these criteria.

Starting A New Search In The Advanced Find Dialog Box

Click **New Search** from the *Advanced Find* dialog box.

Closing The Advanced Find Dialog Box

Click the X at the top right of the box.

Addresses

Creating Contacts

What Are Contacts?

Contacts contain information about the people and businesses you are in touch with. You can store all sorts of information about a person, such as:

- ➤ E-mail address
- ➤ Postal address
- ➤ Phone number
- ➤ Job title.

Getting To Contacts

Click **Contacts** on the Outlook bar.

The Contacts Screen

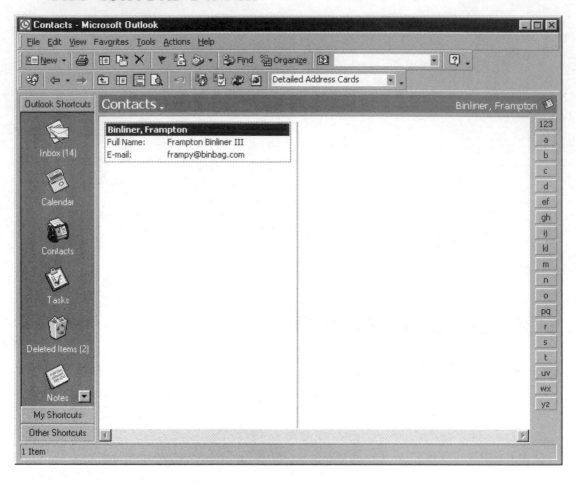

➤ Contacts are shown in the big white area in the middle.

➤ Click a letter tab on the right-hand side of the screen to move to the contacts that start with that letter.

Creating A Contact

1 Click **Contacts** from the Outlook bar.

2 Click **New**.

3 Click on the **General** tab.

756

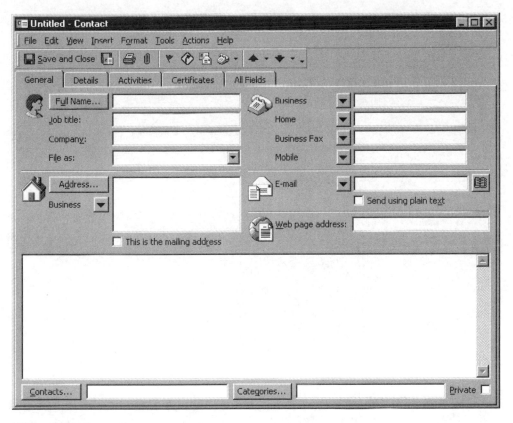

4   Fill in the information you require.

5   If required, click on the **Details** tab and fill in the information you require.

6   If required, click on the **All Fields** tab:

click the drop-down arrow next to *Select from*.

Click on the Field category you require, e.g. *All Contact fields*.

Fill in the information you require, e.g. birthday, assistant's phone number, etc.

7   Click **Save and Close**.

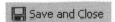

You Can Add Extra Information To The General Tab

If you click the **Full Name** button you can add more detailed information about the name.

Full Name...

Similarly if you click the **Address** button you can add more detailed information about the address.

Address...

If you click the drop down arrows next to the fields, you can get a list of other related fields, which you then fill in.

A Strange Message Appears When I Enter Phone Numbers And Addresses!

A box may appear when you have entered a phone number or an address, checking whether it is correct.

To stop this box from showing again, remove the tick next to *Show this again when phone number is incomplete or unclear.*

Creating A New Contact From An E-mail

When you receive an e-mail, you can add the person who sent it to you as a new contact.

1 Open the e-mail from the sender.

2 Click on their address with the right mouse button – a menu will appear.

3 Click **Add to Contacts**.

4 Enter any more details that you wish.

5 Click **Save and Close**.

Changing The View of Contacts

1 Click on the **View** menu.

2 Click **Current View**.

3 Click on the view you require.

Printing Contacts

1 Double-click the contact to open it.

2 Click on the **Print** icon.

3 Choose the style you require.

4 Click **Print**.

Editing And Deleting Contacts

Editing A Contact

1 Click **Contacts** from the Outlook bar.

2 Double-click on the contact you wish to change.

3 Make any changes you require.

4 Click **Save and Close**.

Deleting A Contact

1   Click on the contact you wish to delete – it will go blue.

2   Press **Delete**.

Using The Address Book

Address books are used to store e-mail addresses. They can make addressing e-mails much quicker and easier.

➤ An icon can be used to address e-mails quickly, rather than typing the whole address.

➤ Nicknames can be used instead of e-mail addresses.

➤ You can create distribution lists which group several addresses together. For instance, you might have to send an e-mail to all of the people in your personnel department. This would normally mean having to type the individual address of each member of the personnel department. However, a distribution list would allow you to type one word or phrase in the address line, and send the e-mail to everyone within that distribution list.

There are three address books in Outlook, although you have equal access to all three of them. A brief explanation of them appears below.

➤ **Outlook Address Book**
This is automatically created from the Contacts in your contact folder (although they need to have an e-mail address in order to be included!).

➤ **Personal Address Book**
This is created and updated by you. It stores e-mail addresses and distribution lists.

Personal Address Books are stored on each computer and are unique for each person.

➤ **Global Address List**
The administrator of your system maintains this address book. They can add or remove addresses. This list is usually the e-mail addresses of all the other people who work at your organization.

Displaying An Address Book

1   Click on the **Tools** menu.

2   Click **Address Book**.

3   Click the drop-down arrow next to *Show names from the*.

4   Click on the address book you want to see.

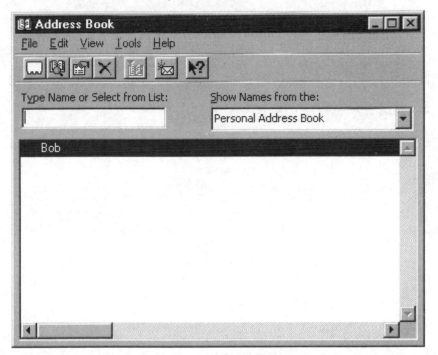

You Might Only Have The Personal Address Book!

Unless you are connected to a network, you will only see the Personal Address Book.

Using The Address Book For E-mail

You can use the address books to add the address quickly.

1   Click **Inbox** from the Outlook bar.

2   Click **New**.

3   Click **To**.

4   If necessary, click the drop-down arrow next to *Show Names from the* and choose the address book you wish to use.

5   Click on the name you wish to use from the left-hand side.

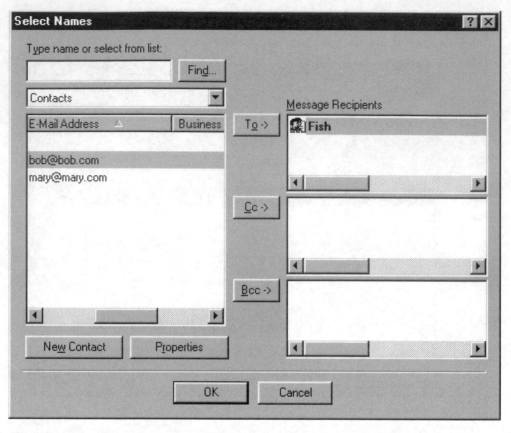

6   Click **To**, **Cc** or **Bcc** – the name will appear on the right, in the relevant box.

7   Click **OK**.

Adding a New Address To The Address Book

Just create a new contact (see page 755)!

Using Personal Distribution Lists

What Is A Distribution List?

A distribution list allows you to group a set of e-mail addresses together (e.g. all the people in the personnel department). When you want to write to everyone in that group, you can use the distribution list instead of typing out all the individual addresses.

Distribution Lists May Already Have Been Set Up By Your Administrator!

Check with them first, before you start creating anything!

Creating A Personal Distribution List With New Contacts

If you want to create a distribution list, but haven't already created the contacts:

1   Click on the **File** menu.

2   Click **New**.

3   Click **Distribution List**.

4   Type in a name for your distribution list.

Name: |

5   Click **Add New**.

6   Type the member's name into the *Display Name* box.

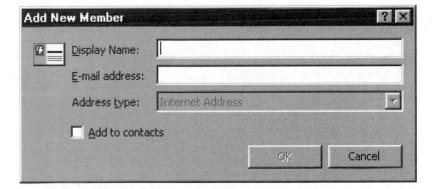

7   Type the e-mail address of the member into the *E-mail address* box.

8   Click in the box next to *Add to contacts* – the box will be ticked, and the member will be added to your contacts.

9   Click **OK**.

763

10   Repeat steps 5 to 9 for everyone else you wish to add.

11   Click **OK.**

12   Click **Save and Close.**

Creating A Personal Distribution List From Your Contacts

If you want to create a distribution list that contains people you already have in your Contacts:

1   Click on the **File** menu.

2   Click **New.**

3   Click **Distribution List.**

4   Type in a name for your distribution list.

5   Click **Select Members.**

6   Click on a name you wish to add.

7   Click **Add.**

8   Repeat steps 6 and 7 for everyone else you wish to add.

9   Click **OK.**

10   Click **Save and Close.**

Sending An E-mail Using A Personal Distribution List

1   Click the **Inbox** from the Outlook bar.

2   Click **New.**

3   Click **To.**

4   If necessary, click the drop-down arrow next to *Show names from the* and choose the address book which contains the distribution list.

5   Click on the distribution list you wish to use.

6   Click **To.**

7   Click **OK.**

All The Addresses In The Distribution List Will Be Visible To The Recipient!

When a recipient receives a message using a distribution list, every name on the list appears in their message window. So the members of your distribution list cannot be kept secret from other members!

Editing A Personal Distribution List

1   Click on the **Tools** menu.

2   Click **Address Book**.

3   Click the drop-down arrow next to *Show names from the.*

4   Click on *Personal Address Book.*

5   Double-click on the name of your distribution list.

6   Click on **Select Members** to add a new member from your contacts

or

click on **Add New** to add a new member who is not one of your contacts

or

click on the member you wish to delete.

Click **Remove**.

7   Click **OK**.

You Might Only Have The Personal Address Book!

Remember, unless you are connected to a network, you will only see the personal address book.

Deleting A Personal Distribution List

1   Click on the Tools menu.

2   Click **Address Book**.

3   Click the drop-down arrow next to *Show names from the.*

4   Click on *Personal Address Book*.

5   Click on the name of the distribution list you wish to delete.

6   Press **Delete**.

7   Click **Yes** to confirm you wish to delete.

Chapter 10

Quick Reference

Web Jargon

A Web Browser

➤ This is the software that you need to look at the World Wide Web.

➤ Internet Explorer is a browser. Another popular browser is Netscape Navigator.

The Modem (Modulator–Demodulator)

➤ The modem is a piece of hardware that connects your computer to the telephone socket.

➤ It converts digital information which is stored on your computer into analogue information that can pass down the phone lines.

Internet Service Provider (ISP) And Servers

➤ Just as you need a telephone service provider to give you your telephone service, you need an **Internet Service Provider** to give you access to the Internet.

➤ ISPs have **servers** – high capacity computers that can store a lot of information. The servers hold Web pages and work like the post office for e-mails – storing and sending letters around the Internet.

➤ ISPs provide you with your e-mail address and space to store any Web pages you create on their server.

URL (Uniform Resource Locator)

➤ This is the term used for the address of a Web page, e.g. http://www.happy.co.uk.

➤ You type URLs into your browser so that your ISP knows where to get the information you require.

Web Pages, Websites And Home Pages

➤ **Web pages** are the pages of information you can see over the Web.

➤ Each Web page is stored as a file on a server.

➤ A **Website** is a collection of files stored in the same folder on the server.

➤ The **Home page** is the first page you see when you connect to a Website. It works a bit like the front cover of a magazine, telling you what information you can find on the Web pages inside that site.

Example Website

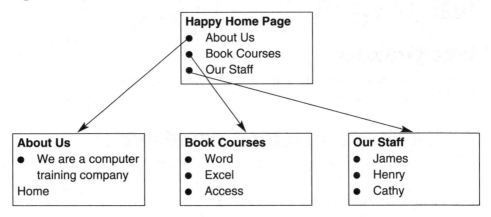

Hyperlink

➤ These are the links in Web pages that take you to other Web pages, so that you don't get stuck at the same page forever.

➤ They are usually underlined text or pictures, and your mouse will change to a pointing hand when you position it over one.

HTML (HyperText Markup Language)

➤ Every Web page is written in the computer language called HTML.

➤ You do not have to know HTML to use the Web, because the browser translates it into pictures and text.

➤ HTML is essentially made up of tags and codes that instruct your browser what to show. For example, there is a tag called <strong> that instructs your browser to make something bold. So '<strong>Kermit the Frog</strong>' would appear as **Kermit the Frog**.

HTTP (HyperText Transfer Protocol)

➤ This is a set of rules that all computers connected to the Internet have agreed to abide by. This means that HTML means the same to all browsers.

➤ When http:// appears at the beginning of a Web address it is saying that it agrees to abide by the rules of HTTP.

E-mail Software

➤ E-mail software allows you to send mail over the Internet.

➤ E-mail software usually comes free with your browser.

➤ Internet Explorer 5 has Microsoft Outlook Express 5. Other examples are Pegasus and Eudora.

Search Engine Support

	Google	AltaVista	Excite	Infoseek	Lycos	Yahoo!
US Address	www.google.com	www.altavista.com	www.excite.com	www.infoseek.com	www.lycos.com	www.yahoo.com
UK Address	www.google.co.uk	www.altavista.co.uk	www.excite.co.uk	www.infoseek.co.uk	www.lycos.co.uk	www.yahoo.co.uk
Natural English	Yes	Yes	Yes	Yes	Yes	Not recommended
Phrase	"Double Quotes"	"Double Quotes"	"Double Quotes"	"Double Quotes"	"Double Quotes"	"Double Quotes"
AND Search	It uses AND by default	+in front of word	+in front of word AND	+in front of word	+in front of word	+in front of word
OR Search	OR	By default	By default and OR	By default		By default
NOT Search	– in front of word	– in front of word	– in front of word AND NOT	– in front of word	– in front of word	– in front of word
Wildcard	No	Asterisk (*)	No	No	No	Asterisk (*)
Proximity Search	No	Advanced text search	No	No	Advanced Search	No
Case Sensitive	No	Yes	No	No	No	No
Date Search	Advanced Search	Advanced text search	No	No	No	in Options
Page Titles	allintitle:	title:				t:
Domain Names	site:	Domain:				u:
Counts Results	Yes	Yes	No	Yes		Yes

Index